The Best Test Preparation for the

SAT Subject Test

Latin

With REA's TEST*ware*® on CD-ROM

Ronald B. Palma, M.A.
Holland Hall School, Tulsa, OK

Research & Education Association
Visit our website at
www.rea.com

Research & Education Association
61 Ethel Road West
Piscataway, New Jersey 08854
E-mail: info@rea.com

The Best Test Preparation for the
SAT LATIN SUBJECT TEST
With TEST*ware*® on CD-ROM

Published 2009

Copyright © 2007 by Research & Education Association, Inc.

Printed in the United States of America

Library of Congress Control Number 2006904624

ISBN 13: 978-0-7386-0253-0
ISBN 10: 0-7386-0253-1

G08-0101

About the Author

Ronald B. Palma has been teaching Latin and other classics courses at Holland Hall School in Tulsa, Oklahoma, for the past 32 years. He holds an A.B. in Classics from Cornell University and an M.A. in Classics from the University of Cincinnati, where he did doctoral work funded by a Louise Taft Semple Fellowship. He has co-authored *Ecce Romani: A Latin Reading Program* (Prentice-Hall, 2005), now in its third edition, and served as series editor for *Review and Test Preparation Guide for the Beginning Student* and *Review and Test Preparation Guide for the Intermediate Student*, both published by Prentice-Hall. Palma has received numerous fellowships and awards for both teaching and scholarship, including Rockefeller and Fulbright grants, the Summer Fellowship of the Classical Society of the American Academy in Rome, a Presidential Scholar Award from the U.S. Department of Education, a Special Recognition Award from the College Board, and the Excellence in Pre-Collegiate Teaching Award from the American Philological Association.

The author, who invites comments on this book, may be reached by e-mail at rpalma@hollandhall.org.

Author Acknowledgments

I would like to acknowledge and thank several people for their invaluable professional and personal support in the production of this book: Gianfranco Origliato, my former editor at Research & Education Association, who invited me to undertake this project, and his successor, Senior Editor Diane Goldschmidt. I would also like to thank Kate Rabiteau of Educational Testing Service for providing me with the current information about the SAT Latin Subject Test and my colleague, Prof. Tom Benedicktson, Dean of the College of Arts and Sciences at the University of Tulsa, for providing careful and creative proofreading of the manuscript. Finally, thanks to Lorie Donovan, Project Manager, and her staff at Publication Services, for their patience and professionalism in guiding me through the "birthing pains" of production. **Quare habe tibi quicquid hoc libelli, qualecumque.**

Ron Palma
Holland Hall School
Tulsa, Oklahoma

Dedication

This book is dedicated to my longtime friend and colleague, Gil Lawall, who has passed the torch to many.

Ron Palma
Holland Hall School
Tulsa, Oklahoma

About Research & Education Association

Founded in 1959, Research & Education Association is dedicated to publishing the finest and most effective educational materials—including software, study guides, and test preps—for students in middle school, high school, college, graduate school, and beyond. Today, REA's wide-ranging catalog is a leading resource for teachers, students, and professionals. We invite you to visit us at *www.rea.com* to find out how "REA is making the world smarter."

Staff Acknowledgments

In addition to our author, we would like to thank Larry B. Kling, Vice President, Editorial, for his overall direction; Pam Weston, Vice President, Publishing, for setting the quality standards for production integrity and managing the publication to completion; John Cording, Vice President, Technology, for coordinating the design, development, and testing of REA's TESTware® software; Heena Patel and Michelle Boykins, Technology Project Managers, for their design contributions and software testing efforts; Diane Goldschmidt, Senior Editor, for coordinating revisions; Christine Saul, Senior Graphic Designer, for designing the cover; Jeff LoBalbo, Senior Graphic Designer, for coordinating pre-press electronic file mapping; Aquent Publishing Services, for typesetting the manuscript, and Kathy Caratozzolo of Caragraphics, for typesetting revisions.

CONTENTS

SECTION 6: Imperatives

SECTION 7: Verbals

SECTION 8: Subjunctive Verbs

SECTION 9: Special Aspects of the SAT Latin Subject Test

SECTION 10: Practice Tests

Index

Quick Study Guide

INSTALLING REA's TEST*ware*®

SYSTEM REQUIREMENTS

Pentium 75 MHz (300 MHz recommended), or a higher or compatible processor; Microsoft Windows 98, NT 4 (SP6), ME, 2000, or XP; 64 MB Available RAM; Internet Explorer 5.5 or higher (Internet Explorer 5.5 is included on the CD); minimum 60 MB available hard-disk space; VGA or higher-resolution monitor, 800x600 resolution setting; Microsoft Mouse, Microsoft Intellimouse, or compatible pointing device.

INSTALLATION

1. Insert the SAT Latin Subject Test TEST*ware*® CD-ROM into the CD-ROM drive.
2. If the installation doesn't begin automatically, from the Start Menu, choose the RUN command. When the RUN dialog box appears, type d:\setup (where *d* is the letter of your CD-ROM drive) at the prompt and click OK.
3. The installation process will begin. A dialog box proposing the directory "Program Files\REA\SATLatin" will appear. If the name and location are suitable, click OK. If you wish to specify a different name or location, type it in and click OK.
4. Start the SAT Latin Subject Test TEST*ware*® application by double-clicking on the icon.

REA's SAT Latin Subject Test TEST*ware*® is **EASY** to **LEARN AND USE**. To achieve maximum benefits, we recommend that you take a few minutes to go through the on-screen tutorial on your computer. The "screen buttons" are also explained there to familiarize you with the program.

TECHNICAL SUPPORT

REA's TEST*ware*® is backed by customer and technical support. For questions about **installation or operation of your software**, contact us at:

Research & Education Association
Phone: (732) 819-8880 (9 a.m. to 5 p.m. ET, Monday–Friday)
Fax: (732) 819-8808
Website: www.rea.com
E-mail: info@rea.com

Note to Windows XP Users: In order for the TEST*ware*® to function properly, please install and run the application under the same computer-administrator level user account. Installing the TEST*ware*® as one user and running it as another could cause file access path conflicts.

THE SAT SUBJECT TEST IN
LATIN

SECTION 1

The Basics

CHAPTER 1

Excelling on the SAT Latin Subject Test

Chapter 1

EXCELLING ON THE SAT LATIN SUBJECT TEST

Whether you are a Latin II, III, or IV student, you are to be congratulated for putting your knowledge of Latin on the line by taking the SAT Latin Subject Test! This book is designed to help you strengthen your specific weaknesses and to facilitate a comprehensive review of all that you've learned. Inside you will find targeted information about the exam, as well as tips on how best to prepare for it.

ABOUT THE SAT LATIN SUBJECT TEST

Who Takes the Test and What Is It Used For?

Students planning to attend college should take the SAT Latin Subject Test if:

(1) They have studied Latin and any of the colleges they apply to require SAT Subject Tests for admission;

OR

(2) The student wishes to demonstrate proficiency in Latin.

The SAT Latin Subject Test is designed for students who have a wide-ranging knowledge of Latin. Recommended preparation includes two to four years of Latin study in high school.

Who Administers the Test?

The SAT Latin Subject Test is developed by the College Board and administered by Educational Testing Service (ETS). The test development process involves the assistance of educators throughout the country, and is designed and implemented to ensure that the content and difficulty level of the test are appropriate.

When Should the SAT Latin Test be Taken?

If you are applying to a college that requires SAT Subject Test scores as part of the admissions process, you should take the SAT Latin Subject Test toward the end of your junior year or at the beginning of your senior year. If your scores are being used only for placement purposes, you may be able to take the test in the spring of your senior year. For more information, be sure to contact the colleges to which you are applying.

When and Where is the Test Given?

The SAT Latin Subject Test is administered twice a year at many locations throughout the United States; most test centers are at high schools. For more information on specific testing dates and locations, consult the registration bulletin or your high school guidance counselor.

To receive information on upcoming administrations of the exam, consult the publication *Taking the SAT Subject Tests*, which may be obtained from your guidance counselor or by contacting:

College Board SAT Program
PO Box 025505
Miami, FL 33102
Phone: (866) 756-7346
Web Contact: *http://www.collegeboard.com/inquiry/sathome/html*
Web site: *http://www.collegeboard.com*

Is There a Registration Fee?

Yes. There is a registration fee to take the SAT Latin Subject Test. Consult the publication *Taking the SAT Subject Tests* for information on the fee structure. Financial assistance may be granted in certain situations. To find out if you qualify and to register for assistance, contact your academic advisor.

CONTENT AND FORMAT OF THE TEST

The SAT Latin Subject Test is a one-hour exam consisting of approximately 70 multiple-choice questions. Each question has four answer choices, lettered (A) through (D). The questions are organized into six categories (Parts A–F in the following table).

Skills Tested	Approximate Percentage of Score	Number of Questions
Grammar & Syntax (Parts A, D, and E)	30	20
Derivatives (Part B)	5	4–5
Translation (Part C)	20	14
Reading Comprehension (Part F)	45	30–35

The parts that follow are arranged in the sequence of their appearance on the exam. Questions in each part are arranged in order of difficulty, easy to difficult.

PART A: Recognition of Forms

Select the specific grammatical form (noun, pronoun, adjective, adverb, and verb) of a Latin word. Eight questions.

PART B: Derivatives

Pick the Latin root word of the English derivative given in context. Four questions.

PART C: Translation

Discriminate the correct meaning of Latin to English sentences or parts of sentences. Fourteen questions.

PART D: Sentence Completion

Complete the Latin sentence by choosing the correct Latin form. Seven questions.

PART E: Syntax Substitution

Choose an alternate way of expressing the same thought in Latin (substitution, e.g. participial phrase for relative clause). Five questions.

PART F: Reading Comprehension

Answer English questions on short passages of adapted Latin (about eight lines). There are three to five sight passages, including one of verse. Uncommon words are glossed. This section includes questions on specific points of grammar and scansion of the first four feet of the dactylic hexameter. Five to 15 questions per passage.

ABOUT THIS BOOK AND TEST*ware*®

This book and the accompanying software will provide you with an accurate and complete representation of the SAT Latin Subject Test. Inside you will find a course review designed to provide you with the information and strategies needed to do well on the exam, as well as two full-length practice tests based on the actual exam. REA's practice tests contain every type of question you can expect to encounter on the SAT Latin Subject Test. Following each test, you will find an answer key with detailed explanations to help you master the test material.

Practice Tests 1 and 2 are included in two formats: in TEST*ware*® format on the enclosed CD and in printed form in this book. **We recommend that you begin your preparation by first taking the computerized version of your test.** The software provides enforced timed conditions and instantaneous, accurate scoring, which make it all the easier to pinpoint your strengths and weaknesses.

Some Special Features

Here are some special features of this book:

- Informal style that talks directly to you with your needs in mind, ***to make you feel comfortable***

- Periodic interjection of humor, ***to keep you in good spirits***

- Analysis of the content and format of the exam, ***to give you insight***

- References to currently available College Board exam materials, ***to inform you***

- Glossaries of terms commonly used in the study of Latin, ***to help you understand***

- Quick-study tables that consolidate major concepts, ***to help you summarize***

- Easy-to-use organizational style, ***to help you find your way***

- Clear and simple explications of forms and their uses, plus memory devices, ***to help you recall***

- Unadapted and adapted sententiae and passages from Roman literature, ***to make readings authentic***

- Questions in each chapter that simulate the format and content of those on the exam, ***to help you gauge your progress***

- Stumper and Ambush questions, ***to challenge you***

- Detailed explanations of answers to questions, ***to help you learn from your mistakes***

- Webliographies of additional resources, ***to extend your review***

- Two complete practice exams, ***to help you assess your readiness***

HOW TO USE THIS BOOK AND TEST*ware*®

To begin your studies, read the suggestions for test taking and take Practice Test 1 on CD-ROM to determine your strengths and weaknesses. Next, study the course review material focusing on your specific problem areas. The course review includes the information you need to know when taking the exam. Then take Practice Test 2 on CD-ROM to become familiar with the format and feel of the SAT Latin Subject Test. If time allows, take Practice Test 1 and 2 in this book to further increase your level of confidence for the test.

To best utilize your study time, follow one of the Study Schedules found at the end of this chapter.

SSD Accommodations for Students With Disabilities

Many students qualify for extra time to take the SAT Subject Tests and our TEST*ware*® can be adapted to accommodate your time extension. This allows you to practice under the same extended time accommodations that you will receive on the actual test day. To customize your TEST*ware*® to suit the most common extensions, visit our website at *www.rea.com/ssd*.

How This Book is Organized

The content of this book is divided into sections and chapters, which are further subdivided into segments that contain notes on finer points of the content. The stated purpose of the SAT Latin Subject Test is to evaluate your ability <u>to read Latin</u>. Because the test evaluates your mastery of the mechanics of reading Latin, with special emphasis on grammar and syntax, the majority of the presentations in this book are devoted to helping you review Latin forms and their uses. These sections are therefore organized according to the parts of speech recommended for review by the College Board, namely, nouns, pronouns, adjectives, adverbs, and verbs:

Section 1: The Basics

Section 2: Nouns

Section 3: Pronouns

Section 4: Adjectives and Adverbs

Section 5: Indicative Verbs

Section 6: Imperative Verbs

Section 7: Verbals

Section 8: Subjunctive Verbs

Section 9: Special Aspects of the SAT Latin Subject Test

Section 10: Practice Tests

Most chapters begin with a reference chart of Latin forms (everyone's favorite!), which is accompanied by a brief discussion of the most common uses of these forms. In these presentations, alternative nomenclature is provided when forms or uses are labeled or described; for example, purpose clauses are also referred to as final clauses. Traditional terms, such as "passive periphrastic," are used for convenience. Glossaries of terms are included at appropriate points in this book, but by no means should this suggest that you will be tested on terminology, which is simply a means to the end of understanding Latin, and not an end in itself.

The presentations in each chapter have been designed to supplement your preparation, whether you have learned Latin using the grammar-translation method (e.g., Amsco's *Lingua Latina*, "Jenney" *First Year Latin* and *Second Year Latin*, *Latin for Americans*, *Our Latin Heritage*) or the reading-based method (e.g., *The Cambridge Latin Course, Ecce Romani, The*

Oxford Latin Course). Use this review guide to supplement the text from which you learned Latin because the latter is the resource with which you will be most familiar. Illustrative Latin sentences with English translations are provided to support the presentations in each chapter. These sentences reflect cultural and literary themes appropriate to the intermediate level of study. The presentation in each chapter ends with a quick-study condensation, followed by practice questions covering the content of that chapter. These questions simulate the styles of questions on the various parts of the actual exam, such as recognition, completion, and translation. A "Stumper" question that will challenge your mastery is included at the end of each set of practice questions. Occasionally, you will come across an "Ambush" question that will evaluate your continuing command of the material from a previous chapter or chapters. The answers to all practice questions are provided and discussed, with references back to the content of the chapter.

In the final section, you will find chapters on parts of the exam that warrant special attention by virtue of the style of their questions, such as syntax substitution, which is the replacement of one Latin word or expression with another that has equivalent meaning. Separate presentations on translation and reading comprehension are provided in the final chapters.

As you make your way through this book, please make liberal use of the various reference tools provided, such as the quick-study reviews within individual chapters and sections, as well as the table of contents; the section, chapter, and segment headings; the back-referencing notations that appear in the discussions of the answers; and the index. This "connective tissue" will help you to move about easily in the book so that you can reinforce what you do know and repair what you do not. The content and organization of each section and chapter are designed to lead you to eventual success on the complete practice tests provided at the end of this book and thus to success on the SAT Latin Subject Test. **Io triumphe!**

TEST-TAKING TIPS

Although you may be unfamiliar with standardized tests such as the SAT Latin Subject Test, there are many ways to acquaint yourself with this type of examination and help alleviate your test-taking anxieties.

Become comfortable with the format of the exam. When you are practicing to take the SAT Latin Subject Test, simulate the conditions under which you will be taking the actual test. Stay calm and pace yourself. After simulating the test only a couple of times, you will boost your chances of doing well, and you will be able to sit down for the actual exam with much more confidence.

Know the directions and format for each section of the test. Familiarizing yourself with the directions and format of the exam will not only save you time, but it will also ensure that you are familiar enough with the SAT Latin Subject Test to avoid nervousness (and the mistakes caused by being nervous).

Do your scratchwork in the margins of the test booklet. You will not be given scrap paper during the exam, and you may not perform scratchwork on your answer sheet. Space is provided in your test booklet to do any necessary work or to draw diagrams.

If you are unsure of an answer, use a guessing strategy. Wrong answers are penalized, but you can guess wisely by using the process of elimination. Go through each answer to a question and rule out as many of the answer choices as possible. By eliminating two answer choices, you give yourself a fifty-fifty chance of answering correctly because there will only be two choices left.

Mark your answers in the appropriate spaces on the answer sheet. Each numbered row will contain four ovals corresponding to each answer choice for that question. Fill in darkly, completely, and neatly the circle that corresponds to your answer. You can change your answer, but remember to erase your old answer *completely*. Any stray lines or unnecessary marks may cause the machine to score your answer incorrectly. When you have finished working on a section, you may want to go back and check to make sure your answers correspond to the correct questions. Marking one answer in the wrong space will throw off the rest of your test, whether it is graded by machine or by hand. When taking the test, you may occasionally want to check your answer sheet to be sure that you are filling in the oval that corresponds to the question you are answering.

You don't have to answer every question. You are not penalized if you do not answer every question. The only penalty results from answering a question incorrectly. Try to use the guessing strategy, but if you are truly stumped by a question, remember that you do not have to answer it.

Work quickly and steadily. You have a limited amount of time to work on each section, so you need to work quickly and steadily. Avoid focusing on one problem for too long. Taking the practice tests in this book will help you to learn how to budget your time and pace yourself.

Keep track of your scores. By doing so, you will be able to gauge your progress and discover your general and particular weaknesses in each section. You should carefully study the reviews that cover your areas of difficulty because this will build your skills in those areas. To help you budget your time for studying, we have provided a detailed study schedule.

SCORING THE SAT LATIN SUBJECT TEST

The SAT Latin Subject Test, like all other Subject Tests, is scored on a 200–800 scale.

How Do I Score My Practice Test?

Your exam is scored by crediting one point for each correct answer and deducting one-third of a point for each incorrect answer. There is no deduction for answers that are omitted. Use the worksheet below to calculate your raw score and to record your scores for the two practice tests you take. To determine your scaled score, you will need to use the Score Conversion Chart for the SAT Latin Subject Test that can be found on page 581 of this book.

Scoring Worksheet

$$\underline{\hspace{2cm}} - (\underline{\hspace{2cm}} \times \frac{1}{3}) = \underline{\hspace{2cm}}$$

| number correct | number incorrect (do not include unanswered questions) | Raw Score (round to nearest whole point) |

	Raw Score	**Scaled Score**
Practice Test 1	_____	_____
Practice Test 2	_____	_____

THE DAY OF THE TEST

Before the Test

Make sure you know where your test center is well in advance of your test day so you do not get lost on the day of the test. On the night before the test, gather the materials you will need the next day:

- Your admission ticket
- Two forms of identification (e.g., driver's license, student identification card, or current alien registration card)
- Two No. 2 pencils with erasers
- Directions to the test center
- A watch (if you wish) but not one that makes noise because it may disturb other test-takers

On the day of the test, you should wake up early (after a good night's rest) and have breakfast. Dress comfortably so that you are not distracted by being too hot or too cold while taking the test. Also, plan to arrive at the test center early. This will allow you to collect your thoughts and relax before the test, and it will also spare you the stress of being late. If you arrive after the test begins, you will not be admitted to the test center and you will *not* receive a refund.

During the Test

When you arrive at the test center, try to find a seat where you feel most comfortable. Follow all the rules and instructions given by the test supervisor. If you do not, you risk being dismissed from the test and having your scores canceled.

Once all the test materials are passed out, the test instructor will give you directions for filling out your answer sheet. Fill this sheet out carefully because this information will appear on your score report.

After the Test

When you have completed the SAT Latin Subject Test, you may hand in your test materials and leave. Then go home and relax! You should receive your score report, which includes your scores, percentile ranks, and interpretive information, about three weeks after you take the test.

ONLINE AND PRINTED RESOURCES FOR THE SAT LATIN SUBJECT TEST

Online Resources from the Learning Center at Collegeboard.com

Testing Tips

http://www.collegeboard.com/student/testing/sat/lc_two/tipsTwo.html

General tips on prepping for and taking the SAT Latin Subject Test.

Latin Sample Questions

http://www.collegeboard.com/student/testing/sat/lc_two/latin/prac/pracStart.html?latin

Sample questions with answers and test taking tips (one sample question from each of the six parts).

Taking the Subject Tests

http://www.collegeboard.com/prod_downloads/sat/satguide/SAT2_Lat_Span_ELPT.pdf

Eighteen sample test questions, with answers, from all six parts of the test. Includes estimated difficulty levels.

Released SAT Latin Subject Tests and Published Articles about those Tests

The College Board Latin Achievement Test (1987 complete test)

Duclos, Gloria S., Doris L. Kays, and Kathleen A. Rabiteau, "An Analysis of Candidate Performance on the Published (1987) Latin Achievement Test," *Classical Outlook* 66, no. 2 (1988–89): 43–48.

The SAT II: Latin Subject Test (1994 minitest, 54 questions)

Crooker, Jill M., and Kathleen A. Rabiteau, "An Analysis of Candidate Performance on the Published SAT II Latin Minitest (1994)," *Classical Outlook* 74, no. 4 (1996–97): 131–37.

Real SAT II: Subject Tests (Latin, Modern Hebrew, Italian) (1998 complete test)

Crooker, Jill M., and Kathleen A. Rabiteau, "An Interwoven Fabric: The AP Latin Examinations, the SAT II Latin Test (1998), and the National Standards for Classical Language Learning," *Classical Outlook* 77, no. 4 (1999–2000): 148–53. (This test is available from the College Board in the book *Real SAT II: Subject Tests*, Item #007034, or as the booklet cited above, Item #430351.)

STUDY SCHEDULE FOR THE SAT LATIN SUBJECT TEST

There are two ways to use this book in preparation for the SAT Latin Subject Test. Plan A is a comprehensive eight-week overview of the basics of Latin and is perhaps the best way to prepare. Plan B is a more incremental and condensed schedule that helps you to focus only on those areas of your command of Latin that require formal review. Whichever plan you choose, be advised that it is best to develop consistency in your preparation, which means that you should develop the habit of reviewing every day. Finally, take full advantage of the design of this study guide by making complete use of the explanations of answers to the practice questions, which direct you back to the original presentations to help you learn from your mistakes.

Plan A

Week	Activity
1	Read the introduction to this book, which summarizes the content and organization of the SAT Latin Subject Test and explains how to use the resources of this study guide in order to increase your chances for success on the exam. Look over the table of contents and leaf through the pages. Also, look through the various glossaries (Grammar and Syntax, Nouns, and Verbs) provided, in order to remind yourself about the meanings of the terms used in the study of Latin. (Remember to do this again when you begin reviewing nouns and verbs, respectively.) Take Practice Test 1 on CD-ROM in order to establish a reference point for your review.

2	Take this week to review Section 2: Nouns. After you have reviewed the material in each chapter of the section and answered the practice questions, be sure to read and understand thoroughly the explanations of the answers. To summarize your review of nouns, look over the Quick Study of Noun Syntax found at the end of Section 2. Note that it will be best if you approach Sections 2, 3, and 4 as a discrete whole because the forms and functions of nouns, pronouns, and adjectives/adverbs are so similar.
3	Review Section 3: Pronouns and Section 4: Adjectives and Adverbs. Do this in the same manner as Section 2. Be sure to consult the summaries provided in the quick study charts for these sections.
4	Review Section 5: Indicative Verbs and Section 6: Imperatives. Do this in the same manner as previously. Be sure that you consult the quick study synopsis and the tips on translating verbs in the indicative mood at the end of Section 5 and that you understand the relationship between verbs in the imperative mood and nouns in the vocative case.
5	Review Section 7: Verbals. Be sure to spend extra time on the forms and functions of both participles and infinitives. Your understanding of these is critical to your ability to read Latin because they, along with dependent subjunctive clauses, characterize best how Latin differs from English in expressing meaning.
6	Review Section 8: Subjunctive Verbs. This section presents both the forms and functions of subjunctive verbs as they are used in Latin. Spend extra time reviewing how to express the meaning of the various types of dependent clauses, which are summarized at the end of this section.
7	Read Section 9: Special Aspects of the SAT Latin Subject Test. When answering the practice questions on the chapters in Section 9, which cover syntax substitution, translation, and reading comprehension, try to apply all that you have reviewed in the previous sections. Use Section 9 as a warmup for the complete practice tests found at the end of the book.

8	Use your final week or weeks of preparation to take Practice Test 2 on CD-ROM and the SAT Latin Subject Tests found at the end of this book. Hopefully, you will be satisfied with your performance! If you are not, take the time and trouble to backtrack from the answer explanations to the review presentations to discover what you did wrong. Feel free to retake the practice tests, paying special attention to the questions with which you had difficulty the first time.

Plan B

This review plan requires you to organize your prep time around your specific needs. For instance, you may be thoroughly familiar with the basic forms of nouns and indicative verbs, but you might have forgotten (or never fully mastered) the concept of the participle. To implement this plan, take Practice Test 1 on CD-ROM to determine your strengths and weaknesses. Use the answer key, the explanations of answers, and the index and table of contents to redirect you back to the appropriate presentations of the material in order to strengthen your weaknesses. Latin II and III students should remember that they may not have studied every concept evaluated on the test. Structure your review as time allows, but above all, do some review each day. Using this strategy for preparation, even the best students may require as long as four weeks of review for the SAT Latin Subject Test.

Complete your studies for the test by taking Practice Test 2 on CD-ROM and, if time allows, the printed practice tests at the end of this book.

CHAPTER 2
Vocabulary and Derivation

Chapter 2

VOCABULARY AND DERIVATION

The members of the Development Committee for the SAT Latin Subject Test represent a variety of different approaches to teaching Latin. Therefore, the vocabulary of the test is not standardized or taken from a single source. Attention is given to using words commonly found in the most frequently used Latin textbook programs. Potentially difficult words in the reading comprehension section are "glossed," that is, their meanings are provided. At times, a common vocabulary word is substituted for a more difficult one in the Reading Comprehension section. Compound verbs do not usually appear on the exam.

DERIVATIVES

The derivation section of the exam tests your ability to recognize which Latin word is the root of an English derivative word. A word in an English sentence is underlined, and you must choose the correct Latin root word from the four choices. The Latin root may be an adjective, adverb, noun, or verb. To give you an idea of the range and scope of vocabulary preparation needed for this section of the exam, the following words are ones that have appeared on SAT Latin Subject Tests.

agō	**premō**
audiō	**rumpō**
cēdō	**sēcō**
cogō	**sequor**
pōnō	**vīvō**

Note that nine of these ten are verbs.

(To satisfy your curiosity, the one nonverb was **pēs**, **pedis**.) And **pōnō** appeared on two different tests! Be aware, however, that the answer choices may consist of a mixture of parts of speech, as in the following example.

SAMPLE QUESTION

Part B: Derivatives

Senior citizens often suffer a malady known as <u>dementia</u>.

(A) mensa   (C) maneō

(B) mens   (D) mensis

Answer: (B)

TIPS ON PREPARING FOR THE DERIVATIVES SECTION

- Reacquaint yourself with the vocabulary you learned from your textbook. In the sample question, knowing that the stem of **mens** is **ment-**, which appears in the derivative *dementia*, helps you to determine that (B) is the correct answer. While learning Latin, it is likely that you spent time exploring the connections between Latin and English. Exploit your ability to see a Latin word within an English derivative in order to find success on this section of the exam.

- As you do when you read Latin, look at the context in which the derivative is found in order to deduce its meaning, and thus move toward recognition of its Latin root. Pay particular attention to the part of speech of the English derivative, which may give a clue to the part of speech of the Latin root; in the sample, the English derivative *dementia* is a noun, as is its Latin root word, **mens**.

VOCABULARY RESOURCES (ONLINE)

- Advice for Learning Foreign-Language Vocabulary (St. Louis University): http://www.slu.edu/colleges/AS/languages/classical/latin/tchmat/grammar/lvocab2.html

- Two Hundred Essential Latin Words, More or Less
  (Anne Mahoney, Boston University): http://www.bu.edu/mahoa/vocab200.html

- Flashcard Exchange
  (online vocabulary flashcard database, organized by Latin text program): http://www.flashcardexchange.com/directory/1157.html

- Quia online vocabulary games
  (teacher-made review games, organized by Latin text program): http://www.quia.com/dir/latin/vocab.html. See also Latinteach (collection of learning links for Latin instructors and students): http://www.latinteach.com

- Quia online vocabulary games for *Wheelock's Latin*: http://www.quia.com/pages/wh2001gold.html

- Latin Dictionary and Grammar Aid
  (Latin–English and English–Latin search engine, Kevin Cawley, University of Notre Dame): http://www.nd.edu/%7Earchives/latgramm.htm

- Perseus Digital Library Latin Vocabulary Tool
  (search engine for word frequencies in Latin works; Tufts University): http://www.perseus.tufts.edu/cgi-bin/vocab?lang=la

DERIVATION RESOURCES (ONLINE)

- Perseus Digital Library Latin Vocabulary Tool (search engine for Latin roots of English words; Tufts University): http://www.perseus.tufts.edu/cgi-bin/resolveform?lang=Latin

- Languages Online: Latin
  (see "Etymology," organized by text program; E.L. Easton): http://eleaston.com/latin.html

PRACTICE QUESTIONS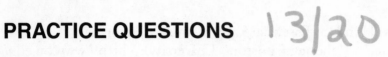

1. The <u>audacious</u> soldier fought in two campaigns.

   (A) audiō   (C) auferō

   (B) augeō   (D) audeō

2. The <u>resumption</u> of work at the factory was on schedule.

   (A) sum   (C) summus

   (B) sūmō   (D) sumptuōsus

3. The salvage diver discovered the remains of the <u>derelict</u>.

   (A) relinquō   (C) religiō

   (B) relēgō   (D) reiciō

4. He scored in the first <u>quartile</u> on this test.

   (A) quaerō   (C) quattuor

   (B) quāre   (D) queror

5. She was most <u>compassionate</u> in her treatment of animals.

   (A) pateō   (C) pareō

   (B) passus   (D) patior

6. Conservatives favored the <u>moratorium</u> on public spending.

   (A) morior   (C) miror

   (B) mōs   (D) moror

7. Her thesis proposed a new process for <u>desalinization</u>.

   (A) salūtō   (C) salvus

   (B) sāl   (D) salūs

8. <u>Auriferous</u> metals are rarely found on hilltops.

   (A) aurum   (C) auricula

   (B) aura   (D) auris

9. The actions of the boy who was cheating on the test were <u>surreptitious</u>.

   (A) petō

   (B) rapiō

   (C) rumpō

   (D) reperiō

10. "It's time to <u>recapitulate</u> (recap) the news," intoned the anchorman.

    (A) caput

    (B) capiō

    (C) capillus

    (D) captō

11. The police officer smiled at the <u>incredulity</u> on the face of the driver stopped for speeding.

    (A) crūdelis

    (B) crēdō

    (C) creō

    (D) crēber

12. The <u>verbose</u> lecturer put everyone to sleep.

    (A) verbum

    (B) verberō

    (C) vērus

    (D) vertō

13. It is <u>illicit</u> for a politician to spend campaign funds for personal reasons.

    (A) legō

    (B) illinc

    (C) licet

    (D) ligō

14. The volleyball player <u>exhorted</u> her teammates to play harder.

    (A) hortus

    (B) hōra

    (C) horreō

    (D) hortor

15. Mediation is one way to <u>adjudicate</u> a disagreement.

    (A) iungō (jungō)

    (B) iūdex (jūdex)

    (C) iuvō (juvō)

    (D) iūrō (jūrō)

16. One of the most difficult experiences a mother can have is
    <u>postpartum</u> depression.

    (A) pareō   (C) pār

    (B) pariō   (D) parō

17. A <u>pecuniary</u> offense often results in a fine.

    (A) pax   (C) pectus

    (B) pecus   (D) spectō

18. "Let's repeat that <u>cadenza</u>," said the conductor to the pianist.

    (A) crescō   (C) cēdō

    (B) caedō   (D) cadō

19. "Do birds have <u>tactile</u> organs?" inquired the boy.

    (A) tangō   (C) tegō

    (B) taceō   (D) tendō

20. The word "co-op" derives from the word <u>cooperate</u>.

    (A) optimus   (C) opus

    (B) ops   (D) optō

Stumper:

The dust storm gave the yard a <u>niveous</u> appearance.

    (A) nitor   (C) nix

    (B) nēve   (D) niteō

Answers

1. (D)	7. (B)	13. (C)	19. (A)
2. (B)	8. (A)	14. (D)	20. (C)
3. (A)	9. (B)	15. (B)	**Stumper:** (C)
4. (C)	10. (A)	16. (B)	
5. (D)	11. (B)	17. (B)	
6. (D)	12. (A)	18. (D)	

CHAPTER 3

Grammar and Syntax

Chapter 3

GRAMMAR AND SYNTAX

For the SAT Latin Subject Test, you are expected to have mastered the basics of Latin grammar and syntax. Note that your exam score is *not* adjusted based upon how many years of Latin you have had, but reflects your general command of the language. The stated purpose of the test is to assess your ability to read Latin. Because a number of different textbook programs are used to teach the language, the exam contains a broad base of anticipated content and skills, roughly approximating the levels of achievement identified on the *National Latin Exam Syllabus* (American Classical League, 2001) and the *National Standards for Classical Language Learning* (American Classical League; American Philological Association, 1997). There is no official syllabus of study for the SAT Latin Subject Test. The syllabus that follows is derived from the teaching experience of the author and from personal study of the exam. This is not an official syllabus, but it serves as a guideline for the grammar and syntax presented for review in this book. Before you begin, you are asked to review some general terms commonly used in the study of Latin grammar and syntax. These terms and those in the glossaries that follow are not tested explicitly on the SAT Latin Subject Test, but your understanding of them is part of your understanding of how Latin works, and thus of your ability to read Latin, which is the main focus of the exam.

Important Notes

1. Macrons (long marks) are provided for all Latin words on the SAT Latin Subject Test and in this book. Thus, **puella** is made distinct from **puellā**, **quaereris** from **quaerēris**, and so on.

2. On the exam and in this book, Latin words containing a consonantal **i** are also given with the **j** spelling, for example, **eius** (**ejus**), **iam** (**jam**), **iaciō** (**jaciō**), and **Iūnō** (**Jūnō**).

GRAMMAR AND SYNTAX GLOSSARY

- **adjective** (**ad** + **iacere/jacere**, *to throw toward*): a class of words that modifies, describes, limits, or specifies a noun or other substantive. In Latin, an adjective may also serve as a noun (see **substantive**) or as an adverb.

- **adverb** (**ad** + **verbum**, *to the word*): the part of speech that consists of a class of words that modify a verb, an adjective, or another adverb.

- **assimilation** (**ad** + **similis**, *similar to*): the phonetic absorption or blending of a consonant by a following consonant for greater ease in pronunciation, such as **ad** + **ferre** = **afferre**.

- **conjugate** (noun, **conjugation**): to give in traditional sequence all forms of a particular tense of a verb.

- **conjunction** (**cum** + **iungere/jungere**, *to join together*): indeclinable words that join together words, phrases, clauses, and sentences, for example **et** (*and*), **sed** (*but*), **aut** (*or*), **nec/neque** (*and not*).

- **context** (**cum** + **texere**, *to join or weave together*): the verbal neighborhood of a word, phrase, or clause in a sentence, used to assist in the determination of meaning.

- **decline** (noun, **declension**): to provide the case forms of a noun, pronoun, or adjective in the singular and plural.

- **enclitic** (from the Greek, "leaning on"): a particle such as **-ne**, **-que**, or **-ve** that is attached to the end of another word, as in **estne?** or **senatus populusque**.

- **gloss** (from the Greek, "tongue or language"): to give the meaning or explanation of an unfamiliar word or word group.

- **grammar** (**grammatica**, *the study of letters or words, philology*): essentially, the study of the forms of words in a language. Study of the forms of words is also referred to as morphology.

- **inflection** (**inflectere**, *to bend, move*): alteration of a word in order to indicate grammatical features such as case, number, person, tense, or mood. With nouns, inflection refers to "declining," and with verbs, to "conjugating."

- **interjection** (**inter** + **iacere/jacere**, *to throw between*): a sudden, short utterance, often emotional, for example **Ecce!** (*Look!*), **Eugepae!** (*Terrific! Cool!*), **Eheu!** (*Alas! Ow!*), **Iō!** (*Hooray!*)

- **macron** (from the Greek, "large"): the mark that designates long syllables in Latin, namely, those that are sustained longer during pronunciation, as in **matellā**.

- **modify** (**modus**, with the sense of *limit*): to qualify or limit the meaning of one word by another.

- **morphology** (from the Greek, "shape"): study of the structure of words, including inflection, derivation, and the formation of compounds.

- **noun** (**nōmen**, *name*): the name of a person, place, thing, or idea.

- **number**: singular or plural.

- **object** (**ob** + **iacere/jacere**, *to put before*): a noun or substantive that receives the action of, or is affected by, the verb in a sentence or one that follows and is governed by a preposition.

- **parse** (**pars ōrātiōnis**, *part of speech*): to identify and describe each individual word in a sentence, namely, its part of speech, grammatical form, and syntactical relationship to the other words in the sentence.

- **part of speech**: a category of words classified according to function, for example adjective, adverb, conjunction, interjection, noun, preposition, pronoun, or verb.

- **preposition** (**prae** + **pōnere**, *to place before*): a short, indeclinable word placed before and linking a noun or substantive (known as the object of the preposition) with another word in the sentence, such as **in flūmine** **natat**, *he is swimming in the river*. The preposition plus its object is known as a prepositional phrase.

- **pronoun** (**prō** + **nōmen**, *for a noun*): a word that substitutes for a noun or noun phrase and designates persons or things previously specified or understood from context, as in **Canis baculum petit. Is id petit.** *The dog fetches the stick. He (The dog) fetches it (the stick).*

- **stem**: in general, the part of a word that is unchanging and provides the root meaning, as well as the part to which the endings that determine contextual meaning are attached. For instance, the stem (or base) of the noun **vox, vōcis**, is **voc-**. Verbs, such as **clāmō, clāmāre, clāmāvi, clāmātus**, have stems in both the present (**clāmā-**) and past (**clāmāv-, clāmāt-**) tenses.

- **substantive** (**sub** + **stāre**, *to stand beneath*): the designation of a pronoun, adjective, participle, or verbal clause that substitutes for (takes on the substance of) a noun, as in **Vox <u>clāmantis</u> in dēsertō**, *The voice of (<u>someone</u>) <u>crying</u> in the wilderness.*

- **synopsis** (from the Greek, "looking at together"): a convenient way to summarize or consolidate all the forms of a given verb by creating and/or translating a single form from each tense, voice, and mood in a designated person and number.

- **syntax** (from the Greek, "to put in order"): refers to the rules for the use of words in a sentence (as opposed to grammar, which is generally concerned with the forms of the words themselves).

- **verb** (**verbum**, *word*): a word that expresses action, occurrence, or existence.

POSSIBLE GRAMMAR AND SYNTAX TOPICS ON THE LATIN SUBJECT TESTS

The superscript numbers indicate how many times a particular form or use has been tested on the published SAT Latin Subject Tests.

	Latin II		**Latin III and IV**	
Nouns				
	nominative:	subject	genitive:	description
		predicate nominative		partitive
	genitive:	possession		objective
	dative:	indirect object		w/ nouns, adjectives and verbs[2]

	Latin II		Latin III and IV	
Nouns (*cont'd*)	accusative:	direct object	dative:	possession[2]
		object prepositions		purpose/ reference = double[1]
		place to which		w/ special verbs[2]
		with special adjectives[2]		agent[3]
		extent space and time	*(locative)* accusative:	place to which (w/o preposition)[2]
	ablative:	object of preposition		subject of infinitive
	(locative)	place where, from which	ablative:	separation
		accompani- ment		cause
		agent[1]		description
		manner		respect/ specification
		time when, w/in which[2]		certain verbs and adjectives
		means/ instrument[1]		
		comparison[1]	locative	
	vocative:	direct address[1]		
	declensions:	1st, 2nd, 3rd, 4th,[1] 5th[1]		
	apposition[1]			

	Latin II	**Latin III and IV**
Pronouns	demonstrative (**hic**,[2] **ille, is**,[2] **īdem, iste**)	
	relative (**quī, quae, quod**)[4]	
	interrogative (**quis, quid**)[3]	indefinite (**aliquis, quīdam, quisque**)
	personal (**ego, tū, vōs, nōs**)	intensive (**ipse**)
	reflexive (**sē**)	
Adjectives	declensions: 1st/2nd, 3rd[3]	
	noun–adjective agreement	
	comparison of regular and irregular adjectives	irregular (**alius, alter**)[1]
	cardinal and ordinal numbers (**ūnus/ prīmus**)	
Adverbs	comparison of regular and irregular adverbs[3]	

	Latin II		**Latin III and IV**
Adverbs *(cont'd)*	interrogative adverb and particle (**nōnne, num, ˉne**)[1]		
Verbs			
	conjugations:	1st, 2nd,[2] 3rd,[2] 4th	
	six tenses of indicative mood		
	active and passive voice		deponent verbs[1]
	irregular verbs (**sum,**[1] **possum, eō, ferō,**[1] **volō, nōlō, mālō, fīo**)*		impersonal verbs (e.g., **licet, placet**)[1]
	imperative mood[1]		participles[5]
	negative command/ prohibition[1]		ablative absolute[4]
			infinitives[3]
			indirect statement[6]
			subjunctive mood
			independent (hortatory)[1]

Latin II	Latin III and IV
Verbs (*cont'd*)	**ut** purpose clause
	result clause[1]
	indirect command[1]
	fear clause[2]
	conditions[3]
	indirect question[1]
	doubt clause[1]
	relative characteristic clause[2]
	relative purpose clause[1]
	cum clauses
	gerund[1]
	gerundive[4]
	passive periphrastic[3]
	supine

*   Irregular verbs are sometimes taught in the third or fourth years.

GRAMMAR AND SYNTAX RESOURCES (ONLINE)

- Latin Site (Eva Easton), http://eleaston.com/latin.html
  Review exercises and activities for main secondary school textbook programs.

- Quia, http://www.quia.com/dir/latin
  Teacher-produced Java games, hangman, pop-ups, quizzes, et al., organized by textbook program.

- *New Latin Grammar* (Allen and Greenough), http://www.hhhh.org/perseant/libellus/aides/allgre (via http://www.perseus.tufts.edu)

- Notre Dame Latin Site (Kevin Cawley, University of Notre Dame), http://www.nd.edu/~archives/latgramm.htm
  Grammatical forms search engine.

- Latin Grammar (Eric Conrad, Ohio State University), http://www.math.ohio-state.edu/~econrad/lang/latin.html
  Paradigm charts, et al., designed by a non-Latin math student.

- Latin Pages (N. Gill, ancienthistory.about.com), Many links to grammar, dictionaries, etc.

- Certamen Questions Database (B. W. Duncan), http://www.geocities.com/bwduncan

- National Latin Exams (Levels II, III–IV Prose, III–IV Poetry, and V, 1997–current year), http://www.nle.org/exams.html#examsprevious
  Printable exams with answers.

- *Ecce Romani*, Books 1 and 2, http://abney.homestead.com/ecce2.html
  Vocabulary and grammar drills, chapter-by-chapter.

- Grammatica (Joan Jahnige, Kentucky Educational Television):
  http://www.dl.ket.org/latin1/review;
  http://www.dl.ket.org/latin1/review/latin2/grammar;
  http://www.dl.ket.org/latin3/grammar;
  http://www.dl.ket.org/latinlit/grammar;
  Vocabulary and grammar drills for *Ecce Romani*.

- Drills for the *Oxford Latin Course* (Margaret Phillips, University Missouri-St. Louis), http://www.umsl.edu/~phillips/oldrills/index.html
  Review materials for *Oxford Latin Course*, chapter-by-chapter, with clickable answers.

- Internet Workbook for the *Oxford Latin Course* (R. Cape, Austin College), http://artemis.austincollege.edu/acad/cml/rcape/latin/grammar-index.html
  Chapter-by-chapter materials with clickable, scored exercises.

- Self-Help Quizzes to accompany the *Oxford Latin Course*, Part I (Barbara McManus), http://www.cnr.edu/home/bmcmanus/oltquizzes.html

- Study guides for the *Oxford Latin Course* (Greg Swann), http://www.presenceofmind.net/Latin/study.html

Wheelock's Latin Resources (Online)

"Wheelock," the Latin textbook most commonly used in colleges, has excellent online support that is helpful to students who are reviewing Latin.

- Official Wheelock's Latin Series Web Site, http://www.wheelock slatin.com/wheelocksflashcards.htm

- Answers to Wheelock's Latin (Richard Armstrong, University of Houston), http://ancienthistory.about.com/od/answerswheelock

- Grammar and Vocabulary Helps (Claude Pavur, St. Louis University), http://www.slu.edu/colleges/AS/languages/classical/latin/tchmat/gr-helps.html

- Grote's Study Guide to Wheelock's Latin (Dale A. Grote, UNC-Charlotte), http://arts.cuhk.edu.hk/Lexis/Wheelock-Latin

Self-scoring unit-by-unit quizzes:

- Exercises for Chapters 1–40 (L. Bowman, University of Victoria, British Columbia), http://web.uvic.ca/hrd/latin/wheelock/

THE SAT SUBJECT TEST IN
LATIN

SECTION 2

Nouns

CHAPTER 4

The Language
of Nouns

Chapter 4

THE LANGUAGE OF NOUNS

In the following three sections, we will review nouns, pronouns, and adjectives all together because they are related in form and function. Although adverbs modify verbs, their forms and functions approximate those of adjectives, therefore, adverbs and adjectives are presented together. The vocative case will not be reviewed until Chapter 23 (Direct Address), and the locative, although not considered a regular case, will be presented for review along with the ablative case. Here is an outline of the sections on nouns and their attendant forms:

Section 4: Adjectives and Adverbs

Chapter 16: Adjectives

Chapter 17: Adverbs

We begin this section with a review of the nomenclature used to describe Latin nouns. Then we will review their various forms and functions. Depending upon your level of study, you may not know everything about Latin nouns, but do your best to remaster what you have learned. The finer points of the syntax of nouns, such as genitive of material or ablative of price, are beyond the scope of this review.

The terms in the following glossary describe the grammar and syntax of nouns. Not only are these descriptive terms used throughout the chapters on nouns, pronouns, and adjectives, but they are also used in test questions on the first and last parts of the exam:

SAMPLE QUESTIONS

Part A: Recognition of Forms

1. The genitive plural of cīvis is

   (A) cīvis   (C) cīvem

   (B) cīvium   (D) cīvibus

Part D: Reading Comprehension

2. The case and number of corporum are

   (A) nominative singular (C) accusative plural

   (B) accusative singular (D) genitive plural

Answers

1. (B)
2. (D)

NOUNS GLOSSARY

- **apposition** (**ad** + **pōnere**, *to place near*): the relationship between a noun and another noun that stands next to and identifies it, for example, **Rōma, urbs aeterna**, *Rome, the eternal city*.

- **base**: see **stem**

- **case**: the designation of the function of a noun, pronoun, or adjective. There are six cases in Latin: nominative, genitive, dative, accusative, ablative, and vocative. Locative is not considered a regular case.

- **declension**: one of five categories of nouns and pronouns and two of adjectives in which the forms are grouped by case, gender, and number. The declension is designated by the spelling of the genitive singular ending. Nouns, pronouns, and adjectives are said to be *declined* when all case forms of the singular and plural are given.

- **gender** (**genus**, *type*): the designation of a noun, pronoun, or adjective as masculine, feminine or neuter. Some nouns have common gender, that is, they can be either masculine or feminine. Because things can be designated as masculine or feminine in Latin, gender must be memorized or determined from contextual clues.

- **noun** (**nōmen**, *name*): the name of a person, place, thing, or idea.

- **number**: singular or plural.

- **predicate** (**prae** + **dīcere**, *to say before*): the designation of a noun or adjective that appears after some form of **esse** and refers to the subject, such as a predicate nominative, **Sōcratēs erat philosophus**, *Socrates was a philosopher*, or a predicate adjective, **Sōcratēs erat sapiens**, *Socrates was wise*.

- **substantive**: see Chapter 3

- **stem**: for nouns, the stem (or base) is found by dropping the genitive singular from the noun, for example, **voc-** is the stem of the noun **vox, vōcis**. The stem is often not easily recognized in the nominative, such as in **vox**, in which the stem **voc-** is disguised by the **x** (**vox** = **vocs**). The stem gives the meaning, whereas the endings indicate the function via case, gender, and number.

THE CASES OF LATIN NOUNS

- **ablative (ab + ferō, ferre, tulī, lātum,** *to carry from*): a case (function) of nouns used in a great variety of ways. The ablative is found with or without prepositions. It commonly expresses time, place, or means, and it is translated by words such as *by*, *from*, *in*, or *with*. The ablative singular is always a vowel, regardless of declension, and the plural always ends in -**s** (-**īs**, -**bus**).

- **accusative (accūsāre,** *to accuse*): the noun case that most commonly identifies the direct object of a sentence. The accusative is therefore also known as the *objective case*. The accusative case, with or without prepositions, also expresses time or place and indicates the subject of an infinitive. The accusative singular generally ends in -**m** and the plural in -**s**.

- **dative (dare,** *to give*): the noun case that indicates the indirect object of a sentence, which is translated by the words *to* or *for*. The dative case is found with verbs of giving or speaking. The indirect object is the secondary object in a sentence, for example, **Pecūniam miserō dedī,** *I gave money to the poor man* or *I gave the poor man money*. (The direct object in this sentence is **pecūniam.**) The dative is also found with certain adjectives and verbs and can indicate possession. In the plural, the forms of the dative case have the same endings as those of the ablative.

- **genitive (genitus,** fr. **gignere,** *to beget*): the noun case generally used to link together two nouns, and expressed in English using the word *of*, such as in **Umbra Caesaris!** *The ghost of Caesar!* or *Caesar's ghost!* The genitive case can also be used with certain nouns, adjectives, and verbs.

- **locative (locus,** *place*): the noun form that designates place. The preposition is not required in Latin with the names of cities, small islands, or with the words **domus,** *home*, and **rūs,** *countryside*.

- **nominative (nōmen,** *name*): the "naming" case that designates the subject or predicate nominative. See also **predicate** (Chapter 3, "Grammar and Syntax Glossary").

- **vocative (vocāre,** *to call, to use the voice*): the noun case of direct address. This case is often found in the context of a verb in the imperative mood. The forms are regularly the same as the nominative, except for second declension nouns ending in -**us** or -**ius**.

CHAPTER 5

The Forms of Nouns

Chapter 5

THE FORMS OF NOUNS

DECLENSION, CASE, NUMBER, AND GENDER

As you know, a noun is the name of a person, place, thing, or idea. In Latin, a noun form such as **tībiae** consists of a stem (or base) and a case ending: **tībi-** (stem) + **-ae** (ending). Nouns, pronouns, and adjectives in Latin are divided into declensions, or categories based upon their endings. Declensions indicate variations in case, gender, and number. The declension to which a noun belongs is derived from the ending of the genitive singular. (By the way, it is said that old Latin teachers never die, they just decline!)

Genitive	Declension
tībi|ae	1st
nās|ī	2nd
ped|is	3rd
man|ūs	4th
facil|ēī	5th

Here are the most common functions of each case in Latin:

    Nominative—subject

    Genitive—possession (*of*)

    Dative—indirect object (*to, for*)

    Accusative—direct object

    Ablative—separation, place/time, means (*from, in, with, by*)

    Vocative—direct address

The noun cases listed in the order of the frequency of their appearance in Latin literature are nominative, accusative, ablative, genitive, and dative.

Nouns have *number*; that is, they can be singular or plural. They also have *gender* (masculine, feminine, neuter, or common gender, that is, either masculine or feminine), which is usually determined by the ending of the nominative singular. Gender can be "declension specific," that is, certain genders are generally found in certain declensions. Nouns of the first and fifth declensions are generally feminine, and those of the second and fourth, masculine. (There are, of course, exceptions.) All three genders are found in the third declension, which is the largest and most varied of the noun declensions. Remember that a Latin noun does not have the articles *a, an*, or *the*. Thus, in the following table, **tībia** can mean *a shinbone, the shinbone*, or simply *shinbone*, depending upon the context. Can you determine what the meanings of the nouns in the following table have in common?

Quick Study of Noun Forms

	1st	2nd	2nd N.	3rd	3rd N.	4th	5th
Singular							
Nominative	tībia	nāsus	brācchium	pēs	caput	manus	faciēs
Genitive	tībiae	nāsī	brācchī	pedis	capitis	manūs	faciēī
Dative	tībiae	nāsō	brācchiō	pedī	capitī	manuī	faciēī
Accusative	tībiam	nāsum	brācchium	pedem	caput	manum	faciem
Ablative	tībiā	nāsō	brācchiō	pede	capite	manū	faciē
Plural							
Nominative	tībiae	nāsī	brācchia	pedēs	capita	manūs	faciēs
Genitive	tībiārum	nāsōrum	brācchiōrum	pedum	capitum	manuum	faciērum
Dative	tībiīs	nāsīs	brācchiīs	pedibus	capitibus	manibus	faciēbus
Accusative	tībiās	nāsōs	brācchia	pedēs	capita	manūs	faciēs
Ablative	tībiīs	nāsīs	brācchiīs	pedibus	capitibus	manibus	faciēbus

First Declension Nouns

Several common first declension nouns are not feminine but masculine, such as the PAIN nouns: **poeta**, *poet*, **agricola**, *farmer*, **incola**, *inhabitant*, and **nauta**, *sailor*.

Second Declension Nouns

Nouns of the second declension have both masculine and neuter genders. The only variation in form between these two genders occurs in the nominative and accusative singular and plural of the neuter noun, where the same form appears in both cases, for example, singular **brācchium**, and plural **brācchia**. Use context to distinguish a singular first declension noun ending in -**a**, such as **tībia**, from a plural second or third declension neuter noun ending in -**a**, such as **brācchia**.

Some nouns whose nominative ends in -**r**, such as **puer** or **vir**, constitute a subcategory of the second declension masculine noun. All other case forms of this type of word are the same as those given in the chart. Avoid confusing the noun **liber**, **librī** (m.), *book*, with the adjective **līber**, **lībera**, **līberum**, *free*.

With words such as **brācchium**, be aware of the fact that the genitive singular form is found both as **brācchī** and as **brācchiī**, depending on the era in which the Latin was written. (The former or contracted spelling was used by pre-Augustan authors and will be the form of preference in this book.)

Note, too, that the stem vowel **i**- and the ending vowel -**i**- both appear in the dative and ablative plural, such as **brācchiīs**.

Third Declension Nouns

The nominative singular of third declension nouns can have a variety of endings. The other case endings of third declension nouns are added to the stem and not to the nominative; for example, the ablative singular of **pēs** (gen. **pedis**) is not **pese**, but **pede** (stem **ped**- + abl. ending -**e**). The third declension is subdivided into two categories, consonant stems and **i**-stems.

Third declension consonant stem nouns—**milēs, mīlit**-; **pax, pāc**; **senātor, senātōr**-

Third declension **i**-stem nouns—**cīvis, cīvis**; **hostis, hostis**; **ignis, ignis**; **mare, maris**

True third declension **i**-stem nouns are generally characterized by forms whose genitive singular has the same number of syllables as the nominative singular, such as **cīvis, cīvis**. Third declension **i**-stem nouns always have **-ium** in the genitive plural (**cīvium**) and can have **-ī** for **-e** (**cīvī** for **cīve**) in the ablative singular and **-īs** for **-ēs** (**cīvīs** for **cīvēs**) in the accusative plural. Some third declension nouns contain features of both consonant and **i**-stem nouns, such as **urbs, urbis** (gen. pl. **urbium**, but abl. sing. **urbe** and acc. pl. **urbēs**).

Be alert for variations in the forms of third declension nouns. Most nouns of this declension have either masculine or feminine gender. Nouns ending in **-or**, like **senātor**, are masculine, and those ending in **-ās** (e.g., **verītās**), **-is** (e.g., **vestis**), **-ō** (e.g., **venātiō**), and **-x** (e.g., **vox**) are feminine.

Fourth Declension Nouns

The macron is the critical element in the forms of the fourth declension. Note that macrons appear in the genitive singular and nominative and accusative plural forms, but not in the nominative singular form. Macrons are provided on the SAT Latin Subject Test, but this doesn't prohibit a question regarding the functional difference between a fourth declension noun with a macron and one without.

Remember that nouns of the second (**dominus**), third (**tempus**), and fourth (**domus**) declensions all have forms ending in **-us**. Use the context to help determine the function. Most fourth declension nouns are masculine. The important nouns **domus** and **manus** are feminine. One important fourth declension word, **domus,** *home,* is unique in that it also contains forms of the second declension masculine noun. These commonly appear as variants in the dative singular (**domuī** or **domō**), accusative plural (**domūs** or **domōs**), and ablative singular (**domū** or **domō**).

Here are some common fourth declension nouns:

aestus, *heat*	**manus,** *hand; band of men*
aquaeductus, *aqueduct*	**metus,** *fear*
arcus, *arch, bow*	**senātus,** *senate*
cantus, *singing*	**sensus,** *feeling, sense*
cāsus, *chance*	**sonitus,** *sound*
cōnsulātus, *consulship*	**spīritus,** *breath, breathing;*
domus, *home*	*spirit, soul*

frūctus, *fruit*   **strepitus**, *noise*

lacus, *lake*   **tumultus**, *commotion*

magistrātus, *official, magistrate*   **versus**, *line of poetry*

Fifth Declension Nouns

Only **diēs** and **rēs** are declined throughout all cases and numbers, although many of the (singular) forms of the other 10 or so nouns in this declension do appear.

All fifth declension nouns are feminine except for **diēs**, *day*, and **merīdiēs**, *noon*, which are masculine. Be especially alert to the ambiguity of the nominative singular and nominative and accusative plural, **faciēs**, and the genitive and dative singular, **faciēī**.

The meaning of the noun **rēs** should not be rendered as *thing*. **Rēs** is often thought of as a catchall word, like the English words "thingamajig" or "whatchamacallit," used by Romans when they couldn't think of the word they wanted. However, **rēs** has a number of different meanings, each of which depends upon its context, including *activity, affair, circumstance, event, issue, item, matter*, and the like.

Here are some common fifth declension nouns:

aciēs, *edge, keenness, line of battle*   **merīdiēs**, *midday, noon*

diēs, *day*   **rēs**, *event, item, situation*, etc.

effigiēs, *likeness, image*   **speciēs**, *appearance*

fidēs, *trust, loyalty*   **spēs**, *hope*

Unusual Noun Forms

The word **deus**, *god,* appears in contracted forms in the plural: **dī** for **deī**, **deum** for **deōrum**, and **dīs** for **deīs**.

To distinguish the dative and ablative plurals of **fīlia** and **dea** from those of **fīlius** and **deus**, the forms **deābus** and **filiābus** are used.

Some nouns of the third declension are irregular. The most common of these are **vīs**, *force, power, strength*, and **mare, maris** (n.), *sea*. In the singular, the forms are **vīs, vīs** (rare), **vī** (rare), **vim, vī**, and in the plural, **vīrēs, vīrium, vīribus, vīrēs** (or **vīrīs**), **vīribus**. Take care not to confuse forms of this word with those of **vir, virī**, *man*, by looking for the macron in the initial syllable of **vīs**.

The forms of **mare** are **mare, maris, marī, mare, marī**, and plural, **maria, marium, maribus, maria, maribus**.

There are only four neuter nouns in the fourth declension, and the most common of these, **cornū**, *horn* or *wing of an army*, and **genu**, *knee*, appear infrequently. In the singular, the forms are **cornū, cornūs, cornū, cornū, cornū**, and in the plural, they are **cornua, cornuum, cornibus, cornua, cornibus**.

Some Latin nouns are found only in the plural, whereas others have one meaning in the singular and another in the plural:

Nouns Found in Plural Only

arma, armōrum	*arms, weapons*
castra, castrōrum	*military camp*
dīvitiae, dīvitiārum	*riches, wealth*
īnsidiae, īnsidiārum	*ambush*
manēs, manium	*shades of the dead*
tenēbrae, tenēbrārum	*darkness*

Nouns with Alternative Meanings

Singular	Plural
aedēs, *house*	**aedēs**, *temple*
cōpia, *abundance*	**cōpiae**, *troops*
fīnis, *end*	**fīnēs**, *boundary*
littera, *letter of alphabet*	**litterae**, *literature*
mōs, *custom*	**mōrēs**, *habits, character*

TIPS ON NOUN FORMS

- Practice with the charts in your text and in this book.

- Review the patterns that appear in the endings of the various noun declensions, for example, most accusative singulars end in -**m**, all ablative singulars end in a vowel, dative and ablative endings are often alike, nominative and accusative endings of neuter nouns are the same, and so on.

- Exceptions to rules and unusual examples of forms are favorite areas of evaluation, for example, the ablative singular of **mare** (**marī**, not **mare**) or the nominative plural of **vīs** (**vīrēs**, not **virī**).

PRACTICE QUESTIONS   12/14

1. The genitive singular of <u>fīlius</u> is
   - (A) fīliōrum
   - (B) fīlī
   - (C) fīliō
   - (D) fīlium

2. The nominative plural of <u>māter</u> is
   - (A) mātrum
   - (B) mātrī
   - (C) mātrēs
   - (D) mātris

3. An alternative way to express <u>videō domūs</u> is
   - (A) videō domō
   - (B) videō domōrum
   - (C) videō domī
   - (D) videō domōs

4. The gender of <u>miser nauta</u> is
   - (A) masculine
   - (B) feminine
   - (C) neuter
   - (D) common

5. The word <u>senātus</u> belongs to the . . . declension.
   - (A) 1st
   - (B) 2nd
   - (C) 3rd
   - (D) 4th

6. The genitive singular of <u>magister</u> is
   - (A) magistrō
   - (B) magistrōrum
   - (C) magistrīs
   - (D) magistrī

7.   Which of the following nouns belongs to the same declension as <u>ager</u>?

(A) pater   (C) liber

(B) frāter   (D) māter

8.   The accusative singular of <u>iter</u> is

(A) itinerum   (C) itineris

(B) itinera   (D) iter

9.   The plural of <u>corpus</u> is

(A) corporī   (C) corporibus

(B) corpora   (D) corporum

10. The dative plural of <u>dea</u> is

(A) deīs   (C) deā

(B) deābus   (D) deae

11. The case and number of <u>ignium</u> is

(A) accusative singular   (C) genitive plural

(B) nominative singular   (D) genitive singular

12. Which of the following cases and numbers is <u>not</u> represented by the form <u>diēs</u>?

(A) nominative singular   (C) accusative plural

(B) accusative singular   (D) nominative plural

13. The alternate of the accusative form <u>cīvēs</u> is

(A) cīvīs   (C) cīvibus

(B) cīvī   (D) cīvium

Stumper:

Which word is accusative in the following sentence?

<u>Corpus hortus domūs cēlābat</u>.

(A) corpus   (C) domūs

(B) hortus   (D) none

Answers

1.	(B)	5.	(D)	9.	(B)	13.	(A)
2.	(C)	6.	(D)	10.	(B)	**Stumper:**	(A)
3.	(D)	7.	(C)	11.	(C)		
4.	(A)	8.	(D)	12.	(B)		

CHAPTER 6
The Nominative Case

Chapter 6

THE NOMINATIVE CASE

As you will recall from the previous chapter, the functions of nouns are indicated by the various cases in which they are found. These cases are the nominative, genitive, dative, accusative, ablative, and vocative. In the ensuing chapters of this section, we will review the main functions of each case so that you can recall how nouns are used and so that you can prepare for the upcoming sections on pronouns and adjectives, which have the same cases, genders, and numbers as nouns. Also in this section, we will meet Bombax ("Boombox"), a ne'er–do–well slave, whose adventures will provide a context for much of our review.

The Forms of the Nominative Case

	1st	2nd	2nd N.	3rd
Singular	tībia	nāsus	brācchium	pēs
Plural	tībiae	nāsī	brācchia	pedēs
	3rd N.	4th	5th	
Singular	caput	manus	faciēs	
Plural	capita	manūs	faciēs	

THE USES OF THE NOMINATIVE CASE

Subject

The nominative, or "naming," case has two uses: as the subject of a sentence and as a predicate nominative. The subject is the person or thing that performs the action of the verb, as in the following sentence:

> **<u>Bacillus</u> vīlicus Bombācem haud multum amat.**
> *The overseer <u>Bacillus</u> dislikes Bombax.*

Predicate Nominative and Predicate Adjective

Because of the meaning of **esse**, its forms cannot take a direct object. **Esse** links the subject with a noun or adjective following the predicate (the verb and associated or dependent words). The linked words are known as predicate nominatives or predicate adjectives, depending upon their function. In English, these words follow the verb and refer back to the subject:

Predicate nominative:	**Bombax <u>parasītus</u> est.**
	Bombax is a <u>moocher</u>.
Predicate adjective:	**Bombax <u>ignāvus</u> est.**
	Bombax is <u>lazy</u>.

Apposition

Apposition (**ad** + **ponere**, *to place beside*) is the relationship between a noun and another noun that stands next to and identifies or limits it. The word in apposition is often bounded by commas and is known as the appositive. An appositive agrees with its noun in case, and usually in number and gender. It can be found in any case, such as the accusative:

Dominus Bombācem, <u>servum</u> ignāvum, vendidit.
The master sold Bombax, the lazy <u>slave</u>.

TIPS ON TRANSLATING THE NOMINATIVE CASE

- Look for the subject at or near the beginning of a Latin sentence. If there is no nominative, look at the personal ending of the verb for the subject:

    Est parasītus.
    <u>He</u> is a moocher.

- Be aware of the distinction in usage between a noun in apposition and a predicate nominative. Whereas a predicate nominative must be nominative, a noun in apposition with another noun may appear in any case.

PRACTICE QUESTIONS 4/4

1. Ignāvō servō mandata dedit. The subject of this sentence is
   (A) Ignāvō   (C) mandata
   (B) servō   (D) he (in the verb dedit)

2. Quis erat . . . ?
   (A) vīlicum   (C) vīlico
   (B) vīlicī   (D) vīlicus

3. Bacillus Bombācem . . . punīre vult.
   (A) servum   (C) servō
   (B) servus   (D) servōrum

4. Bacillus . . . nōn erat.
   (A) dominum   (C) dominus
   (B) dominō   (D) domine

Answers

1. **(D)**
   The sentence reads _He gave orders to the lazy slave_. The subject is in the verb, as none of the other forms can serve as the subject. Answers (A) **Ignāvō** and (B) **servō** are in the dative case and **mandata** is neuter plural, whereas the verb **dedit** is singular.

2. **(D)**
   Vīlicus is a predicate nominative because it follows the verb and restates the subject. Answer (A) is the most likely wrong choice because the verb **erat** cannot take a direct object. Answer (B) is genitive singular or nominative plural, and (C) is dative or ablative singular.

3. **(A)**
   This question is designed to test the fact that a noun in apposition must agree with the noun that it defines or limits and is generally found next to the noun it defines. Therefore, the answer is **servum**, modifying **Bombācem**. Answer (B) is nominative singular and could

modify **Bacillus**, but the position of the missing word makes it more likely to be taken with **Bombācem** than with **Bacillus**, and the case is wrong. Answer (C) is dative or ablative singular and (D) genitive plural, neither of which are correct choices for apposition with **Bacillum**.

4. **(C)**

   Dominus is the correct answer because a predicate nominative, re-stating the subject, is required by the context. The obvious answer is perhaps (A) **dominum**, but an accusative direct object cannot be found with **erat**. Answer (B) is dative/ablative and (D) vocative, neither of which fits the context.

CHAPTER 7

The Genitive Case

Chapter 7

THE GENITIVE CASE

The Forms of the Genitive Case

	1st	2nd	2nd N.	3rd
Singular	tībiae	nāsī	brācchī	pedis
Plural	tībiārum	nāsōrum	brācchiōrum	pedum

	3rd N.	4th	5th
Singular	capitis	manūs	faciēī
Plural	capitum	manuum	faciērum

THE USES OF THE GENITIVE CASE

Possessive Genitive

The genitive case links two nouns together, as in **servus dominī**, the *slave of the master* or *the master's slave*. This linkage very often indicates possession, namely, that someone has custody of or control over something or someone else. In English, possession is expressed by the word *of* preceding the word indicating the possessor. (Note that although *of* is a preposition in English, it is not in Latin.) In English, possession may also be expressed by the use of the apostrophe-S for the singular, *the master's*, and S-apostrophe for the plural, *the masters'*. (Before the Norman invasion, English did have a genitive ending, *-es*, but the *-e* eventually dropped away and was replaced by the apostrophe.)

Genitive of Description

A noun in the genitive case can describe another noun. If it does, the describing noun requires an accompanying adjective:

> **Bombax servus <u>magnae calliditātis</u> est.**
> *Bombax is a slave <u>of great cunning</u>.*

Partitive Genitive

The partitive genitive, found with nouns such as **pars**, *part*, **nihil**, *nothing*, and **satis**, *enough*, and with (neuter) adjectives and pronouns, such as **aliquid**, *something*, **nimium**, *too much*, **plūs**, *more*, and **quid**, *something*, indicates a part of the whole. The partitive genitive is also known as genitive of the whole. So in the sentence **Bombax nihil labōris agit**, *Bombax does no work*, the underlined genitive phrase literally means *nothing of work*.

Cardinal numbers, especially **mīlia**, *thousands*, are also used in this way. The phrase **mille passuum** means *mile*, literally, *a thousand (of) paces*.

The partitive idea is also expressed by a prepositional phrase introduced by **ē/ex** or **dē**, such as **unus ē servīs**, *one of the slaves*, literally *one from the slaves*. Words such as **paucī, -e, -a**, *a few (of)*, and **quīdam, quaedam, quoddam**, *certain (of)* are also used in this way.

Objective Genitive

A genitive phrase can be used to express the object of an emotion or feeling, hence the term objective, and it is usually translated with the word *for*, as in **amor lībertātis**, *love for freedom* and **dēsīderium amīcae**, *longing for a friend*.

Use the context of the sentence to determine how best to phrase this use of the genitive.

Genitive with Certain Nouns, Adjectives, and Verbs

Words whose meaning requires the translation *of* in English take the genitive case:

Noun: **Bombax omnia laudis causā agit.**
                    Bombax does everything for the sake of praise.

Adjective: **Bombax cupidus vīnī semper est.**
                    Bombax is always desirous of wine.

Verb: **Saepe Bombax officī oblīviscitur.**
                    Bombax is often forgetful of his duty.

The following common adjectives are "agreeing adjectives," and are <u>not</u> followed by the genitive case:

extrēmus, *end (of)*　　　　**reliquus**, *remainder (of)*

medius, *middle (of)*　　　　**summus**, *top (of)*

omnis, *all (of)*

Therefore, we have **Bombax <u>in mediā viā</u> ambulābat**, *Bombax was walking <u>in the middle of</u> the road*.

TIPS ON TRANSLATING THE GENITIVE CASE

- Use the context in order to avoid confusing the following forms of the genitive with those of other noun cases:

  ancillae (gen. sing.)　　**ancillae** (dat. sing and nom. pl.)

  servī (gen. sing.)　　　　**servī** (nom. pl.)

  laboris (gen. sing.)　　　**servīs** (dat. and abl. pl.)

  laborum (gen. pl.)　　　　**servum** (acc. sing.)

- Remember that the genitive case generally links two nouns whose meaning may be characterized by the use of the word *of* in translation: **baculum vīlicī**, *the cane of the overseer*.

- Avoid translating certain genitive expressions too literally. For example, **satis temporis** has the best meaning of *enough time* (not *enough of time*), and **dēsīderium lībertātis** means *longing for freedom* (not *longing of freedom*).

PRACTICE QUESTIONS

1. Bombax plūs . . . semper vult.

   (A) cibus　　　　　　(C) cibō

   (B) cibum　　　　　　(D) cibī

2. Bombax servus . . . erat.

   (A) magnae ignāviae　(C) magnas ignāvīas

   (B) magnam ignāviam　(D) magna ignāvia

3. The life of a slave was often <u>full of misery</u>.

   (A) plēna miseria   (C) plēna miseriā

   (B) plēna miseriae   (D) plēna cum miseriā

4. Canes vestīgia <u>fugitīvae ancillae</u> secutī sunt.

   (A) of the runaway maid

   (B) with the runaway maid

   (C) for the runaway maid

   (D) toward the runaway maid

5. For a slave, the price <u>of freedom</u> was hard work.

   (A) lībertātum   (C) lībertātis

   (B) lībertātī   (D) lībertāte

6. Bombax <u>aliquid malī</u> semper agebat.

   (A) of something bad   (C) something bad

   (B) for something bad   (D) with someone bad

7. ... nōmen nōn habēbat.

   (A) Ūnus ē servīs   (C) Ūnus servōrum

   (B) Ūnum servum   (D) Ūnīus servī

8. Servus <u>grātiam beneficī</u> agit.

   (A) gratitude and kindness

   (B) gratitude or kindness

   (C) gratitude for kindness

   (D) kind gratitude

Stumper:

Bombax quinque milia ... ambulāre nōn poterat.

   (A) passūs   (C) passus

   (B) passum   (D) passuum

Answers

1. **(D)**

    The irregular adjective **plūs** is found with the partitive genitive, therefore **plūs cibī**, *more of food* (i.e., *more food*), is the best choice to complete the sentence. Answer (A) **cibus** is a distractor because it has the same ending as **plūs** (which is neuter). Answer (B) is accusative and (C) is dative/ablative; neither is justifiable in the context of this sentence.

2. **(A)**

    The missing expression is a genitive of description, so it gives the meaning *Bombax was a slave of great idleness*. Answer (B) is accusative, which can't follow a form of **esse**. Answer (C) is plural, but the context is singular, and (D) is nominative, so it is not appropriate here.

3. **(B)**

    This question tests knowledge of the genitive case used with certain adjectives, here, **plēnus, -a, -um**. So *full of misery* is correctly translated as **plēna miseriae**. Answers (A) and (C) do not make sense because the nouns accompanying **plēna** are not in the genitive, but in the nominative and accusative cases, respectively. Neither does answer (D) *full with misery* make sense.

4. **(A)**

    This question asks you to recognize that **fugitīvae ancillae** is genitive rather than dative. The context of the sentence requires the sense *of the runaway maid* rather than *to/for the runaway maid*, so the resulting phrase must be (A), genitive, not (C), dative. Answers (B) and (D) are ablative and accusative phrases, respectively, so they are not appropriate choices here.

5. **(C)**

    This question simply asks for knowledge of the genitive singular ending of the third declension noun **lībertās**, which is **lībertātis**. The other answers are (A) **lībertātum**, genitive plural, (B) **lībertātī**, dative singular, and (D) **lībertāte**, ablative singular, none of which correctly translates *of freedom*.

6. **(C)**
    Aliquid malī is a partitive genitive, meaning *something (of) bad*. The sentence reads, *Bombax was always doing something bad*. Answer (A) is a distractor that incorrectly translates the genitive phrase, and answers (B) and (D) are dative, *for*, and ablative, *with*, respectively, neither of which translates the genitive form **malī** correctly.

7. **(A)**
    Given the choices, this sentence requires an alternative to the partitive genitive, which is (A) **Ūnus ē servīs**, *One of the slaves*. Answer (C) is the obvious choice, but correct usage requires the prepositional phrase, **ē servīs**, *out of/from the slaves*. Answers (B) and (D) do not make sense in the context of this sentence, which reads *One of the slaves did not have a name*.

8. **(C)**
    This is an example of the objective genitive, requiring the sense of *for* in **grātiam beneficī**, *The slave is giving gratitude for (a) kindness*. The translations offered in answers (A) and (B) require conjunctions such as **et** or **aut/vel** in the Latin, which are not found in the sentence, and (D) *kind gratitude* is an indefensible translation of the noun **beneficī**.

Stumper: **(D)**
    Numbers are used in expressions of the partitive genitive, as here, **mīlia passuum**, *thousands of paces*, or *miles*. Answer (A) is genitive but singular, whereas **quinque** and **mīlia** both require a plural to complete their meaning. Answer (B) **passum** could serve as the accusative direct object of **ambulāre**, but it does not link grammatically with **mīlia**. Answer (C) is the nominative singular of the fourth declension noun **passus**, and another nominative is not needed in this sentence because **Bombax** is the subject.

CHAPTER 8
The Dative Case

Chapter 8

THE DATIVE CASE

The Forms of the Dative Case

	1st	2nd	2nd N.	3rd
Singular	tībiae	nāsō	brācchiō	pedī
Plural	tībiīs	nāsīs	brācchiīs	pedibus
	3rd N.	4th	5th	
Singular	capitī	manuī	faciēī	
Plural	capitibus	manibus	faciēbus	

USES OF THE DATIVE CASE

Dative as Indirect Object

The dative case, also known as the "giving" or "to/for" case, is used to denote the person to whom or for whom something is done, given, shown, or told. This use of the dative is called the indirect object, that is, the person or thing indirectly affected by the action of the verb, as opposed to the direct object, which directly receives the action of the verb, for example:

> **Bombax speculum amīcae dedit.**
> *Bombax gave a mirror to his girlfriend (gave his girlfriend a mirror).*

In this sentence, the direct object is the accusative form **speculum**, and the indirect object is the dative form **amīcae**. To remember the type of word that produces an indirect object, use the memory device "Give, show, offer, tell, ring the dative bell."*

When determining the meaning of identical forms of the dative or ablative, consider the context of the sentence. Commonly, the form will

---

* David Pellegrino, http://latinteach.com/casemnemonics.html. Go to the Latinteach website, click on "Resources," and then on "Mnemonic Devices."

be dative if it designates a person and ablative (of means) if it designates a thing:

Dative: **Bacillus <u>servō</u> poenam dabat.**
              Bacillus was giving punishment <u>to the slave</u>.

Ablative: **Bacillus servum <u>baculō</u> verberābat.**
              Bacillus was beating the slave <u>with a cane</u>.

The translation of the indirect object with the word *to* is to be distinguished from that of **ad** + accusative, which implies direction or expresses motion toward:

    Bombax epistulam <u>ad amīcam</u> Palaestram mīsit.
    Bombax sent a letter <u>to his girlfriend</u> Palaestra.

In the same way, the translation of the indirect object with the word *for* is to be distinguished from that of **prō** + ablative, which means *in defense of*, *on behalf of*, such as in **prō bonō publicō**, *for the public good.*

Dative of Possession

When used with a form of the verb **esse**, the dative case can show possession. The possessor is put into the dative case:

    Estne baculum <u>Bacillō</u>?
    Does <u>Bacillus</u> have a cane? (Literally, *Is there a cane to Bacillus?*)

This use of the dative case is an alternative to **habēre** + accusative:

    Habetne Bacillus baculum?
    Does Bacillus have a cane?

Datives of Reference and Purpose (the double dative)

The dative case can be used to indicate the person or thing for whose benefit an action is performed. The dative of reference is also known as the dative of advantage. During translation, insertion of the phrase *with reference to* can often clarify the meaning:

    <u>Multīs</u> Bombax ignāvus erat.
    <u>To many</u>, Bombax was lazy. (With reference to many, Bombax was lazy.)

The dative can also show purpose:

Bombax Palaestrae <u>auxiliō</u> erat.
> *Bombax <u>helped</u> Palaestra* (literally, *Bombax was <u>for</u> [<u>the purpose of</u>] <u>a</u> <u>help</u> [with reference] to Palaestra*).

The preceding sentence contains two words in the dative case: **Palaestrae** (reference) and **auxiliō** (purpose). This illustrates what is known as the "double dative," that is, the appearance of the dative of reference and the dative of purpose together. The verb is usually a form of **esse**. The dative of purpose is an alternative to other ways of expressing the idea of purpose or intent, which is a favorite subject for testing on the SAT Latin Subject Exam.

Dative with Certain Types of Verbs

Some verbs are said to be intransitive in Latin, that is, they do not have objects in the accusative case. Certain of these verbs may be followed by the dative case, for example:

Servus <u>vīlicō</u> paret.
> *The slave obeys <u>the overseer</u>.*

Note that in translation, the dative is expressed as a direct object, making the verb **paret** transitive in English. Such verbs are generally noted in word lists and dictionaries by the designation (+ dat.) Verbs of this type express the implicit meaning *to* or *for*, such as **placēre**, *to be pleasing to*:

Ancilla Palaestra <u>Bombācī</u> placēbat.
> *The servant girl Palaestra was pleasing <u>to Bombax</u>* (i.e., *pleased Bombax*).

Here are some additional intransitive verbs that take the dative case. Think of this use of the dative as a dative of reference. Many of these verbs belong to the second conjugation:

SIVs

cēdere, *to grant, yield to*	**parēre**, *to obey*
crēdere, *to trust, believe*	**persuādēre**, *to convince*
favēre, *to favor*	**resistere**, *to oppose*
ignoscere, *to pardon, forgive*	**respondēre**, *to reply*
imperāre, *to order, command*	**servīre**, *to serve*
invidēre, *to envy*	**studēre**, *to be eager*
parcere, *to spare*	

Verbs used impersonally, that is, with the subject "it," can be followed by the dative case. Such verbs include **libet**, *it is pleasing*, **licet**, *it is allowed*, **vidētur**, *it seems*, and the verbal phrase **necesse est**, *it is necessary*:

> **Licetne servō ē fundō exīre?**
> *Is the slave allowed to leave the farm?* (Literally, *Is it allowed to/for the slave to leave the farm?*)

Another verb that can be used impersonally is **placēre**, as in **mihi placet**, *it pleases me*.

Intransitive verbs that are compound—that is, ones that contain certain prepositional prefixes such as **ad**, as in **appropinquāre** (**ad** + **propinquāre**), *to draw near to, approach*—may be followed by a noun in the dative case. Other such prefixes are **ante-**, **circum-**, **con-** (**cum**), **in-**, **inter-**, **ob-**, **post-**, **prae-**, **prō-**, **sub-**, and **super-**. Common verbs of this type include **inferre**, *to carry in, attack*, **occurrere**, *to meet*, **praeficere**, *to set over, appoint*, **praeesse**, *to preside over*, and various other compounds of **esse**:

> **Vīlicus Bacillus servīs praeest.**
> *The overseer Bacillus is in charge of the slaves.*

Think of this dative as a dative of reference as in the preceding example, *Bacillus is in charge with reference to the slaves.*

Note that the spelling of some prepositional prefixes, such as **ad** in **appropinquāre**, changes due to assimilation:

> **cum** + **fīdere** = **confīdere**, *to trust* (literally, *have complete trust in*)
>
> **ob** + **currere** = **occurrere**, *to meet* (literally, *run in front of, against*)
>
> **sub** + **currere** = **succurrere**, *to help, support* (literally, *run beneath*)

Such compound verbs may take both an accusative and a dative object:

>   acc.   dat.
> **Dominus Bacillum servīs praefēcit.**
> *The master placed Bacillus in charge of the slaves.*

Dative with Certain Adjectives

The dative case is used with certain adjectives whose essential meaning requires the word *to* or *for*:

> **Estne Bacillus inimīcus Bombācī?**
> *Is Bacillus unfriendly to Bombax?*

Other examples of such adjectives include the following:

amīcus, *friendly*	**grātus**, *pleasing*
benignus, *kind*	**idōneus**, *suitable*
cārus, *dear*	**propinquus**, *near, related*
difficilis, *difficult*	**similis**, *similar*
dissimilis, *dissimilar*	**utilis**, *useful*
facilis, *easy*	

Dative of Agent with Passive Periphrastic

The dative of agent with the gerundive + a form of **esse** indicates the person who must perform the obligation expressed in the verb:

> **Omnēs servī <u>Bacillō</u> custodiendī erant.**
> *Bacillus had to guard all the slaves* (i.e., *All the slaves had to be guarded by <u>Bacillus</u>*).

TIPS ON TRANSLATING THE DATIVE CASE

- Use other words in the sentence to help you resolve the following ambiguities:

  first declension dative **tībiae** = genitive singular and nominative plural **tībiae**

  second declension dative **nāsō** = ablative singular **nāsō**

  fifth declension dative **faciēī** = genitive singular **faciēī**

  dative plurals of all declensions = ablative plurals of all declensions

  Avoid mistaking the form of the third declension dative singular, such as **pedī** or **capitī**, for the genitive singular or nominative plural of a second declension noun, such as **nāsī**.

- Always look for a direct object as the first step in identifying an indirect object in a Latin sentence. If there is no direct object, or if the sense of the sentence does not require an indirect object, then consider alternative uses of the dative case, for example, possession, purpose, reference, double dative, or completing the meaning of an adjective or verb whose sense requires the translation *to* or *for*. Insertion of a phrase such as *with reference to* often helps to clarify the meaning of the dative.

- Remember that the basic translation of the dative case is *to* or *for*, but that there are other appropriate renderings, as in the following sentence:

  Bacillus alterum servum <u>Bombācī</u> praefēcit.
  Bacillus placed another slave in charge <u>of Bombax</u>.

  Conversely, the words *to* and *for* can be expressed by other cases in Latin, such as **ad patriam**, *to (toward) the fatherland*, and **prō patriā**, *for* or *on behalf of the fatherland*.

PRACTICE QUESTIONS

1. Will the master give <u>the slave</u> her freedom?

   (A) servam

   (C) servae

   (B) servā

   (D) serva

2. Bombācis tunica <u>idōnea cēnae</u> nōn erat.

   (A) suitable with dinner

   (C) a suitable dinner

   (B) suitable for dinner

   (D) for a suitable dinner

3. Necesse est . . . parcere.

   (A) miserōs servōs

   (C) miserōrum servōrum

   (B) miserī servī

   (D) miserīs servīs

4. <u>Dominus fīliō servī pecūniam lībertātī dedit.</u>

   (A) The master gave the slave's son freedom for his money.

   (B) The slave's son gave the master money for his freedom.

   (C) The master gave the slave's son money for his freedom.

   (D) The slaves gave the master's son money for their freedom.

5.   Licēbatne Bacillō servīs praeesse?

(A) Is he permitted to place Bacillus in charge of the slaves?

(B) Did he place the slaves in charge of Bacillus?

(C) Was Bacillus permitted to be in charge of the slaves?

(D) Was Bacillus permitting the slaves to be in charge?

6.   Nihil pecūniae Bombācī erat.

(A) Bombax never has money.

(B) Bombax had no money.

(C) Bombax has no money.

(D) There is no money for Bombax.

7.   Bombax . . . epistulam amōris mīsit.

(A) Palaestram   (C) Palaestrā

(B) Palaestrae   (D) ad Palaestram

8.   The overseer Bacillus was a great help to his master.

(A) magnum auxilium dominī

(B) magnō auxiliō ad dominum

(C) magnum auxilium dominō

(D) magnō auxiliō dominō

Stumper:

Cēna . . . servienda erat.

(A) ab Palaestrā   (C) Palaestrā

(B) Palaestrae   (D) Palaestra

Answers

1.   **(C)**
This is an example of the dative as indirect object. The gender is not an issue, as all forms are in the first declension and are feminine. Answer (A) is accusative, (B) ablative, and (D) nominative, none of which suit the context. The phrasing of the English suggests that *the slave* should be accusative, but the direct object is clearly *freedom*.

2. **(B)**
    This question examines familiarity with the dative case accompanying adjectives whose essential meaning includes the words *to* or *for*, as here, **idōnea cēnae**, *suitable for dinner*. The sentence reads *Bombax did not have a tunic suitable for dinner*. Answer (A) is an ablative phrase, and (C) *a suitable dinner* incorrectly translates **idōnea** as modifying **cēnae**. Answer (D) is a distractor that requires the Latin to read **idōneae cēnae**, *for a suitable dinner* rather than **idōnea cēnae**, *suitable for dinner*. (See "Dative with Certain Adjectives.")

3. **(D)**
    Parcere is a verb that takes a dative object, hence, **miserīs servīs parcere**, *to be sparing to the unfortunate slaves*. Answer (A) is the obvious (but incorrect) answer as the accusative direct object of the verb; (B) is nominative plural, intended to simulate third declension dative singular forms; and (C) is genitive plural, which does not fit the meaning of the sentence. (See "Dative with Certain Types of Verbs.")

4. **(C)**
    This intricate sentence contains two uses of the dative: indirect object (**filiō**) and purpose (**lībertāti**). The noun **servī** in the genitive singular serves as a distractor. Translation (A) incorrectly swaps the phrase **pecūniam lībertātī**, *money for freedom* with *freedom for money*. Translation (B) misinterprets the functions of the nouns **dominus filiō** because **dominus** is nominative and **filiō** dative, rather than dative and nominative, respectively. In (D), if slaves (**servī**) were the subject, a plural verb would be necessary, but the verb **dedit** is singular. (See "Dative as Indirect Object" and "Datives of Reference and Purpose.")

5. **(C)**
    This sentence contains two uses of the dative, one with an impersonal verb, **Licēbatne Bacillō**, *Was Bacillus permitted* (literally, *Was it permitted to Bacillus*) and the other with a compound verb, **servīs praeesse**, *to be in charge of the slaves*. Answer (A) makes the common error of confusing the verb **praeesse**, *to be in charge of*, with **praeficere**, *to place in charge of*. Answer (B) is defensible, grammatically, but it makes less sense than (C) and gives the impersonal verb **Licēbat** a personal subject (*he*). Answer (D) makes **Bacillus** the personal subject of **Licēbat** and mistranslates **praeesse** as **praeficere**. (See "Dative with Certain Types of Verbs.")

6. **(B)**
    Nihil . . . Bombācī erat is an example of the possessive dative, equivalent to **Bombax pecūniam non habet**. This sentence also contains an example of the partitive genitive, **nihil pecūniae**, *nothing of money (no money)*. Answers (C) and (D) do justice to the Latin, but the verb tense in each should be past, not present. In (A), *never* does not render **nihil** correctly. (See "Dative of Possession.")

7. **(D)**
    Because motion is implied in the verb **mīsit**, Bombax is sending the love letter toward Palaestra and the preposition **ad** + accusative is used. Therefore, the dative case in (B) is inappropriate here. Answer (A) *to send someone something* misrepresents an indirect object (*someone*) as a direct object.

8. **(D)**
    Magnō auxiliō dominō is a double dative, expressing both reference (*to his master*) and purpose (*a great help*). Answer (C) seems the most likely answer because it replicates the English, but Latin requires a dative of purpose (**magnō auxilio**) rather than a predicate nominative or accusative (**magnum auxilium**) in this context. The Latin in (A) incorrectly reads *a great help of the master*. In the phrase **ad dominum** in (B), **ad** means *toward* and implies motion, which is not evident in the English here. (See "Datives of Reference and Purpose.")

Stumper: (B)
The passive periphrastic requires a dative of agent when a person is performing the obligatory action of the verb, hence **Palaestrae**, *by Palaestra*. This sentence reads *The dinner had to be served <u>by Palaestra</u>*. Answers (A) and perhaps (C), as ablatives of agent, are tempting answers, but the dative, and not the ablative, is found with a passive periphrastic such as **servienda erat**. Answer (D) **cēna** is preferable to **Palaestra** as the nominative subject, given the sense. (See "Dative of Agent with Passive Periphrastic" and Chapter 25, "The Gerund, the Gerundive, and the Supine.")

CHAPTER 9

The Accusative Case

Chapter 9

THE ACCUSATIVE CASE

The Forms of the Accusative Case

	1st	2nd	2nd N.	3rd
Singular	tībiam	nāsum	brācchium	pedem
Plural	tībiās	nāsōs	brācchia	pedēs
	3rd N.	**4th**	**5th**	
Singular	caput	manum	faciem	
Plural	capita	manūs	faciēs	

THE USES OF THE ACCUSATIVE CASE

Direct Object

The accusative or "objective" case has several major functions, the most important of which is to mark the direct object of most verbs. A direct object is a person or thing that receives the action of the verb or that is directly affected, caused, or produced by the action of the verb, as in the following sentence:

> **Palaestra <u>crīnēs</u> pectēbat.**
> *Palaestra was combing (her) <u>hair</u>.*

Object of Some Prepositions

The accusative extends its role as the objective case by serving as the object of those prepositions that do not take the ablative case:

ad, *to, toward*	**post**, *after, behind*
ante, *before*	**prae**, *in front of*
circum, *around*	**prope**, *near*

in, *into*	**propter**, *because of*
inter, *between*	**super**, *above*
ob, *because of*	**trans**, *across*
per, *through, along*	

Accusative of Place to Which

Prepositions such as **ad** usually accompany a verb of motion and indicate the place toward which a person or object is moving. This use of the accusative case is traditionally called the "accusative of place to which":

> **Palaestra ad hortum ambulat.**
> *Palaestra is strolling toward the garden.*

The preposition **ad** can have multiple meanings in English, such as *to*, *toward*, *at*, *near*, *for the purpose of*, *for*, *until*, and *according to*. Consider carefully the word or words that accompany this preposition in order to determine which of its meanings is most appropriate.

When found with the accusative case, the Latin preposition **in** could mean *against*, as **in hostēs**, *against the enemy*, but it generally means *into* (not *in*):

> **Palaestra in hortum ambulat.**
> *Palaestra is strolling into the garden.*

With the names of cities, small islands, and the words **domus** and **rūs**, the preposition expressing place to which is omitted:

> **Palaestra Rōmam** (not **ad Rōmam**) **semper īre vult.**
> *Palaestra always wants to go to Rome.*

Accusative of Extent of Space or Time

The accusative case is used to express extent of distance or duration of time:

> **Palaestra duās horās in hortō sedēbat.**
> *Palaestra was sitting in the garden for two hours.*

Use the following memory device: "Duration and extent of space require the plain accusative case." With regard to extent of time or space, the words meaning *for* or *during* do not appear in Latin.

Abhinc, *ago, from this point in time*, with the accusative, also express-es duration of time:

Abhinc complūrēs mensēs Palaestra ad villam pervēnerat.
Palaestra had arrived at the villa <u>several months ago</u>.

Accusative Subject of an Infinitive in Indirect Statement

In addition to serving as several kinds of objects, the accusative case is used to express the subject of an infinitive in indirect statement:

Bombax putat <u>Palaestram</u> eum amāre.
Bombax thinks that <u>Palaestra</u> likes him.

Accusative with Gerund or Gerundive to Show Purpose

Ad + the accusative case of the gerund or gerundive is used to express purpose:

Bombax in hortum ambulāvit <u>ad Palaestram videndam</u>.
Bombax strolled into the garden <u>for the purpose of seeing</u> (<u>to see</u>) <u>Palaestra</u>.

The previous two important uses of the accusative case will be dis-cussed further in subsequent chapters.

Exclamatory Accusative

The accusative case, rather than the nominative or vocative, is used in expressing an exclamation, such as the following:

Iam nunc Palaestra ex hortō excesserat. "<u>Mē miserum!</u>" gemuit Bombax.
Palaestra had just now left the garden. Bombax groaned,"Rats!"

A famous example of this usage is Cicero's exclamation:

Ō tempora! Ō mōrēs!
Oh, the times! Oh, the character (of the people)!

TIPS ON TRANSLATING THE ACCUSATIVE CASE

- Remember that, except for neuter nouns, the accusative case is characterized in all declensions by the ending -**m** in the singular (-**am**, -**um**, -**em**, -**um**, -**em**) and a long vowel + -**s** in the plural (-**ās**, -**ōs**, -**ēs**, -**ūs**, -**ēs**).

- The accusative endings of neuter nouns, singular and plural, are the same as those of the nominative.

- Do not confuse endings of the accusative singular, as in **nasum**, with genitive plural endings, as in **nasōrum** (second declension), **pedum** (third), **manuum** (fourth), or **faciērum** (fifth).

- The accusative case is used mainly to express an object (of a verb, of a preposition, etc.)

- In a Latin sentence, the direct object is often found near the verb.

- Do not confuse **in** (+ acc.), meaning *into* or *against*, with **in** (+ abl.), meaning *in* or *on*.

- The accusative case is used to express duration of time and extent of space (as opposed to the ablative, which is generally used to express points or limits of time).

PRACTICE QUESTIONS

1. Bombax napped <u>for eight hours</u>.
   - (A) octō hōrīs
   - (C) octō hōras
   - (B) octāvā hōrā
   - (D) octāvam hōram

2. Bacillus īrātus erat propter . . . servī.
   - (A) fugā
   - (C) fuga
   - (B) fugae
   - (D) fugam

3. Bombax cum Palaestrā <u>trēs horās</u> in hortō sedēbat.
   - (A) three hours ago
   - (C) within three hours
   - (B) for three hours
   - (D) at the third hour

4. In hortō, statua . . . piscīnam posita erat.

    (A) prope   (C) dē

    (B) prō   (D) sine

ago (from this time)

5. Bombax ad villam <u>abhinc quattuor mensēs</u> pervēnit.

    (A) four months later   (C) within four months

    (B) after four months   (D) four months ago

6. "Nōlī <u>in mē</u> baculum vertere!" implorābat Bombax.

    (A) in me   (C) into me

    (B) against me   (D) on me

thirty thousand paces = 30 miles

7. <u>Triginta mīlia passuum abhinc septem diēs iter fēcit.</u>
    ^ paces

    (A) In seven days, he traveled three miles.

    (B) Seven days ago, he traveled 3,000 miles.

    (C) Seven days ago, he traveled for 30 miles.

    (D) Within seven days, he traveled 30 miles.

8. Bombax <u>Delphōs</u> iter facere volēbat.

    (A) from Delphi   (C) to Delphi

    (B) near Delphi   (D) in Delphi

9. Bombax in agrōs cucurrit ad fugiendum.

    (A) as he was fleeing   (C) at the point of flight

    (B) in order to flee   (D) toward the fugitive

Stumper:

Nēmo cogitat . . . dīligentem servum esse.

    (A) Bombax   (C) Bombāce

    (B) Bombācem   (D) Bombācis

Answers

1. **(C)**
    For eight hours expresses extent of time, therefore the accusative case is needed. The ablative case, expressing other elements of time, appears in two of the other options: answer (A) *(with)in eight hours* and answer (B) *in/on the eighth hour*. Note in this mistaken translation the use of the ordinal *eighth* (**octāvam**) rather than the cardinal number *eight* (**octō**). Answer (D) **octāvam hōram**, *for the eighth hour*, expresses an extent of time. (See "Accusative of Extent of Space or Time.")

2. **(D)**
    The preposition **propter** takes the accusative case, hence **fugam**. If **propter** is properly identified as a preposition, the two choices are answer (A) is ablative and (D) is accusative. Answer (B) is a red herring, because the meaning of **propter**, *because of* might suggest an object in the genitive case; however, this is incorrect. Answer (C) **fuga**, a subject form, does not fit the grammatical requirements.

3. **(B)**
    This is another accusative extent of time, this time in Latin. Answer (A) is provided as a distractor because the word *ago* in the answer would be expressed in the accusative case (i.e., **abhinc trēs hōrās**, *three hours ago*); however the adverb **abhinc** is missing. *Within three hours* and *at the third hour*, both indicating a point in time, require the ablative. (See "Accusative of Extent of Space or Time.")

4. **(A)**
    This question requires a specific knowledge of which prepositions are found with the accusative case and which with the ablative. **Prope** is the only choice found with the accusative, hence **prope piscīnam**, *near the fishpool*.

5. **(D)**
    This sentence reads *Bombax arrived at the villa four months ago*. Answers (A) and (B) require that the Latin be **post quattuor mensēs** or **quattuor post mensibus**, and answer (C) the ablative phrase **quattuor mensibus**. (See "Accusative of Extent of Space or Time.")

6. **(B)**
    This question asks you to discriminate among various meanings of the preposition **in**. The sentence reads *"Don't turn the switch against me,"* *implored Bombax.* Answers (A) and (D) are incorrect because **in** meaning *in* or *on* is found with the ablative case. Answer (C) *into me* makes less sense than *against me*. (See "Accusative with Gerund or Gerundive to Show Purpose.")

7. **(C)**
    This sentence contains two constructions with the accusative: for extent of distance, **triginta milia passuum**, *thirty thousand paces* (30 miles), and for a time expression, **abhinc septem diēs**, *seven days ago*. In answer (A), the time frame and mileage are incorrect; in (B), the time frame is correct, but the mileage is not; and in (D), the distance is correct, but the time frame is incorrect. (See "Accusative of Extent of Space or Time.")

8. **(C)**
    The preposition **ad** is understood with the name of a city as the accusative of place to which. The context of the sentence implies that Bombax wished to travel to or from Delphi because the idiom **iter facere** expresses motion. This eliminates answers (B) and (D) due to sense. Because **Delphōs** has an accusative plural ending (because the name **Delphi** is plural) with the understood preposition *ad*, answer (C) is correct. For (A) to have been correct, the form **Delphīs** (i.e., **ē Delphīs**) would have been necessary. (See "Accusative of Place to Which.")

9. **(B)**
    In this sentence, **ad fugiendum** is a gerund of purpose, meaning *for the purpose of fleeing* or *(in order) to flee*. Answer (D) is omitted because **fugiendum** does not mean *fugitive*. The translations in neither (A) *as* nor (C) *at the point of* correctly translate the preposition **ad**. (See "Accusative with Gerund or Gerundive to Show Purpose.")

Stumper: **(B)**
    The noun **Bombācem** is accusative singular and serves as the subject of the infinitive **esse** in this indirect statement. Answer (A) **Bombax**, which might be taken as the obvious answer, is incorrect because the form is nominative. Answers (C) and (D) are eliminated because **Bombāce** and **Bombācis** are in the wrong cases, namely, ablative and genitive, respectively. (See "Accusative Subject of an Infinitive in Indirect Statement.")

CHAPTER 10

The Ablative Case and the Locative Case

Chapter 10

THE ABLATIVE CASE AND THE LOCATIVE CASE

The Forms of the Ablative Case

	1st	2nd	2nd N.	3rd
Singular	tībiā	nāsō	brācchiō	pede
Plural	tībiīs	nāsīs	brācchiīs	pedibus

	3rd N.	4th	5th
Singular	capite	manū	faciē
Plural	capitibus	manibus	faciēbus

THE USES OF THE ABLATIVE CASE

The ablative case is the "busiest" of all the cases because it has more uses than any other. It combines the functions of three original cases, and thus it can express the multiple ideas of separation (*from*), place and time (*in*, *at*), and means or instrument (*by*, *with*). The ablative case is generally used to modify or limit the meaning of the verb in some way.

Because there are nearly 20 different uses of the ablative case, your review here will be limited to the most common uses, that is, those which involve the stated or implied use of prepositions, especially **ā/ab**, *away from*, *by*, **cum**, *with*, **dē**, *down from*, **ē/ex**, *out of*, and **in**, *in/on*. For this reason the ablative is known as "the prepositional case." When you are translating the ablative case, remember that English often requires a preposition when Latin only implies its use, such as **brevī tempore**, *in a short time*. On the SAT Latin Subject Test, you are not expected to differentiate among these by syntactical label, for example, "ablative of means," but you are expected to be able to recognize, comprehend, and translate the meanings of the various uses of the ablative case in context.

When the ablative with an implied or "understood" preposition appears, you should always base your final decision about its meaning on what makes the best sense, which may require some experimentation with the wording. The review of the ablative case presented in this chapter is divided into three categories: ablatives with a preposition, those with or without a preposition, and those without a preposition. The uses of the ablative case are listed in the following table in the sequence in which they are reviewed in this chapter.

With a Preposition	With or Without a Preposition	Without a Preposition
With certain prepositions	Manner	Time when
	Separation	Time within which
Place where	Cause	Means or instrument
Place from which		Comparison
Accompaniment		Degree of difference
Agent		Description or quality
		Respect or specification
		With certain verbs and adjectives

The Ablative Case with a Preposition

The prepositions that take the ablative case may be conveniently remembered by the "ablative astronaut," SID SPACE:

Sub, *under*

In, *in, on*

Dē, *about, down from*

Sine, *without*

Prō, *in front of, for*

Ā/ab, *from, by*

Cum, *with*

Ē/ex, *from**

---

* SID SPACE was created by Sally Davis. See David Pellegrino, http://latinteach.com/prepmnemonics.html.

Ablative of Place Where

> **Bombax et Palaestra <u>sub arbore</u> sedent.**
> *Bombax and Palaestra are sitting <u>beneath a tree</u>.*

> **Bombax nōmen suum <u>in arbore</u> scrībere vult.**
> *Bombax wants to carve his own name <u>on the tree</u>.*

Notes

1. Do not confuse **in** + ablative, meaning *in*, *on*, with **in** + accusative, meaning *into*, *against*. (See Chapter 9, "Accusative as Object of Some Prepositions.")

2. Prepositional phrases are often found just preceding the verb.

3. A noun, most often in the genitive case, can come between a preposition and its object, as in the title of the great poem by Lucretius, **Dē Rērum Nāturā**, *On the Nature of Things*.

Ablative of Place from Which

Motion away from a person or place is indicated by a prepositional phrase with **ā/ab**, *away from*, **dē**, *down from*, or **ē/ex**, *out of*, + the ablative case:

> **Palaestra <u>ex hortō</u> discedit.**
> *Palaestra is departing <u>from the garden</u>.*

Notes

1. Remember that the word **ā** is the same as **ab**, and **ē** is the same as **ex**. The consonant is added to simplify pronunciation when these prepositions appear before words beginning with vowels, for example, **ab urbe** and **ex arbore**.

2. With the names of cities, small islands, and the words **domus** and **rūs**, the preposition is omitted in expressions of place from which:

> **Palaestra <u>domō</u> (not ē domō) semper exīre vult.**
> *Palaestra always wants to leave (from) <u>the house</u>.*

3. The preposition is often expressed or emphasized by appearing as the prefix of a compound verb, such as **exīre** in the preceding example.

The Ablative with a Specific Preposition

Ablative of Accompaniment (with cum)

This ablative with the preposition **cum** expresses the person with whom someone does something, that is, it answers the question "With whom?"

> **Palaestra <u>cum Bombāce</u> ad aquam habendam ambulat.**
> *Palaestra is walking <u>with Bombax</u> to obtain water.*

Note that when it is found with a personal pronoun, **cum** is attached as an enclitic:

> **"Palaestra <u>mēcum</u> ambulat," Bombax dīcēbat.**
> *"Palaestra is walking <u>with me</u>," Bombax said.*

Ablative of Personal Agent (with ā/ab)

The person who completes the action of a passive verb is given in the ablative + **ā/ab**, meaning *by* (see Chapter 8, "Dative of Agent"):

> **Aqua ad culīnam <u>ā Palaestrā</u> portābitur.**
> *The water will be carried to the kitchen <u>by Palaestra</u>.*

To help with the identification of the ablative of agent when translating, think of these three words beginning with the letter **p**: there must be a **p**assive verb, a **p**reposition, and a **p**erson.

The Ablative With or Without a Preposition

Ablative of Manner (with or without cum)

A prepositional phrase introduced by **cum** and known as the ablative of manner answers the question "How?" The ablative of manner is translated *with* whether **cum** is stated or implied, for example, **summā cum laude**, *with highest praise*, or **magnā vōce**, *with a loud voice*:

> **Palaestra <u>cum gaudiō</u> laborat.**
> *Palaestra does her work <u>with joy</u>.*

Ablative of Separation (with or without ā/ab or ē/ex)

The ablative of separation expresses the distancing of one person or thing from another person or thing, and it is often translated using the preposition *from*, for example, **prohibēre**, *to restrain from*. Look for words such as **carēre**, *to lack*, **līberāre**, *to set free*, **prīvāre**, *to deprive*, or **removēre**, *to remove*, as in:

> **Palaestra ad aquam portandam <u>vīribus carēbat</u>.**
> *Palaestra <u>lacked the strength</u> to carry the water.*

If a preposition is used in the Latin, look for **ā/ab** or **ē/ex**:

> **Bombax ollam sumpsit et Palaestram <u>ā labōre līberāvit</u>.**
> *Bombax took up the water jar and <u>freed</u> Palaestra <u>from the work</u>.*

Ablative of Cause (with or without ā/ab, dē, or ē/ex)

The reason that something is done can be expressed by the ablative case. When found with a preposition, **ā/ab**, **dē**, or **ē/ex** is used. When translating the ablative of cause without a preposition, insert the phrase *because of* to clarify the meaning:

> **Bombax <u>amōre</u> Palaestram adiuvit.**
> <u>*Because of his love*</u> *Bombax helped Palaestra.*

Sometimes cause is expressed by **ob** or **propter**, *because of, on account of*:

> **<u>Propter amōrem</u> Bombax Palaestram adiuvit.**
> <u>*Because of his love*</u>, *Bombax helped Palaestra.*

The Ablative without a Preposition

When translating an ablative form or phrase without a preposition, provisionally insert the prepositions *from*, *with*, *down from*, *out of*, or *in/on* until you find the clearest way to express the meaning in English.

Ablative of Time (when and within which)

The ablative case without a preposition is used to express time when, that is, a specific point in time, as in **prīmā hōrā**, *at the first hour*. The ablative can also express time within which, for example **duōbus proximīs annīs**, *within the past two years*, meaning sometime between two years ago and the present. The ablative of time is translated using *at*, *in*, *on*, or *within*:

Time when:	**Cēna undecimā hōrā in triclinium ferētur.**
	Dinner will be brought into the dining room at the eleventh hour.
Time within which:	**Tribus hōrīs omnia consumpta erunt.**
	Within three hours, everything will have been eaten.

Notes

1. The words **ante**, *before*, and **post**, *after*, may be used to express time as prepositions with the accusative, for example, **ante prīmam lūcem**, *before dawn* (literally, *before first light*), or as adverbs with the ablative, such as **tribus post mēnsibus**, *three months later* (literally, *afterward by three months*).

2. Common words and phrases expressing time include:

aestāte, *in summer*	**eō tempore**, *at that time*
brevī tempore, *in a short time*	**hieme**, *in winter*
eōdem tempore, *at the same time*	**merīdiē**, *at midday*

Remember that duration of time, that is, the inclusive passage of time, is expressed by the accusative case and is translated using the word *for*, as in **multōs diēs**, *for many days*. (See Chapter 9, "Accusative of Extent of Space or Time.")

Ablative of Means or Instrument

This ablative, perhaps the most important of those used without a preposition, denotes the means or instrument by which an action is accomplished and is always *a thing* and never a person. (See "Ablative of Personal Agent" for the equivalent of the ablative of means with a person.) Translate the ablative of means using the words *by* or *with*. The meaning of this use of the ablative may be clarified by insertion of the phrase *by means of*:

> **Rādix coquus carnem cultrō scindēbat.**
> *Radix the cook was cutting the meat with (by means of) a knife.*

Ablatives of Comparison and Degree of Difference

The comparative degree of the adjective or adverb may be followed by the ablative of comparison. This is an alternative to the expression of comparison using **quam** (which will be covered in the chapter on adjectives). Note that in the ablative of comparison the word *than* is not expressed in Latin:

> **Nōnne glīrēs suāviōrēs porcō erunt?**
> *Surely the dormice will be tastier than the <u>pork</u>?*

Both the ablative and the **quam** construction with a comparative adjective are often found with the ablative of degree of difference, which expresses how much one person or thing differs from another by using words such as **multō**, *by so much*, or **paulō**, *by so little*:

> **Glīrēs <u>multō</u> suāviōrēs porcō erunt.**
> *The dormice will be <u>much</u> tastier than the pork* (literally, *tastier by much*).

Ablative of Description or Quality

A noun in the ablative case with a modifying adjective, when used to describe the character, quality, or size of someone or something, is known as ablative of description. This use of the ablative has the same function as the genitive of description (see Chapter 7, "Genitive of Description"):

> Ablative: **Rādix erat coquus <u>exīmiā arte</u>.**
> *Radix was a chef <u>of outstanding skill</u>.*
>
> Genitive: **Rādix erat coquus <u>exīmiae artis</u>.**
> *Radix was a chef <u>of outstanding skill</u>.*

Ablative of Respect or Specification

The ablative case can indicate in what regard something is true. Because the ablative of respect is found without a preposition, its meaning may be clarified by the insertion of the implied words *with respect to*:

> **Asparagus salsus <u>sapōre</u> erat.**
> *The asparagus was salty <u>in taste</u>* (literally, *with respect to its taste*).

Ablative with Certain Verbs and Adjectives

Verbs found with the ablative include the deponent verbs **fruor**, *to enjoy*, **fungor**, *to perform*, **potior**, *to possess*, **ūtor**, *to use*, and **vescor**, *to feed on*:

> **Rādix in culinā <u>officiīs fungēbatur</u>.**
> *Radix <u>was carrying out his duties</u> in the kitchen.*

The ablative is also found with the adjectives **dignus**, *worthy of*, and **indignus**, *unworthy of*:

> **Eratne cēna parata ā coquō <u>digna laude</u>?**
> *Was the dinner prepared by the cook <u>worthy of praise</u>?*

One other major use of this case, the ablative absolute, will be reviewed with participles in Chapter 24.

TIPS ON TRANSLATING THE ABLATIVE CASE

- Prepositional phrases with the ablative are relatively easy to translate, assuming your recollection of the meanings of the prepositions. Be sure that you review these.

- Note that both **ā/ab** and **ē/ex** can have the sense of *from*; however, **ā/ab** can also have the meaning of *by*, as in the ablative of agent:

  > **Cēna <u>ā convīvīs</u> laudābātur.**
  > *The dinner was praised <u>by the guests</u>.*

  Consider both possibilities when translating **ā/ab**.

- Be sure to determine whether the Latin preposition **in** is followed by an object in the ablative case (in which case it means *in* or *on*) or the accusative case (in which case it means *into* or *against*).

- Ablative expressions without the preposition are often ambiguous in meaning. When translating the ablative without a preposition, it is helpful to try the implied prepositions *by*, *from*, *in*, or *with*:

Manner: ("In what way?")	**Rādix anserem <u>magnā arte</u> coquēbat.** *Radix cooked the goose <u>with great skill</u>.*
Means: ("With what?")	**Rādix anserem <u>cultrō</u> scidit.** *Radix carved the goose <u>with a knife</u>.*

PRACTICE QUESTIONS   11/12

1. Rādix <u>magnitūdine</u> bōlētōrum fēlix erat.

    (A) by means of the size   (C) because of the size

    (B) according to the size   (D) except for the size

2. <u>Within three hours</u>, the dessert will have been served.

    (A) Tertiā hōrā   (C) Trēs hōrās

    (B) Tribus hōrīs   (D) Tertiās hōrās

3. Gustātiō huius cēnae dignissima . . . erat.

    (A) laudis   (C) laudī

    (B) laude   (D) laus

4. Secunda mensa <u>magnā cūrā</u> parāta erat.

    (A) with great care   (C) by means of great care

    (B) because of great care (D) with respect to great care

5. Rādix optimus coquus . . . dubiō erat.

    (A) prō   (C) sub

    (B) dē   (D) sine

6. <u>Bombax paulō altior Bacillō erat</u>.

    (A) Bacillus was much taller than Bombax.

    (B) Bombax was a little taller than Bacillus.

    (C) Bombax was much taller than Bacillus.

    (D) Bacillus was a little taller than Bombax.

7. For the dinner, Radix created dishes <u>of great beauty</u>.

   (A) magna pulchritūdō

   (B) magnae pulchritūdinī

   (C) magnā pulchritūdine

   (D) magnam pulchritūdinem

8. Rādix convīvās <u>culinā</u> prōhibēbat.

   (A) from the kitchen

   (B) by means of the kitchen

   (C) in the kitchen

   (D) with respect to the kitchen

9. Bombax had loved Palaestra <u>for two years</u>.

   (A) secundō annō   (C) duōbus annīs

   (B) duōs annōs   (D) secundum annum

10. Bacillus Bombācem . . . verberabat.

   (A) cum baculō   (C) baculō

   (B) baculum   (D) ā baculō

11. Coquus . . . sālis semper ūtēbātur.

   (A) nimium   (C) nimīo

   (B) nimius   (D) nimiam

Stumper:

   <u>Alterō servō ā Bacillō verberātō</u>, Bombax dīligentius laborābat.

   (A) While Bacillus was beating another slave

   (B) After Bacillus had been beaten by another slave

   (C) As Bacillus is beating another slave

   (D) Because another slave was beaten by Bacillus

Answers

1. **(C)** [ablative of description]

    The sentence reads *Radix was happy because of the size of the mush-rooms.* Answers (B) and (D) do not make sense in this context, and they are not justifiable grammatically from the Latin provided. Answer (A) is justifiable because **magnitūdine** could conceivably be an ablative of means, but **magnitūdō** is not an implement.

2. **(B)** [ablative of time (within which)]

    This sentence reads *Within three hours, the dessert will have been served.* Answer (A) **tertiā hōrā** is singular and therefore incorrect, as is answer (D) **tertiās hōrās**, because the ordinal number **tertiās** appears instead of the cardinal **trēs**. Answer (C) is an example of extent of time with the accusative, *for three hours*, and is therefore an incorrect translation of **tribus hōrīs**.

3. **(B)** [ablative with special adjective]

    Because the adjective **dignus, -a, -um**, *worthy of* takes the ablative case, answer (B) **(dignissima) laude**, *most worthy of praise*, is the correct response. Answer (A) is a red herring because the meaning *worthy of* suggests that a genitive is required. It is not. Answer (C) is dative, which does not fit the sense. Answer (D) is tempting because **dignissima** is feminine nominative singular, as is **laus**. However, the sentence does not make sense with **dignissima laus** as the subject (which is **gustatiō**).

4. **(A)** [ablative of manner]

    With great care makes the best sense of the choices given. The sentence reads *The dessert course had been prepared with great care.* This answers the question "How or in what manner had the dessert been prepared?" The word **magnā** in the ablative preceding a noun in the ablative strongly suggests that **magnā cūrā** is ablative of manner. Answers (B) and (C) do not make sense in this context, and the wording of (C) requires that **magnā cūrā** be taken as an ablative of means, but **cūrā** is not an implement.

5. **(D)** [ablative with preposition]

    All options contain prepositions that take the ablative case, but only **sine** supplies a word whose meaning is consistent with the context: *Radix was the best cook, without a doubt.*

6. **(B)** [ablatives of degree of difference and comparison]
    This sentence contains an ablative of degree of difference (**paulō altior**, *a little taller*), together with an ablative of comparison (**Bacillō**, *than Bacillus*). The sentence is comparing Bombax with Bacillus, so (A) and (D) are out. Answer (C) is not appropriate because **paulō** is translated as *much*.

7. **(C)** [ablative of description]
    The appearance of the word *of* in the phrase *of great beauty* tempts an identification as genitive of description, but there is no genitive option among the answers. Because the ablative case may also be used to describe someone or something, (C) is correct. Answer (B) looks temptingly like a genitive, but it is in fact a dative, which is unsuited to the context here. The nominative and accusative in (A) and (D), respectively, have no grammatical justification for expressing the phrase *of great beauty*.

8. **(A)** [ablative of separation]
    The meaning of the verb **prōhibēbat** suggests the answer *from the kitchen* by default. This is a verb of separation because it means to keep someone or something away. The translations in answers (B) *by means of*, (C) *in*, and (D) *with respect to* are not consistent with the meaning of this verb. Therefore, **culīnā prōhibēbat** is an example of the ablative of separation: (*Radix*) *kept the guests* (*away*) *from the kitchen*.

9. **(B)** [accusative of extent of space or time]
    This is a sneaky one because it tests your knowledge of the accusative of duration of time, reviewed in the previous chapter. Answer (A) *in the second year* is an ablative of time when. Answer (C) means (*with*)*in two years*, an ablative of time within which, and (D) *for the second year* is an ablative of extent of time, but is singular with an ordinal number and not plural with a cardinal number.

10. **(C)** [ablative of means]
    The clause *Bacillus was beating Bombax* . . . sets up use of the ablative of means or instrument because it suggests the use of an implement or tool, namely, that Bombax was being beaten *with* something. Because the ablative of means is found without a preposition, (A) and (D) are out. Answer (B) makes no sense in this context because **Bacillus** is the subject and **Bombācem** is the direct object.

11. **(C)** [ablative with a special verb]

As an alert Latin student, you no doubt immediately spotted the deponent verb **ūtēbātur**, one of the special deponents that takes an object in the ablative case, which is **nimiō** in this sentence. The other forms are (A) nominative/accusative neuter, (B) nominative, and (D) accusative. Complicating matters is the appearance of the partitive genitive in this sentence, **nimiō sālis**, *too much (of) salt*. If you answered this one correctly, way to go! (See Chapter 7, "Partitive Genitive.")

Stumper: **(D)** [ablative absolute]

The underlined portion of this sentence is an ablative absolute, which you haven't yet reviewed. This ablative absolute contains a past participle, **verberātō**, which means that the action of the beating has already taken place, relative to the working (**laborābat**). The action in (A) and (C) is happening at the same time as that of the main verb (-ing), so these must be omitted from consideration. Answers (B) and (D) are both translated in the past, but it is the <u>slave</u> who has been beaten, not Bacillus, therefore (B) is incorrect.

A SPECIAL CASE: THE LOCATIVE

You will remember that *place to which* is expressed by the accusative with a preposition such as **ad** (see Chapter 9, "Accusative of Place to Which") and *place from which* is expressed by the ablative with a preposition such as **ē/ex** (see "Ablative of Place from Which"). Convention in Latin requires that the preposition be omitted in expressing place to which and place from which with the names of cities and towns, small islands (all except Sicily and Sardinia), and the nouns **domus**, **domūs** (f.), *home*, and **rūs**, **rūris** (n.), *countryside*. (Recall that the noun **domus** has forms in both the second and fourth declensions; see Chapter 5, "Fourth Declension Nouns.")

The accusative or ablative ending of the place name or noun reflects the preposition that would be found with that case if expressed directly, as in **domum**, *toward home* (not **ad domum**) or **Rōmā**, *from Rome* (not **ē Rōmā**). When the preposition **ad** is found before the names of cities, towns, and small islands, it has the meaning *at* or *near*, for example **ad Mediolānum**, *near Milan*. With the names of cities or towns, small islands, **domus** and **rūs**, *place where* is indicated by the locative case. Depending upon the declension of the noun, the endings of the genitive, dative, or ablative are used in the locative case. The context of the sentence will generally assist you in determining the meaning. For plural nouns in the locative case, the ablative ending is used, as in **Cūmīs**, *in/at Cumae*, and **Gādibus**, *in/at Gades*. Note that many place names have only plural forms because their names are plural, such as **Cūmae**, **Delphī**, and **Pompēiī**. Place constructions appear frequently on the SAT Latin Subject Test.

For a surefire way to remember the use of **domum** without a preposition, check out the memorable graffiti scene from the Monty Python film *The Life of Brian*.

The Forms of Place Names

	1st Declension	2nd Declension	3rd Declension
Accusative	**Capuam**, *to Capua*	**Mediolānum**, *to Milan*	**Carthāginem**, *to Carthage*
Ablative	**Capuā**, *from Capua*	**Mediolānō**, *from Milan*	**Carthāgine**, *from Carthage*
Locative (genitive)	**Capuae**, *in* or *at Capua*	**Mediolānī**, *in* or *at Milan*	**Carthāginī**, *in* or *at Carthage*

The context, particularly the verb, will help you to determine the precise meaning of ambiguous forms of place names:

> **Vergilius Athēnīs studēbat.**
> *Vergil studied in Athens.*

> **Vergilius Athēnīs navigāvit.**
> *Vergil sailed from Athens.*

PRACTICE QUESTIONS 6/7

1. Aeneās classem . . . ducēbat.

 (A) Ītaliam   (C) ad Ītaliam

 (B) Ītaliae   (D) Ītaliā

2. Aeneas cum Sibyllā <u>Cūmīs</u> profectus est.

   (A) from Cumae   (C) up to Cumae

   (B) to Cumae   (D) near Cumae

3. After leaving Troy, Odysseus sailed <u>for home</u>.

   (A) domus   (C) ad domum

   (B) domum   (D) in domum

4. Navigāvitne Aeneās <u>Syrācūsās</u>?

   (A) away from Syracuse   (C) to Syracuse

   (B) in Syracuse   (D) within Syracuse

5. Dum Aeneās . . . manēbat, Dīdō eum amābat.

   (A) Carthāgine   (C) Carthāginem

   (B) Carthāginī   (D) Carthāginibus

   accusative

6. Vergilius <u>Brundisiō</u> <u>Neāpolim</u> iter fēcit.

   (A) from Brundisium to Naples

   (B) to Brundisium from Naples

   (C) up to Brundisium from Naples

   (D) from Brundisium and Naples

Stumper:

   Vergilius <u>rūrī</u> morārī semper volēbat.

   (A) from the country   (C) in the country

   (B) to the country   (D) into the country

Answers

1. **(C)**
   Italy is a country, not a city or small island, and therefore it requires the preposition **ad**. The other cases are irrelevant, although (A) **Ītaliam** is a sneaky attempt to get you to nibble a red herring of an accusative!

2. **(A)**

Cūmīs is either the ablative or dative form of **Cūmae** (a name that is plural), meaning either *from Cumae* or the locative *in Cumae*. Because the verb **profectus est**, *he set out*, predisposes the former meaning, **Cūmīs** must mean *from Cumae*, giving the sentence the meaning *Aeneas set out from Cumae with the Sibyl.*

3. **(B)**

Sailed for home is motion toward a place, therefore **ad** + accusative is expected. However, the word **domus** gets special treatment among place expressions and drops the preposition, thereby omitting answers (C) and (D). The nominative **domus** in answer (A) has no meaning here.

4. **(C)**

Among the choices, answers (B) and (D) can be omitted because one can't sail in a city. Because **Syrācūsās** is accusative (the name **Syrācūsae** is plural), the place preposition **ad** is understood, giving the translation *to Syracuse.* Answer (A) requires **Syrācūsīs**, *from Syracuse.*

5. **(B)**

The sentence in this question begins *While Aeneas remained . . . ,* implying *at* or *in* Carthage. These prepositions require the locative case, which for the singular third declension noun **Carthāgō** is equivalent to the dative, **Carthāginī**. None of the other answers makes sense with **manēbat**: Answer (A) means *from Carthage*, (C) means *to Carthage*, and (D) does not translate.

6. **(A)**

The ablative **Brundisiō (ē Brundisiō)** and accusative **Neāpolim (ad Neāpolim)** mean *from Brundisium* and *to Naples.* Answers (B) and (C) require **Brundisium Neāpoli**, and (D) requires **Brundisiō et Neāpoli**.

Stumper: **(C)**

The verb **mōrārī**, *to stay* creates a context that requires the locative case, meaning *in* or *at a place.* The locative form **rūrī** thus means *in the countryside.* Remember that **rūs** is a word that does not take a preposition in place expressions. Answer (A) *from the country* requires the ablative form **rūre**; (B) *to the country* and (D) *into the country* require the accusative form **rūs**, which is neuter.

Quick Study of Noun Syntax

Case	Function	Description of Function	Example
Nominative (Chapter 6)			
	subject	expresses who or what is performing the action	**Servus labōrat.** *The slave is working.*
	predicate nominative	restates the subject	**Senex servus est.** *The old man is a slave.*
Genitive (*of*, apostrophe-S or S-apostrophe) (Chapter 7)			
	possessive	expresses whose, of whom, or of what; links two nouns	**amīca puerī** *the girlfriend of the boy or the boy's girlfriend*
	descriptive	with accompanying adjective, describes another noun	**fēmina magnae pulchritūdinis** *a woman of great beauty*
	partitive	indicates a part of the whole	**satis temporis; plūs vīnī** *enough (of) time; more wine*
	objective	expresses object of emotion	**cupiditās pecūniae** *the desire for money* (literally, *of money*)
	with special words	requires translation *of*	**plēnus īrae** *full of anger* **amōris grātiā** *for the sake of love*

Quick Study of Noun Syntax (cont'd)

Case	Function	Description of Function	Example
Dative (*to* or *for*) (Chapter 8)			
	indirect object	indicates *to* whom or *for* whom something is done, shown, told, or given	**Puer puellae osculum dedit.** *The boy gave a kiss to the girl* or *The boy gave the girl a kiss.*
	possession	shows ownership	**Est canis puerō.** *The boy has a dog* (literally, *there is a dog to/for the boy*).
	reference	indicates "with reference" to whom an action is done	**Mihi imāgō apparuit.** *A vision appeared to me.*
	double dative	dative of reference + dative of purpose	**Suīs salūtī fuit.** *He was the salvation of his men* (literally, *for the salvation for his men*).
	with verbs	intransitive verbs	**crēde mihi** *trust me* (literally, *be trusting to me*)
		impersonal verbs	**licet mihi** *I am permitted* (lit., *it is permitted to me*)
		compound verbs	**occurrere amīcō** *to meet a friend*
	with adjectives	adjectives that require the meaning *to* or *for*	**similis patrī** *similar to the father*

Case	Function	Description of Function	Example
	agent	the person who must perform a necessary action	**tibi agendum est** *you must do it* (literally, *it must be done by you*)
Accusative (Chapter 9)			
	direct object	receives action of verb	**Brūtus Caesarem necāvit.** *Brutus killed Caesar.*
	object of preposition	accompanies **per, prope**, etc.	**per viam** *along the road* **prope arborem** *near the tree*
	place to which	expresses motion toward with **ad**	**ad urbem** *toward the city*
	duration of time	expresses passage of time	**trēs diēs** *for three days* **abhinc duōs mensēs** *two months ago*
	subject of infinitive	subject of infinitive in indirect statement	**Audiō theātrum clausum esse.** *I hear that the theater is closed.*
	gerundive of purpose	**ad** + gerundive expresses purpose or intent	**ad forum videndum** *to see the forum*
	exclamatory	expresses an exclamation	**Mē miserum!** *How unhappy I am!*

Quick Study of Noun Syntax (cont'd)

Case	Function	Description of Function	Example
Ablative (*by*, *from*, *with*, etc.) (Chapter 10)			
With a preposition	place where	used with prepositions (e.g., **in**, *in*, *on*, **sub**) to indicate location	**in mensā** *on the table* **sub plaustrō** *beneath the wagon*
	accompaniment	expresses partnership (*with*)	**Puer cum cane ambulat.** *The boy walks with his dog.*
	personal agent	indicates the person who completes the action of a passive verb (*by*)	**Lūna ab amantibus conspicitur.** *The moon is seen by the lovers.*
	place from	used with prepositions, (e.g., **ā/ab**, **dē**, or **ē/ex**) to express motion away	**ab urbe** *away from the city* **dē caelō** *down from the sky* **ē villīs** *from the villas*
With or without a preposition	manner	indicates how (*with*)	**magnō (cum) murmure** *with a great rumbling*
	separation	indicates the distancing of one person or thing from another, following certain verbs (with or without **ā/ab** or **ē/ex**)	**(ē) timōre sē liberāvit** *he freed himself from fear*

Case	Function	Description of Function	Example
Without a preposition	cause	*because of*, with or without **ā/ab, dē, ē/ex**	**(ex) vulnere dolēbat** *he was in pain from (because of) his wound*
	time when	expresses a point in time	**sextō annō; aestāte** *in the sixth year; in the summer*
	time within	expresses time during which	**quinque mensibus** *in or within five months*
	means	indicates the instrument or tool with which an action is performed (*with, by*)	**Mīles gladiō hostem vulnerāvit.** *The soldier wounded his enemy with a sword*
	comparison	expresses comparison between two persons or things (*than*)	**Hic mons altior illō est.** *This mountain is higher than that.*
	degree of difference	indicates the extent to which one person/thing differs from another (*much, less*)	**Hic mons multō altior est.** *This mountain is much higher, literally, higher by much.*
	description	with accompanying adjective, describes some characteristic (a person of . . .)	**Erat vir magnā fortitūdine.** *He was a man of great courage.*
	respect or specification	expresses in what regard or respect something is true	**meā sententiā** *in my opinion*

Quick Study of Noun Syntax (*cont'd*)

Case	Function	Description of Function	Example
	with certain verbs	accompanies specific deponent verbs	**Frūaminī vītā.** *You should enjoy life.*
	ablative absolute	phrase consisting of a noun or pronoun + participle in ablative (*after, when, since, while, etc.*)	**hōc factō** *after this was done* **multīs clāmantibus** *while many are/were shouting* **Caesare consule** *while Caesar is/was consul*
Vocative (Chapter 23)			
	direct address	naming or speaking directly to a person	**"Tite, claude iānuam."** *"Titus, close the door."* **"Fer auxilium mātrī, fīlī."** *"Help your mother, son."*
Locative (*in* or *at*) (Chapter 10)			
	place where	indicates location without a preposition (names of cities, small islands, **domus, rūs**)	**Rōmae maneō.** *I am staying in Rome.*

PRACTICE QUESTIONS   24/26

1. Fīlius senātōris . . . est.

   (A) mīlēs   (C) mīlitis

   (B) mīlitem   (D) mīlite

2. Cleopātra venēnō mortem sibi intulit.

   (A) without poison   (C) for poison

   (B) poison   (D) with poison

3. Aeger morbō . . . mortuus est.

   (A) quintō diē   (C) quintī dīeī

   (B) quinque diēs   (D) quintum diem

4. Eratne Caesar parvus magnitūdine?

   (A) by means of his size

   (B) with respect to his size

   (C) despite his size

   (D) instead of his size

5. Silvae sunt plēnae arborum.

   (A) with trees   (C) trees

   (B) of trees   (D) from trees

6. Līberī aliquid . . . semper volunt.

   (A) novum   (C) novus

   (B) novī   (D) novō

7. Erat auxiliō amīcō.

   (A) He helped a friend.   (C) The help was friendly.

   (B) A friend helped him. (D) His friend was helpful.

8. <u>Viginti annōs</u> vir pauper erat.

    (A) After 20 years

    (C) For 20 years

    (B) Within 20 years

    (D) On the 20th year

9. Puer rumpēns per ianuam clamāvit, "Ignosce . . . !"

    (A) mē

    (C) mihi

    (B) meum

    (D) meī

10. Manūs ūtilēs <u>multīs rēbus</u> sunt.

    (A) for many tasks

    (C) many tasks

    (B) with many tasks

    (D) because of many tasks

11. Adulescens . . . cum parentibus habitābat.

    (A) domō

    (C) domus

    (B) domum

    (D) domī

12. Cicerō . . . erat.

    (A) consulem

    (C) consulī

    (B) consule

    (D) consul

13. Hospitēs . . . manēbant.

    (A) in ianuam

    (C) per ianuam

    (B) propter ianuam

    (D) ad ianuam

14. <u>Duōbus mensibus Athēnās</u> navigābit.

    (A) Within two months/from Athens

    (B) After two months/from Athens

    (C) For two months/to Athens

    (D) In two months/to Athens

15. Multī Rōmam . . . visitāre volunt.

    (A) urbs aeterna

    (C) urbem aeternam

    (B) urbis aeternae

    (D) urbe aeternā

16. Hannibal in Ītaliā <u>sēdecim annōs</u> manēbat.

    (A) within 16 years   (C) after 16 years

    (B) for 16 years   (D) 16 years ago

17. Catilīna erat vir <u>parvae dignitātis</u>.
    The expression equivalent in meaning to the underlined phrase is

    (A) parvae dignitātī   (C) parvam dignitātem

    (B) parvā dignitāte   (D) parva dignitās

18. Rōma maior urbs . . . erat.

    (A) Brundisium   (C) Brundisiī

    (B) Brundisiō   (D) Brundisiīs

19. <u>Illā nocte</u> multī senātōrēs <u>Rōmā</u> fugērunt.

    (A) For that night . . . to Rome.

    (B) After that night . . . from Rome.

    (C) On that night . . . from Rome.

    (D) Because of that night . . . to Rome.

20. Mīlitēs <u>in hostēs</u> impetum faciēbant.

    (A) toward the enemy   (C) from the enemy

    (B) against the enemy   (D) through the enemy

21. Scelestī servī dignī . . . sunt.

    (A) suppliciō   (C) supplicī

    (B) supplicium   (D) supplicia

22. <u>Multa servīs facienda sunt</u>.

    (A) Many things must be done to the slaves.

    (B) Slaves have to do many things.

    (C) Many slaves must do things.

    (D) The slaves are doing many things.

23. Gracchus nōn scīvit . . . interfectum esse.

   (A) frātrem   (C) frātre

   (B) frāter   (D) frātrum

24. Mihi nōmen est Perdix.

   (A) My name is Perdix.   (C) Perdix gave me a name.

   (B) Perdix has my name. (D) Perdix was my name.

25. Senex prudentiā carēbat.

   (A) Age and wisdom were lacking.

   (B) The old man lacked wisdom.

   (C) The wise man was old.

   (D) He lacked the wisdom of age.

Stumper:

   Cēna . . . placēbat.

   (A) imperātōrī   (C) imperātōre

   (B) imperātōrem   (D) imperātōris

Answers

1.	(A) pred. nom.	15.	(C) apposition
2.	(D) abl. means	16.	(B) acc. extent time
3.	(A) abl. time	17.	(B) abl. descr.
4.	(B) abl. respect	18.	(B) abl. compar.
5.	(B) gen. w/ adj.	19.	(C) abl. time; abl. place from
6.	(B) partitive gen.	20.	(B) acc. prep. phrase
7.	(A) double dative	21.	(A) abl. with adj.
8.	(C) acc. extent time	22.	(B) dative of agent
9.	(C) dat. with verb	23.	(A) acc. subj. infin.
10.	(A) dat. with adj.	24.	(A) dat. possession
11.	(D) locative	25.	(B) abl. separation
12.	(D) pred. nom.	**Stumper:**	(A) dat. w/ impersonal
13.	(D) acc. prep. phrase		
14.	(D) abl. time within; acc. place to which		

THE SAT SUBJECT TEST IN
LATIN

SECTION 3

Pronouns

CHAPTER 11

Demonstrative Pronouns

Chapter 11

DEMONSTRATIVE PRONOUNS

AN INTRODUCTION TO PRONOUNS

A pronoun (**prō** + **nōmen**, *for a noun*) takes the place of a noun, for example, **videō senātōrem** (noun), *I see the senator*, and **videō eum** (pronoun), *I see him* (i.e., *the senator*). The pronoun keeps the writer from continually having to repeat a name or designation. Pronouns, of which there are many types, are a major component of Latin, and they appear often on the SAT Latin Subject Test.

In this section, we will review pronouns in the following order: demonstrative, relative, indefinite, personal (including possessive adjectives) interrogative, indefinite, reflexive, and intensive. We will review both the forms and uses of pronouns, most of which can also be used as adjectives. Such pronouns may be referred to as "adjective pronouns"; **hic**, for example, can mean *this one* or *he* as a pronoun and *this* as an adjective. The forms of pronouns are often similar to one another or have the same endings. During your review, observe the commonalities among pronouns, such as **hōs**, **illōs**, **eōs**, **istōs**, **ipsōs**, **quōs**, **quōsdam**, **nōs**, and **vōs**, which are all forms of pronouns in the masculine accusative plural. It is important that you rely on your knowledge of corresponding noun endings to assist your memory because many pronouns have the same endings as nouns. In the following chart, the forms in boldface have the same endings as those of first and second declension nouns.

The Forms of Demonstrative Pronouns

	Singular			Plural		
	Masculine	**Feminine**	**Neuter**	**Masculine**	**Feminine**	**Neuter**
Nominative	hic	haec	hoc	hī	hae	haec
Genitive	huius	huius	huius	hōrum	hārum	hōrum
Dative	huic	huic	huic	hīs	hīs	hīs
Accusative	hunc	hanc	hoc	hōs	hās	haec
Ablative	hōc	hāc	hōc	hīs	hīs	hīs

	Singular			Plural		
	Masculine	**Feminine**	**Neuter**	**Masculine**	**Feminine**	**Neuter**
Nominative	ille	illa	illud	illī	illae	illa
Genitive	illīus	illīus	illīus	illōrum	illārum	illōrum
Dative	illī	illī	illī	illīs	illīs	illīs
Accusative	illum	illam	illud	illōs	illās	illa
Ablative	illō	illā	illō	illīs	illīs	illīs

	Singular			Plural		
	Masculine	**Feminine**	**Neuter**	**Masculine**	**Feminine**	**Neuter**
Nominative	is	ea	id	eī	eae	ea
Genitive	eius	eius	eius	eōrum	eārum	eōrum
Dative	eī	eī	eī	eīs	eīs	eīs
Accusative	eum	eam	id	eōs	eās	ea
Ablative	eō	eā	eō	eīs	eīs	eīs

THE FORMS OF DEMONSTRATIVE PRONOUNS

The demonstrative pronoun (**demonstrāre**, *to point out*), which can serve as both a pronoun and an adjective, designates a particular person or thing.

Demonstrative Pronouns

	Singular	**Plural**
hic, haec, hoc	*this one here*	*these ones here*
ille, illa, illud	*that one over there*	*those ones over there*
is, ea, id	*he, she, it* or *this one*	*these ones, those ones*
īdem, eadem, idem	*the same one*	*the same ones*
iste, ista, istud	*that one over there* (*often shows contempt*)	*those ones over there* (*often shows contempt*)

You might be interested to know that **ille** and **illa** are the predecessors of the French and Spanish definite articles **le** and **la** (French) and **el** and **la** (Spanish), as in Spanish **la casa**, *the house*.

The pronoun **īdem, eadem, idem** consists of **is, ea, id** + the suffix **-dem**. The following forms vary from **is, ea, id** (the letter **-m** changes to **-n** in these forms for reasons of pronunciation):

> accusative singular, masculine and feminine: **eundem** and **eandem**

> genitive plural: **eōrundem, eārundem, eōrundem**

Use the macron to distinguish between the masculine form **īdem** (for **isdem**) and the neuter **idem**. The neuter plural form **eadem**, *the same* (*things*) is often used as a substantive. The demonstrative **iste, ista, istud** has the same forms as **ille, illa, illud**.

THE USES OF DEMONSTRATIVE PRONOUNS

Hic and **ille** have the same distinctions in meaning as in English, that is, **hic** refers to *this one right here*, and **ille** to *that one over there*. When used as adjectives, these words have the same forms and meanings as the pronouns, but simply modify a noun in the sentence:

Demonstrative pronoun: **Hic in forō ambulābat.**
This man (or *He*) *was strolling in the forum.*

Demonstrative adjective: **Hic vir in forō ambulābat.**
This man was strolling in the forum.

In the first sentence, with no other information as to the identity of the person or thing to which the pronoun refers, **Hic** is translated as *This man* or *He* because the pronoun is masculine. For testing purposes on the substitution section of the SAT Latin Subject Test, **hic** and **ille** are used interchangeably. Use the context to distinguish the feminine form **haec** from the neuter form **haec**, which appears often as a pronoun, *these things*, and the feminine form **illa** from the neuter form **illa**. Don't confuse the demonstrative **hic**, *this*, with the adverb **hīc**, *here*.

It is important to note that the demonstrative pronoun **is**, **ea**, **id**, *this one* or *that one*, substitutes for the pronoun of the third person, *he*, *she*, *it*, which Latin does not have. (This demonstrative will be reviewed more thoroughly in the discussion on personal pronouns in Chapter 14.)

TIPS ON TRANSLATING DEMONSTRATIVE PRONOUNS

- Many of the forms of demonstrative pronouns have endings that are approximate or identical to those of first and second declension nouns.

- The forms of **hic** and **ille** and those of their plurals, **hī** and **illī**, have the distinct meanings of *this*, *that*, *these*, and *those*, respectively.

- The demonstrative pronoun **is**, **ea**, **id** very often takes the meaning of one of the personal pronouns *he*, *she*, or *it*.

- Demonstrative pronouns may also serve as adjectives. Determine the function, and therefore the meaning, from the context.

- Remember that the demonstrative pronoun **eum** or **eam** may be translated as *it* if the antecedent is masculine or feminine:

Longa erat ōrātiō sed eam audiēbam.
The speech was long, but I listened to it (not her).

PRACTICE QUESTIONS

1. The accusative singular of īdem is

   (A) idem   (C) eundem

   (B) eandem   (D) eōrundem

2. Nōlī eī crēdere!

   (A) them   (C) that

   (B) him   (D) yourself

3. Tribunus haec dixit quod īrātus erat.

   (A) this thing   (C) these things

   (B) those things   (D) that thing

4. Senātōrēs in Cūriā congregant. Vīdistīne . . . ?

   (A) eum   (C) ea

   (B) eī   (D) eōs

5. In Cūriā hic senātor prope illōs sedēbat.

   (A) that . . . this man   (C) this . . . them

   (B) these . . . those men (D) this . . . these men

6. That acquaintance of yours always disrupts public assemblies.

   (A) Īdem   (C) Hic

   (B) Is   (D) Iste

7. Censor nōmina illōrum in tabulā scrībit.

   (A) his   (C) them

   (B) their   (D) that

8. Does a praetor do the same things as a consul?

   (A) illa   (C) eōs

   (B) istōs   (D) eadem

9. <u>Frāter huius senātor est</u>.

   (A) This senator has a brother.

   (B) The brother of that man is a senator.

   (C) This man's brother is a senator.

   (D) He is the brother of this senator.

10. Dabatne aedīlis <u>hīs illa</u>?

   (A) these things to her   (C) that thing to them

   (B) those things to them (D) her to these

Stumper:

   <u>Is eīs dē hōc dīcet</u>.

   (A) He will tell this about them.

   (B) He is telling him about this.

   (C) He is telling them about that.

   (D) He will tell them about this.

Answers

1. **(C)**
   The form **eundem** is the equivalent of the pronoun **eum** + the suffix -**dem**, which is masculine accusative singular. Answer (A) is neuter, (B) has the correct case but the incorrect gender (feminine), and (D) has the correct gender but the incorrect case and number (genitive plural).

2. **(B)**
   The verb **crēdere** takes an object in the dative, accounting for the appearance of **eī**, which is dative singular. Answer (A) misdirects you into considering **eī** as the nominative plural masculine form, producing the translation *them*, which is actually a translation of an accusative form (vs. the nominative **eī**, *they*). This does not fit the context here. Answer (C) *that* cannot be a translation of the demonstrative **eī** without a meaning such as *that person* as a pronoun. Answer (D) requires that the **eī** be the personal or reflexive pronoun **tibi**, *yourself* (singular because the imperative is singular). (See Chapter 8, "Dative with Certain Types of Verbs.")

3. **(C)**

This question examines your ability to discriminate between singular and plural forms of the demonstrative pronoun **hic**, **haec**, **hoc** and between the meanings of *this* and *that*. This demonstrative pronoun means *this/these*, so (B) and (D) are not options because they contain translations of **ille** (*that* and *those*). The context requires that **haec** be the accusative direct object of **dixit**. Familiarity with the forms of this pronoun leads to the conclusion that **haec** is accusative plural neuter, *these things*. The sentence reads *The tribune said these things because he was angry*.

4. **(D)**

This sentence completion calls for the simple direct object form **eōs**, *Did you see them?* referring to the senators (masculine and plural). Answer (A) is singular, the incorrect number; (B) is dative singular or nominative plural, the incorrect cases, given the context of this sentence; and (C) is **ea**, feminine singular or nominative or accusative plural neuter. Answer (C) as a neuter plural form **ea**, *those things*, is justifiable grammatically, but **ea** has no possible antecedent (**senātōrēs** is not neuter and **Cūriā** is not plural). Furthermore, **ea**, as the third person form *she*, could not be the subject of **Vīdistīne**.

5. **(C)**

This question asks for discrimination between the meanings of **hic** and **ille** and between their functions as adjective and pronoun. **Hic**, as a demonstrative adjective, modifies **senātor**, *this* (*senator*) and **illōs**, *them* serves as the pronoun object of the preposition **prope**. For (A), the Latin would be **ille** . . . **hunc**. In (B), the answer *these* is plural, but in the sentence, **hic** is singular. For (D), the correct Latin would be **hic** and **hōs**. The sentence reads *In the Senate House, this senator was sitting near those* (*senators*).

6. **(D)**

The English translation of the underlined phrase contains an overtone or suggestion of contempt or distaste, requiring that the answer be (D) **Iste**. The pronouns supplied in the other answers do not carry such meaning.

7. **(B)**

Illōrum is a genitive (plural) form of the demonstrative pronoun, which can be deduced from the context. Answer (B) *their* is the only plural answer that expresses the idea of possession. Answer (A) *his* (Latin **eius**) is singular; (C) *them* is not genitive (*of them* would be correct); and (D) *that* is both singular and an adjective, despite having the proper basic meaning of **ille, illa, illud**.

8. **(D)**
    The phrase *the same things* in the question requires a neuter plural pronoun in Latin. Answer (A) fills the bill, but it does not include the meaning of *the same*. Answers (B) and (C), although plural, are both masculine and therefore do not accurately translate *things*. Furthermore, as with **illa** in (A), these pronouns do not carry the meaning of *the same* found in **eadem**.

9. **(C)**
    This sentence is tricky because your mind's eye wants to read it as (D) *He is the brother of this senator* or something equivalent. The sentence reads *The brother of this* (*man*) *is a senator*. The genitive form **huius** does not modify **senātor** or **frāter**, which are nominative. Answer (A) is incorrect because **est** does not mean *has*, and (B) **huius** has a meaning of *this* rather than *that*. Note that the apostrophe is used instead of the more familiar word *of* to indicate possession in the translation given in the correct answer, (C).

10. **(B)**
    Was the aedile giving those things to them? The verb of giving implies the appearance of both a direct object (**illa**, *those things*) and an indirect object (**hīs**, *to them*). The Latin of (A) would read *these things to her*, **haec eī**; (C) *that thing to them*, **illud eīs**; and (D) *her to those*, **eam hīs**.

Stumper: (D)
The fact that **dicet** is in the future tense eliminates (B) and (C), which have verbs in the present tense. In (A), the meanings of **hōc** and **eīs** are transposed, leaving (D), *He will tell* (*to*) *them about this.*

CHAPTER 12

The Relative Pronoun and the Interrogative Pronoun

Chapter 12

THE RELATIVE PRONOUN AND THE INTERROGATIVE PRONOUN

The Forms of the Relative Pronoun

	Singular		
	Masculine	**Feminine**	**Neuter**
Nominative	quī	quae	quod
Genitive	cuius	cuius	cuius
Dative	cui	cui	cui
Accusative	quem	**quam**	quod
Ablative	**quō**	**quā**	**quō**

	Plural		
	Masculine	**Feminine**	**Neuter**
Nominative	**quī**	**quae**	quae
Genitive	**quōrum**	**quārum**	**quōrum**
Dative	quibus	quibus	quibus
Accusative	**quōs**	**quās**	quae
Ablative	quibus	quibus	quibus

THE FORMS OF THE RELATIVE PRONOUN

In the preceding chart, the forms in **boldface** have the same endings as the corresponding cases of first and second declension nouns. The underlined forms have endings that belong to the third declension. Also note the similarities of forms of the relative pronoun to those of the demonstrative pronoun.

THE USES OF THE RELATIVE PRONOUN

The relative pronoun **quī**, **quae**, **quod**, *who*, *which*, *that*, is so called because it introduces an explanatory or descriptive clause that "relates" to another word or other words in its sentence or in a previous sentence. The verb of this clause is in the indicative, and therefore its meaning is expressed as a fact. The noun or pronoun that the relative clause modifies is known as the antecedent (**ante** + **cēdere**, *to go before*), which is usually found immediately prior to the relative pronoun. The pronoun that introduces the relative clause agrees with its antecedent in gender and number, but not necessarily in case. In its clause, the relative pronoun performs a function independent of that of its antecedent, as in the following example:

nom.   acc.

Spurius erat <u>senātor</u> [<u>quem</u> audīvī] ōrātiōnem habēns.

relative clause

Spurius was the <u>senator</u> [<u>whom</u> I heard] giving a speech.

The relative pronoun **quem** agrees with its antecedent **senātor** in gender (masculine) and number (singular), but not in case. **Senātor** serves as the predicate nominative in the main clause and **quem** is the direct object of the verb **audīvī** in the relative clause.

When reading, be sure to relate the relative pronoun to its antecedent. If the antecedent is a <u>person</u>, use *who*, *whom*, or *whose* when translating. If the antecedent is a <u>thing</u>, use *which* or *that*. The relative pronoun can also introduce other types of clauses that have their verbs in the subjunctive mood. These clauses, such as the relative clause of purpose and the relative clause of characteristic, will be presented in Chapter 31.

The relative clause is a self-contained unit of thought, often framed by commas. When translating a relative clause, it is helpful to bracket the clause as a separate sense unit within the sentence:

Ōrātiō [quam audīvī] erat longa.
The speech [that I heard] was long.

When translating, avoid pulling words out of the relative clause and inserting them into the main clause, and vice versa.

The antecedent of a relative pronoun is sometimes given in the context of the preceding sentence, leading to a situation where the relative pronoun is found at the beginning of the succeeding sentence. When translating this "linking **quī**," substitute a demonstrative, such as *this* or *these*, or a personal pronoun, such as *him*, for example:

Spurius dē rēbus urbānīs dīcēbat. <u>Quibus</u> verbīs dictīs, omnēs eum laudābant.
Spurius was speaking about urban affairs. <u>These</u> (literally, Which) words having been spoken, everyone praised him.

<u>Quem</u> octō servī ē forō lectīcā ferēbant.
Eight slaves carried <u>him</u> (literally, whom) from the Forum in a limo.

In the first set of sentences, the form **Quibus** refers to Spurius's speech about urban affairs, **dē rēbus urbānīs**, mentioned in the previous sentence. In the second example, the relative pronoun **quem** refers back to **eum** (Spurius) in the previous sentence. In such situations, English requires that you avoid translating a word such as **quem** as a relative pronoun (*whom, which,* etc.)

English sometimes omits the relative pronoun without loss of meaning, such as the omission of the word *whom* from the sentence in the first example: *Spurius was the senator I heard giving a speech.* Latin does not omit the relative pronoun, but it sometimes does omit the antecedent when it is indefinite, for example:

Sunt (eī) <u>quī</u> prope rostra stant ut ōrātiōnem audiant.
There are those <u>who</u> are standing near the Rostra to hear the speech.

A relative clause has the same basic meaning as that of a participle, when the participle is translated as a clause:

Relative clause: **Multitūdō ōrātōrem <u>quī rostra</u> <u>ascendēbat</u> impediēbat.**
The crowd hindered the orator <u>who was</u> <u>mounting</u> the Rostra.

Participle: **Multitūdō ōrātōrem rostra <u>ascendentem</u> impediēbat.**
The crowd hindered the orator <u>who was mounting</u> the Rostra.

This is a good time to remind you that both dependent clauses and participles are found much more often in Latin than in English.

The Interrogative Pronoun

	Singular		
	Masculine	**Feminine**	**Neuter**
Nominative	**quis**	**quis**	**quid**
Genitive	**cuius**	**cuius**	**cuius**
Dative	**cui**	**cui**	**cui**
Accusative	**quem**	**quem**	**quid**
Ablative	**quō**	**quō**	**quō**

THE FORMS OF THE INTERROGATIVE PRONOUN

In the preceding chart, note that the masculine and feminine forms are identical. Note, too, the similarities of the forms of the interrogative pronoun to those of the relative pronoun. The plural forms of the interrogative <u>pronoun</u> are the same as those of the relative pronoun **quī, quae, quod**. (For the forms of the relative pronoun, see the first chart in this chapter.)

<u>Ē quibus</u> lictor fascēs accipiet?
From <u>whom</u> will the attendant receive the bundle of rods with the axe?

The forms of the interrogative <u>adjective</u> are also the same as those of the relative pronoun, and they are translated *Which . . . ?*

<u>Quem consulem</u> lictōrēs prōsequentur?
<u>Which consul</u> will the attendants accompany?

THE FUNCTION OF THE INTERROGATIVE PRONOUN

The interrogative (**inter** + **rogāre**, *to ask in the presence of*) pronoun is **quis**, *who* for both masculine and feminine genders, and **quid**, *what*, for neuter. The interrogative pronoun introduces a direct question with an indicative verb and an indirect question clause with a subjunctive verb:

indicative

Direct question: **Quis fascēs lictōrī dabit?**
Who will give the bundle of rods with the axe to the attendant?

subjunctive

Indirect question: **Nesciō lictōrem cui fascēs det.**
I do not know the attendant to whom he is giving the rods and axe.

The interrogative pronoun will usually be the first word in a direct question, which will end with a question mark.

In an indirect question clause with a subjunctive verb, the interrogative pronoun is not found at the beginning of the sentence but at the beginning of its clause. There is no question mark. (Direct questions will be reviewed in Chapter 23, and indirect questions will be covered in Chapter 31.) Take care to distinguish the forms of the interrogative pronoun **quis**, **quis**, **quid** from those of the relative pronoun **quī**, **quae**, **quod**, both of which are commonly found.

TIPS ON TRANSLATING RELATIVE AND INTERROGATIVE PRONOUNS

- When you translate, be sure that the function of the relative pronoun is <u>independent</u> of that of its antecedent, that is, decide the meaning of the case based on its use in its own clause. Remember, however, that the number and gender of the relative pronoun and its antecedent must agree.

- The nominative form of the relative pronoun is translated as *who* or *which/that*, the genitive as *whose/of whom*, and the dative, accusative, and ablative, as *whom* or *which/that*. Because the latter cases require objects, such as *to/for whom*, *whom*, or *with whom*, remember that the English objective word *whom* must end in *-m*, in the manner of the singular form of the direct object in Latin. For example, **Cui crēdis?** means not <u>*Who*</u> *do you trust?* but <u>*Whom*</u> *do you trust?*

- When deciding whether the nominative or accusative case of the relative or interrogative pronoun is required, turn the sentence around. For instance, consider the sentence *Which laws were often broken by the Romans?* Is *Which laws* the subject or direct object of the verb? By reversing the phrasing to read *The Romans broke which laws?* you can clearly identify *Which laws* in the original as the object accusative.

- On paper or in your head, bracket the relative clause, which begins with a relative pronoun and ends with a verb. Remember that the relative clause describes a noun, pronoun, or other word group in its sentence or in a previous sentence.

- Be aware that a relative pronoun can also introduce a relative clause that has its verb in the subjunctive mood.

- The preposition **cum** is attached to the end of the relative pronoun in prepositional phrases, such as **quōcum** or **quibuscum**, *with whom* or *with what*.

- The relative pronoun and the interrogative pronoun and adjective have the same forms in the plural. In the singular, the relative pronoun and interrogative adjective have three gender-specific forms of each case (**quī**, **quae**, and **quod**, etc.), and the interrogative pronoun has two (**quis** and **quid**, etc.)

- When translating, be aware that some forms of the relative pronoun, such as **quam** and **quod**, have alternative functions and meanings, for example:

    Impediēbant eum <u>quod</u> ōrātiōnem habitūrus erat.
    They were obstructing him <u>because</u> he was going to give a speech.

PRACTICE QUESTIONS

1. Senēs . . . in forō vīdī senātōrēs erant.

    (A) quis   (C) quem

    (B) quī   (D) quōs

2. The accusative singular feminine of <u>quis</u> is
   (A) quam   (C) quae
   (B) quem   (D) quā

3. Aedificium <u>quod</u> faciēbant basilica erat.
   (A) when   (C) because
   (B) that   (D) whom

4. <u>At what hour</u> will the citizens leave the assembly?
   (A) Quam hōram   (C) Quā hōrā
   (B) Quae hōra   (D) Quid hōrae

5. Consul <u>cui</u> fascēs datī sunt imperium tenēbat.
   (A) whose   (C) who
   (B) whom   (D) to whom

6. The senators <u>with whom</u> the consul was walking were his enemies.
   (A) quōcum   (C) quibus
   (B) post quōs   (D) quibuscum

7. Consul <u>cuius</u> nōmen Cicerō erat senātum consultum ultimum tenēbat.
   (A) to whom   (C) whose
   (B) who   (D) with whom

8. . . . lēgī cīvēs semper parent?
   (A) Quō   (C) Cui
   (B) Quem   (D) Quis

9. <u>Which laws</u> did Roman citizens disregard?
   (A) Quās lēgēs   (C) Quārum lēgum
   (B) Quae lēgēs   (D) Quibus lēgibus

10. Ā quibus omnēs lēgēs parēbuntur?

    (A) For whom   (C) From which

    (B) From whom   (D) By whom

11. Quī quae vult dīcit, quae nōn vult audiet.

    If stated, the antecedent of each quae would be the form

    (A) eās   (C) ea

    (B) eam   (D) id

12. Plēbēs quī ambulābant per Viam Sacram ad comitiam ībant.

    The most accurate substitute is

    (A) ambulātūrī

    (B) postquam ambulāverant

    (C) ambulantēs

    (D) quod ambulābant

13. Saxa quibus basilica aedificata erat gravissima fuērunt.

    (A) for whom   (C) to which

    (B) with which   (D) by whom

14. Perīcula timidus quae nōn sunt videt.

    The antecedent of quae is

    (A) dangers

    (B) the fearful person

    (C) those things

    (D) she (understood)

Stumper:

Sunt quibus dīversae opīniōnēs essent.

    (A) There are those who had different opinions.

    (B) They are the ones whose opinions are different.

    (C) Those who had opinions were different.

    (D) They are the different ones who had opinions.

Answers

1. **(D)**

   The context of the missing relative pronoun suggests the word *whom* to complete the meaning of the verb, that is, *I saw whom*. *Whom* is an object form in English, so an object form in Latin is required, leaving the choices of (C) and (D), which are both accusative. Because the antecedent **senēs** is plural, (C) **quem**, which is singular, must be eliminated. Answer (A) **quis** is an interrogative pronoun that does not relate back to an antecedent, and (B) **quī** is a relative pronoun in the nominative case, which seems to be the correct answer, at first glance. Remember that the function of a relative pronoun in its clause is separate from that of its antecedent. The sentence reads *The old men whom I saw in the Forum were senators*.

2. **(B)**

   Option (A) **quam** seems the obvious correct answer, but this form is the accusative singular feminine form of the relative pronoun **quae**, not that of the interrogative pronoun **quis**. Answer (C) **quae** is feminine nominative (singular or plural), and (D) **quā** is the feminine ablative singular form of the relative **quae**.

3. **(B)**

   The relative pronoun **quod** in this sentence modifies **aedificium** and is the direct object of the verb **faciēbant**, giving the translation *The building that they were making*. Answer (A) *when* is not an option for translating **quod**. **Quod** can have a causal meaning, such as *because*, as in (C), but this meaning does not make sense in the context of this sentence. Answer (D) *whom* has a personal meaning, whereas the relative pronoun **quod** is neuter and cannot have a personal meaning.

4. **(C)**

   The underlined phrase *At what hour* requires an ablative of time. Because the sentence is a direct question, an interrogative adjective is needed. The ablative singular form of **quī, quae, quod**, which serves as the interrogative adjective, is therefore **quā**. **Quā hōrā**, *At what hour* accurately completes the meaning of the sentence. The accusative, nominative, and partitive genitive phrases in (A), (B), and (D), respectively, have no grammatical meaning in this context.

5. **(D)**

   In this sentence, **datī sunt** takes a dative indirect object, **cui**, *to whom*, the antecedent of which is **consul**. The sentence reads *The consul to whom the fasces were given held the imperium.* Answer (A) *whose* is possessive genitive, the form of which would be **cuius**. Answer (B) *whom* is object accusative, the form of which is **quem**, and (C) *who* is subject nominative, the form of which is **quī**.

6. **(D)**

   With whom is a phrase requiring the preposition **cum**. Because the antecedent **senātōrēs** is plural, the relative pronoun must also be plural. Hence (A), which is singular, must be eliminated. Answer (B) **post quōs**, *after whom* changes the meaning of the original prepositional phrase, and (C) breaks the general rule that the ablative of accompaniment must be found with the preposition **cum**.

7. **(C)**

   Cuius is the genitive singular form of the relative pronoun. It links **nōmen** with its antecedent **consul**. The sentence then reads *The consul whose name was Cicero . . .* In the Latin sentence, (A) requires the dative form **cui**, (B) requires the nominative form **quī**, and (D) requires the ablative form **quōcum**.

8. **(C)**

   This is a bit tricky. Success on this question requires that you know that the verb **parēre** takes a dative object (see Chapter 8). Only **cui** is dative and is therefore the correct answer. This form is an interrogative adjective modifying **lēgī**. Answer (A) **quō** is ablative; (B) **quem** perhaps the most obvious answer, is accusative; and (D) **quis** is nominative. The sentence reads *Which law do (the) citizens always obey?*

9. **(A)**

   Basically, this question asks you to decide whether the English phrase *Which laws?* serves as the subject or direct object of the verb. By turning the sentence around (*Roman citizens disregarded which laws?*), you can determine that the answer must be the object accusative form **quās lēgēs**. Answer (B) **quae lēgēs** is nominative, (C) **quārum lēgum** is genitive, and (D) **quibus lēgibus** is dative or ablative.

10. **(D)**
This sentence contains the simple prepositional phrase **Ā quibus**, *By whom* as the interrogative phrase to be translated. Answer (A) *For whom* is dative. Answers (B) *From whom* and (C) *From which* are ablative, but they require the preposition phrase **Ē quō** or **Ē quibus**. The sentence reads *By whom will all laws be obeyed?*

11. **(C)**
This sentence says *He who says (the things) that he wants will hear (the things) that he does not want (to hear).* Because the sense requires that the form **quae** be the neuter plural of the relative pronoun, the antecedent is understood as the neuter plural *things. That* is the direct object in both instances, and the only pronoun among the answers that is accusative plural neuter is **ea** (**quae**). If (A) **eās** were the antecedent, the relative would be **quās**; if (B) **eam**, then the relative would be **quam**; if (D) **id**, then **quod**.

12. **(C)**
This question asks you to substitute a similar construction for the relative clause **quī ambulābant**. The present active participle **ambulantēs** can be translated as the relative clause *who were walking.* Answer (A) **ambulātūrī**, *about to walk*, is a future active participle; (B) **postquam ambulāverant**, *after they had walked*, is a time clause; and (D) **quod ambulābant**, *because they were walking*, is a causal clause.

13. **(B)**
Quibus is tricky here because it is an ablative without a preposition, leading to some contextual guesstimation. The form could also be dative, of course, but the sense does not permit this use, unless it would be incorrectly taken as a possessive dative with the verb **erat**. Therefore (A) and (C), which are dative, are eliminated. So we are left with *The stones . . . the basilica had been built were extremely heavy.* Answer (D) *by whom* does not relate to **saxa**, the antecedent of **quibus**. Nor is a preposition found before **quibus**, which would be required for an ablative of agent, also meaning *by whom*, with the passive verb. Such a sentence would not make sense: *The stones by whom . . .* Therefore, **saxa quibus** must mean *The stones with which* or *by means of which.*

14. **(A)**

This sentence by Publilius Syrus reads *The fearful (person) sees dangers that are not even (there).* Among the answers, the antecedent of **quae** that gives the most meaningful translation is *dangers*, **perīcula**, which is the direct object of **videt**. **Quae** agrees with **perīcula** as a neuter plural, leading to the meaning *Dangers that*. **Quae** does not agree with (B) **timidus** in gender or number. Answer (C) is grammatically conceivable, but the ensuing translation does not make sense, and (D) requires that the relative clause have a singular verb.

Stumper: **(A)**

This sentence reads, literally, *There are those to whom there were different opinions*, that is, those who had different opinions. Thus **quibus dīversae opīniōnēs essent** is an example of dative of possession (see Chapter 8). Also, the antecedent of the relative pronoun **quibus** is missing. In the sentence, the adjective **dīversae** clearly modifies **opīniōnēs**, which removes (C) and (D). The translations of the relative pronoun and verb tense are wrong in (B). The relative clause of characteristic with the subjunctive, **quibus . . . essent**, that appears in this sentence will be covered in Chapter 31.

CHAPTER 13

Indefinite Pronouns

Chapter 13

INDEFINITE PRONOUNS

The Forms of Indefinite Pronouns and Adjectives

Indefinite Pronoun	Indefinite Adjective
Masculine, Feminine, Neuter	**Masculine, Feminine, Neuter**
quidam, **quae**dam, **quid**dam, *a certain one*	**qui**dam, **quae**dam, **quod**dam, *a certain*
ali**quis**, *some/anyone*, ali**quid**, *some/anything*	ali**qui**, ali**qua**, ali**quod**, *some*, *any*
quisque, *each one, everyone* **quid**que, *each one, everything*	**quis**que, **quae**que, **quod**que, *each, every*
quisquam, *anyone*, **quid**quam/ quicquam, *anything*	(**ūllus, -a, -um**, *any*)

THE USES OF INDEFINITE PRONOUNS AND ADJECTIVES

The indefinite pronoun (literally, *without limit*) does not specify the identity of the person or thing to which it refers. As with other pronouns, the indefinite pronoun may also be used as an adjective. Most contain the forms of the interrogative pronoun **quis**, **quis**, **quid** in the singular and the relative pronoun **quī**, **quae**, **quod** in the plural (the nominative singular forms are given in boldface in the chart above; for the other case forms of these pronouns, see the charts in the previous chapter). To these forms are added a prefix, such as in **aliquis**, or a suffix, such as in **quīdam**, **quisque**, or **quisquam**. Only the **quis** or **quī** part of the indefinite pronoun changes form, as the context requires.

Quīdam, Quaedam, Quiddam, *a certain one*

Pronoun: **Consul quendam ad tabulārium mīsit.**
The consul sent a certain man to the Records Office.

Adjective: **Quīdam consul virum ad tabulārium mīsit.**
A certain consul sent a man to the Records Office.

Observe in the preceding chart that the nominative and accusative singular neuter of the pronoun **quīdam** is **quiddam** and the adjective **quoddam**.

As with the demonstrative pronoun **īdem**, the accusative singular and genitive plural forms of **quīdam** contain **-n-** instead of **-m-**. In the masculine and feminine, the accusative singular forms are **quendam** and **quandam** and, in the genitive plural of the masculine, feminine, and neuter, they are **quōrundam, quārundam, quōrundam**.

Aliquis, Aliquid, *someone*, *something*

Pronoun: **Tribūnus alicui nuntium dedit.**
The tribune gave a message to someone.

Adjective: **Aliquī nuntiī scripta legere volunt.**
Some messengers want to read what was written.

The pronoun **aliquis** combines the adjective **alius**, *other*, with the interrogative pronoun **quis**, *who*. With the adjective **aliquī**, the forms of the relative **quī, quae, quod** are used except in the nominative singular feminine, which is **aliqua**, not **aliquae**.

Quisque, Quidque, *each one/thing, everyone/thing*

Pronoun: **"Suus cuique mōs," scripsit Terentius.**
"To each his own way," wrote Terence.

Adjective: **Quid quisque homō putet, philosophus cognoscere vult.**
A philosopher wishes to find out what every person thinks.

Observe that the adjectival form of **quisque, quaeque, quodque** is the same as the relative pronoun **quī, quae, quod**, except for the masculine nominative singular, which is **quisque**, not **quīque**.

Quisquam, Quidquam/Quicquam, *anyone, anything*

Pronoun:

Iūstitia (Jūstitia) numquam nocet cuiquam.
Justice never harms <u>anyone</u>.

Adjective:

The irregular adjective **ūllus, -a, -um,** *any,* serves as the adjectival form of **quisquam,** for example:

Sī <u>ūllō</u> modō potest . . .
If it can (be done) in <u>any</u> way . . .

Quicquam is used as an alternative to **quidquam** because the assimilation of the sound **d** by the sound **q** makes **quicquam** easier to pronounce.

Other Indefinite Pronouns

Quārē habē tibi <u>quicquid</u> hoc libellī, <u>qualecumque</u>. (Catullus)
And so, have for yourself <u>whatever</u> this (is) of a little book, <u>such as it is</u> (i.e., take the book for what it's worth).

There are other variations of the indefinite pronoun, such as **quisquis, quaequae, quidquid** (or **quicquid**) and **quicumque, quaecumque, quodcumque,** both meaning *whoever* or *whatever.* The latter, an indefinite relative pronoun, is declined the same as the relative pronoun: the suffix -**cumque** is unchanging.

The use of **quis, quis, quid,** *anyone, anything,* instead of **aliquis** or **quisquam,** as an indefinite is reserved for subordinate clauses introduced by conjunctions such as **cum, nē, nisi, num, sī,** or **ut.** The most common use is **sī quis,** *if anyone:*

<u>Sī quis</u> aliquid novī aget, in actīs diūrnīs scrībetur.
<u>If anyone</u> does something unusual, it will be written in the public record.

Indefinite Pronouns and Adjectives

From quī, quae, quod		From quis, quis, quid
Pronoun	**Adjective**	**Pronoun**
quīcumque, *whoever*	aliquī, *some, any*	aliquis, *someone, anyone*
quīdam, *a certain one*	quīdam, *a certain*	quisquam, *anyone*
	quisque, *each, every**	quisque, *each one*
		quisquis, *whoever*

* These forms, except for the nominative singular masculine **quisque**, derive from **quī, quae, quod**.

TIPS ON TRANSLATING INDEFINITE PRONOUNS

- Indefinite pronouns and adjectives are formed from the pronouns **quī, quae, quod** and **quis, quis, quid**. Exploit your knowledge of these relative and interrogative pronouns and adjectives.

- Use the context to determine the function of the indefinite pronoun or adjective, as in the following examples:

  Indefinite pronoun: **Vir in actīs diūrnīs <u>aliquid</u> scrīpsit.**
  The man wrote <u>something</u> in the public record.

  Indefinite adjective: **<u>Aliquī vir</u> in actīs diūrnīs scrīpsit.**
  <u>Some man</u> wrote in the public record.

- Remember that indefinite pronouns and adjectives are non-specific, that is, they are translated by words such as *any*, *each*, *some*, or *whoever*.

- Avoid confusing the conjunction **quamquam**, *although*, and the adverbs **quōque**, *also*, and **quidem**, *indeed*, with forms of the indefinite pronoun and adjective.

PRACTICE QUESTIONS

1. Suntne <u>aliquae lēgēs</u> malae?
    (A) all laws   (C) some laws
    (B) many laws   (D) certain laws

2. The Senate wishes to remove <u>certain praetors</u> from their provinces.
    (A) quīdam praetōrēs   (C) aliquōs praetōrēs
    (B) quōsdam praetōrēs   (D) quōsque praetōrēs

3. Sī <u>quis</u> in forum ierit, splendida aedificia vidēbit.
    (A) who   (C) someone
    (B) anyone   (D) whoever

4. <u>Quisquis</u> amat, valeat; pereat quī nescit amāre! (Pompeiian wall inscription)
    (A) Anyone   (C) A certain one
    (B) Someone   (D) Whoever

5. <u>Aliquis aliquid dē quōquam dīcere potest</u>.
    (A) He can say anything whatever about this.
    (B) Some people can speak about anything to anyone.
    (C) Every person has something to say about this certain person.
    (D) Anyone can say anything about anyone.

6. <u>Alicui quidem rogantī quam iubentī (jubentī) libentius parēmus</u>.
    This sentence means
    (A) You can catch more flies with honey than with vinegar.
    (B) Oil and water don't mix.
    (C) Birds of a feather flock together.
    (D) The end justifies the means.

7. Īdem is to eundem as quīdam is to

   (A) quōrundam   (C) quendam

   (B) quemquam   (D) quemque

8. Can there be a reason <u>for anyone</u> to speak out against his own country?

   (A) quicquid   (C) quibusque

   (B) quōdam   (D) cuiquam

Stumper:

    . . . . remedia graviōra perīculīs sunt.

   (A) Quādam   (C) Quīdam

   (B) Quaedam   (D) Quoddam

Answers

1. **(C)**

   Selecting the correct answer here requires knowledge of the meaning of the indefinite adjective **aliquī, aliqua, aliquod**, *some* or *any*. The Latin of (A) would be **omnēs lēgēs**, (B) **multae lēgēs**, and (D) **quaedam lēgēs**. The sentence reads *Are <u>some</u> laws bad?* (See **"Aliquis, aliquid."**)

2. **(B)**

   Proper translation of the underlined phrase requires knowledge of the meaning of the adjective **quīdam, quaedam, quoddam**, *a certain*, which the context requires in its accusative plural form, **quōsdam**. Answer (A) has the correct adjective, but in the nominative instead of the accusative. Answers (C) and (D) have the correct case endings, but neither is the correct Latin word: **aliquōs** means *some* or *any*, and **quōsque** means *each* or *every*. (See **"Quīdam, Quaedam, Quiddam."**)

3. **(B)**

   When introduced by conjunctions such as **sī**, the pronoun **quis** means *anyone*. Translation (A) *who* for **quis** requires that the pronoun be an interrogative and that the sentence be a direct question, which it is not. Answers (C) *someone* and (D) *whoever* are not acceptable meanings of the pronoun **quis**. The Latin for the former would be **aliquis** and for the latter **quīcumque** or **quisquis**. The sentence reads *If anyone comes* *into the forum, he will see magnificent buildings*. (See "Other Indefinite Pronouns.")

4.   **(D)**

This quote is part of a Pompeiian wall inscription about love. The indefinite pronoun **quisquis** is the nominative subject of the sentence and means *whoever*. The Latin for (A) and (B) is **aliquis**, and for (C) it is **quīdam**. The sentence reads *Whoever loves, let him prosper; he who does not know (how) to love, let him be undone*. (See "Other Indefinite Pronouns.") Note the appearance of the jussive subjunctives **valeat** and **pereat**, *Let him . . .*

5.   **(D)**

This sentence contains a mouthful of three indefinite pronouns: **aliquis**, *anybody*; **aliquid**, *anything*; and a form of **quisquam** (or **quicquam**), *anyone* (or *anything*). The first is the nominative subject, the second the accusative direct object, and the third the object of an ablative preposition. Answers (A), (B), and (C)—all containing various elements of correctness—are designed to test your knowledge of the meanings of various indefinite pronouns. In (A), the object **aliquid** cannot mean *whatever*. In (B), **quisque** does not mean *some people*, nor does **dē quōquam** mean *to anyone*. The *about this certain person* of (C) requires the ablative of the indefinite pronoun **quīdam**, which is **quōdam**, not **quōquam**.

6.   **(A)**

This sentence says, literally, *We more readily obey someone (who is) asking (rather) than ordering*. The verb **parēre** takes a dative object, hence the participial phrase **alicui . . . rogantī quam iubentī (jubentī)**. Don't be fooled into thinking that **quidem** in this sentence is another indefinite pronoun! (See **"Aliquis, Aliquid"** and Chapter 8, "Dative with Certain Types of Verbs.")

7.   **(C)**

This analogy compares the singular subject and object forms of the demonstrative pronoun **īdem** with the indefinite pronoun **quīdam**. These forms illustrate the effect of assimilation in producing the spelling changes of **eundem** and **quendam**. (See **"Quīdam, Quaedam, Quiddam."**)

8. **(D)**

For anyone requires the dative of **quisquam**, which is **cuiquam**. Answer (A) **quicquid** is nominative or accusative singular neuter, meaning *whatever*. Answer (B) **quōdam** is ablative singular of **quīdam**, *a certain person*, and (C) **quibusque** is a plural of **quisque**, which does not fit the singular sense here. (See **"Quisquam, Quidquam/Quicquam"** and "Other Indefinite Pronouns.")

Stumper: (B)

The various possible answers tell you that what is missing is a form of **quīdam, quaedam, quoddam**, the indefinite adjective. The missing adjective modifies **remedia**, which is the neuter plural subject of the verb **sunt**. Of the choices, the neuter plural form of the adjective that agrees with **remedia** is **quaedam**. Answer (A) **quādam** is ablative singular feminine, (C) **quīdam** is nominative singular masculine, and (D) **quoddam** is nominative/accusative singular neuter. This sentence reads *Some solutions are worse than the problems.* (See **"Quīdam, Quaedam, Quiddam."**)

CHAPTER 14

Personal Pronouns

Chapter 14

PERSONAL PRONOUNS

The Forms of Personal Pronouns

	1st person (*I*, *we/us*)		2nd person (*you*)	
	Singular	**Plural**	**Singular**	**Plural**
Nominative	**ego**	**nōs**	**tū**	**vōs**
Genitive	**meī**	**nostrum, nostrī**	**tuī**	**vestrum, vestrī**
Dative	**mihi**	**nōbīs**	**tibi**	**vōbīs**
Accusative	**mē**	**nōs**	**tē**	**vōs**
Ablative	**mē**	**nōbīs**	**tē**	**vōbīs**

In Latin, there is no pronoun of the third person. For the forms of the demonstrative pronoun **is**, **ea**, **id**, *he*, *she*, *it*, which serves as the pronoun of the third person, see the chart in Chapter 11. Personal pronouns have the following English meanings:

	1st person	2nd person	3rd person
Singular	*I*	*you*	*he, she, it*
Plural	*we, us*	*you*	*they, them*

THE USES OF PERSONAL PRONOUNS

Pronouns of the First and Second Persons (*I*, *we/us*, and *you*)

The personal pronoun substitutes for a previously stated noun or pronoun and designates a specific person, as in the following example:

> **Puer puellam basiat. "Ego tē amō!" dīcit.**
> *The boy kisses the girl. "I love you!" he says.*

The subject forms are **ego**, *I*, and **tū**, *you* (singular). The subject plurals are **nōs**, *we* and **vōs**, *you* (plural), respectively. Avoid confusing the form **nōs** with that of **vōs**.

To distinguish between the forms **tū** and **tē** of the second person pronoun, recall two famous sayings:

> **Et tū, Brūte?**
> *You, as well, Brutus?* (Caesar in Shakespeare's *Julius Caesar*)

> **Nōs moritūrī tē salutāmus.**
> *We who are about to die salute you.* (gladiatorial greeting to the emperor in the arena)

The Pronoun of the Third Person (*he*, *she*, *it*, and *they*)

The demonstrative pronoun **is, ea, id** that you reviewed in the previous chapter designates the person or thing about which the speaker or writer is talking or writing, and it therefore serves as the pronoun of the third person, *he*, *she*, *it*. The subject plurals are **eī, eae, ea**, *they*. Here are examples of the use of this demonstrative as the pronoun of the third person:

> **Nōlī eī ea dīcere.**
> *Don't say those things to him/her.*

> **Mitte epistulam ad eum.**
> *Send the letter to him.*

> **Nōs eōs nōn amāmus.**
> *We do not like them.*

> **Īte cum eīs!**
> *Go with them!*

> **Eīs id facient.**
> *They will do it for them.*

> **Is eam amat.**
> *He likes her.*

When the gender is ambiguous (such as **eī** in the first example), Latin, as a patriarchal language, prefers the masculine. Remember that third person pronouns may cross gender boundaries when expressing meaning:

> **Accēpistīne epistulam?**
> *Did you receive the letter?*

> **Eam accēpī.**
> *I did receive it* (not *her*).

Emphatic Use of the Personal Pronoun

When found in the nominative case, personal pronouns in Latin are often used to indicate a change of subject or to intensify the subject indicated by the ending of the verb. (In English, a word to be emphasized is stressed by voice inflection.) Here is an example of the emphatic use of the personal pronoun in Latin:

> **Sī valēs, bene est. Ego valeō.**
> *If you are well, I am glad. I (me, myself, and I) am well.*

THE FORMS AND USES OF POSSESSIVE ADJECTIVES

Possessive Adjectives of the First and Second Persons

The genitive case of the personal pronoun is <u>not</u> used to indicate possession. This is reserved for the possessive adjectives: **meus, -a, -um,** *my*; **noster, nostra, nostrum,** *our*; **tuus, -a, -um,** *your* (singular); and **vester, vestra, vestrum,** *your* (plural). Possessive adjectives are thus first/second declension adjectives that correspond to the personal pronouns **ego, nōs, tū,** and **vōs.**

> **Pater <u>noster</u>, quī es in caelō . . .**
> <u>Our</u> *Father, who are in heaven . . .* (rather than **Pater <u>nostrī</u>,** *the Father <u>of us</u>*)

> **<u>Mea</u> culpa.**
> <u>My</u> *fault.*

The genitive forms of the personal pronoun (**meī, tuī, nostrum/nostrī,** and **vestrum/vestrī**) are primarily used with adjectives and verbs that require the genitive case or with special uses, such as the partitive genitive:

> **Multī <u>nostrum</u> fortūnae crēdunt.**
> *Many <u>of us</u> trust to luck.*

Nostrum is used partitively, whereas **nostrī** is used objectively, as in **desidērium <u>nostrī</u>,** *longing <u>for us</u>.* (See Chapter 7, "Partitive Genitive" and "Objective Genitive.")

Expressing Possession in the Third Person

To express possession in the third person, Latin uses either a pronoun or an adjective. Because there is no possessive adjective corresponding to the third person pronoun **is, ea, id**, the genitive form of the pronoun **eius (ejus)**, *of him, of her, of it* is used to express *his, hers, its.* (Note how much the Latin word **eius** sounds like the English word *his!*) The plurals are **eōrum, eārum, eōrum**, *of them* (i.e., *their, theirs*):

> **Fortuna eius (ejus) bona est.**
> *His* (or *her*) *luck* (i.e., *the luck of him* or *her*) *is good.*

Possession in the third person can also be expressed by using the adjective **suus, -a, -um**. This adjective corresponds to the reflexive pronoun **sē**. The reflexive adjective **suus, -a, -um** can be singular or plural and has the meaning *his own, her own,* or *their own*:

> **Dī cuique suum fātum concēdunt.**
> *The gods grant to each* (*person*) *his own fate.*

Personal Pronouns and Possessive Adjectives

	Singular		Plural	
	Personal Pronoun	**Possessive Adjective**	**Personal Pronoun**	**Possessive Adjective**
1st person	**ego**	**meus, -a, -um**	**nōs**	**noster, nostra, nostrum**
	I	*my, mine*	*we*	*our/s*
2nd person	**tū**	**tuus, -a, -um**	**vōs**	**vester, vestra, vestrum**
	you (alone)	*your/s* (sing.)	*you* (all)	*your/s* (pl.)
3rd person	**is, ea, id**		**eī, eae, ea**	
	he, she, it		*they*	

TIPS ON TRANSLATING PERSONAL PRONOUNS

- Personal pronouns are irregular but similar to each other in case form.

- Personal pronouns are often used to show emphasis.

- **Is**, **ea**, **id**, a demonstrative pronoun (*this* or *that person*) and a demonstrative adjective (*this* or *that*), also serves as the pronoun of the third person (*he, she, it*).

- Possessive adjectives and pronouns serve the function of the possessive genitive of the personal pronoun: **meus, -a, -um**, *mine* replaces **meī**, *of me*. The possessive adjectives **meus**, *my* and **noster**, *our/s*, **tuus**, *your/s* and **vester**, *your/s*, and **suus**, *his/her/its own*, correspond to the personal and reflexive pronouns **ego**, *I*, and **nōs**, *we/us*, **tū**, *you* (singular) and **vōs**, *you* (plural), and **sē**, *himself/herself/itself*.

- The possessive adjective need not be expressed in Latin when the sense may be inferred without it, as in **Mātrem audiō**, *I hear (my) mother*. Conversely, the possessive adjective, if used, clarifies or emphasizes, for example **Mātrem meam audiō**, *I hear my mother* (as opposed to *your mother*).

- Pronominal phrases such as **nōs omnēs**, *all of us*, appear often.

- **Mihi** often appears in contracted form as **mī** in poetry, for the sake of the meter.

- When pronouns of the first and second persons appear with **cum**, the preposition is attached to the end of the pronoun as an enclitic, such as **mēcum**, **tēcum**, **nōbīscum** or **vōbīscum**.

   Pax vōbīscum.
   Peace be with you.

PRACTICE QUESTIONS

1.   . . . omnēs līberī esse volumus.

   (A) Nōbīs   (C) Eī

   (B) Vōs   (D) Nōs

2. The plural of <u>tibi</u> is

   (A) vōbīs   (C) vestrum

   (B) vōs   (D) tuī

3. Amīcī, Rōmānī, cīvēs, . . . venīte!

   (A) nōbīscum   (C) cum vōbīs

   (B) ad vestrōs   (D) cum nōbīs

4. Illum librum emī sed <u>eum</u> nōn lēgī.

   (A) him   (C) it

   (B) his   (D) them

5. <u>Tē tua, mē mea delectant</u>.

   (A) My things please you, your things please me.

   (B) Your things please me, my things please you.

   (C) Your and my things please both you and me.

   (D) Your things please you, my things please me.

6. <u>Dic mihi haec</u>.

   (A) She is speaking to me.

   (B) Tell me these things.

   (C) Tell her this for me.

   (D) This woman is talking to me.

7. <u>Nec tēcum possum vīvere nec sine tē</u>. (Martial)

   (A) I can live neither with you nor without you.

   (B) I can live with you and I cannot live without you.

   (C) You can neither live with me nor without me.

   (D) I not am able to live with you or near you.

8. He lost <u>his (someone else's)</u> <u>money</u>.

   (A) eōrum pecūniam   (C) suam pecūniam

   (B) eius (ejus) pecūniam   (D) eam pecūniam

9. Not <u>for ourselves</u> alone.

   (A) nōs   (C) nōbīs

   (B) nostrīs   (D) ad nōs

10. Vidēsne . . . in speculō?

   (A) tē   (C) vestrum

   (B) vōs   (D) tibi

Stumper:

   <u>I am helping you.</u>

   (A) Tulī auxilium ad tē.

   (B) Vōbīs auxiliō sum.

   (C) Tū auxilium mihi das.

   (D) Auxilium tibi venit.

Answers

1. **(D)**
   The missing pronoun must be **Nōs**, in order to agree with the verb **volumus**, *we wish*. The appearance of the pronoun, in addition to the personal ending of the verb, emphasizes that it is *we* who wish to be free. Answer (A) is the wrong form of the pronoun, and neither (B) **Vōs**, *You*, nor (C) **Eī**, *They*, agrees with the verb. The sentence reads *We all* (or *All of us*) *wish to be free*.

2. **(A)**
   Tibi is dative singular. Therefore, its plural is **vōbīs**. Answer (B) **vōs** is nominative or accusative plural, (C) **vestrum** is genitive plural, and (D) **tuī** genitive singular.

3. **(A)**
   Nōbīscum to accompany **venīte**, for a translation of *You* (plural) *come with us*, makes the best sense. Answers (B) **ad vestrōs**, *toward yours*, and (C) **cum vōbīs**, *with you*, make no sense in the context of this sentence. Remember that the preposition **cum** is attached to the pronoun, eliminating (D).

4. **(C)**

This question asks you to remember that a masculine pronoun can be translated *it* when referring to a thing (e.g., **librum**). Answer (A) *him* is a possible translation of the pronoun **eum**, but this meaning does not make sense in the specific context given. Answer (B) *his* is not a possible translation of **eum**, and (D) *them* is plural, whereas **eum** is singular. This sentence reads *I bought that book, but I didn't read it.* (For the demonstrative **is, ea, id**, see "The Pronoun of the Third Person.")

5. **(D)**

This sentence reads *Your (things) please you (and) my (things) please me.* The pronouns **tē** and **mē** are in the accusative singular and serve as direct objects in this sentence. **Tua**, *yours*, and **mea**, *mine*, serve as corresponding possessive adjectives used as neuter substantives, *your things* and *my things*, because no nouns are provided. Answers (A) and (B) are the same, but the wording is reversed. (This is a confusing sentence!) The translation in (C) does not give the meaning of the Latin, wherein each person is pleased by his own things, not both persons by both things.

6. **(B)**

Dic, *Tell* is an imperative, immediately eliminating (A) and (D), which do not contain imperatives. In (C), the translation *her* is incorrect for the demonstrative **haec**, which can be feminine, but it is not in the dative case, as required by the translation *Tell (to) her* . . . This form would be **huic**. In the correct answer, **haec** serves as a pronoun in the accusative plural neuter form, meaning *these things*.

7. **(A)**

The meaning of this sentence depends both on correct translation of **nec . . . nec**, *neither . . . nor* and on seeing that **cum** and **sine** are opposites, and that therefore their prepositional phrases **tēcum**, *with you*, and **sine tē**, *without you*, contrast. Answer (B) says the same thing in both clauses, (C) turns the thought around, and (D) **sine** is mistranslated as *near*.

8. **(B)**

In (A), the pronoun **eōrum**, *their*, is plural, whereas *his* is required in the sentence. Answer (C) contains the reflexive adjective *his own*, but the sentence reads *his (someone else's)*. In (D), **eam** serves as a demonstrative adjective *this* or *that (money)*, which does not indicate possession. Answer (B) may be rendered *his money*, that is, the money of someone other than the subject.

9.   **(C)**

The word *for* in the English sentence suggests the use of the dative case. Therefore, (A) **nōs**, which is nominative or accusative and not dative, (B) **nostrōs**, which is accusative and an adjective, and (D) **ad nōs**, which is a prepositional phrase requiring a verb of motion, are all inappropriate.

10.   **(A)**

The appearance of the word **speculō**, *mirror*, suggests that someone is looking at himself or herself, requiring the reflexive/personal pronoun *you*. This is because the subject of **vīdes** is in the second person, that is, *you are looking at yourself.* Answers (A) and (B) are both possible, but the verb is singular, therefore (B) is incorrect because the object pronoun **vōs** is plural. Answer (C) **vestrum**, *of you* or *your*, does not fit the sense, and (D) is in the dative case, which is not justifiable here. The sentence reads *Do you see yourself in the mirror?* (For the reflexive use of the personal pronoun, see the next chapter.)

Stumper: **(B)**

I am helping you may be rendered in Latin as a double dative, *I am for a help to/for you*, **Vōbīs auxiliō sum**. Answer (A) has the verb in the wrong tense, (C) transposes *you* and *me*, and (D) *Help is coming to/for you* does not indicate from whom the help is coming. (See Chapter 8, "Double Dative.")

CHAPTER 15

Reflexive and Intensive Pronouns

Chapter 15

REFLEXIVE AND INTENSIVE PRONOUNS

Reflexive Pronouns

Singular and Plural

	Masculine, Feminine, and Neuter
Nominative	——
Genitive	**suī**
Dative	**sibi**
Accusative	**sē**
Ablative	**sē**

THE FUNCTION OF THE REFLEXIVE PRONOUN

The reflexive pronoun (**reflectere**, *to bend* or *turn back*) refers back to the subject of the clause or sentence in which it is found. Pronouns of the first and second persons, singular and plural, also serve as reflexive pronouns, as in **ego mē videō**, *I see myself*, and **tū tē vidēs**, *you see yourself*. (For the forms of personal pronouns, see the table at the beginning of Chapter 14.) The reflexive pronoun **sē** for the third person has the same form for the singular and plural and for all genders, namely, **is sē videt**, *he sees himself*, **ea sē videt**, *she sees herself*, and **eī sē vident**, *they see themselves*.

There is no nominative form of the reflexive pronoun, because it must refer back to the subject. Observe that the other forms of the reflexive pronoun are similar to those of the singular pronouns of the first and second persons.

Use the context to distinguish in meaning between the accusative and ablative forms **sē**. Note that the form **sē** is sometimes found as **sēsē**. The accusative form **sē** is commonly found as the subject of the infinitive in indirect statement.

THE REFLEXIVE ADJECTIVE

As indicated in Chapter 14, when expressing possession in the third person, Latin prefers to use the adjective **suus, -a, -um**, *his own, her own, its own* (plural, *their own*), instead of the genitive form of the pronoun **suī**, *of himself*, and so on. The adjective of the third person may therefore be designated as a "reflexive adjective." Remember that when you see a form of the reflexive adjective, the meaning refers back to the subject, in the same manner as the reflexive pronoun **sē**, as in the following examples:

Reflexive pronoun:	**Nōnne puella sē in spēculō agnoscit?** *Surely the girl recognizes herself in the mirror?*
Reflexive adjective:	**Nōnne fīlia patrem suum agnoscere potest?** *Surely a daughter can recognize her own father?*

Suus, -a, -um assumes the gender and number of its antecedent, which is the subject. In the second sentence just above, **patrem** is a masculine singular noun, therefore the rules of agreement in Latin require that the form of the modifying adjective be masculine and singular, hence **suum**. But because it is a reflexive adjective, **suum** refers back to the feminine subject **fīlia** and is translated *her own* (*father*) and not *his own father*. This requires the translation of a masculine form as feminine! Note that the reflexive adjective can appear as a substantive (noun), as in the following sentence:

Suōs vetuit nōs adiūvāre.
He forbade his men from helping us.

Make careful distinction between the meaning of the possessive pronoun **eius (ejus)**, . . . , *his, hers, its*, and that of the reflexive adjective **suus, sua, suum**, . . . , *his own, her own, its own*. Here are some examples to help you distinguish between the two:

Possessive pronoun:	**Pater sē culpāvit quod fīlium eius (ejus) nōn agnōvit.** *Father blamed himself because he did not recognize his (someone else's) son.*

Possessive pronoun:	**Nōnne mātrēs fīliōs <u>eārum</u> agnoscere possunt?** *Surely mothers can recognize <u>their</u> sons (the sons of others)?*
Reflexive adjective:	**Pater sē culpāvit quod fīlium <u>suum</u> nōn agnōvit.** *Father blamed himself because he did not recognize <u>his own</u> son.*
	Nōnne mātrēs fīliōs <u>suōs</u> agnoscere possunt? *Surely mothers can recognize <u>their own</u> sons?*

THE INTENSIVE PRONOUN

The intensive pronoun **ipse**, **ipsa**, **ipsum**, *himself, herself, itself* (plural, *themselves*), stresses or emphasizes the identity of the person or thing to which the pronoun refers. The intensive pronoun has the same case, gender, and number as the noun or pronoun with which it is found, and it generally follows the noun or pronoun emphasized, as in **ego ipse**, *I myself*, **ea ipsa**, *she herself*, **sē ipsum**, *he himself*, and **ōrātōrēs ipsī**, *the speakers themselves*.

The intensive pronoun **ipse**, **ipsa**, **ipsum** has the same endings as the demonstrative pronoun **ille**, **illa**, **illud**, except for the nominative and accusative singular neuter, which are **ipsum** and **illud**, respectively. (For the forms of **ille**, see the chart in Chapter 11.) Because both reflexive and intensive pronouns have similar appearance (**sē** and **ipse**) and are translated using the word *-self*, their uses must be clearly distinguished. The reflexive pronoun completes the meaning of its sentence, whereas the intensive pronoun merely adds emphasis without changing the meaning, as in the following examples:

Reflexive:	**Docetne rhētor <u>sē</u> linguam Latīnam?** *Is the teacher of oratory teaching <u>himself</u> Latin?*
Intensive:	**Docetne rhētor <u>ipse</u> linguam Latīnam?** *Is the teacher of oratory <u>himself</u> teaching Latin?*

TIPS ON TRANSLATING REFLEXIVE AND INTENSIVE PRONOUNS

- Distinguish between the reflexive and the intensive pronoun by looking at both the placement of the word and its function. With the reflexive pronoun, the action of the verb is directed at the subject. Unlike the intensive pronoun, the case function of a reflexive pronoun is <u>independent</u> of that of the noun to which it refers, as in the following:

  nom. acc.
  Pater <u>se</u> culpāvit.
  Father blamed himself.

- Intensive pronouns generally follow the nouns with which they combine and (unless they are substantives) behave like adjectives, that is, they agree with the noun in case, gender, and number:

  nom. nom.
  Pater <u>ipse</u> mē nōn agnovit.
  Father <u>himself</u> did not recognize me.

Quick Study of Pronouns

Latin Form	Translation	Type	Function
hic, ille, is	*this one, that one*	demonstrative	points out specifically
quī, quae, quod	*who, which, that*	relative	describes, explains
quis, quis, quid	*who? what?*	interrogative	introduces a question
quīdam, aliquis	*a certain one, someone, anyone*	indefinite	identifies vaguely
ego, tū, is, ea, id	*I, you, he, she, it*	personal	designates with reference to writer
mē, tē, sē	*myself, yourself, him/herself/itself*	reflexive	restates the subject
ipse, ipsa, ipsum	*he himself, she herself, it (itself)*	intensive	emphasizes

PRACTICE QUESTIONS

Enjoy the following "sentence story"!

1. Ille consul <u>sibi</u> potestātem habēre volēbat.

   (A) himself
   (C) for him (someone else)

   (B) for himself
   (D) for them

2. The senators blamed <u>him</u> for his rival's death.

   (A) eum
   (C) ipsum

   (B) ipse
   (D) sē

3. <u>Consul dīcit suum competītōrem sē occidisse</u>.

   (A) The consul says that his rival killed him (someone else).

   (B) The consul says that he (someone else) killed his rival.

   (C) The consul says that his (someone else's) rival killed himself.

   (D) The consul says that his rival killed himself.

4. Some senators called for <u>his</u> removal.

   (A) suī
   (C) eius (ejus)

   (B) suum
   (D) ipsīus

5. Iste sciēbat <u>quōsdam</u> senātōrēs sibi inimīcōs esse.

   (A) some
   (C) any

   (B) all
   (D) several

6. <u>Certē īrātī senātōrēs consulī ipsō sē opposuit</u>.

   (A) Surely the consul himself confronted the angry senators.

   (B) Surely the angry senators themselves confronted the consul.

   (C) Surely the consul confronted the angry senators themselves.

   (D) Surely the angry senators confronted the consul himself.

7. <u>Senātōrēs suōs sēcum dūcēbant</u>.

(A) The senators brought his men with them.

(B) They were bringing with them the senators' men.

(C) The senators brought their men with them.

(D) The senators brought their men with him.

8. "You must give <u>yourself</u> up to justice!" shouted someone from the crowd.

(A) sē   (C) tū

(B) vōbīs   (D) tē

9. "<u>I myself</u> am not a crook!" exclaimed the consul.

(A) Meus ipse   (C) Ille ipse

(B) Ego ipse   (D) Mē ipse

Stumper:

Iste <u>sē ipsum</u> puniendum esse nōn crēdidit.

(A) they themselves   (C) he (someone else)

(B) he himself   (D) that one

Answers

1. **(B)**
For himself requires the dative form of the reflexive pronoun **sē**, which is **sibi**. The Latin of (A) is the intensive pronoun (**ille consul**) **ipse**, *that consul himself*. Answer (C) requires the pronoun of the third person **eī**, *for him* (a second party), and (D) *for them* is not reflexive because the subject is **ille consul**, *that consul*.

2. **(A)**
The pronoun **eum** fits the need for an accusative form of the third person pronoun, referring to the consul. Answers (B) and (C) are intensive (nom. sing. masc. and nom./acc. sing. neut.), neither of which is appropriate to the sense here. The pronoun **sē** is a reflexive pronoun of the third person in the accusative, but must refer back to **senātōrēs** as its antecedent, which doesn't fit the sense.

3. **(D)**

This sentence contains both a reflexive adjective (**suum**) and a reflexive pronoun (**sē**), both referring to the consul's rival (**competītōrem**), which is found within an indirect statement. Therefore, the sentence reads *The consul says that his (own) rival killed himself.* Answers (A) and (B) require **eum**, rather than **sē** (note the ambiguity of the Latin here), and (C) requires the substitution of **eius (ejus)** for **suum**.

4. **(C)**

His is not a reflexive adjective because the subject to which it refers is **senātōrēs**, which is plural. Therefore, (A) and (B) are to be discounted. Answer (D) **ipsius** is indeed genitive and suggests the idea of possession found in the word *his*, but the meaning of the sentence does not provide an opportunity for the use of an intensive pronoun. (See "The Intensive Pronoun.")

5. **(A)**

This question reviews the material in a previous chapter. The indefinite pronoun **quīdam** can mean "some" in the plural. The sentence reads *That one* (i.e., *the consul) knew that some senators were unfriendly to him.* Answer (B) requires **omnēs**, (C) **aliquōs**, and (D) the adjective **complūrēs**.

6. **(D)**

This sentence contains both an intensive pronoun, (**consulī**) **ipsō**, (*the consul*) *himself*, which is dative after the compound verb **opposuit**, and a reflexive pronoun, **sē** (**opposuit**), (*opposed*) *themselves* (*to*). In (A), the translation wrongly has the consul confronting the senators. In (B), the Latin requires that the intensive pronoun **ipsī** follow **senātōrēs** instead of emphasizing the consul. Answer (C) is a combination of the variations found in (A) and (B), and is therefore incorrect.

7. **(C)**

The reflexive adjective **suus, -a, -um** sometimes serves as a substantive, as here, where **suōs** without a modified noun means *their (own) men.* Note the masculine gender. **Sēcum**, *with themselves* behaves as other reflexive pronouns when found with **cum**, which is enclitic. In (A), the translation *his men* is not reflexive with regard to the subject, **īrātī senātōrēs**, which is plural. Answer (B) omits **suōs** in its translation and (D) *with him*, does not correctly translate **sēcum**, which is reflexive. (See "The Reflexive Adjective.")

8. **(D)**

The sentence illustrates the use of the personal pronoun as reflexive. *Yourself* or **tē** is the direct object of the verb *to give up* and refers back to the subject of that verb, *you*. Answer (A) is in the wrong person (third), and (B) and (C) are in the wrong cases, dative and nominative, respectively.

9. **(B)**

This sentence illustrates the use of the intensive pronoun emphasizing a personal pronoun, which is a common type of expression. Therefore, **Ego ipse** is the correct rendering of *I myself*. Answer (A) offers an impossible combination of a possessive adjective (**meus**, *my*) and an intensive pronoun (**ipse**, *himself*). Answer (C) is not an intensive, but a reflexive, pronoun in the third person and is found in the incorrect case (accusative). Answer (D) **Ille ipse** gives the incorrect meaning *He himself*. (See "The Intensive Pronoun.")

Stumper: **(B)**

This sentence, which combines an intensive with a reflexive, reads *That one* (i.e., *the consul*) *believed that he himself must not be punished*. **Sē ipsum** serves as the subject accusative of the infinitive **puniendum esse** in an indirect statement and refers back to the subject of the main clause, **iste**. Answer (A) *they themselves* is impossible as a translation because **sē ipsum** is singular. Answer (C) *he* (someone else) is not reflexive, as required by **sē ipsum** in the sentence. Answer (D) is rendered by the pronoun **illum** or **istum** in Latin.

THE SAT SUBJECT TEST IN
LATIN

SECTION 4

Adjectives and Adverbs

CHAPTER 16

Adjectives

Chapter 16

ADJECTIVES

INTRODUCTION TO ADJECTIVES

The forms of adjectives (**ad** + **iacere/jacere**, *to throw toward*) are the same as or similar to those of nouns. Adjectives modify nouns and can even stand as nouns themselves. They are organized into two classes based on their forms. One class has endings of the first and second declensions of nouns and is identified by the masculine, feminine, and neuter forms of the nominative singular, such as **laetus, laeta, laetum** (in dictionary format, **laetus, -a, -um**). The other class has endings of the third declension, such as **tristis, tristis, triste** (**tristis, -is, -e**).

First/second declension adjective:

Rōmānī quī rūrī habitābant laetī saepe erant.
Romans who lived in the country were often <u>happy</u>.

Third declension adjective:

Rōmānī quī in urbe habitābant tristēs saepe erant.
Romans who lived in the city were often <u>unhappy</u>.

An adjective must agree with its noun in case, number, and gender. In the first of the preceding examples, **laetī** modifies **Rōmānī**. Both are nominative, plural, and masculine. In the second example, **tristēs** also modifies **Rōmānī**, and both are also nominative, plural, and masculine. <u>However, an adjective is not required to have the very same ending as the noun in order for it to agree with the noun.</u> If the adjective belongs to a different declension from the noun, the endings will be spelled differently, as in the second set of examples that follow:

Same Declensions	
First/second declension adjective and first/second declension noun:	**laetī Rōmānī**, *happy Romans*
Third declension adjective and third declension noun:	**agrestis amnis**, *country stream*
Different Declensions	
Third declension adjective and first/second declension noun:	**tristēs Rōmānī**, *unhappy Romans*
First/second declension adjective and third declension noun:	**perīculōsum flūmen**, *dangerous river*

Quick Study of the Forms of Adjectives in the Positive, Comparative, and Superlative Degrees

	Singular			Plural		
	Masculine	**Feminine**	**Neuter**	**Masculine**	**Feminine**	**Neuter**
Nominative						
1st/2nd	**laetus**	**laeta**	**laetum**	**laetī**	**laetae**	**laeta**
	laetior	laetior	laetius	laetiōrēs	laetiōrēs	laetiōra
	laetissimus	laetissima	laetissimum	laetissimī	laetissimae	laetissima
3rd	**tristis**	**tristis**	**triste**	**tristēs**	**tristēs**	**tristia**
	tristior	tristior	tristius	tristiōres	tristiōrēs	tristiōra
	tristissimus	tristissima	tristissimum	tristissimī	tristissimae	tristissima
Genitive						
1st/2nd	**laetī**	**laetae**	**laetī**	**laetōrum**	**laetārum**	**laetōrum**
	laetiōris	laetiōris	laetiōris	laetiōrum	laetiōrum	laetiōrum
	laetissimī	laetissimae	laetissimī	laetissimōrum	laetissimārum	laetissimōrum
3rd	**tristis**	**tristis**	**tristis**	**tristium**	**tristium**	**tristium**
	tristiōris	tristiōris	tristiōris	tristiōrum	tristiōrum	tristiōrum
	tristissimī	tristissimae	tristissimī	tristissimōrum	tristissimārum	tristissimōrum

Quick Study of the Forms of Adjectives in the Positive, Comparative, and Superlative Degrees (continued)

	Singular			Plural		
	Masculine	**Feminine**	**Neuter**	**Masculine**	**Feminine**	**Neuter**
Dative						
1st/2nd	**laetō**	**laetae**	**laetō**	**laetīs**	**laetīs**	**laetīs**
	laetiōrī	laetiōrī	laetiōrī	laetiōribus	laetiōribus	laetiōribus
	laetissimō	laetissimae	laetissimō	laetissimīs	laetissimīs	laetissimīs
3rd	**tristī**	**tristī**	**tristī**	**tristibus**	**tristibus**	**tristibus**
	tristiōrī	tristiōrī	tristiōrī	tristiōribus	tristiōribus	tristiōribus
	tristissimō	tristissimae	tristissimō	tristissimīs	tristissimīs	tristissimīs
Accusative						
1st/2nd	**laetum**	**laetam**	**laetum**	**laetōs**	**laetās**	**laeta**
	laetiorem	laetiōrem	laetius	laetiōrēs	laetiōrēs	laetiōra
	laetissimum	laetissimam	laetissimum	laetissimōs	laetissimās	laetissima
3rd	**tristem**	**tristem**	**triste**	**tristēs**	**tristēs**	**tristia**
	tristiōrem	tristiōrem	tristius	tristiōrēs	tristiōrēs	tristiōra
	tristissimum	tristissimam	tristissimum	tristissimōs	tristissimās	tristissima

	Singular			Plural		
	Masculine	**Feminine**	**Neuter**	**Masculine**	**Feminine**	**Neuter**
Ablative						
1st/2nd	**laetō**	**laetā**	**laetō**	**laetīs**	**laetīs**	**laetīs**
	laetiōre	laetiōre	laetiōre	laetiōribus	laetiōribus	laetiōribus
	laetissimō	laetissima	laetissimō	laetissimīs	laetissimīs	laetissimīs
3rd	**tristī**	**tristī**	**tristī**	**tristibus**	**tristibus**	**tristibus**
	tristiōre	tristiōre	tristiōre	tristiōribus	tristiōribus	tristiōribus
	tristissimō	tristissimā	tristissimō	tristissimīs	tristissimīs	tristissimīs

FORMS OF FIRST/SECOND DECLENSION ADJECTIVES

Some first/second declension adjectives end in **-er** in the masculine nominative singular, for example **miser, misera, miserum**, as does the noun **puer** (stem **puer-**). Therefore, the stem of the adjective is **miser-**. Common adjectives of this type include **asper**, *rough, harsh*, and **līber**, *free*. Other examples of this type drop the **-e-** from the stem, such as **noster, nostra, nostrum**, as does the noun **ager** (stem **agr-**). Therefore, the stem of the adjective **noster** is **nostr-**. Common adjectives of this type include **aeger**, *ill*, **dexter**, *right*, **pulcher**, *pretty*, **sacer**, *holy*, **sinister**, *left*, and the possessives **noster**, *our*, and **vester**, *your* (plural)

Nine common adjectives of the first/second declensions are irregular in that they have **-īus** in the genitive singular and **-ī** in the dative singular in all genders, as in the following sentence:

Estne pōmerīum terminus <u>totīus</u> urbis Rōmae?
Is the pomerium the boundary <u>of the entire</u> city of Rome?

Except for the variation in the nominative and accusative singular neuter, these two cases have the same endings as the demonstrative pronoun **ille, illa, illud** (see Chapter 11). The irregular adjectives are the following:

alius, alius, aliud, *another*	**alter, altera, alterum**, *the other*
nūllus, -a, -um, *none*	**neuter, neutra, neutrum**, *neither*
sōlus, -a, -um, *alone*	**uter, utra, utrum**, *each (of two)*
tōtus, -a, -um, *whole, entire*	
ūllus, -a, -um, *any*	
ūnus, -a, -um, *one*	

Use the mnemonic UNUS NAUTA to remember these adjectives:

Ūnus, **N**ūllus, **Ū**llus, **S**ōlus, then **N**euter, **A**lter, **U**ter, **T**ōtus, **A**lius*

THE FORMS OF THIRD DECLENSION ADJECTIVES

Third declension adjectives are generally formed in the same way as third declension **i**-stem nouns, that is, they have **-ī** as the ending of the ablative singular and **-ium** as the ending of the genitive plural. (See Chapter 5

---

* See David Pellegrino, http://latinteach.com/adjmnemonics.html.

for noun forms and the preceding table for adjective forms.) The nominative and accusative cases of the neuter plural end in **-ia**:

> **Flōrēs in <u>omnī</u> hortō circum piscīnam crescunt.**
> *In <u>every</u> garden flowers grow around the fishpool.*

> **In villīs Rōmānīs peristȳlia <u>similia</u> porticibus erant.**
> *In Roman villas there were peristyles <u>similar</u> to porticoes.*

Adjectives of the third declension belong to one of three different categories, as revealed by the gender differentiation in the nominative case. Of these, the "two termination" adjectives—those with two different endings—are the most common.

	Three Termination	Two Termination	One Termination
Masculine	**celer** nuntius	**omnis** nuntius	**fēlix** nuntius
Feminine	**celeris** fibula	**omnis** fibula	**fēlix** fabula
Neuter	**celere** animal	**omne** animal	**fēlix** animal

THE USES OF ADJECTIVES

Adjectives as Modifiers

Adjectives that modify (i.e., limit or describe) other words can be single words, participles, or relative clauses:

Single word as modifier:
> **Plūrimī Rōmānī villās rusticās rūrī habent.**
>
> *<u>A large number of</u> Romans have farm estates in the country.*

Participle as modifier:
> **Servī <u>habitantēs</u> in hīs villīs strenuē laborant.**
>
> *Slaves <u>living</u> on these estates work hard.*

Relative clause as modifier:
> **Servī [<u>quī dīligentissimī sunt</u>] laudantur.**
>
> *The slaves [<u>who are very industrious</u>] are praised.*

Adjectives as Substantives

Plural forms of both first/second and third declension adjectives are sometimes used as nouns. When an adjective substitutes for, or "takes the substance of," a noun in this way, it is called a substantive, meaning it can "stand by itself." Substantive adjectives appear in English, as in the title of the classic film *The Good, the Bad, and the Ugly*. **Labor omnia vincit**, *Labor conquers all (things)*, serves as the motto of the State of Oklahoma.

Here are several more examples:

Multī in Campāniam sē mōvērunt.
Many (people) have moved into Campania.

Tulēruntne omnēs bona sēcum?
Did they all bring their possessions with them?

The following adjectives are commonly found as substantives:

First/Second Declension	Third Declension
bona, *the goods (property)*	**maiōrēs**, *ancestors*
bonī/malī, *good/bad people*	**minōrēs**, *descendants*
multa, *many things*	**omnēs**, *all men, everyone*
multī/paucī, *many/few people*	**omnia**, *all things, everything*
Rōmānī, *Romans*	

Adjectives as Adverbs

Where English uses an adverb, Latin often uses an adjective. When you translate, let the best sense dictate the phrasing, as in the following sentence:

Aestāte laetī ad ōram maritimam proficiscuntur.
In the summertime, they gladly go to the seacoast (rather than *the glad* [*people*] *go to the seacoast*).

COMPARISON OF ADJECTIVES

Adjectives in Latin have three degrees: positive, comparative, and superlative. These terms refer to the degree of intensity, or magnitude, of the meaning of the adjective, as in the English *big, bigger, biggest*. The positive adjective "posits" or puts forward some general characteristic of a noun. The comparative is used when comparing two persons or things, and the superlative is used when comparing three or more. Expression of the forms of adjectives and adverbs according to their degrees is called "comparison."

Comparison of Adjectives

Positive Adjective	Comparative Adjective	Superlative Adjective
M, F, N	**M, F, N**	**M, F, N**
laetus, laeta, laetum	**laetior, laetior, laetius**	**laetissimus, -a, -um**
happy	*happier, more happy, rather happy, too happy, quite happy*	*happiest, most happy, very happy, exceedingly happy*

As with any adjective in the positive degree, the forms of the comparative and superlative degree must agree with their nouns in case, number, and gender:

Positive: **Rusticus est laetus.**
The country man is happy.

Comparative: **Rusticus est laetior.**
The country man is rather happy.

Superlative: **Rusticus est laetissimus.**
The country man is very happy.

Comparative Adjectives

In comparative forms, the endings of third declension nouns are added to the base or stem of the adjective + **-ior-**, for example **trist-** + **-ior** = **tristior** (gen., **tristiōris**). (For these forms, see the chart at the beginning of this chapter and note that the neuter nominative and accusative singular forms, such as **tristius**, are the exception to this pattern.)

The forms of comparative adjectives do <u>not</u> belong to the **i**-stem declension of nouns, that is, they do not have **-ī** in the ablative singular,

-ium in the genitive plural, or **-ia** in the neuter nominative and accusative plurals. The forms are **tristiōre**, **tristiōrum**, and **tristiōra**, respectively.

When two persons or things are compared, the comparative form of the adjective is used in the appropriate case, number, and gender, along with either of the following constructions:

- Ablative of comparison (see also Chapter 10, "Ablatives of Comparison and Degree of Difference"):

    Hoc flūmen celerius <u>illō</u> est.
    This river is faster <u>than</u> that one.

- Comparison with **quam**:

    Hoc flūmen celerius <u>quam</u> illud est.
    This river is faster <u>than</u> that one.

Notes:

1. When **quam** is used, the two items compared are found in the same case, regardless of which case it is.

2. Be alert to the fact that the word **quam** has a number of other uses and meanings, such as the following:

    - **Quam**, *whom*, *that*, in a relative clause:

        Estne illa <u>quam</u> scis prūdens?
        Is that woman <u>whom</u> you know wise?

    - **Quam**, *How* . . . in an exclamation or a question:

        <u>Quam</u> prūdens es!
        <u>How</u> wise you are!

        <u>Quam</u> prūdens es?
        <u>How</u> wise are you?

    - **Quam** + superlative adjective or adverb, *as . . . as possible*:

        Quisque <u>quam prūdentissimus</u> esse vult.
        Everyone wishes to be <u>as wise as possible</u>.

Superlative Adjectives

Superlatives of regular adjectives, such as **prūdentissimus** in the preceding example, contain the double consonants **-ss-**, **-rr-**, or **-ll-** and have endings that belong to the first/second declensions. These endings give superlatives the appearance of positive adjectives. Because most positive adjectives end in **-s**, like **prūdens** (gen., **prūdentis**), the most common superlative form contains **-ss-**, such as **prūdentissimus, -a, -um**.

Adjectives whose positive form ends in **-r**, like **celer**, have **-rr-** in their superlative forms, as in **celerrimus, -a, -um**. Other adjectives such as these include **acer**, *sharp, fierce,* **asper**, *rough, harsh,* **celer**, *swift,* **celeber**, *famous,* **līber**, *free,* **miser**, *unhappy,* and **pulcher**, *pretty.*

Most third declension adjectives that end in **-lis** form their superlatives regularly, like **fidēlis** (**fidēlissimus**), **nōbilis** (**nōbilissimus**), and **ūtilis** (**ūtilissimus**). However, several adjectives ending in **-lis** duplicate the consonant **-l-** rather than **-s-** in the superlative degree:

> **facilis, -is, -e** (**facillimus, -a, -um**), *easy*
>
> **difficilis, -is, -e** (**difficillimus, -a, -um**), *difficult*
>
> **dissimilis, -is, -e** (**dissimillimus, -a, -um**), *unlike*
>
> **gracilis, -is, -e** (**gracillimus, -a, -um**), *slender*
>
> **humilis, -is, -e** (**humillimus, -a, -um**), *humble, poor*
>
> **similis, -is, -e** (**simillimus, -a, -um**), *similar*

To remember these six adjectives, use the device FUDGE DISH:

> **F**acilis **U** **D**ifficilis **G**racilis **E**, then **D**issimilis **I** **S**imilis **H**umilis*

The superlative adjective or adverb is often found with the genitive plural in a partitive expression, for example **prūdentissimus <u>omnium</u>**, *wisest <u>of all</u>*.

Here is a summary of the formation of the superlative degree of regular adjectives:

Positive	Superlative
<u>lātum</u> **flūmen**, *wide river*	<u>lātissimum</u> **flūmen**, *widest river*
<u>celere</u> **flūmen**, *fast river*	<u>celerrimum</u> **flūmen**, *fastest river*
<u>difficile</u> **flūmen**, *difficult river*	<u>difficillimum</u> **flūmen**, *most difficult river*

* See Pellegrino, http://latinteach.com/adjmnemonics.html.

Irregular Adjectives

The following adjectives are considered irregular because their comparative and superlative forms do not follow the pattern of formation of other adjectives. Review these important words, which provide the roots of many derivatives in English. Conversely, use your knowledge of English derivatives to help you remember the meanings of these adjectives.

Comparison of Irregular Adjectives

Positive	Comparative	Superlative
bonus, -a, -um, *good*	**melior, melius,** *better*	**optimus, -a, -um,** *best*
malus, -a, -um, *bad*	**peior, peius (pejor, pejus),** *worse*	**pessimus, -a, -um,** *worst*
magnus, -a, -um, *big*	**maior, maius (major, majus),** *bigger*	**maximus, -a, -um,** *biggest*
parvus, -a, -um, *small*	**minor, minus,** *smaller*	**minimus, -a, -um,** *smallest*
multus, -a, -um, *many*	**plūs** (gen., **plūris**), *more*	**plūrimus, -a, -um,** *most*

A WORD OR TWO ABOUT ADJECTIVES AND WORD ORDER

Roman writers, especially poets, often separated an adjective from its noun for visual or phonetic effect, as in the following line from the *Aeneid*, spoken by Laocoon:

> **"O miserī, quae tanta insānia, cīvēs?"**
> *"O pitiable citizens, what madness is this?"*

In the following line, Horace describes a maiden embraced by a youth while both are surrounded by roses:

> Quis multā **gracilis** [tē] **puer** in rosā?
> *What **slender boy** (embraces) [you] amid many a rose?*

Although an adjective or adverb generally precedes the word that it modifies (with a few exceptions, such as **rēs publica** and **populus Rōmānus**), an adjective can also be found after the noun it modifies.

When two adjectives modify the same noun, they can be connected with **et**, as in the following sentence:

> **Tiberis erat flūmen celere et turbidum.**
> *The Tiber was a swift, wild river.*

(Note that the conjunction is omitted in English.) It is important to be familiar with the forms of adjectives and nouns and to think clearly about your options regarding the words that may or may not go together in a noun-adjective combination.

TIPS ON TRANSLATING ADJECTIVES

- Remember that adjectives can have different endings from the nouns they modify, but they must agree with those nouns in case, number, and gender.

- The ablative singular of positive adjectives of the third declension ends in **-ī**, unlike the ablative singular of third declension nouns, which ends in **-e**, as in **omnī tempore**, *at every moment*.

- In some instances, adjectives in Latin may be translated as nouns or adverbs in English.

- Adjectives have three degrees of meaning, positive, comparative, and superlative, that have variable translations.

- Comparison of two persons or things may be expressed either with **quam** or the ablative of comparison.

PRACTICE QUESTIONS

1. Rōma . . . quam Pompēii erat.

   (A) paulō minor   (C) multō minor

   (B) paulō maior   (D) multō maior

2. Hard work overcomes <u>all things</u>.

   (A) omnēs   (C) omnia

   (B) omnī   (D) omnibus

3. Caesar was more powerful <u>than Cicero</u>.

   (A) Cicerōne   (C) quam Cicerōne

   (B) Cicerō   (D) Cicerōnis

4. Eratne Caesar . . . omnium?

   (A) nōbilissimus   (C) nōbilissimum

   (B) nōbilius   (D) nōbilior

5. <u>Bonum</u> is to <u>melius</u> as <u>multum</u> is to

   (A) plūrimus   (C) plūrimum

   (B) plurium   (D) plūs

6. The genitive singular of <u>alter</u> is

   (A) alterī   (C) alteriīs

   (B) alterīus   (D) alterō

7. <u>Paucī sed bonī</u>.

   (A) The few are the good.

   (B) Few men, but good ones.

   (C) The good are few.

   (D) Few possessions, but good ones.

Stumper:

   <u>Facile consilium damus aliī</u>.

   (A) We give easy advice to others.

   (B) We are giving someone else advice about that which is easy.

   (C) We give advice to another easily.

   (D) The easiest advice is that which we give to others.

Answers

1. **(D)**
    This sentence expresses a comparison between Rome and Pompeii. Because you should know that Rome was much larger than Pompeii, (D) is preferable to (B). Answers (A) **paulō minor**, *a little smaller*, and (C) **multō minor**, *much smaller*, are not correct because they are not true. This comparative construction is an example of the ablative of degree of difference. This sentence reads *Rome was much bigger than Pompeii*. (See Chapter 10, "Ablatives of Comparison and Degree of Difference.")

2. **(C)**
    Omnia, *all things* appears as a substantive in this sentence. Answer (A) **omnēs** can be accusative plural, as required, but would have the meaning *all people* as the masculine/feminine form. Answer (B) is dative or ablative singular and (D) is dative or ablative plural, neither of which fits the meaning of *all things* as the direct object in this sentence. (See "Adjectives as Substantives.")

3. **(A)**
    Cicerōne is an ablative of comparison. Answer (B) is only possible if it is accompanied by **quam**, which it is not. In (C), both options that express comparison appear together, that is, **quam** and the ablative, which is incorrect. Answer (D) is genitive and irrelevant to the required English meaning. (See "Comparative Adjectives" and Chapter 10, "Ablatives of Comparison and Degree of Difference.")

4. **(A)**
    Was Caesar the most noble Roman of all? The appearance of **omnium** in this sentence keys the need for the superlative adjective *most . . . of all*. Based on the answers provided, a form of the adjective **nōbilis** is missing. This adjective must modify **Rōmānus**, which is a nominative in apposition to the subject **Caesar**. This requirement eliminates (C), which is a superlative adjective, but in the accusative case. Answers (B) and (D) are comparative forms, respectively, neither of which correctly completes the idiomatic use with **omnium**. Because of its similarity to **Rōmānus**, the neuter comparative form **nōbilius** surely distracted you! (See "Superlative Adjectives.")

5. **(D)**

This analogy compares positive and comparative forms of irregular adjectives in the neuter gender. As **melius** is the comparative form of **bonum**, you are asked to provide the comparative form of **multum**, *much*, which is **plūs**, *more*. Answers (A) and (C) are both superlative, not comparative, and in (B) the genitive plural form **plūrium** is reminiscent of the nominative or accusative singular neuter ending -**um**, but the declension is wrong. (See "Irregular Adjectives.")

6. **(B)**

Alter is an irregular adjective, which takes the unexpected genitive and dative singular endings of -**īus** and -**ī**, respectively. The remaining forms of **alter, altera, alterum** have endings of the regular first/second declension adjective. Answer (A) is dative, (C) is dative and ablative plural, and (D) is ablative singular, which are all inconsistent with the requested genitive singular form. (See "Forms of First/Second Declension Adjectives.")

7. **(B)**

This sentence contains examples of adjectives used as substantives. **Paucī** means *the few* or *few people*, just as **bonī** means *the good* or *good people*. The sentence reads *Few men, but good ones*. (A form of the verb **esse** is often understood in mottoes.) Answers (A) and (C) omit the conjunction **sed** from their translations, and (D) would require that the substantives be neuter, as implied by the word *possessions*, that is, goods. (See "Adjectives as Substantives.")

Stumper: **(C)**

This sentence provides an example of the neuter form of the adjective **facilis** used as an adverb, **facile**, *easily*. In (A) **aliī** cannot be translated as *to others*, which would require the dative plural form **aliīs**. The translation in (B) does not render **facile** correctly. Answer (D) *easiest* translates the superlative and not the positive degree as required by the form **facile** in the sentence. Also, as mentioned, *to others* is not the correct translation of **aliī**. (See "Adjectives as Adverbs" and "Irregular Adjectives.")

CHAPTER 17
Adverbs

Chapter 17

ADVERBS

INTRODUCTION TO ADVERBS

Adverbs answer implied questions such as "when?" (e.g., **saepe**, *often*), "where?" (e.g., **ibi**, *there*), and "how?" (e.g., **benigne**, *kindly*), and thus can indicate time, place, or manner. Adverbs usually modify verbs (**ad + verbum**, *to the verb*), but can also modify adjectives or other adverbs. Some adverbs may be formed from adjectives. Many particles, both interrogative (e.g., **nōnne**) and negative (e.g., **haud**, **nē**, **neque/nec**, **nōn**), are also adverbs, as well as words such as **ut**, which introduces a dependent clause. In general, an adverb appears as closely as possible to the word it modifies. Here are some examples:

Adverb not formed from an adjective:	**Avēs in arboribus <u>saepe</u> cantant.** *Birds <u>often</u> sing in the trees.*
Adverb from a first/second declension adjective:	**Avēs bācās ē rāmīs arboris <u>cupidē</u> ēdunt. (cupidus, -a, -um)** *Birds <u>eagerly</u> eat berries from the tree's branches.*
Adverb from a third declension adjective:	**Avēs in caelō <u>frequenter</u> volant. (frequens, frequentis)** *Birds are flying in the sky <u>in large numbers</u>.*

ADVERBS NOT FORMED FROM ADJECTIVES

Many adverbs have unchangeable forms whose meanings must be memorized. These are usually categorized by their associated meanings of <u>time</u>, such as **herī**, *yesterday*, **hodiē**, *today*, and **crās**, *tomorrow*; <u>place</u>, such as **hinc**, *from here*, **illinc**, *from there*, and **undique**, *everywhere*; or <u>manner</u>, such as **sīc**, *thus, so*, **valdē**, *very*, and **vix**, *barely, hardly*.

Many positive adverbs end in **-m**, including **clam**, *secretly*, **interim**, *meanwhile*, and **statim**, *immediately*.

Note that some adverbs, such as **multum**, *much*, and **prīmum**, *at first*, can also appear to be adjectives modifying neuter nouns, in which case the meaning is adjectival, such as **prīmum nōmen**, *first name*.

Rather than having the regular positive adverb ending **-ē**, a few positive adverbs derived from first/second declension adjectives are formed by adding **-ō** to the stem, such as **certō** (but also **certē**), *surely*, **continuō**, *immediately*, **falsō**, *falsely*, **meritō**, *deservedly*, **prīmō** (but also **prīmum**), *at first*, **rārō** (but also **rārē**), *seldom*, **sērō**, *late*, and **subitō**, *suddenly*.

POSITIVE ADVERBS DERIVED FROM ADJECTIVES

Adverbs can also be derived from adjectives. Adverbs derived from adjectives are usually translated with *-ly*. For example, **laetē** (from **laetus**, **-a**, **-um**) means *happily*.

Adverbs derived from first/second declension adjectives add **-ē** to the stem, as in the following examples:

Positive Adjective	Stem	Positive Adverb
laetus, -a, -um, *happy*	**laet-**	**laetē**, *happily*
miser, misera, miserum, *sad*	**miser-**	**miserē**, *sadly*

Adverbs derived from third declension adjectives have several variations in stems, plus the ending **-ter**:

Positive Adjective	Stem	Positive Adverb
neglegēns, *careless*	**neglegent-**	**neglegenter**, *carelessly*
audax, *bold*	**audac-**	**audacter**, *boldly*
fortis, *brave*	**fort(i)-**	**fortiter**, *bravely*

COMPARISON OF ADVERBS

As with adjectives, adverbs may be used to express comparisons between two persons or things (comparative degree) or three or more (superlative degree). The comparative form of the adverb has the same form as that of the nominative singular of the neuter adjective, as in **laetius**, *happier* (adjective) and **laetius**, *more happily* (adverb). The superlative form of the adverb has the same relationship to the positive form of the adverb as the superlative form of the adjective has to its positive. For example, **laetissimē**, *most happily*, is to **laetē**, *happily*, as **laetissimus, -a, -um**, *most happy*, is to **laetus, -a, -um**, *happy*. The same rules for the duplication of consonants apply to adverbs as to adjectives (see Chapter 16, "Superlative Adjectives").

The forms of positive, comparative, and superlative adverbs do not change. Here are some examples of how the various forms of the adverb are translated:

Positive adverb:	**Avēs in arboribus <u>laetē</u> cantant.**
	The birds are <u>happily</u> singing in the trees.
Comparative adverb:	**Avēs in arboribus <u>laetius</u> cantant.**
	The birds are <u>rather happily</u> singing in the trees.
Superlative adverb:	**Avēs in arboribus <u>laetissimē</u> cantant.**
	The birds are <u>most happily</u> singing in the trees.

Quick Study Comparison of Regular Adjectives and Adverbs

	Adjectives	Adverbs
Positive	**laetus, -a, -um**, *happy*	**laetē**, *happily*
Comparative	**laetior, laetior, laetius**, *happier*	**laetius**, *more happily*
Superlative	**laetissimus, -a, -um**, *happiest*	**laetissimē**, *most happily*

Quick Study Comparison of Irregular Adjectives and Adverbs

	Positive	Comparative	Superlative
	Masculine, Feminine, Neuter	**Masculine, Feminine, Neuter**	**Masculine, Feminine, Neuter**
Adjective	**bonus, -a, -um,** *good*	**melior, melius,** *better*	**optimus, -a, -um,** *best*
Adverb	**bene,** *well*	**melius,** *better*	**optimē,** *best*
Adjective	**malus, -a, -um,** *bad*	**peior, peius (pejor, pejus),** *worse*	**pessimus, -a, -um,** *worst*
Adverb	**male,** *badly*	**peius (pejus),** *worse*	**pessimē,** *worst*
Adjective	**magnus, -a, -um,** *great*	**maior, maius (major, majus),** *greater*	**maximus, -a, -um,** *greatest*
Adverb	**magnopere,** *greatly*	**magis,** *more*	**maximē,** *most*
Adjective	**parvus, -a, -um,** *small*	**minor, minus,** *smaller*	**minimus, -a, -um,** *smallest*
Adverb	**paulum,** *little*	**minus,** *less*	**minimē,** *least*
Adjective	**multus, -a, -um,** *many*	**plūs** (gen., **plūris**), *more*	**plurimus, -a, -um,** *most*
Adverb	**multum,** *much*	**plūs,** *more*	**plurimum,** *most*

N.B.: Be aware that a few adjectives are compared by using the adverbs **magis**, *more* and **maximē**, *most*, for example, **magis idōneus**, *more suitable*, and **maximē idōneus**, *most suitable*.

THE USES OF ADVERBS

Adverbs modify a verb, an adjective, or another adverb:

With a verb: **Arborēs lūce sōlis <u>celeriter</u> crescunt.**
Trees grow <u>quickly</u> in sunlight.

With an adjective: **Succīdere arborem est <u>valdē</u> <u>malum</u>.**
To cut down (i.e., Cutting down) a tree is <u>very</u> <u>wrong</u>.

With another adverb: **<u>Ita</u> <u>verō</u>, nihil tam pulchra quam arbor est.**
<u>Truly</u> <u>yes</u>, there is nothing so lovely as a tree.

TIPS ON TRANSLATING ADJECTIVES AND ADVERBS

- Use the context to help you distinguish an adverb from an adjective, especially in the comparative and superlative forms. Look for the noun modified if you suspect that the word is an adjective, and look for the verb if you suspect that the word is an adverb, as in the following sentences:

  Adjective: **Avis <u>melius</u> <u>carmen</u> cum nōn ēsurit cantat.**
  A bird sings a <u>better</u> <u>song</u> when it is not hungry.

  Adverb: **Cum nōn ēsurit, avis <u>melius</u> <u>cantat</u>.**
  A bird <u>sings</u> <u>better</u> when it is not hungry.

- Look for the adjective or adverb in the general neighborhood of its noun or verb, and be aware that in poetry the modifier is sometimes deliberately placed in an unexpected position for poetic effect.

- Be familiar with the variations used in English to express the different degrees of adjectives and adverbs. Use the context when considering which option makes the best sense, for example:

  Aliquando Rōma <u>calidior</u> est.
  Sometimes Rome is <u>rather hot</u> (or <u>too hot</u>, in preference to <u>hotter</u>).

- Be especially familiar with forms of the third declension adjective, irregular adjectives, and the comparison of adjectives and adverbs (especially **quam** or the ablative with comparatives), all of which may receive attention on the SAT Latin Subject Test.

PRACTICE QUESTIONS

1. Flōrēs in hortō prope arborēs <u>dulcēs</u> redolent odōrēs.

   Based on the sense, the noun modified by <u>dulcēs</u> is

   (A) Flōrēs   (C) arborēs

   (B) hortō   (D) odōrēs

2. Crescuntne flōrēs <u>celerius</u> arboribus?

   (A) quickly   (C) as quickly as

   (B) more quickly   (D) most quickly

3. The form of the adverb that means <u>too easily</u> is

   (A) facilius   (C) facillimē

   (B) facilis   (D) magis facilis

4. Which of the following adverbs has a meaning pertaining to place?

   (A) postridiē   (C) undique

   (B) paulisper   (D) vix

5. <u>Ītalia est pulcherrima</u> means

   (A) Italy is rather beautiful.   (C) Italy is too beautiful.

   (B) Italy is very beautiful.   (D) Italy is beautiful.

6. Nōnne sōl maior <u>quam lūna</u> est?

   The best substitute for the underlined phrase is

   (A) lūnā   (C) lūnam

   (B) lūna   (D) lūnae

7. Illud opus in hortō nōn . . . est

   (A) facilis   (C) facile

   (B) facilium   (D) facilī

8. The positive adverb of the adjective <u>gravis</u> is

    (A) grave   (C) graviter

    (B) gravius   (D) gravidus

9. <u>Līberē, līberius, līberrimē</u>

    (A) Freely, very freely, too freely

    (B) Freely, too freely, relatively freely

    (C) Free, rather free, very free

    (D) Freely, rather freely, most freely

10. Hoc flūmen . . . quam illud fluit.

    (A) lentior   (C) lentē

    (B) lentissimē   (D) lentius

11. Herī vespērī per rīpam <u>quam diūtissimē</u> ambulābāmus.

    (A) for a long time

    (B) for as long as possible

    (C) for a very long time

    (D) for a rather long time

12. Canis nōmine Fīdō . . . est.

    (A) fidēlissimus omnium   (C) fidēlissimē omnium

    (B) fidēlissimus omnibus   (D) maxīmē fidelis omnium

13. <u>Parvus</u> is to <u>paulum</u> as <u>magnus</u> is to

    (A) magis   (C) magnopere

    (B) maximē   (D) magnum

14. <u>Multa ignoscendō fit potens potentior.</u> (Publilius Syrus)

    (A) Many things become more powerful through forgiveness.

    (B) By being forgetful of power, many become more powerful.

    (C) By forgiving many things, a powerful man becomes more powerful.

    (D) Being so powerful over many things, he becomes forgiving.

15.   Hī hortī . . . quam illī sunt. Quī hortī . . . omnium sunt?

   (A) minōrēs; minimī   (C) minōrēs; minimē

   (B) minōrī; minimōrum   (D) minōribus; minimī

Stumper:

   Faster, Higher, Stronger (Olympic motto)

   (A) Citius, Altius, Fortius

   (B) Citus, Altus, Fortis

   (C) Citissimē, Altissimē, Fortissimē

   (D) Citō, Altē, Fortiter

Answers

1.   Adjective **(D)**
   This sentence reads *The flowers in the garden near the trees give off a sweet scent*. Based purely on the ending, the adjective **dulcēs** could modify **Flōrēs**, **arborēs**, or **odōrēs**, but based upon the sense, **odōrēs** is the most likely noun modified. The position of the noun **odōrēs**, perhaps a poetic counterpart to **Flōrēs** at the front of the sentence, is meant to distract you, because **odōrēs** would logically be found beside **dulcēs**.

2.   Adverb **(B)**
   The form **celerius** can be a comparative adjective in the nominative or accusative singular neuter form, or a comparative adverb. If **celerius** were an adjective, it would modify either the noun **flōrēs** or the noun **arboribus**, which are neither singular nor neuter. Therefore, **celerius** must be an adverb modifying the verb **Crescunt**. As an adverb, the form **celerius** is comparative, hence (B) *more quickly*. The Latin of (A) is **celeriter**, the positive adverb; (C) the correlative expression **tam celeriter quam**; and (D) the superlative adverb **celerrimē**. The sentence reads *Do flowers grow more quickly than trees?*

3.   Adverb **(A)**
   Too easily is a comparative (*too*) adverb (*easily*). *Too* is one of the options for translating the comparative degree of adjectives and adverbs. Of the forms provided, (A) **facilius** is correct. Answer (B) **facilis** is a positive adjective, *easy*; (C) **facillimē** is a superlative adverb, *very easily*;

and (D) **magis facilis**, *more easily*, which is an improper use of the comparative adverb **magis**.

4.   Adverb **(C)**
Answers (A) **postridiē**, *on the next day*, and (B) **paulisper**, *for a short while*, pertain to time, and (D) **vix**, *scarcely*, expresses manner, leaving **undique**, *on all sides,* as an adverb answering the question "where?" and expressing place.

5.   Adjective **(B)**
This question tests knowledge of the potential variations used to express the meaning of the superlative adjective. Here, the form is **pulcherrima**. Answers (A), (C), and (D) are all unacceptable. Answers (A) *rather beautiful* and (C) *too beautiful* are variations of ways to express the comparative degree, and (D) *beautiful* expresses the positive degree.

6.   Adjective **(A)**
This sentence, which reads *Isn't the sun larger than the moon?*, contains an expression of comparison between the sun and the moon. Of the choices offered, only the ablative of comparison, (A) **lūnā**, can substitute for the **quam** comparative construction that appears in the sentence. Answer (B) **lūna** is nominative, (C) **lūnam** is accusative, and (D) **lūnae** is genitive or dative.

7.   Adjective **(C)**
The demonstrative adjective **illud** reveals the gender of **opus** to be neuter. Therefore, by the rules of agreement, the missing adjective must have a neuter ending. Furthermore, the adjective must have a nominative case ending because it is modifying the subject, **opus**. The question of degree doesn't arise because all answers appear in the positive degree. These limitations rule out (A) **facilis**, which does not have a neuter ending, and (D) **facilī**, which is not nominative, but dative. Answer (B) provides distraction because it has an ending that is identifiable as a potential nominative or accusative neuter form of the second declension. However, it is not. **Facilium** is genitive and plural. This sentence reads *The work in the garden is not easy*.

8.   Adverb **(C)**
Only two of the four answers can be adverbs: (B) **gravius** the comparative and (C) **graviter** the positive. Because the positive is requested,

the correct answer is **graviter**. Answers (A) **grave** and (D) **gravidus** are positive adjectives. (See "Positive Adverbs Derived from Adjectives.")

9. Adverb **(D)**

This series represents the sequence of the various degrees of the adverb **liberē**. The meaning of the word is irrelevant because all answers have to do with being free. We are concerned with (1) the correct part of speech, adjective or adverb, and (2) the appropriate sequence of the translations relative to the forms. The forms are adverbs and are given in the standard order of positive, comparative, and superlative, so the correct answer is (D). Answer (C) translates adjectives, rather than adverbs. Answer (A) reverses the comparative and superlative, and (B) gives redundant translations of the comparative form.

10. Adverb **(D)**

The need for a comparative adverb to accompany **quam illud** in order to complete the meaning of the sentence *This river flows more slowly than that one* leads to (D) **lentius**. Answer (A) **lentior** is comparative, but is an adjective. Answers (B) **lentissimē** and (C) **lentē** are incorrect forms of the degree of the adverb required by the context here.

11. Adverb **(B)**

The idiomatic expression **quam** + superlative is translated *as . . . as possible*, which makes (B) **quam diūtissimē** correct. Answer (A) requires the positive adverb **diū**, (B) the superlative adverb **diūtissimē** by itself, and (D) the comparative adverb **diūtius**. The sentence reads *Yesterday evening we walked along the riverbank for as long as possible*. (See Chapter 16, "Comparative Adjectives.")

12. Adjective **(A)**

Given the answers, the missing part of the sentence is the common phrase containing the superlative adjective plus the genitive plural form **omnium**, *-est of all*. The best immediate choices are (A) and (C), both of which contain a superlative. Answer (A) is correct because (C) **fidēlissimē** is an adverb, and an adjective is needed to modify **Fīdō**, as the sense suggests. Answer (B) **fidēlissimus omnibus** contains the wrong form of **omnis**, and (D) provides a tempting but incorrect phrase using the superlative adverb **maximē**. (For superlatives with **omnium**, see Chapter 16, "Superlative Adjectives.")

13. Adjective **(C)**

Because **paulum**, *little*, is the positive adverb corresponding to the positive irregular adjective **parvus**, *small*, we are looking for the adverbial equivalent of the positive irregular adjective **magnus**, *big*. This is (C) **magnopere**, *greatly*. Answer (A) **magis** is the <u>comparative</u> adverb formed from **magnus**, (B) **maximē** is the <u>superlative</u> adverb formed from **magnus**, and (D) **magnum** is the positive adjective of **magnus** in the neuter form, which matches, incorrectly, with the positive adverb **paulum**.

14. Adjective **(C)**

Don't let the gerund in this sentence fool you into translating the adjectives incorrectly. **Multa** is used as a substantive, *many things*, here, as is **potens**, *a (the) powerful man*. In (A), the translation makes **multa** the subject, which it is not possible because the verb **fit** is singular. This version also omits the word **potens**. In (B), the object of **ignoscendō** is *many things*, not *power*, and **potentior** does not agree with **multa**. Answer (D) omits the word **potentior** and ignores the substantive adjective **potens** as the subject of the verb fit. The sentence reads *By overlooking many things* (or *overlooking much*), *a powerful* (*man*) *becomes more powerful*.

15. Adjective **(A)**

Read these sentences as *These gardens are <u>smaller</u> than those. Which gardens are the <u>smallest</u> of all?* These translations require comparative and superlative forms of the irregular adjective **parvus** to complete their meanings. In both sentences, the adjectives modify the nominative subject **hortī**. Answer (B) **minōrī** is not a nominative form, but dative, and **minimōrum** is genitive. The missing adjective in the second sentence must modify **hortī** and not the genitive plural form **omnium**. Answer (C) contains an adverb **minimē**, and (D) **minōribus** is in the ablative case, which is a diversion to fool you into considering the possible need for the ablative of comparison here.

Stumper: (A)

The translation of **Citius**, **Altius**, **Fortius**, *Higher*, *Faster*, *Stronger* requires comparative adverbs (or adjectives in the neuter), which are found in (A). Answer (B) gives the positive adjectives, which are incorrect in both degree and part of speech. Answers (C) and (D) offer adverbs, but in the wrong degrees, namely superlative and positive.

THE SAT SUBJECT TEST IN
LATIN

SECTION 5

Indicative Verbs

CHAPTER 18

The Language of Verbs

Chapter 18

THE LANGUAGE OF VERBS

The terms listed and defined below are traditionally used to describe the forms and functions of Latin verbs and will be used throughout the succeeding sections. As with the terminology of nouns, these terms are not tested explicitly on the SAT Latin Subject Test, but your understanding of them is assumed as part of your ability to work with the Latin language. Such terms include conjugation, person, number, tense, voice, and mood. As with nouns, adjectives, pronouns, and adverbs, questions implying knowledge of the descriptive terms of Latin verbs appear on the first and last parts of the exam.

SAMPLE QUESTIONS

Part A: Recognition of Forms

1.   The pluperfect passive subjunctive of <u>trahunt</u> is

   (A) traherentur   (C) tractī essent

   (B) traxissent   (D) tractī erant

Part F: Reading Comprehension

2.   The tense and voice of <u>dedisse</u> is

   (A) present active   (C) perfect passive

   (B) perfect active   (D) present passive

Answers

1.   (C)

2.   (B)

You will begin with a review of the language of verbs, that is, the terms used to designate verb forms. Then you will move on, chapter by chapter, to review the various forms and functions of verbs. Verbs, as you have learned, are words that express action, occurrence, or existence. Depending upon your level of study, you may not know everything about Latin verbs (which have, by the way, nearly 300 variations in form), but do your best to remaster those things that you have learned. Some subtleties of Latin verb usage, such as the so-called historical present, subordinate clauses in indirect statement, or subjunctive by attraction, are omitted from this review. Here are the contents of the sections on verbs:

Section 5: Indicative Verbs

Chapter 18: The Language of Verbs

Chapter 19: Indicative Verbs, Active and Passive

Chapter 20: Deponent Verbs

Chapter 21: Irregular Verbs

Chapter 22: Impersonal Verbs

Section 6: Imperative Verbs

Chapter 23: Direct Address

Section 7: Verbals

Chapter 24: Participles

Chapter 25: Gerund, Gerundives, Supine

Chapter 26: Infinitives

Section 8: Subjunctive Verbs

Chapter 27: Forms of the Subjunctive

Chapter 28: Independent Subjunctives

Chapter 29: Conditional Sentences

Chapter 30: **Ut** Clauses

Chapter 31: **Q**-Word Clauses

Chapter 32: **Cum** Clauses

VERBS GLOSSARY

- **clause** (**claudere**, *to close, enclose*): a group of words containing a subject and a verb and standing as part of a compound or complex sentence. Clauses in Latin have a variety of functions. In general, they can serve to express either main (or independent) thoughts or subordinate (or dependent) thoughts. The function and meaning of a clause is usually determined by an introductory word followed by a verb in either the indicative or subjunctive mood, for example:

  Cum Caesar dictātor erat, senātōrēs eum occīdērunt.
  When Caesar was dictator, senators killed him.

  The main clause is **senātōrēs eum occīdērunt** and the subordinate or dependent clause is **Cum Caesar dictātor erat**. (See also **phrase**.)

- **conjugation** (**cum + iugāre/jugāre**, *to join together*): a category of the verb whose designation depends upon the stem vowel appearing in the present active infinitive. There are four conjugations of verbs in Latin: first, **cantāre**; second, **censēre**; third, **cognoscere** (sometimes divided into "third" and its variation, "third -iō"); and fourth, **sentīre**. Verbs that do not conform to the patterns of these conjugations are said to be "irregular." To conjugate a verb means to give in traditional sequence all forms of a particular tense.

- **coordinate** (**cum + ordō, ordinis**, *with order* or *arrangement*): the connecting or joining of two equal verbal elements, such as *She smiled and he smiled back*. The conjunction that joins the two elements is known as a coordinating conjunction. (See also **subordinate**.)

- **finite verb** (**finis**, *end*): a verb that is limited by person and number, such as **mittit**, *he sends*, or **dormiēmus**, *we will sleep*. Infinitives are not so limited.

- **infinitive** (**in + finis**, *without end*): a form of the verb without person or number, that is, without limit, as opposed to a finite verb. This verb has as its English meaning *to* + the meaning of the verb. Regular verbs have three tenses of the infinitive in the active voice: present, **cantāre**, *to sing*; perfect, **cantāvisse**, *to have sung*; and future, **cantātūrus esse**, *to be about to sing*. In the passive, the forms are **cantātus esse**, *to have been sung*, and **cantātus īrī**, *to be about to be sung*, which is rarely found.

- **intransitive verb** (**in** + **trans** + **īre**, *not to go across*): an intransitive verb, such as **currere**, *to run*, cannot take a direct object. (In English, one may be said to "run a machine," but not in Latin.) A transitive verb, on the other hand, expresses an action that is carried from the verb to the object, as in **epistulam mittere**, *to send a letter*.

- **noun clause**: see **substantive clause**.

- **participle** (**particeps**, *sharing*, from **pars, partis** + **capere**, *to take part*): a word that "participates" in the functions of both a verb and an adjective. Regular verbs have two participles in the active voice, as in **faciēns** (stem **facient-**), *doing*, and **factūrus**, -*a*, -**um**, *about to do* (present and future tenses), and two passive participles, **factus**, -**a**, -**um**, *having been done*, and **faciendus**, -**a**, -**um**, *about to be done* (perfect and future tenses, passive). The future passive participle is also known as the gerundive. There are no present passive or perfect active participial forms.

- **phrase** (from the Greek, "to show or point out"): a series of related words that do <u>not</u> contain a subject or verb (as opposed to a clause), such as **ad insulam**, *toward the island*, a prepositional phrase, and **ad insulam īre**, *to go to the island*, an infinitive phrase. (See also **clause**.)

- **principal part** (**princeps**, fr. **primus** + **capere**, *first, foremost*): a series of verb forms that provide the key elements from which all other forms of that verb are derived. There are usually four principal parts given in the dictionary form of a Latin verb: **tangō, tangere, tetigī, tactus**. **Tangō**, *I touch* (first person singular, present tense active); **tangere**, *to touch* (present active infinitive); **tetigī**, *I touched* (first person singular, perfect tense active); **tactus**, *having been touched* (perfect passive participle).

- **stem**: the unchanging part of a verb to which the characteristic vowel and endings are added. (The term "root" is also used; the term "base" is reserved for nouns.) As indicated by the principal parts, such as **tangō, tangere, tetigī, tactus**, each verb has three stems: the present stem (**tange-**), the perfect active stem (**tetig-**), and the perfect passive stem, (**tact-**). Such stems are used to create the active and passive forms of verb tenses in Latin.

- **subordinate** (**sub** + **ordō**, **ordinis**, *beneath order, arrangement*): also known as dependent or secondary, this term refers to the dependency of one thought or clause upon another within a sentence. In a sentence that contains more than one item of information, the subordinate or dependent clause is less important than the main clause, that is, it "hangs down" from (**dē** + **pendēre**) the main clause and cannot stand alone. Subordinate clauses modify or extend the meaning of a noun or main clause, and they are joined to the main clause by pronouns (**quī**), adverbs (**cum**, **ut**), or subordinating conjunctions (**sī**, **quoniam**). (For an example, see **clause**.)

- **substantive clause**: also known as a substantive noun clause or noun clause, this clause takes the place of a noun. A substantive clause, in taking the place of an accusative direct object in a sentence, contains a statement, command, or question.

Statement:	**Dīxit [sē senātōrem esse].** *He said [that he was a senator].*
Command:	**Senātor lībertō imperāvit [ut sē ad forum comitārētur].** *The senator ordered the freedman [to accompany him to the Forum].*
Question:	**Lībertus rogāvit [quid senātor vellet].** *The freedman asked [what the senator wanted].*

  This type of clause is found as an indirect command, indirect question, or fear clause with the subjunctive and as a result clause following certain verbs.

- **synopsis**: see Chapter 3.

- **transitive verb**: see **intransitive verb**.

- **verbal**: verbs that perform the functions of nouns or adjectives. The gerund, the supine, and infinitives are verbal nouns. Participles, including the gerundive, are verbal adjectives.

The Elements of Latin Verbs

The elements of Latin verbs consist of the information in the verb form that defines its meaning: tense, voice, mood, person, and number, such as **portātus esset**, pluperfect passive subjunctive, third person singular. The following verbal elements will be presented for review in the chapters that follow.

- **mood** (**modus**, *manner* or *way*): one of three attitudes of mind or modes of speech that determines whether the action of the verb communicates a fact (indicative), a command (imperative), or a possibility, wish, or other nonfactual expression (subjunctive):

    - **indicative** (**index**, *forefinger* = *indicator*): a verbal mood that indicates a statement of fact or an assertion, as well as a direct question:

        Puella nōmen Drūsillam habet.
        The girl is named Drusilla.

        Estne Drūsilla nōmen puellae?
        Is Drusilla the girl's name?

        The indicative is the most common of the three moods of verbs used in Latin.

    - **imperative** (**imperāre**, *to order*): a verb that expresses a positive or negative command, admonition, or entreaty in the second person singular or plural, such as **Siste!** (*You*) *stop!*

    - **subjunctive** (**sub** + **iungere/jungere**, *to subjoin* or *subordinate*): the mood of finite verbs that is used to express a hypothetical action, often requiring in English translation an auxiliary word such as *may*, *might*, *should*, or *would*. The subjunctive has a variety of uses, either as a verb in a main clause with an independent meaning or in a subordinate clause with a dependent meaning. There are four tenses of the subjunctive, active and passive: present, imperfect, perfect, and pluperfect.

- **number**: an indication of whether the subject of the verb is singular or plural, as in **sentiō**, *I feel* (singular), or **sentīmus**, *we feel* (plural). This term does <u>not</u> refer to the conjugation of a verb!

- **person**: the person or thing performing the action of the verb, as in **sternuērunt**, *they sneezed*. A verb is referred to as being in the first person (*I*, singular, *we*, plural), second person (*you*, singular, *you*, plural), or third person (*he/she/it*, *they*), depending on the ending of the verb. The personal endings of the perfect tense of the active voice are different from those found in the other tenses of the active.

- **tense** (**tempus**, *time*): the element of a verb that expresses the time of the action of a verb. There are six tenses in Latin: present, imperfect, future, perfect, pluperfect, and future perfect. These are divided into two systems, the present and the perfect. The present system of the indicative mood consists of the present, imperfect, and future tenses (active or passive) and the perfect system consists of the perfect, pluperfect, and future perfect tenses (active or passive). The present system expresses *continuous* action and the perfect system *completed* action. The subjunctive mood lacks the future and future perfect tenses. Within a Latin verb, tense is often revealed by an infix or "tense indicator," which stands between the stem and the personal ending. For **vidēbat**, *he was seeing*, the stem is **vid-**, the stem vowel is **-ē-**, the tense indicator is **-ba-**, and the personal ending is **-t**. The designation of time and the use of tenses is more exact in Latin than in English.

- **voice**: the aspect of a Latin verb that expresses whether the subject is <u>doing</u> the action of the verb or <u>receiving</u> the action. There are two voices in Latin, active and passive, each characterized by its own set of personal endings (except for the perfect tense active, which is unique). The active and passive voices are found in both the indicative and subjunctive moods.

  - **active** (**agere**, *to do*): the active voice is used when the verb expresses the doer of the action, such as **Canis os videt**, *The dog <u>sees</u> (is actively observing) the bone*. In meaning, the distinction between active and passive in Latin is generally the same as that found in English.

  - **passive** (**patior, patī, passus sum**, *to endure*): the aspect of a verb that expresses the action of the verb as done to the subject, as in **Os ā cane vidētur**, *The bone <u>is seen</u> by the dog*. The active and passive voices are found in both the indicative and subjunctive moods.

Special Forms of Verbs

- **defective verb** (**dē** + **facere**, *to be lacking, deficient*): a verb that lacks one or more forms that are regularly inflected in other verbs, such as, **coepī**, *I began*, **meminī**, *I remember*, and **ōdī**, *I hate*, all of which have lost the forms of the present system.

- **deponent verb**: verbs that have "placed aside" (**dē** + **pōnere**) some of their verbal information. Deponent verbs are passive in form and active in meaning, and therefore they have no fourth principal part, as in **loquor** (*I speak*), **loquī** (*to speak*), **locūtus sum** (*I have spoken*). Such verbs have the forms of the regular passive voice. Deponents must be memorized or you must deduce their meaning from context.

- **gerund** (**gerere**, *to carry on*): a verbal noun that has characteristics of both a verb and a noun, such as **gerendum**, *carrying on*. Only the singular forms of the genitive, dative, accusative, and ablative cases, second declension, appear.

- **gerundive** (**gerere**, *to carry on*): a verbal adjective formed by adding -**ndus**, -**a**, -**um** to the present stem of the verb, as in **gerendus**, **gerenda**, **gerendum**, *carrying on*. This form also serves as the future passive participle, for example **agenda**, *(things) about to be done*. As with any adjective, the gerundive agrees with a noun or pronoun.

- **impersonal verb**: verbs that are found in the third person singular with the ending -**t** and have a nonpersonal subject, as in the following example:

  Senātōrī cūriam intrāre licet.
  It is allowed to the senator to enter the Senate House (i.e., *The senator is allowed . . .*)

  Impersonal verbs are found with the accusative, dative, or genitive case, and they may be followed either by an infinitive or a verb in the subjunctive.

- **irregular verb**: a verb, such as **sum**, **eō**, or **volō**, that does not conform to the patterns of formation found with regular verbs. Verbs in this small but important category can stand alone in a sentence, or, like **sum**, they can serve as an auxiliary verb with another verb form, such as **captus est**. Irregular verbs can combine with prepositional prefixes to form verbs with related meanings, for example **absum** or **adsum**.

- **periphrastic** (from the Greek, "roundabout"): this term describes a verb that expresses its meaning in a peripheral way, that is, it uses an auxiliary or helping verb to complete its meaning. The <u>active</u> periphrastic is a more emphatic or definitive way of expressing the future tense, as in the following sentence:

  Hannibal Rōmānōs <u>oppugnātūrus erat</u>.
  Hannibal <u>was about to attack</u> the Romans.

  The <u>passive</u> periphrastic uses the gerundive, accompanied by a form of **esse**, to express necessity or obligation, as in **Carthāgō <u>dēlenda est</u>**, *Carthage <u>must be destroyed</u>*.

- **supine** (**supīnus**, *lying on the back*): a verbal noun formed from the fourth principal part of the verb. Supines are found only with the accusative and ablative endings of the fourth declension noun, such as **mīrābile <u>dictū</u>**, *wonderful <u>to say</u>*.

CHAPTER 19

Forms of the Indicative: Active and Passive

Chapter 19

FORMS OF THE INDICATIVE: ACTIVE AND PASSIVE

INDICATIVE AND SUBJUNCTIVE

This chapter is devoted to helping you recall the forms of regular finite verbs in the indicative mood, the most common category of verbs in Latin. The indicative mood expresses a fact or an assertion, as well as a direct question, whereas the subjunctive mood expresses hypothetical situations:

Indicative: **Catella passerem habet quī ad sōlam dominam pīpiat.**
Catella has a songbird that sings only to its mistress. (fact)

Subjunctive: **Utinam hic passer mihi pīpiet.**
If only this sparrow would sing for me. (nonfact)

There are six tenses of the indicative, active and passive. Because indicative verbs are the ones most frequently found in Latin, you probably learned these first and extended from them your knowledge of additional verb forms. In this chapter, the forms of the indicative mood will be presented together in the active and passive voices, according to tense. Note that the forms and meanings of the imperative, participle, and infinitive will be covered in subsequent sections.

ACTIVE AND PASSIVE

Voice is the aspect of the verb that expresses who or what is doing the action. The active voice expresses the doer of the action and the passive voice expresses the action of the verb as done to the subject:

Active: **Cum passer mortuus est, Catella lūgēbat.**
When her songbird died, Catella mourned.

Passive: **Cum passer mortuus est, ā Catellā lūgēbātur.**
When the songbird died, it was mourned by Catella.

THE PRESENT SYSTEM OF INDICATIVE VERBS

There are two systems of indicative verbs in Latin, the present and the perfect. The present system, with verbs in the present, imperfect, and future tenses, contains elements that are attached to the present stem and express <u>ongoing</u> action. The perfect system, consisting of verbs in the perfect, pluperfect, and future perfect tenses, contains elements that are attached to the perfect stem, active and passive, and express <u>completed</u> action.

The present stem of the verb is formed by dropping the **-re** from the present active infinitive (i.e., its second principal part). Remember that the stem vowel of the present stem determines the conjugation to which a verb belongs:

Principal Parts	Stem	Stem Vowel	Conjugation
parō, parāre	**parā-**	-ā-	1st
sedeō, sedēre	**sedē-**	-ē-	2nd
mittō, mittere	**mitte-**	-e-	3rd
audiō, audīre	**audī-**	-ī-	4th

The third conjugation has a subcategory called the "third **-iō**," for example, **faciō**, **facere**. Verbs such as this belong to the third conjugation (note the infinitive), but have nearly the same forms as those of the fourth conjugation, **audiō**, **audīre**. Third **-iō** verbs are not treated as a separate category in this book.

You must commit to memory the principal parts of Latin verbs or be familiar with the patterns that can occur within the third and fourth principal parts, which provide the perfect active and passive stems. For these, refer to your textbook.

Passive verbs are often found with the ablative of personal agent (see Chapter 10, "Ablative of Personal Agent"), which indicates the person *by whom* the action of the verb is performed, as in the following sentence:

Passer quī ā Catellā lūgēbātur nōmen Pīpī habēbat.
The songbird that was mourned by Catella had the name "Pipi."

As you review, pay close attention to the similarities between forms of the active and passive voices in the present system, such as **mittimus** (active), *we send*, and **mittimur** (passive), *we are sent*.

Personal Endings of the Present System of Active and Passive Voices

	Active		Passive	
	Singular	**Plural**	**Singular**	**Plural**
1st	**-ō** or **-m**, *I*	**-mus**, *we*	**-r**, *I*	**-mur**, *we*
2nd	**-s**, *you* (alone)	**-tis**, *you* (all)	**-ris**, *you* (alone)	**-minī**, *you* (all)
3rd	**-t**, *he, she, it*	**-nt**, *they*	**-tur**, *he, she, it*	**-ntur**, *they*

Present Indicative: Active and Passive

mittō, mittor, *I send, am sent*   **mittimus, mittimur**, *we send, are sent*

mittis, mitteris, *you* (alone) *send, are sent*   **mittitis, mittiminī**, *you* (all) *send, are sent*

mittit, mittitur, *he sends, is sent*   **mittunt, mittuntur**, *they send, are sent*

- Formation: present stem + personal endings, for example, **lugēre** provides the stem **lugē-**, to which is added a personal ending, such as **-t**, giving **luget**, *she mourns*. In the forms of the present tense of third conjugation verbs such as **mittere**, the stem vowel changes from **-e-** to **-i-** (or **-u-**), hence, **mittō, mittis, mittit**, and so on, and **mittunt**.

- The present tense expresses ongoing action in present time.

- The present tense form **mittō** can be translated alternatively *I send, I am sending, I do send*. Use the context to help you decide which option to use when translating.

Imperfect Indicative: Active and Passive

mittēbam, mittēbar, *I was sending, was sent*	**mittēbāmus, mittēbāmur,** *we were sending, were sent*
mittēbās, mittēbāris, *you were sending, were sent*	**mittēbātis, mittēbāminī,** *you were sending, were sent*
mittēbat, mittēbātur, *he was sending, was sent*	**mittēbant, mittēbantur,** *they were sending, were sent*

- Formation: present stem + tense indicator **-ba-** + personal ending (except that the first person singular of the active ends in **-m**, not **-ō**, e.g., **mittēbam**). Thus, **mitte** + **ba** + **t** = **mittēbat**, *he was sending*. The following memory device might be of assistance:

    "What do those imperfect sheep say?"
    "Ba."*

- Forms of the imperfect tense of verbs belonging to the **-iō** conjugations have the present stem ending in **-iē-** throughout the tense, for example, **faciēbam, faciēbās, faciēbat**, and so on and **audiēbam, audiēbās, audiēbat**, and so on. This jingle may help you remember the two vowels of an **-iō** verb in the imperfect tense:

    Imperfect forms insert long **ē**

    In **-iō** verbs before the **b**.

- The imperfect tense expresses ongoing or continuous action in past time. Note that the imperfect (**in** + **perficere**, *not completed*) tense is not a completed action and, therefore, is not part of the perfect system of verbs. Don't be confused by the fact that the term "imperfect" includes the word "perfect"! The action of the imperfect tense when compared to that of the perfect has been described as similar to that of a motion picture compared to a snapshot.*

---

* LeaAnn A. Osburn; see David Pellegrino, http://latinteach.com/verbmnemonics.html.
* John C. Traupman, *Lingua Latina* 1 (Amsco School Publications, 1999), 239.

- The imperfect tense form **mittēbam** can be translated alternatively *I was sending, I kept on sending, I used to send,* or simply *I sent.*

Future Indicative: Active and Passive

mittam, mittar, *I will send, be sent*	**mittēmus, mittēmur,** *we will send, be sent*
mittēs, mittēris, *you will send, will be sent*	**mittētis, mittēminī,** *you will send, be sent*
mittet, mittētur, *he will send, be sent*	**mittent, mittentur,** *they will send, be sent*

- Formation: The forms of the future tense depend on the <u>conjugation to which the verb belongs</u>. For first and second conjugations, use the present stem + tense indicator -**bi**- + personal endings, as in **parā<u>bō</u>, parābis, parābit** and **parābimus, parābitis, parā<u>bunt</u>**. Note the exceptions in spelling, as indicated by the underlining. For third and fourth conjugations, as with the verb **mittere** in the preceding table, the tense indicator -**bi**- is replaced by the vowel -**e**- (except in the first singular, where the ending is -**am**). The forms of the future tense of -**iō** verbs include the vowel -**i**-: **audiam, audiēs, audiet** and **audiēmus, audiētis, audient**. The following memory device may help you remember these variations in the forms of the future tense:

    Conjugations one and two, in the future **bō**, **bi**, **bu**;
    Conjugations four and three, in the future **a** then **e**.*

- Because of the ambiguity between verb forms of the <u>present tense of the second conjugation</u>, such as **docet** (**docēre**), and those of the <u>future tense of the third conjugation</u>, such as **discet** (**discere**), it is important that you know principal parts of verbs and that you also make full use of the context of the sentence when making decisions about tense.

- Here are some tips for "telling the future":

    1. Know the principal parts of the verbs in question. In a second conjugation verb, such as **docet**, the vowel -**ē**- is the stem vowel of the present tense, as indicated in the first principal part **doceō**. In a third conjugation verb, such as **discet**, the vowel -**e**- represents the future tense.

---

* Pellegrino, http://latinteach.com/verbmnemonics.html.

2. Look for other indications of the future tense in the context of the sentence, like the adverb **crās**, *tomorrow*, or a verb having a more obvious form of the future tense, such as **docēbit**.

3. Guess future! There are many more verbs in the third conjugation than in the second, making it much more likely that a verb with an **-e-** vowel is in the future tense than in the present.

- Remember that the macron has a grammatical function in distinguishing the future passive, as in **mittēris**, *you will be sent*, from the second person singular forms of third conjugation verbs in the present passive, as in **mitteris**, *you are being sent*. Avoid confusing either passive form with the future perfect active **mīseris**, *you will have sent*.

- Future time may also be expressed by the use of the active periphrastic, consisting of the future active participle plus forms of **esse**, for example, **missūrus est**, *he is about to send, going to send*. The active periphrastic is a more emphatic or definitive expression of the future tense. We'll review more about this later.

THE PERFECT SYSTEM OF INDICATIVE VERBS

Verbs in the perfect system are generally characterized by stem changes that appear in the third and fourth principal parts, for example, in the verb **mittō**, **mittere**, <u>**mīsī**</u>, <u>**missus**</u>, the perfect active stem is **mīs-** and the perfect passive stem is **miss-**. (Note that the fourth principal part is in fact the perfect passive participle, which will be reviewed in Chapter 24.)

Except for the forms of the perfect active, which have unique personal endings, verbs in the perfect system are formed from the perfect stem, active or passive, plus various forms of the verb **esse**, as in **mīserat** (pluperfect active), *he had sent*, **mīserit** (future perfect active), *he will have sent*, **missus est** (perfect passive), *he has been sent*, **missus erat** (pluperfect passive), *he had been sent*, and **missus erit** (future perfect passive), *he will have been sent*. All <u>passive</u> forms of the perfect system (perfect, pluperfect, and future perfect) are <u>compound</u>, that is, they consist of two parts, as in **missus est**.

The meanings of the tenses in the perfect system express action in past time that is <u>completed</u>.

Perfect Indicative: Active and Passive

mīsī, missus sum,
I sent, have been sent

mīsimus, missī sumus,
we sent, have been sent

mīsistī, missus es,
you sent, have been sent

mīsistis, missī estis,
you sent, have been sent

mīsit, missus est,
he sent, has been sent

mīsērunt, missī sunt,
they sent, have been sent

- Active formation: perfect active stem **mīs-** + personal ending **-t** = **mīsit**, *he sent*. (For personal endings, see the table below.)

- Passive formation: perfect passive stem **miss-** + first/second declension adjectival endings **-us, -a, -um** + detached form of **esse** in the present tense, as in **missus est**, *he has been sent*.

- Although the spelling of the stem of the perfect tense active is variable, it often includes **-s-, -u-, -v-,** or **-x-**, or a reduplication, such as **cucurrī (currere)** or **tradidī (tradere)**. Be alert for forms that have perfect stems matching or approximating those of the present tense, such as **leg-** (present) and **lēg-** (perfect) of the verb **legere**, and **ven-** (present) and **vēn-** (perfect) of the verb **venīre**. Also remember that, for some verbs, the perfect active stem is the same as the present; for example, **occurrit** means both *he meets* and *he met*. Use the context for further assistance regarding the accurate translation of ambiguous verb forms.

- Recall the famous words of Julius Caesar to help you with the perfect stems of three important verbs:

  Vēnī, vīdī, vīcī.
  I came, I saw, I conquered.

- Remember the third principal parts of the important verbs **dedī (dare)**, *I gave*, and **stetī (stāre)**, *I stood*.

- The personal endings of the perfect tense active, which are added to the perfect stem, are unique:

Personal Endings of the Perfect System of the Active Voice

	Singular	Plural	Singular	Plural
1st	-ī, *I*	-imus, *we*	mīsī	mīsimus
2nd	-istī, *you*	-istis, *you*	mīsistī	mīsistis
3rd	-it, *he, she, it*	-ērunt, *they**	mīsit	mīsērunt

* Note that when it appears as an ending, **-ērunt** belongs to the perfect tense, whereas the freestanding form **erunt**, *they will be*, is a form of the future tense of the irregular verb **esse**.

- The ending of the participial form **missus, -a, -um** must agree in gender and number with the subject, for example <u>senātor</u> <u>missus</u> est, *the senator has been sent*, and <u>cīvēs</u> missī sunt, *the citizens have been sent*. The personal ending of the form of **esse** must agree in number with the subject, as in <u>tribunus</u> missus est, *the tribune (<u>he</u>) has been sent*. The double forms of verbs in the perfect passive system may be found either as **missus est** or **est missus** without any change in meaning.

- The perfect tense (**perficere** = **per** + **facere**, *finish*) expresses action completed in immediate past time.

- The form **mīsī** can be translated *I sent*, *I have sent*, or *I did send*. Avoid using *was* in translating the perfect passive, such as **missus est**. The word *was* is ambiguous in English: it is not concise in its expression of whether an action is ongoing (*was being*, imperfect tense) or completed (*has been*, perfect tense).

- Do <u>not</u> translate the form of the helping verb **esse** as a main verb; for example, **missus est** does <u>not</u> mean *he is sent*.

- In Latin verse, you may find an alternate form of the perfect tense in the third person plural. This form accommodates the meter or poetic context. For example, **fuēre** substitutes for **fuērunt**. Avoid translating these variant forms as present active infinitives by confirming the presence of the perfect stem, which is **fu-** in this example. Forms of the perfect tense may also be abbreviated or compressed; for example, **dōnāvērunt** becomes **dōnārunt**, *they gave*, and **sperāvistī** becomes **sperāstī**, *you hoped*.

Pluperfect Indicative: Active and Passive

mīseram, missus eram,
I had sent, had been sent

mīseramus, missī eramus,
we had sent, had been sent

mīseras, missus erās,
you had sent, had been sent

mīserātis, missī erātis,
you had sent, had been sent

mīserat, missus erat,
he had sent, had been sent

mīserant, missī erant,
they had sent, had been sent

- Active formation: perfect active stem **mīs** + imperfect tense of **esse** (**eram, erās, erat**, etc.) = **mīserat**, *he had sent*.

- Passive formation: perfect passive stem **miss-** + first/second declension adjectival endings **-us, -a, -um** + detached form of **esse** in the imperfect tense, as in **missus erat**, *he had been sent*.

- The pluperfect is the tense that expresses completed action in the remote past, that is, an action that was completed in past time before another action completed in past time. The pluperfect tense (**plus** + **quam** + **perficere**, *more than completed*) is also known as the "past perfect" because it expresses "past-past" time, such as *Cicero had returned to the Forum before the Senate convened*. Both verbs are in past time, but the "returning" happened and was completed before the "convening." Avoid the temptation to translate the pluperfect tense as an imperfect by using the word *was*.

Future Perfect Indicative: Active and Passive

mīserō, missus erō, *I will have sent, will have been sent*

mīserimus, missī erimus, *we will have sent, will have been sent*

mīseris, missus eris, *you will have sent, will have been sent*

mīseritis, missī eritis, *you will have sent, will have been sent*

mīserit, missus erit, *he will have sent, will have been sent*

mīserint, missī erunt, *they will have sent, will have been sent*

- Active formation: perfect active stem **mīs** + future tense of **esse** (**erō, eris, erit**, etc.) = **mīserit**, *he will have sent*.

- Passive formation: perfect passive stem **miss-** + first/second declension adjectival endings **-us, -a, -um** + detached form of **esse** in the future tense, such as **missus erit**, *he will have been sent*.

- Note that the expected form **-erunt** in the third person plural changes to **-erint**, such as in **mīserint**, *they will have sent*, in the active voice. Avoid confusing the future perfect active form **mīserint**, *they will have sent*, with that of the perfect active form, as found in **mīsērunt**, *they have sent*. Also note that the future passive form is **missī erunt** (not **missī erint**).

- The future perfect is the tense of finite indicative verbs expressing action that will have been completed before another action in future time begins. For example, *Cicero will have returned to the Forum <u>before</u> the Senate will convene*. The future perfect tense is often best translated by the <u>present</u> tense in English because *When Cicero returns* makes better sense than *When Cicero will have returned*.

- The future perfect is the least common of the six verb tenses in Latin.

Quick Study Synopsis of an Indicative Verb in the Active and Passive Voices

mittō, mittere, mīsī, missus		
	Active	**Passive**
Present System		
Present	**mittit**, *he is sending, sends*	**mittitur**, *he is being sent, is sent*
Imperfect	**mittēbat**, *he was sending, sent*	**mittēbatur**, *he was being sent, was sent*
Future	**mittet**, *he will send*	**mittētur**, *he will be sent*
Perfect System		
Perfect	**mīsit**, *he sent, has sent, did send*	**missus est**, *he has been sent, was sent*
Pluperfect	**mīserat**, *he had sent*	**missus erat**, *he had been sent*
Future Perfect	**mīserit**, *he will have sent*	**missus erit**, *he will have been sent*

TIPS ON TRANSLATING VERBS IN THE INDICATIVE MOOD

Pay special attention to forms of the indicative that are, or appear to be, ambiguous, as in the following examples:

- Forms of the imperfect and future tenses:

susurrābat	vs.	**susurrābit**
he was whispering		*he will whisper*

- Forms of the present and perfect tenses in the third singular:

Labor omnia <u>vincit</u>.	vs.	**Labor omnia <u>vīcit</u>.**
conquers		*conquered*
<u>Legit</u> volūmen.	vs.	**<u>Lēgit</u> volūmen.**
<u>*He reads*</u> *the scroll.*		<u>*He read*</u> *the scroll.*

- Forms of the present and future tenses:

persuadet	vs.	**crēdet**
he convinces		*he will believe*
regeris	vs.	**regēris**
you are being ruled		*you will be ruled*

- Forms of the third plural:

<u>erunt</u>, *they will be*

vīd<u>ērunt</u>, *they have seen*

vīd<u>erant</u>, *they had seen*

vīd<u>erint</u>, *they will have seen*

vīsī <u>erunt</u>, *they will have been seen*

- Forms of the passive voice:

monentur	vs.	**monitae sunt**
they are warned		*they have been warned* (not *they are warned*)

- Forms of the active and passive voices:

mīseris	vs.	**mitteris**
you will have sent		*you are being sent*
		mittēris
		you will be sent

Be clear about how the time of each of the six tenses is best expressed in English:

- Present system

Present:	continuous present	*are . . . -ing*
Imperfect:	continuous past	*were . . . -ing*
Future:	continuous future	*will be . . . -ing*

- Perfect system

Perfect:	completed past	*has been . . . -ed*
Pluperfect:	completed before another past action	*had been . . . -ed*
Future Perfect:	completed before another future action	*will have been . . . -ed*

SAMPLE QUESTIONS

Part A: Recognition of Forms

1. The pluperfect of <u>vincimur</u> is

    (A) victī erāmus   (C) victī sumus

    (B) vīcerat   (D) victī essēmus

Part D: Sentence Completion

2. Simul multa. . . .

    (A) agitur   (C) actī erant

    (B) acta sunt   (D) agēris

Answers

1. (A)   2. (B)

PRACTICE QUESTIONS

1. The future passive equivalent of <u>scrībit</u> is

    (A) scrībitur   (C) scriptus est

    (B) scrībēbātur   (D) scrībētur

2. The perfect tense equivalent of <u>audis</u> is

    (A) auditus est   (C) audiēbās

    (B) audīvistī   (D) auditis

3. Heri <u>lēgistī</u> librum quem priōre diē emerās.

    (A) you are reading   (C) you will read

    (B) you did read   (D) you want to read

4. The active equivalent of <u>tenēbāminī</u> is

    (A) tenēbās   (C) tenētis

    (B) tenēbātis   (D) tenēbāris

5. The active of <u>missus erat</u> is

   (A) mittēbat   (C) mīserat
   (B) mittēbātur   (D) missus est

6. Pater suum fīlium <u>cognōverat</u>.

   (A) recognized   (C) has recognized
   (B) had recognized   (D) was recognizing

7. <u>Vocābāmur</u> ā pārentibus nostrīs.

   (A) We will be called (C) We were called
   (B) We are called   (D) We were calling

8. The plural of <u>tenuit</u> is

   (A) tenuerant   (C) tenuerint
   (B) tenuērunt   (D) tenent

9. Prīmā lūce sōl <u>surget</u>.

   (A) arose   (C) has risen
   (B) will rise   (D) rises

10. The future tense of <u>ducō</u> is

   (A) ducam   (C) ducēmus
   (B) ducēbam   (D) ducor

11. <u>Dormiēbatne</u> ignāvus discipulus?

   (A) Will . . . sleep? (C) Was . . . sleeping?
   (B) Can . . . sleep?   (D) Were . . . sleeping?

12. The personal subject of <u>trahiminī</u> is

   (A) tū   (C) nōs
   (B) ego   (D) vōs

13. Proximō mense ad Hispāniam <u>mittēris</u>.
    - (A) you will be sent
    - (C) you will have sent
    - (B) you are being sent
    - (D) you will send

14. The singular of <u>parābāmus</u> is
    - (A) parāmus
    - (C) parō
    - (B) parābō
    - (D) parābam

15. Which of the following belongs to the second conjugation?
    - (A) custodiō
    - (C) iungō (jungō)
    - (B) navigō
    - (D) iubeō (jubeō)

16. The passive of <u>portāvērunt</u> is
    - (A) portātī erant
    - (C) portātī erunt
    - (B) portātī sunt
    - (D) portantur

17. <u>Duxī</u> equum ad aquam.
    - (A) I lead
    - (C) I led
    - (B) Lead
    - (D) To have led

18. Dī hominēs semper <u>amāverint</u>.
    - (A) they had loved
    - (C) they will have loved
    - (B) they did love
    - (D) they will love

19. Baculum ā cane <u>receptum est</u>.
    - (A) has been fetched
    - (C) is being fetched
    - (B) had been fetched
    - (D) has fetched

20. Si ad Crētam navigāveris, ā pīrātīs <u>capiēris</u>.
    - (A) you are being captured
    - (B) you will have captured
    - (C) you are capturing
    - (D) you will be captured

Stumper:

Consul <u>factūrus es</u>.

(A) you are becoming

(B) you are about to become

(C) you have become

(D) you will have become

Answers

1.	(D)	7.	(C)	13.	(A)	19.	(A)
2.	(B)	8.	(B)	14.	(D)	20.	(D)
3.	(B)	9.	(B)	15.	(D)	**Stumper:**	(B)
4.	(B)	10.	(A)	16.	(B)		
5.	(C)	11.	(C)	17.	(C)		
6.	(B)	12.	(D)	18.	(C)		

CHAPTER 20

Deponent Verbs

Chapter 20

DEPONENT VERBS

PASSIVE VERBS AND DEPONENT VERBS

Deponent verbs have "put aside" (**dēpōnere**) their active forms and passive meanings. Therefore, they are verbs that have only <u>passive forms</u> and <u>active meanings</u>, such as **loquitur**, *he is speaking* (not *he is being spoken*). Such verbs have also been called "fake passives." Deponent verbs occur in all four conjugations and have the same forms as regular passive verbs. Even forms such as the perfect passive participle have active meanings, as in **locūtus**, *having spoken* (not *having been spoken*).

DEPONENT VERBS

Deponent verbs have only <u>three</u> principal parts:

loquor	(*I speak*, first person singular, present tense passive)
loquī	(*to speak*, present passive infinitive)
locūtus sum	(*I have spoken*, first person singular, perfect tense passive)

As with nondeponent verbs, the conjugation of a deponent verb is determined from its second principal part: first, **hortārī**; second, **verērī**; third, **loquī**; and fourth, **orīrī**. The deponent verb in the preceding list belongs to the third conjugation because its present infinitive form is **loquī**. (The forms of passive and deponent infinitives will be discussed further in Chapter 26.) The present active stem is then **loque-** (from the hypothetical present active infinitive form **loquere**). The deponent verb has a present active stem that is used in some forms, such as the gerundive **loquendum**, or the imperfect subjunctive **loquerētur**. There are no deponent verbs in English, but there are a large number in Latin, many of which are found in compound forms. Here are some examples of how deponent verbs are translated in context:

> **Glūkōs medicus sē ipsum curāre <u>conātus est</u>. <u>Mortuus est</u>.**
> *Dr. Glukos <u>tried</u> to cure himself. <u>He died</u>.*

> **Hypoxia sē languere semper <u>querēbatur</u>.**
> *Hypoxia <u>was</u> always <u>complaining</u> that she felt faint.*

Synopsis of a Deponent Verb

loquor, loquī, locūtus sum

Present	**loquuntur**, *they are speaking*
Imperfect	**loquēbantur**, *they were speaking*
Future	**loquentur**, *they will speak*
Perfect	**locūtī sunt**, *they have spoken*
Pluperfect	**locūtī erant**, *they had spoken*
Future Perfect	**locūtī erunt**, *they will have spoken*

Note that other forms of deponent verbs, such as imperatives, participles, and infinitives, will be covered in subsequent chapters.

COMMON DEPONENT VERBS

First Conjugation

> **arbitror, arbitrārī, arbitrātus sum**, *think, judge*
>
> **cōnor, cōnārī, cōnātus sum**, *try, attempt*
>
> **hortor, hortārī, hortātus sum**, *encourage, urge on*
>
> **mīror, mirārī, mirātus sum**, *wonder*
>
> **moror, morārī, morātus sum**, *stay, remain*

Second Conjugation

> **polliceor, pollicērī, pollicitus sum**, *promise*
>
> **reor, rērī, ratus sum**, *think*
>
> **tueor, tuērī, tutus sum**, *protect, aid*
>
> **vereor, verērī, veritus sum**, *fear, be afraid*

Third Conjugation

loquor, loquī, locūtus sum, *speak, talk*

nanciscor, nanciscī, nactus sum, *obtain*

nascor, nascī, nātus sum, *be born*

proficīscor, proficīscī, profectus sum, *set out, depart*

queror, querī, questus sum, *complain, lament*

sequor, sequī, secūtus sum, *follow*

ūtor, ūtī, ūsus sum (+ abl.), *use*

Third -iō Conjugation

ēgredior, ēgredī, ēgressus sum, *go out, leave*

ingredior, ingredī, ingressus sum, *go in, enter*

morior, morī, mortuus sum, *die*

patior, patī, passus sum, *endure, suffer, allow*

prōgredior, prōgredī, prōgressus sum, *go forward, proceed*

regredior, regredī, regressus sum, *go back, return*

Fourth Conjugation

experior, experīrī, expertus sum, *test, try*

orior, orīrī, ortus sum, *rise, get up*

potior, potīrī, potītus sum (+ abl. or gen.), *possess, obtain*

ADDITIONAL INFORMATION ABOUT DEPONENT VERBS

Semideponent Verbs

The subcategory of deponent verbs called "semideponents" consists of verbs that are active in the present system and passive in the perfect system, such as **audeō, audēre, ausus sum**, *I dare, to dare, I (have) dared.* In addition to **audeō**, the most common semideponents are **gaudeō**,

gaudēre, gāvīsus sum, *rejoice, be glad*, and **soleō, solēre, solitus sum**, *be accustomed*. Note that all three verbs belong to the second conjugation. Be careful to distinguish between **audeō** and **audiō**!

> **Nūper vespillō Diaulus nunc medicus fierī <u>ausus est</u>.**
> *Diaulus, recently an undertaker, now <u>has dared</u> to become a doctor.*

Deponent Verbs with Ablative Direct Objects

In Chapter 10, you met a small number of deponent verbs that take their direct objects in the <u>ablative</u> case rather than in the accusative, such as **ūtor, ūtī, ūsus sum** in the following sentence:

> **Symmachus <u>discipulīs</u> quī manūs gelātās habēbant ūtēbātur.**
> *Symmachus kept using <u>apprentices</u> who had cold hands.*

These verbs are:

> **fruor, fruī, frūctus sum**, *enjoy, have benefit of*
>
> **fungor, fungī, fūnctus sum**, *perform, discharge*
>
> **potior, potīrī, potītus sum**, *obtain, get possession of*
>
> **ūtor, ūtī, ūsus sum**, *use, make use of*
>
> **vēscor, vēscī**, *eat, feed on*

Use the memory device PUFFV ("puffy") to remember the first letters of these deponent verbs with the ablative case.*

Deponent Verbs with Additional Meanings

The common deponent **morior** in the perfect system means *is dead* as well as *died*; **mortuus est** means *he is dead* as well as *he died*.

The verb **vidēre** has a special sense when it appears in the passive, namely, that *to be seen* means *to seem*. In its passive forms, this verb can behave like a deponent verb, i.e., can have an active meaning: **videor, vidērī, vīsus sum**, *I seem, to seem, I have seemed*. (For this verb as an impersonal with the dative case, see Chapter 8, "Dative with Certain Types of Verbs.")

---

* David Pellegrino, http://latinteach.com/casemnemonics.html.

TIPS ON TRANSLATING DEPONENT VERBS

•   Deponent verbs may be recognized through familiarity or from context. First, know the principal parts of the most common deponents by knowing which verbs are deponent. Secondly, use common sense to help you to determine whether a verb is passive or deponent, as in the following example:

   Aegrī multum dolōrem patiēbantur.
   The sick were enduring much pain.

   You can deduce that **patiēbantur** is deponent because its meaning as a passive verb, *were being endured*, does not make sense in this context.

•   Be alert to the peculiarities of some deponent verbs, such as semideponents and deponents with ablative objects.

•   When working with deponent verbs, take care to distinguish among those that look alike, such as **mīror**, *wonder at*, **morior**, *die*, and **moror**, *delay*, or **nanciscor**, *obtain*, and **nascor**, *be born*.

PRACTICE QUESTIONS

1.   Iuvenālis (Juvenālis) <u>loquēbātur</u>, "Mens sāna in corpore sānō."

   (A) was said   (C) was saying

   (B) will say   (D) kept on being said

2.   Glūkōs in cubiculum <u>ingressus est</u> ut cum Anēmiā loquerētur.

   (A) entered   (C) has been entered

   (B) is entering   (D) having entered

3.   "Anemia, it is important for you <u>to get out</u> of the house every day," advised Glukos.

   (A) ēgredere   (C) ēgressus esse

   (B) ēgrediendī   (D) ēgredī

4. Anēmia mortua ā Mercuriō ad īnferōs <u>ducētur</u>.

    (A) will lead   (C) is leading

    (B) is led   (D) will be led

5. Quamobrem Mercurius . . . <u>potītus est</u>?

    (A) cadūceum   (C) cadūceōs

    (B) cadūceō   (D) cadūceōrum

6. <u>Verērisne</u> morī?

    The closest meaning to that of the underlined word is

    (A) Timētisne   (C) Timēbisne

    (B) Timēsne   (D) Timērēsne

7. Aescūlapius omnēs Rōmānōs <u>tuētur</u>.

    (A) will protect   (C) is being protected

    (B) should protect   (D) protects

8. Medicī Rōmānī sē ipsōs cūrāre <u>ausī sunt</u>.

    (A) were dared   (C) have been dared

    (B) dared   (D) are daring

SENTENTIAE ANTIQUAE

1. Cūra pecūniam crescentem . . . (Horace)

    (A) sequitur   (C) secutūrus esse

    (B) sequī   (D) secūtus es

2. Nōn nōbīs sōlum <u>nātī sumus</u>. (Cicero)

    (A) we have been born   (C) we were being born

    (B) we are being born   (D) we had been born

3. In bibliothēcīs . . . dēfunctōrum immortālēs animae. (Pliny the Elder)

   (A) loquēbātur

   (B) locūtī erant

   (C) loquor

   (D) loquuntur

4. <u>Nōn prōgredī est regredī</u>. (motto)

   (A) We're advancing backwards rapidly.

   (B) The good old days were best.

   (C) Man never accomplished anything without hard work.

   (D) Forward not backward.

5. Stick to the subject, the words <u>will follow</u>. (Cato)

   (A) sequuntur

   (B) secūta erunt

   (C) sequantur

   (D) sequentur

Stumper:

   Ō <u>passī</u> graviōra, dabit deus hīs quoque fīnem! (Vergil)

   (A) to suffer

   (B) having been suffered

   (C) having suffered

   (D) they suffered

Answers

1. **(C)**
   Lōquēbatur is in the imperfect tense and therefore is translated *he was saying*. The sentence reads *Juvenal <u>was saying</u>, "A sound mind in a sound body."* Answers (A) and (D) also express the meaning of the imperfect tense, but in the passive voice, whereas **loquor** is a deponent verb. Answer (B) requires the future tense form **loquētur**.

2. **(A)**
   As with verbs in the regular passive voice, verb forms such as **ingressus est** provide the various past tenses of deponent verbs. **Ingressus est** is a form of the perfect tense, therefore Answer (A) *entered* is correct. The sentence reads *Glukos <u>entered</u> the room to speak with Anemia.* Answer (C) is also given in the perfect tense, but it is passive. Answer (B) *is entering* is a common incorrect translation of a passive form of the perfect system because of the appearance of the verb **est**. Answer (D)

would require the past participle **ingressus**, which is only a component of the perfect passive verb form.

3. **(D)**
    The phrase *to get out of* is expressed by the infinitive **ēgredī**. Although (A) **ēgredere** appears to be an infinitive, it is not, because **ēgredior** is a deponent verb and has forms only in the passive. This form is an alternative to the second person singular present tense form **ēgrederis**. Answer (B) **ēgrediendī** is a gerund or gerundive, and (C) **ēgressus esse** is an infinitive, but it appears in the wrong tense (perfect).

4. **(D)**
    The appearance of a regular passive verb form is designed to keep you honest. **Ducētūr**, *she will be led* is the future tense of the passive of the regular verb **dūcere**. The sentence reads *The deceased Anemia will be led by Mercury to the underworld*. The other answers give translations in the active voice, in anticipation of the incorrect identification of **dūcētur** as a deponent verb.

5. **(B)**
    This question tests your alertness to the fact that certain deponent verbs take a direct object in the ablative case. **Potior** is one of these verbs, and therefore **cadūceō** is the correct answer, leading to the meaning *For what reason did Mercury come into possession of the caduceus?* Answer (A) is the anticipated incorrect answer because **cadūceum** is accusative. Answers (C) and (D) are in the plural and therefore incorrect here because *caduceus* is singular. (For special deponents, see "Deponent Verbs with Ablative Direct Objects.")

6. **(B)**
    Vererīsne is in the present tense, second person singular *Are you afraid?* The equivalent in the active voice is **Timēs**. Answer (A) is plural and (B) is future tense. **Vererī** is a second conjugation verb, and therefore **Vererīs** is present tense, not future (which is **Verēbēris**). Answer (D) is a form of the imperfect subjunctive. Note the deponent infinitive **morī**, *to die*.

7. **(D)**
    In this question, you must decide between the present and future tenses, either of which could conceivably be expressed by the form **tuētur**. Because this verb belongs to the second conjugation, the form is in the

present tense, making (D), not (A), the correct answer. The Latin of (B) *should protect* is the subjunctive form **tueātur**. Answer (C) is not possible because the translation *is being protected* is passive, and **tueor** is a deponent verb. The sentence reads *Aesculapius protects all Romans*. (For the ambiguity between forms of the present and future tenses, see Chapter 19.)

8. **(B)**

Audeō is a semideponent verb, which has active meanings in the perfect system. **Ausī sunt** is in the perfect tense and has **medicī Rōmānī** as its subject. The sentence therefore reads *Roman doctors ventured to take care of themselves*. Answers (A) and (C) offer translations that are passive, which are not appropriate for a deponent form. Answer (D) is a red herring because it contains the translation *are*, which gives a meaning of **sunt** but not of **ausī sunt**. (See "Semideponent Verbs.")

Sententiae Antiquae Answers

1. **(A)**

Horace's sentence reads *Worry follows increasing money*. Therefore, a main verb is necessary to complete the meaning of the sentence. Answers (B) and (C), which are infinitives, do not serve this function. Answer (D) **secūtus es**, *you have followed*, does not have a personal ending that agrees with the nominative subject **cūra**.

2. **(A)**

Cicero's sentence reads *We have not been born for ourselves alone*. Because of the meaning *be born* in English, the verb **nascor** appears to be passive, but it is deponent. Therefore, the underlined form **nātī sumus** is a form of the perfect tense, which is translated *we have been born*, or better, *we are born* with the sense of *we are alive*. The translations in Answers (B), (C), and (D) are in the wrong tenses, namely, the present, imperfect, and pluperfect.

3. **(D)**

Pliny says *The undying souls of the dead speak in libraries*. The nominative subject **immortālēs animae** requires a plural verb, a fact that drops (A) and (C) from consideration. Answer (B) appears to be a likely option, but the verb **locutī erant** does not agree in gender with the subject **animae**.

4. **(D)**

The Latin reads literally *Not to go forward is to go backward*. The deponent infinitives **prōgredī** and **regredī** are examples of the subjective infinitive, which is the infinitive used as a noun subject (*going forward* and *going backward*). (For the subjective infinitive, see Chapter 26.)

5. **(D)**

Will follow requires a future tense in the Latin, so **sequentur** is the correct answer because **sequor** belongs to the third conjugation. Answer (A) **sequuntur** means *they are following*, (B) **secuta erunt** means *they will have followed*, and (C) **sequantur** means *let them follow*, a form of the jussive subjunctive. Only the first person singular form of the future tense contains an -**a**- vowel, **sequar**.

Stumper: **(C)**

Passī is the past participle of **patior** (from which, by the way, the English word "passive" is derived). Perfect passive participial forms may only be translated (literally) in the active voice if the verb is deponent, that is, as *having suffered* rather than as (B) *having been suffered*. Answer (A) *to suffer* translates the infinitive form **patī**, which is similar in appearance to the participial form **passī**. Answer (D) *they suffered* expresses a main verb, **passī sunt**, which includes the past participle in its form.

CHAPTER 21

Irregular Verbs

Chapter 21

IRREGULAR VERBS

REGULAR AND IRREGULAR VERBS

Look at the list of principal parts in the following chart. You will remember that irregular verbs do not conform to the patterns found in regular verbs. Irregular verbs are among the most commonly used verbs in Latin, as they are in many languages. They can stand alone, like **est**, become parts of other verb forms, such as **missus est** or **missus esse**, or be combined with prepositional prefixes to form a host of verbs that are related to them in meaning, as in **abesse**. Some tenses of irregular verbs conform to the patterns of regular verbs and contain familiar personal endings, but many of the forms of irregular verbs are unpredictable and must be memorized.

Principal Parts of Irregular Verbs

sum, esse, fuī, *be*

possum, posse, potuī, *be able*, *can*

eō, īre, iī (or **īvī**), *go*

ferō, ferre, tulī, lātus, *carry*, *bring*

volō, velle, voluī, *wish*, *want*

nōlō, nōlle, nōluī, *be unwilling*

mālō, mālle, māluī, *prefer*

fīō, fierī, factus sum, *become*, *happen*

Here are some examples of irregular verbs in context:

Habentne magistrī in memōriā sē discipulōs <u>fuisse</u>?
Do teachers ever remember that they themselves <u>were</u> students?

Rōmānī Athēnās <u>iērunt</u> ut linguam Graecam discerent.
Romans <u>went</u> to Athens in order to learn the Greek language.

<u>Veli</u>tne quisquam magister <u>fierī</u>?
<u>Would</u> anyone <u>wish</u> <u>to become</u> a teacher?

THE PRESENT INDICATIVE ACTIVE OF IRREGULAR VERBS

The forms of the present tense of irregular verbs are the most unpredict-able of the six tenses. Here are the forms of the present indicative of the common irregular verbs listed in the preceding table, except for **nōlo** and **mālō**, which approximate those of **volō**. Look for patterns within the irregularities and try to remember what you have previously learned about these verbs. Notice from the principal parts given above that only two irregular verbs, **ferō** and **fīō**, have passive forms.

Conjugations of the Present Tense of Irregular Verbs

	esse, *be*		**posse**, *be able*		**īre**, *go*	
	Singular	Plural	Singular	Plural	Singular	Plural
1st	**sum**	**sumus**	**possum**	**possumus**	**eō**	**īmus**
2nd	**es**	**estis**	**potes**	**potestis**	**īs**	**ītis**
3rd	**est**	**sunt**	**potest**	**possunt**	**it**	**eunt**

	ferō, *bring*		**velle**, *wish*		**fierī**, *become*	
	Singular	Plural	Singular	Plural	Singular	Plural
1st	**ferō**	**ferimus**	**volō**	**volumus**	**fīō**	**fīmus**
2nd	**fers**	**fertis**	**vīs**	**vultis**	**fīs**	**fītis**
3rd	**fert**	**ferunt**	**vult**	**volunt**	**fit**	**fiunt**

INDICATIVE ACTIVE OF IRREGULAR VERBS

All tenses of irregular verbs, except for the forms of the present, behave as their regular verb counterparts (stem + ending). For complete conju-gations of these forms, consult your textbook. For the forms, functions, and translations of imperatives, participles, and infinitives of these verbs, see the chapters in Sections 6, and 7.

Quick Study Synopses of Irregular Verbs

	esse	posse	īre
Present	est, *he is*	potest, *he is able*	it, *he is going*
Imperfect	erat, *he was*	poterat, *he was able*	ībat, *he was going, went*
Future	erit, *he will be*	poterit, *he will be able*	ībit, *he will go*
Perfect	fuit, *he has been, was*	potuit, *he has been able, could*	iit (or **īvit**), *he has gone, went*
Pluperfect	fuerat, *he had been*	potuerat, *he had been able*	ierat (or **īverat**), *he had gone*
Future Perfect	fuerit, *he will have been*	potuerit, *he will have been able*	ierit (or **īverit**), *he will have gone*

	ferre	velle	fierī
Present	fert, *he is bringing*	vult, *he is wishing*	fit, *he is becoming*
Imperfect	ferēbat, *he was bringing*	volēbat, *he was wishing*	fiēbat, *he was beoming*
Future	feret, *he will bring*	volet, *he will wish*	fiet, *he will become*
Perfect	tulit, *he has brought*	voluit, *he has wished*	factus est, *he has become*
Pluperfect	tulerat, *he had brought*	voluerat, *he had wished*	factus erat, *he had become*
Future Perfect	tulerit, *he will have brought*	voluerit, *he will have wished*	factus erit, *he will have become*

Sum, Esse, Fuī, *be, exist*

The forms of **esse** vary the most of any irregular verb. Remember that the third person plural of the future tense is **erunt** (be careful to distinguish this form from that of the third person plural of the perfect tense, **fuērunt**).

Although both **eram** and **fuī** may be translated *I was*, the former is in the imperfect tense, and thus the action is understood as <u>ongoing</u>, that is, *I was, over a period of time*. **Fuī** is in the perfect tense and shows <u>completed</u> action, as in *I was, and am no longer*.

Forms of the irregular verb **esse** may accompany participles in order to create other verb forms, such as **missus <u>erat</u>**, **missus <u>esset</u>**, **missus <u>esse</u>**, **missūrus <u>esse</u>**, **mittendus <u>est</u>**. Note that when this type of combination occurs, there is a change in the meaning of the form of **esse**: **missus <u>est</u>** means *he <u>has been</u> sent*, not *he <u>is</u> sent*. In a line of verse, forms of **esse** may be omitted from a two-part verb, such as **missūrus (esse)**, due to considerations of meter or dramatic effect.

Do not confuse the irregular verb **sumus**, *we are*, with the adjective **summus, -a, -um**, *the top of*.

Possum, Posse, Potuī, *be able, can*

The forms of **posse** derive from the adjective **potis**, meaning *able, capable*, which is attached as a prefix to various forms of **esse**. Before forms of **esse** beginning with **s-**, the **-t-** of **potis** is altered or assimilated to **-s-**, hence **potis** + **sum** = **possum** (as opposed to **potsum**). The **-t-** is retained before a vowel, as in **poteram** or **potuistī**.

When translating, note that in English, the past tense of *can* is *could*. Also be careful to distinguish the imperfect indicative **poteram** from the pluperfect indicative **potueram**, and the forms of the verb **posse** from those of the regular verb **pōnō, pōnere, posuī, positus**, *put, place*.

Eō, īre, lī (īvī), *go*

This verb behaves as the regular fourth conjugation verb **audiō** except for the future tense, where it changes to first/second conjugation forms, such as **ībō, ībīs, ībit**.

The alternative perfect tense form **īvī** is found much less often than **iī**; for example, the form **īveram** appears less commonly than **ieram**. The forms of the perfect tense of **īre** made from the **i-** stem are **iī, īstī, iit** and **iimus, īstis, iērunt**. Those made from the stem **īv-** are **īvī, īvistī, īvit** and **īvimus, īvistis, īvērunt**.

Distinguish **eō**, *I go*, from the adverb **eō**, *to this place*, by using context.

Ferō, Ferre, Tulī, Lātus, *bring, carry*

This irregular verb has the endings of a regular third conjugation verb, such as **mittere**, in the present system, although the stem vowel **-e-** is missing occasionally, such as from **ferre**, *to bring*. Take special note of these forms of the present tense: **fers, fert**, and **fertis**.

This verb has a passive voice, the forms of which are constructed and translated in a regular manner, as in the synopsis **fertur**, **ferēbātur**, **ferētur**, **lātus est**, **lātus erat**, **lātus erit**.

Avoid confusing the forms of **ferō**, **ferre** with those of **feriō**, **ferīre**, *strike*, *hit*.

Volō, Velle, Voluī, *wish*, *want*

Nōlō, Nōlle, Nōluī, *be unwilling*, *not wish*

Mālō, Mālle, Māluī, *prefer*, *want more*

These verbs often have the endings of regular third conjugation verbs, except for forms in the present tense (see the preceding chart, and also note the irregular forms of the present infinitives **velle**, **nōlle**, and **mālle**). The tenses of the perfect system are regularly formed.

Remember that the verb **nōlō** (**nōn** + **volō**) can become a compound form in the present tense, such as the singular, **nōlō**, **nōn vīs**, **nōn vult** and the plural, **nōlumus**, **nōn vultis**, **nōlunt**.

Volō, **velle** should be carefully distinguished from **volō**, **volāre**, *fly*, and from forms of the noun **vīs**, *force*, *strength*, by using the context.

Be careful not to confuse forms of the irregular verb **mālō** (**magis** + **volō**, *wish more*) with those of the adjective **malus**, **-a**, **-um**, *bad*.

Fiō, Fierī, Factus Sum, *become*, *happen*; *be made*

Fīō has forms much like the regular fourth conjugation verb **audiō**. The irregular verb **fierī** serves as the passive of the present system of the verb **facere**, for example **faciuntur**, *they are being made* has the same meaning as **fīunt**, *they become*. In the perfect system, passive forms appear as deponent verbs, such as **factī sunt**, *they have become*. **Fierī** can have either the active meanings *become*, *occur*, or *happen* or the passive meanings *be done* or *be made*. Consider both options when translating.

TIPS FOR TRANSLATING IRREGULAR VERBS

- Practice with the forms of irregular verbs and know the principal parts so that you are familiar with the patterns within the irregularity of each verb. Be able to make distinctions in tense and meaning among forms that are similar, such as **erunt**, **fuērunt**, **iērunt** or **erant**, **fuerant**, **ierant**.

- When translating, consider the irregular verb in the context of the sentence in which it is found.

  Other cues to the identity of an irregular verb may be provided in the sentence, as in the following example:

  Dum complūrēs in atrium intrābant, iam nunc multī in peristȳliō erant.
  While several people were entering the atrium, there were already many in the garden.

  In this sentence, the verb **intrābant** may be more familiar to you as a form of the imperfect tense than the irregular verb **erant**, leading you to the deduction that **erant** might be translated best in the imperfect tense.

- It is important to remember that forms of the imperfect tense **eram**, **erās**, **erat**, and so on, refer to <u>ongoing action</u> in the past and the forms of the perfect tense, **fuī**, **fuistī**, **fuit**, and so on, refer to <u>completed</u> action in the past.

- Remember that although the word "been" is used in translating forms of verbs in the perfect system of **esse**, such as in **fuit**, *he has been*, the verb has a meaning in the active voice.

- Remember that the forms of the irregular verb **fīō, fierī, factus sum** may be translated with meanings that are either active (*become, happen*) or passive (*be done* or *be made*), depending upon the context.

- The irregular verbs **ferre**, **īre**, and **sum** have many compound forms. These often exhibit assimilation, for example **afferre** (**ad** + **ferre**), *carry toward*, and **auferre** (**ab** + **ferre**), *carry away.*

SAMPLE QUESTIONS

Part A: Recognition of Forms

1. The present indicative passive of <u>fers</u> is

   (A) ferēris   (C) feriminī

   (B) ferēbāris   (D) ferris

Part C: Translation

2. Ad tabernam prope forum <u>eunt</u>.
    (A) they have gone   (C) they are going
    (B) they were   (D) they are

Part D: Sentence Completion

3. Cum Rōmae . . . , sē gerent similēs Rōmānīs.
    (A) fuērunt   (C) futūrī
    (B) erunt   (D) esse

Part F: Reading Comprehension

4. The tense and mood of <u>fīet</u> are
    (A) present indicative   (C) present subjunctive
    (B) imperfect indicative (D) future indicative

Answers

1. (D)   2. (C)   3. (B)   4. (D)

PRACTICE QUESTIONS

1. The perfect active indicative of <u>sunt</u> is

   (A) fuērunt   (C) fuerant

   (B) fuerint   (D) fuissent

2. The perfect active indicative of <u>potes</u> is

   (A) potuistis   (C) potueris

   (B) potuerās   (D) potuistī

3. Ego magister <u>factus eram</u>.

   (A) I was being made   (C) I had become

   (B) I was becoming   (D) I have been made

4. When <u>will we be able</u> to live in peace and harmony?

   (A) potuerimus   (C) poterimus

   (B) poterāmus   (D) possumus

5. <u>We went</u> to school.

   (A) imus   (C) iimus

   (B) eāmus   (D) ierāmus

6. Which verb is not in the present tense?

   (A) fuit   (C) vult

   (B) fert   (D) it

7. Coals <u>had been brought</u> to Newcastle.

   (A) ferēbant   (C) ferēbantur

   (B) lātī erant   (D) lātī sunt

8. Ubi lēgēs nōn valent, <u>poterit</u>ne populus līber esse?

   (A) will be able   (C) is able

   (B) was able   (D) will have been able

9. <u>Does</u> any student <u>prefer</u> to stay at home?

    (A) Maluitne?   (C) Mavultne?

    (B) Malēbatne?   (D) Maletne?

10. <u>Nōn ferēmus</u>.

    (A) We are not enduring.

    (B) We shall not be endured.

    (C) We shall not endure.

    (D) We have not endured.

Stumper:

The prince <u>had become</u> a pauper.

(A) factus est   (C) fēcit

(B) factus erat   (D) fēcerat

SENTENTIAE ANTIQUAE

1. <u>Annī eunt modō fluentis aquae</u>. (Ovid)

    The basic meaning of this thought is

    (A) Time flies.

    (B) O the times, O the values!

    (C) Seize the day.

    (D) Make haste slowly.

2. If <u>you prefer</u> peace and quiet, take a wife of equal station. (Quintilian)

    (A) malēbās   (C) māvīs

    (B) māluerās   (D) maluistī

3. In this Republic, <u>there were</u> once men of great character and reliability. (Cicero)

    (A) fuerant   (C) essent

    (B) erant   (D) sunt

4. <u>Possunt quia posse videntur.</u> (Vergil)

    (A) They could since they seemed to be able.

    (B) They can since they seemed to be able.

    (C) They could since they seem to be able.

    (D) They are able since they seem to be able.

5. <u>Magnae rēs nōn fiunt sine perīculō.</u> (Terence)

    The basic meaning of this thought is

    (A) Always carry an umbrella.

    (B) No pain, no gain.

    (C) Only the simple things matter.

    (D) We have nothing to fear but fear itself.

Answers

1. **(A)**
    The perfect tense forms of **esse** have regular endings. Answer (B) is in the future perfect tense, (C) is in the pluperfect indicative, and (D) is in the pluperfect subjunctive.

2. **(D)**
    The verb **posse** has the endings of regular verbs in the perfect tense, plus the stem **potu-**, hence **potuistī**, *you were* or *have been able* is equivalent in the perfect tense to the present tense form **potes**, *you are able*. Answer (A) is in the perfect tense and is in the second person, but is plural. Answer (B) **potuerās** is pluperfect, *you had been able*, and (C) **potueris** is future perfect, *you will have been able*.

3. **(C)**
    The perfect system of the passive voice of **facere** is translated as a deponent verb, that is, with the active meaning of *happen* or *become*. The form **factus eram** is in the pluperfect tense, therefore the verb means *I had become*. Answers (A) and (B) require **fiēbam** and (C) requires **factus sum**.

4. **(C)**

Answer (A) is to be distinguished from the correct answer because the perfect stem is found in (A) **potuerimus**, making this form future perfect. The underlined translation *will we be able* in the sentence calls for **poterimus**, a form in the future tense. Answer (B) **poterāmus** is pluperfect, *we had been able*, and (D) **possumus** is present, *we are able*.

5. **(C)**

We went requires a form of the imperfect or perfect tense of the verb **ire**. Because no form of the imperfect tense is available among the choices, (C) **iimus** is correct. Answer (A) **imus** is in the present indicative, and (B) **eāmus** is in the present tense of the subjunctive mood. Answer (D) is pluperfect, *we had gone*.

6. **(A)**

Answer (A) **fuit** contains the perfect stem **fu-** and therefore is a form of the perfect tense of **esse**, *he has been* or *he was*. Answers (B), (C), and (D) are all in the present tense.

7. **(B)**

The translation *had been brought* requires a passive form of the pluperfect tense of **ferre**, thus, **lātī erant**. Answer (A) is in the active voice and (C) and (D) are in the wrong tenses, that is, imperfect and perfect. Remember that among irregular verbs, only **ferō** and **fīō** have passive forms.

8. **(A)**

Poterit is in the future tense and is thus translated *will be able*. The sentence reads *When the laws are not strong, will the people be able to be free?* Answer (B) translates a verb in the imperfect or perfect tense, (C) is in the present tense, and (D) is in the future perfect.

9. **(C)**

Does prefer requires the present tense in Latin, leading to the answer **māvult**, which is a compound form of the verb **volō**. Answer (A) **māluit** is perfect tense (note the tense indicator **-u-**), (B) **mālēbat** is imperfect tense, and (D) **mālet** is future tense.

10. **(C)**

The **-e-** vowel present in **ferēmus** makes this a form of the future tense. It cannot be translated in the present tense because **ferre** is an irregular verb, rather than a verb of the third conjugation. Answer (A) requires the present tense (**ferimus**), (B) the future passive (**ferēmur**), and (D) the perfect tense (**tulimus**).

Stumper: **(B)**

The tense of the underlined verb is pluperfect, eliminating (A) and (C), which are in the perfect tense. Because *had become* is equivalent to *had been made*, the passive form **factus erat** is required rather than the active form **fēcerat**. (See **"Fīō, Fierī, Factus Sum."**)

Sententiae Antiquae Answers

1. **(A)**

Ovid's sentence reads *The years go (by) in the manner of flowing water*. The verb **eunt** is the present tense of **īre**. The subject of this sentence is **annī**, *years*, which leads to the immediate conclusion that the sentence has something to do with time.

2. **(C)**

You prefer requires the present tense of the irregular verb **mālle** in the second person, which is **māvīs**. Answer (A) **mālēbas** means *you were preferring*; (B) **mālueras**, *you had preferred*; and (D) **maluistī**, *you (have) preferred*.

3. **(B)**

The underlined verb *there were* is translated by a form of the imperfect tense of the verb **esse**, which is **erant**. (**Fuērunt** is not an option given here.) Answer (A) **fuerant**, *they had been* is pluperfect tense; (C) **essent** is imperfect tense, but subjunctive; and (D) **sunt**, *they are* is present tense.

4. **(D)**

This question tests command of forms of the verb **posse** and also the use of the passive of **vidēre** as a deponent verb. The correct answer is *They are able because they seem to be able*. **Possunt** is in the present tense, so (A) and (C), containing the translation *could*, which expresses the past tense in English, are incorrect. Answer (B) translates the present tense form **videntur** as *seemed*, which is in the past tense, and therefore also incorrect. (See Chapter 20, "Additional Information about Deponent Verbs.")

5. **(B)**

Terence's sentence reads *Great events don't come about without risk*. Of the answers available, the closest in meaning to this is (B) *No pain, no gain*.

CHAPTER 22

Impersonal Verbs

Chapter 22

IMPERSONAL VERBS

Impersonal verbs are found in the third person singular and have the ending **-t** and the nonpersonal subject "it," for example, **Claudiō placet**, *it is pleasing* (*to*) *Claudius* or *Claudius is pleased*. Some impersonal verbs, such as **placet**, can be used personally, that is, with a subject that is expressed, as in the following example:

> **Bōlētī placent Claudiō.**
> *Mushrooms please Claudius.*

Impersonal verbs may also appear as gerunds or infinitives. There are about 15 of these verbs that appear commonly in Latin, many of which belong to the second conjugation. Most are followed by an infinitive phrase, but some may also be followed by a subjunctive clause. When there is need for variation in tense, the tense change appears in the impersonal, such as **placet**, **placēbat**, **placēbit**. Forms of the impersonal verb are found in both the indicative and subjunctive moods. Because impersonal verbs are common in Latin but rare in English, the literal translation of an impersonal construction in Latin should be rephrased in English, as in this example:

> **Pudēbatne Claudium claudum esse?**
> *Was Claudius ashamed to be lame?* (Literally, *Was it shaming Claudius to be lame?*)

The subject of the sentences in this chapter is the life and times of the emperor Claudius, as he is portrayed in the film series *I, Claudius*.

IMPERSONAL VERB + (ACCUSATIVE OR DATIVE) + (INFINITIVE OR SUBJUNCTIVE)

Impersonal Verbs with the Accusative or Dative Case

With the accusative:

accidit, accidere, accidit, *it happens*

decet, decēre, decuit, *it is proper, fitting; one should*

iuvat, iuvāre, *it pleases*

necesse est, *it is necessary*

oportet, oportēre, oportuit, *it is fitting; one ought* or *must*

With the dative:

libet, libēre, libuit, *it is pleasing, agreeable*

licet, licēre, licuit, *it is allowed, permitted; one may*

opus est, *there is need, it is necessary*

placet, placēre, placuit, *it pleases; one likes*

vidētur, vidērī, *it seems* (See also Chapter 20, "Deponent Verbs with Additional Meanings.")

Observe the function of the impersonal verbs **necesse erat** and **libēbat** in the following sentences. Note that the impersonal is accompanied by a noun in either the accusative or dative case, plus an infinitive:

acc.   infin.

Caligulā occīsō, necesse erat <u>militēs</u> novum imperātōrem <u>eligere</u>.
When Caligula was killed, it was necessary <u>for the soldiers</u> <u>to select</u> a new emperor.

dat.   infin.

Libēbatne <u>Claudiō</u> imperātor <u>fierī</u>?
Was it agreeable <u>to Claudius</u> <u>to become</u> (<u>that he become</u>) emperor?

The semideponent verb **soleō, solēre, solitus sum,** *be accustomed, usual,* and the verb **debeō, debēre, debuī, debitus,** *owe, ought, be obligated, should,* can appear to be impersonal verbs because their forms are often found in the third person and are accompanied by an infinitive. However, they always have personal subjects, as in the following examples:

Caligula crūdēlis esse <u>solēbat</u>.
Caligula <u>was in the habit of</u> being cruel.

Caligula propter crūdēlitātem punīrī <u>debet</u>.
Caligula <u>ought</u> to be punished for his cruelty.

Impersonal verbs may also be accompanied by a subjunctive clause, with or without **ut**, as in this example:

subjunctive

Licēbatne Claudiō [(ut) fīliam frātris uxōrem duceret?]
Was Claudius permitted [to marry (i.e., that he marry) his niece?]

IMPERSONAL VERB + ACCUSATIVE + (GENITIVE OR INFINITIVE)

This type of impersonal verb expresses <u>feelings or emotion</u> and is followed by the accusative (of the person or persons feeling the emotion) and the genitive (of the cause or reason for the emotion), as in this sentence:

acc.   gen.

Nōn taedēbat <u>Tiberium</u> <u>vitae</u> Capreīs.
<u>*Tiberius*</u> *was not bored <u>with life</u> on Capri* (literally, *It was not boring Tiberius of life on Capri*).

When such impersonal verbs are used, some rephrasing of the English is necessary in order to clarify the meaning of the Latin. Such verbs may be accompanied alternatively by an infinitive phrase, in place of the genitive case, as in this sentence:

acc.   infin.

Nōn paenituit Tiberium Rōmā <u>egredi</u>.
Tiberius did not regret <u>leaving</u> Rome (literally, *It did not make Tiberius feel regret to leave Rome*).

Impersonal verbs with the accusative + genitive or infinitive:

---

miseret, miserēre, miseruit, *it makes one* (acc.) *feel pity* or *feel sorry for something* (gen.)

paenitet, paenitēre, paenituit, *it makes one* (acc.) *regret* or *repent of something* (gen.)

piget, **pigēre**, **piguit**, *it annoys, disgusts, causes one* (acc.) *to be ashamed of something* (gen.)

pudet, **pudēre**, **puduit**, *it shames, makes one* (acc.) *ashamed of something* (gen.)

taedet, **taedēre**, **taesum est**, *it bores, makes one* (acc.) *tired of something* (gen.)

PASSIVE VERBS USED IMPERSONALLY

Intransitive verbs (i.e., verbs that do not take a direct object), may be used in the third person singular of the passive, with the implied subject "it," for example:

> **Ab imperātōre ad mūnera perventum est.**
> *The emperor arrived at the public show* (literally, *It was arrived by the emperor . . .*)

Such verbs are used impersonally when the writer or speaker wishes to emphasize the action, rather than the person/s performing the action. Good English requires rephrasing of passive verbs used impersonally, such as **fortiter pugnābātur**, which is best translated as *the fighting was fierce*, whereas a literal rendering would give *it was fought fiercely*. Verbs such as **parcere**, *spare*, **persuādēre**, *convince*, **pugnāre**, *fight*, and compound forms of **venīre**, such as **pervenīre**, *arrive*, appear impersonally in the passive.

TIPS ON TRANSLATING IMPERSONAL VERBS

- An impersonal verb differs from a personal verb by requiring the nonpersonal subject "it" in most cases. After working out the meaning of the impersonal verb and its accompanying forms, recast the wording in comprehensible English.

- The impersonal verb is often found at the front of a Latin sentence, but it could be located anywhere.

- Be alert to the fact that the case of the noun or pronoun that accompanies the impersonal verb can be accusative, dative, or genitive.

- Note the tense of the impersonal verb and also whether it is accompanied by an infinitive phrase or a subjunctive clause.

SAMPLE QUESTIONS

Part C: Translation

1.   <u>Eum domī manēre oportet</u>.

    (A) He ought to stay home.

    (B) It is appropriate that he stay home.

    (C) It was necessary for him to stay home.

    (D) He must stay home.

Part D: Sentence Completion

2.   Hoc dīcere . . . nōn licet.

    (A) vestrōs   (C) vōbīs

    (B) vōs   (D) tē

Answers

1.   (A)   2.   (C)

PRACTICE QUESTIONS

1.   In pictūrā moventī *Sum Claudius*, multōs venēnō necāre . . . placēbat.

    (A) Līviae   (C) Līviā

    (B) Līviam   (D) Līvia

2.   <u>Nōn decēbat Caligulam</u> dīcere "Ōderint, dum metuant."

    (A) Caligula was not allowed

    (B) It was not necessary for Caligula

    (C) Caligula was not ashamed

    (D) It was not appropriate for Caligula

3. <u>Julia was weary of exile</u>.

   (A) Iūlia (Jūlia) exsilī taedēbat.

   (B) Iūliae (Jūliae) exsilium taedēbat.

   (C) Iūliam (Jūliam) exsilī taedēbat.

   (D) Iūliam (Jūliam) exsilium taedēbat.

4. Vidēbātur . . . Claudium stultum esse.

   (A) Līvia   (C) Līviae

   (B) Līviam   (D) Līviā

5. <u>Piget Līviam linguae haesitātiōnis Claudī.</u>

   The basic meaning of this sentence is that

   (A) Claudius feels pity for Livia's stuttering.

   (B) Claudius's stuttering is agreeable to Livia.

   (C) Livia permits Claudius to stutter.

   (D) Claudius's stuttering disgusts Livia.

6. "<u>Oportuit</u> Germānōs signa legiōnum reddere!" exclamābat Augustus.

   (A) Ought   (C) Can

   (B) Did   (D) Might

7. <u>Debēbat</u>ne Claudius Britanniam vincere?

   (A) Was forbidden   (C) Was obligated

   (B) Was permitted   (D) Was encouraged

8. <u>Women were not allowed</u> to be emperors.

   (A) Fēminīs nōn licet   (C) Fēminae nōn licēbant

   (B) Fēminae nōn licēbat (D) Fēminīs nōn licēbat

9. Tacitus scrīpsit Nerōnem Rōmam incendere <u>nōn paenitēre</u>.

   (A) did not regret   (C) is not punished

   (B) is not permitted   (D) ought not

10. Caligulā imperātōre, <u>accidit</u> ut equus senātor fieret.

    (A) it happened   (C) it pleased

    (B) it was appropriate   (D) it was necessary

SENTENTIAE ANTIQUAE

1. Infāmiae suae neque <u>pudet et taedet</u>. (Cicero, *Against Verres*)

    These words refer to

    (A) shame and weariness (C) misery and repentance

    (B) regret and pity   (D) pleasure and pain

2. A liar <u>ought</u> to have a good memory. (Quintilian)

    (A) licet   (C) oportet

    (B) placet   (D) decet

3. <u>Decet verēcundum esse adulescentem</u>. (Plautus)

    (A) It is shameful for a young person to be modest.

    (B) A young person can regret being modest.

    (C) It is proper for a young person to be modest.

    (D) There is need for young people to be modest.

4. Quodque libet facere . . . licet. (Seneca)

    (A) victor   (C) victōrī

    (B) victōrem   (D) victōris

5. Placeat . . . quidquid deō placuit. (Seneca)

    (A) hominem   (C) hominī

    (B) homō   (D) homine

Stumper:

> <u>Aedificāre in tuō propriō sōlō nōn licet quod alterī noceat</u>. (legal axiom)

(A) You are allowed to build whatever you like on your own property.

(B) If someone hurts himself while building on your property, you are at fault.

(C) You are allowed to build on your own property only what does not harm another.

(D) No one should harm another while in a building on your property.

Answers

1. **(A)**
   When used impersonally, **placēre** takes a dative object, therefore the missing form of the word **Līvia** should appear in the dative case, which is (A). The sentence reads *In the movie* I, Claudius, *it was pleasing <u>to Livia</u> to kill many (people) with poison*. Answer (B) **Līviam**, an accusative, is an obvious but incorrect answer. Answers (C) **Līviā** and (D) **Līvia** have no function in this sentence. (See "Impersonal Verb + [Accusative or Dative] + [Infinitive or Subjunctive].")

2. **(D)**
   Because all the verbs are given in the imperfect tense, you are asked to select the correct meaning of (**nōn**) **decēbat** (**Caligulam**), which is *it was (not) appropriate (for Caligula)*. The sentence reads *It was not appropriate for Caligula to say, "Let them hate (me), so long as they fear (me)."* Answer (A) *was allowed* requires **licēbat**, (B) *was necessary* requires **necesse erat**, and (C) *was ashamed* needs **pudēbat**.

3. **(C)**
   Taedēbat, as a verb expressing emotion, takes an accusative of the person and a genitive of the cause or reason for the emotion. In (C), **Iūliam** (**Jūliam**) is accusative and **exsilī** genitive, giving the literal meaning *It was not wearying <u>Julia of exile</u>*. Answers (A), (B), and (D) do not have the correct combination of accusative and genitive forms: (A) has nominative and genitive, (B) dative/genitive and accusative, and (D) accusative and accusative. (See "Impersonal Verb + Accusative + [Genitive or Infinitive].")

4. **(C)**

This sentence reads *It seemed to Livia that Claudius was foolish*. The missing noun must be the dative form **Līviae** after the impersonal verb **vidēbātur** (see Chapter 8, "Dative with Certain Types of Verbs"). Answers (A), (B), and (D) are all in the incorrect case, the nominative, accusative, and ablative, respectively.

5. **(D)**

Piget, another verb expressing emotion, is found with the accusative, **Liviam**, and genitive, **linguae haesitātiōnis**. (**Claudī** is simply a possessive genitive, unrelated to the use of the impersonal verb here.) Answer (A) would require an exchange of Livia and Claudius in the sentence and the appearance of the lookalike verb **pudet**. Answers (B) and (C) mistranslate **piget** as *is agreeable* and *permits*, respectively. (See "Impersonal Verb + Accusative + [Genitive or Infinitive].")

6. **(A)**

Of the choices of meanings for **oportuit** in this sentence, *ought* is the most appropriate. Answer (B) *did* simply translates the tense of **oportuit**. Answers (C) *can* requires the verb **posse**, and (D) *might* requires the subjunctive mood. The sentence reads *"The Germans ought to return the legionary standards," exclaimed Augustus*. The accusative form **Germānōs** is consistent with the appearance of the irregular verb **oportuit**. (See "Impersonal Verb + [Accusative or Dative] + [Infinitive or Subjunctive].")

7. **(C)**

This question tests your knowledge of the meaning of the verb **debēre**, which has the sense of obligation, that is, something one ought to do or should do. Hence, the sentence reads *Was Claudius obliged to conquer Britain?* The answers *forbid, permit*, and *encourage* require other verbs.

8. **(D)**

The impersonal verb **licēbat** is found with the dative case, therefore (D) **fēminīs licēbat** is correct. Answer (A) **fēminīs licet** has the incorrect tense. Answer (B) **fēminae** is singular when a plural is required (*women*) and (C) **fēminae** incorrectly serves as the subject of the impersonal verb.

9. **(A)**
    The impersonal verb **paenitet** means *regret* (as in penance and peni-tent), therefore (A) is correct. The sentence reads *Tacitus writes that Nero did not regret burning Rome*. The infinitive **paenitēre** is used in an indirect statement. Answer (B) requires the verb **licēre**, (C) requires the verb **punīre** (etymologically akin to **paenitēre**), and (D) requires **oportēre**.

10. **(A)**
    This sentence reads *While Caligula was Emperor, it happened that a horse became a senator*. The meaning of the verb **accidit** is *it happens* or *it happened*. The imperfect tense of the subjunctive **fieret** in the substantive result clause requires that **accidit** be translated as a past tense in this sentence. Answer (B) requires **decēbat** in the Latin, (C) requires **placēbat**, and (D) requires **necesse erat**.

Sententiae Antiquae Answers

1. **(A)**
    The meanings of the impersonals **pudet** and **taedet** are *it is shameful* and *it is wearisome*, respectively, so (A) is correct. Answer (B) requires the verbs **paenitet** and **miseret**, and (C) and (D) require words that do not relate to impersonal verbs. The sentence reads *(Verres) is neither ashamed of nor bored with his own ill fame*.

2. **(C)**
    The word *ought* requires the impersonal verb **oportet**. Answer (A) **licet** means *permitted* or *allowed*, (B) **placet** means *pleased*, and (D) **decet** means *fitting* or *appropriate*.

3. **(C)**
    Because **decet** means *it is fitting* or *it is appropriate*, (C) is the best re-sponse. Answers (A) *shameful* and (B) *regret* do not give acceptable mean-ings of the impersonal verb **decet**. Answer (D) gives the wrong sense of **decet** and translates **adulescentem** as plural.

4. **(C)**
    Seneca's statement, *A victor is allowed to do whatever he likes*, requires that the word **victor** be in the dative case after the impersonal verb **licet**, namely, *it is permitted to the victor*. The nominative, accusative, and genitive cases found in (A), (B), and (D) are not relevant in this sentence.

5. **(C)**
This sentence reads *Let whatever has been acceptable to god be acceptable to* <u>*mankind*</u>. The dative form **deō** with the impersonal verb **placuit** prompts recognition of the fact that the case of the missing noun will also be dative, that is, **hominī**. Answer (A) is accusative, (B) is nominative, and (D) is ablative. Note the appearance of the independent jussive subjunctive form **placeat**, *let it be acceptable* (see Chapter 28, "Jussive and Hortatory Subjunctives").

Stumper: **(C)**
Neither (B) nor (D) contains in their translations the proper meaning of the impersonal verb **licet**. Answer (A) seems likely until you notice that *whatever you like* does not correctly render **quod alterī noceat**, which means *(the type of thing) that may be harmful to another* in the original sentence. This is a relative clause of characteristic with the subjunctive. (See Chapter 8, "Dative with Certain Types of Verbs.")

THE SAT SUBJECT TEST IN
LATIN

SECTION 6

Imperatives

CHAPTER 23

Direct Address: Commands, Direct Questions, and the Vocative Case

Chapter 23

DIRECT ADDRESS: COMMANDS, DIRECT QUESTIONS, AND THE VOCATIVE CASE

THE IMPERATIVE MOOD

You will remember that the term "mood" indicates the way in which a verb functions in a sentence. Now that we have reviewed the indicative, we will review the second mood of the three, the imperative, which expresses a command or prohibition. The imperative mood appears less often than the indicative and subjunctive moods. This chapter will present the positive and negative imperatives of regular, deponent, and irregular verbs, as well as the vocative case of nouns, which is often found in association with imperatives. Although the imperative has forms in both the present and future tenses, only the present tense will be reviewed in this book.

COMMANDS AND PROHIBITIONS

Positive Imperatives of Regular Verbs

The present imperative (**imperāre**, *to order*) does just what it says: it orders or commands an action, such as **Tacē!** (*You alone*) *be quiet!* and **Tacēte!** (*You all*) *be quiet!* Note that the imperative commands someone in the second person, or *you*, which is "understood" in both Latin and English.

Imperatives of Regular Verbs

	Singular	Plural
1st conjugation (**stāre**)	**stā**, (*you alone*) *stand*	**stāte**, (*you all*) *stand*
2nd conjugation (**sedēre**)	**sedē**, (*you alone*) *sit*	**sedēte**, (*you all*) *sit*
3rd conjugation (**legere**)	**lege**, (*you alone*) *read*	**legite**, (*you all*) *read*
4th conjugation (**audīre**)	**audī**, (*you alone*) *listen*	**audīte**, (*you all*) *listen*

The present imperative in the singular has the same form as the present stem of the verb: both are formed by dropping **-re** from the present infinitive. Thus the present stem and present imperative singular of the verb **mittere** are both **mitte**. The plural is formed by adding **-te** to the present stem, except in verbs of the third conjugation, where the stem vowel changes from **-e-** to **-i-**. For example, from the present stem **mitte-** comes the plural imperative form **mittite**.

Polite commands in the first and third persons (*Let us . . . , Let him . . .*) are expressed with the present subjunctive, such as the well-known verse often sung or played at graduation ceremonies:

> **<u>Gaudeāmus</u> igitur, iuvenēs (juvenēs) dum sumus.**
> *<u>Let us</u> therefore <u>rejoice</u> while we are young.*

When identifying and translating imperatives, observe punctuation that signifies direct address, such as quotation marks and exclamation points, as in the following example:

> **"Cavē canem!" Doofus in murō suprā stercus scrīpsit.**
> *"<u>Watch out for</u> the dog!" Doofus wrote on the wall above the poop.*

The verbs **dīcere**, **dūcere**, **facere**, and **ferre** have irregular forms of the present imperative: **dīc**, **dūc**, **fac**, and **fer**. The plurals are regular: **dīcite**, **dūcite**, **facite**, and **ferte** (but note the dropped **-i-** in **ferte**). This rhyme may help your memory:

> **Dūc, dīc, fac, and fer**, should have an **-e**, but it isn't there.*

---

* Keith Berman; see David Pellegrino, http://latinteach.com/verbmnemonics.html.

Positive Imperatives of Deponent Verbs

Singular	Plural
conārī, *(you alone) try*	**conāminī**, *(you all) try*

The present imperative in the singular is an abbreviation of the second person <u>singular</u> of the present passive. In the preceding example, **conāris**, *you are trying*, becomes **conāre**, *(you) try*.

Note that the plural form of the present imperative is the same as the second person <u>plural</u> of the present passive. Imperatives of deponent verbs in the other conjugations are formed and translated in the same way.

Positive Imperatives of Irregular Verbs

	Singular	Plural
esse	**es**, *(you alone) be*	**este**, *(you all) be*
īre	**ī**, *(you alone) go*	**īte**, *(you all) go*
ferre	**fer**, *(you alone) bring*	**ferte**, *(you all) bring*

Negative Imperatives (Prohibitions)

Negative commands in Latin are expressed by the present imperative of the irregular verb **nōlō** in the singular or plural, **nōlī** or **nōlīte**, plus the present active infinitive of the verb giving the command, as in the following sentences:

> **"<u>Nōlī dormīre</u> in ludō, Doofe!" admonuit grammaticus Tuxtax.**
> *"<u>Don't sleep</u> in class, Doofus!" admonished the teacher Tuxtax.*

> **"<u>Nōlīte dormīre</u> in ludō, discipulī!" admonuit grammaticus Tuxtax.**
> *"<u>Don't sleep</u> in class, students!" admonished the teacher Tuxtax.*

Avoid translating **nōlī** in a prohibition as *(I) don't want to. . . .*

In poetry, **nē** + the positive imperative expresses a prohibition, such as:

> **Equō <u>nē crēdite</u>, Teucrī!** (Vergil)
> *<u>Don't trust</u> the horse, Trojans!*

DIRECT QUESTIONS

A direct question is an inquiry addressed to a person or persons. It can be introduced by a variety of "question words," followed by a verb in the indicative mood. Question words can indicate that the person asking the question wants to prompt a preconceived answer, which is known in English as a "leading question." Look for the question mark when identifying a direct question.

Nōnne (which may be considered a double negative, **nōn** + **-ne**) asks for the answer *yes*; that is, the person asking the question would like you to agree:

> **<u>Nōnne</u> Doofus molestus discipulus est?**
> *Doofus <u>is</u> an annoying student, <u>isn't he</u>?* or *<u>Isn't</u> Doofus an annoying student?*

The answer *yes* in Latin is commonly expressed by **ita**, **ita vērō**, **vērō**, or a repeat of the verb, as in the following exchange:

> **"Nōnne Doofus molestus discipulus est?" "Est."**
> *"Isn't Doofus an annoying student?" "He is."*

Num calls for the answer *no*, for example,

> **<u>Num</u> Doofus litterās memoriā tenēre potest?**
> *Doofus <u>can't</u> remember the alphabet, <u>can he</u>?* or *Surely Doofus <u>can't</u> remember the alphabet?*

The answer *no* is commonly expressed by **minimē**, **minimē vērō**, or **nōn**, which would give the answer **nōn potest** in the preceding example.

The enclitic particle **-ne** is usually attached to the verb, which is placed at the beginning of the sentence. This type of question simply asks for information, such as a *yes* or *no* answer:

> **Erant<u>ne</u> omnēs grammaticī Graecī?**
> *Were all teachers Greek?* (*Yes* or *no*, your choice)

Here are some other common words that can introduce a direct question:

Cum? *When?*	**Quō?** *Where to?*
Cur? *Why?*	**Quōmodō?** *How?*
Quālis? *What sort of?*	**Quot?** *How many?*
Quam? *How? To what extent?*	**Quotiēns?** *How often?*

Quandō? *When?*   **Ubi?** *Where? When?*

Quantum? *How big? How much?*   **Unde?** *From where?*

For the interrogative pronoun **quis, quis, quid**, see Chapter 12.

There are other types of questions in Latin, such as rhetorical questions and double questions, the details of which are beyond the scope of this book. Questions expressed with the verb in the subjunctive mood, such as the deliberative question and the indirect question, are presented in upcoming chapters.

THE VOCATIVE CASE

It is appropriate to review the vocative case at this time because this noun form so often accompanies the imperative mood of verbs. The vocative or "calling" case (**vocāre**, *to use the voice*) is used to identify or name a person or thing to whom a command, question, or statement is addressed directly. As you will remember after looking at the following examples, the form of the vocative is the same as the nominative for all declensions, singular and plural, except for second declension masculine nouns, where there is a change in the ending. For second declension nouns ending in **-us**, the ending changes to **-e**; for nouns ending in **-ius**, the **-us** is dropped. The plural form of the vocative of a noun from any declension is always the same as the nominative plural.

> **"Respondē Latīnē, <u>Doofe</u>," praecipit Tuxtax.**
> *"Reply in Latin, <u>Doofus</u>," instructs Tuxtax.*

> **Tuxtax gemuit, "<u>Efflūvī</u>, dōnā mihi pācem!"**
> *"<u>Effluvius</u>, give me a break!" groaned Tuxtax.*

> **"Claudite librōs, <u>discipulī</u>, et mentēs aperīte!"**
> *"Close your books, <u>students</u>, and open your minds!"*

Be alert for punctuation that helps to differentiate nominative forms from vocative:

Direct statement: **Tuxtax Doofum reprehendit.**
                                      Tuxtax (nominative) *is scolding Doofus.*

Direct address: **Tuxtax, Doofum reprehendit.**
                                      Tuxtax (vocative), *he* (someone else) *is scolding Doofus.*

In the second example, the comma defines **Tuxtax** as vocative and the sentence as one of direct address. (By the way, the name Tuxtax means *plenty of whacks*.)

The vocative form of the adjective **meus** is **mī**, as in the following:

> **Cēnābis bene, <u>mī Fābulle</u>, apud mē.** (Catullus)
> *You will dine well at my place, <u>my</u> (<u>friend</u>) <u>Fabullus</u>.*

TIPS ON TRANSLATING DIRECT ADDRESS

- When identifying and translating imperatives, direct questions, and vocative forms, observe punctuation that signifies direct address, such as exclamation points, quotation or question marks, and commas.

- Avoid translating **nōlī** in a prohibition as (*I*) *don't want to*. . . .

- Be careful to distinguish forms of the vocative singular from those of other noun cases, such as ablative (**senātōre**) and genitive (**Marcī**). Context will usually help.

PRACTICE QUESTIONS

1. . . . bene, discipule!

   (A) Notāte   (C) Notāre

   (B) Notā   (D) Nōlīte notāre

2. "Extende manum, . . . !" admonuit īrātus Tuxtax.

   (A) Errōnius   (C) Errōnī

   (B) Erroniī   (D) Errōniō

3. Semper . . . vēritātem, Doofe.

   (A) dīcite   (C) dīc

   (B) nōlīte dīcere   (D) dīcī

4. <u>Doofus is here, isn't he?</u>

    (A) Num Doofus adest?

    (B) Nōnne Doofus adest?

    (C) Estne hīc, annōn?

    (D) Adestne Doofus?

5. . . . diem, discipulī!

    (A) Carpe   (C) Nōlī carpere

    (B) Carpite   (D) Carpī

6. Ignosce mihi, . . .

    (A) grammaticus   (C) grammaticum

    (B) grammaticī   (D) grammatice

7. <u>Nōlī obdormīre!</u>

    (A) Don't fall asleep!

    (B) I don't want to fall asleep!

    (C) Don't want to fall asleep!

    (D) I wish you wouldn't fall asleep!

8. The vocative singular of <u>my friend</u> is

    (A) mī amīce   (C) mī amīcō

    (B) meus amīcus   (D) meī amīcī

9. <u>Num studēs?</u>
    The expected answer is

    (A) Ita vērō   (C) Studeō

    (B) Nōn sciō   (D) Minimē

10. <u>Quō</u> hodiē īre vīs?

    (A) When   (C) With whom

    (B) Where to   (D) Why

SENTENTIAE ANTIQUAE

1. <u>Disce aut discede</u>. (school motto)

   (A) Teach or leave.   (C) Behave or depart.

   (B) Learn or leave.   (D) Dance or die.

2. <u>Saepe stilum verte bonum libellum scriptūrus</u>. (Horace)

   (<u>stilum vertere</u> = *to turn over the stylus, to erase*)

   (A) Good reading leads to good writing.

   (B) Write much to write well.

   (C) Use a good pencil when writing.

   (D) Much editing makes for good writing.

3. . . . , ō Venerēs Cupidīnēsque! (Catullus)

   (A) Lūge   (C) Lūgēte

   (B) Lūgērī   (D) Lūgēre

4. Ō rūs, <u>quandō</u> ego tē aspiciam? (Horace)

   (A) how   (C) where

   (B) when   (D) why

5. . . . in arma properāre, Rōmānī! (anonymous)

   (A) Nōlō   (C) Nōlle

   (B) Nōlī   (D) Nōlīte

6. <u>Nōnne iubēbis</u> (<u>jubēbis</u>) Catilīnam in vincula dūcī? (Cicero)

   (A) You won't order, will you?

   (B) Will you order?

   (C) Surely you won't order?

   (D) You will order, won't you?

7.   . . . Catulle, dēsinās ineptīre. (Catullus)

   (A) Misere   (C) Miser

   (B) Miserī   (D) Miserō

8.   Ludī magister, . . . sīmplicī turbae. (Martial)

   (A) parce   (C) parcere

   (B) parcite   (D) parsus

Stumper:

   Crēde mihi, miserōs prūdentia prīma relinquit. (Ovid)

   (A) Trust me, good sense makes people unhappy.

   (B) Believe me, for the unhappy the first thing to go is good
        sense.

   (C) I believe that unhappiness makes people judgmental.

   (D) To believe that I am unhappy abandons good sense.

Answers

1. **(B)**
    The punctuation reveals this sentence to be a direct command. Be-
cause **discipule**, a single student, is being addressed, the answer must be
a singular form of the imperative, which is (B) **Notā**. Answer (A) is plural,
(C) is an infinitive, and (D) is a negative command.

2. **(C)**
    The context requires the vocative form of the name **Efflūvius**, based
on the answers provided. This name ends in **-ius**, so the **-us** is dropped,
leaving **Efflūvī** as the vocative. Answer (A) is nominative singular, (B) is
nominative plural, and (D) is dative or ablative singular and irrelevant to
the context. (See "The Vocative Case.")

3. **(C)**
    The implied meaning of this sentence requires the singular com-
mand because **Doofe** is in the vocative case. The verb **dīcō** has an irregular form of the singular imperative, which is **dīc**. The remaining answers
are incorrect because (A) and (B) are in the plural and (D) is a present
passive infinitive.

4. **(B)**
    The phrasing of the original sentence calls for a question word in the Latin that produces a positive answer. Thus **Nōnne Doofus adest** is correct. Answer (A) reads *Doofus isn't here, is he?*; (C) reads *Is he here or not?*; and (D) reads *Is Doofus here?* (See "Direct Questions.")

5. **(B)**
    This sentence tempts you to choose (A) **Carpe** to complete Horace's famous saying, but the vocative form **discipulī** is plural, requiring (B) **Carpite**. Answer (C) doesn't make sense, given the implied meaning of the command, and (D) is a present passive infinitive, which could easily be mistaken as a form of the imperative, if the verb **carpere** belonged to the fourth conjugation.

6. **(D)**
    Given the forms of the answers, the word **grammaticus**, *teacher* clearly belongs to the second declension, leading to the choice of (D) **grammatice** as the correct answer. The imperative **Ignosce** in the sentence requires that the missing form be vocative singular. Answer (A) is nominative, (B) is genitive singular or nominative plural, and (C) is accusative singular.

7. **(A)**
    This sentence provides an example of a singular negative command or prohibition, *Don't fall asleep!* Answers (B) and (C) are typical mistaken translations of the negative imperative, and (D) requires a subjunctive verb expressing a wish. (See "Negative Imperatives [Prohibitions].")

8. **(A)**
    The correct translation of *my friend* as a vocative requires familiarity with the fact that the vocative form of the possessive adjective **meus** is irregular. Thus, **mī amīce** is correct. Answer (B) is nominative, not vocative. Answer (C) **mī amīcō** is the contracted form of **mihi** + the dative form of **amīcus**. Answer (D) **meī amīcī** is nominative or vocative plural. (See "The Vocative Case.")

9. **(D)**
    The interrogative particle **Num** in the sentence, which reads *You don't study, do you?*, prompts the answer **Minimē**, *No, I don't.* Answer (A) **Ita vērō** means *Yes*; (B) **Nōn sciō** means *I don't know*; and (C) **Studeō** means *I do study.* (See "Direct Questions.")

10. **(B)**

This question simply asks for the meaning of the interrogative adverb **Quō?**, which is *To where?* The sentence reads (*To*) *where do you want to go today?"* Answer (A) *when* would use **ubi**, **cum** or **quandō**; (C) *with whom* would use **quōcum** or **quibuscum**; and (D) *why* would use a word such as **cur**, **quārē**, or **quamobrem**.

Sententiae Antiquae Answers

1. **(B)**

This motto plays on the imperative singular forms of the verbs **discere**, *to learn*, and **dīscedere**, *to leave*. Answer (A) requires familiarity with the meaning of the verb **discere**, which is not *to teach* (this is **docēre**). Answer (C) suggests wrongly that **disce** might mean *behave*, given the derivative *discipline*. Answer (D) is just for fun.

2. **(D)**

Horace's saying reads *Turn* (*your*) *stylus often* (*if you're*) *going to write a book* (*that's*) *good.* By *turn your stylus often*, he means that erasing or frequent editing is necessary for good writing. **Verte** is a singular command addressed to the reader, and **scriptūrus** is a future active participle modifying you, the reader (the subject of **Verte**).

3. **(C)**

You might be familiar with this famous opening line from Poem 3. The punctuation requires an imperative, which must be plural, because the vocatives **Venerēs** and **Cupīdinēs** are plural. Answer (C) **Lūgēte** fits the requirements. Answer (A) **Lūge** is a singular imperative, (B) **Lūgērī** is a present passive infinitive, and (D) **Lūgēre** is a present active infinitive, none of which fit the context of the sentence.

4. **(B)**

This sentence reads *O countryside, when shall I see you?* The question simply asks for the meaning of the interrogative adverb **quandō**. Answer (A) *how* is **quōmodō** or something similar, (C) *where* is **ubi**, and (D) *why* is **cur**.

5. **(D)**

This sentence is a negative command in the plural, as required by the punctuation and by the vocative plural form **Rōmānī**. **Nōlīte** is the form needed to supplement the infinitive **properāre**, therefore completing the negative imperative. The sentence reads *Don't rush to arms, Romans!* Answer (A) **Nōlō** means *I don't wish*, (B) **Nōlī** is the singular imperative, and (C) **Nōlle** is the present active infinitive.

6.   **(D)**
The interrogative particle **Nōnne** requires phrasing in translation that produces a positive response. This is (D) *You will, won't you?* The sentence reads *You will order that Catiline be put into chains, won't you?* Answers (A) and (C) require the negative particle **Num** and (B) the enclitic **-ne**.

7.   **(C)**
This line from Poem 8 reads **Miser Catulle, dēsinās ineptīre**, *Poor Catullus, stop playing the fool.* As an adjective modifying **Catulle**, which is vocative, **Miser** must therefore also be vocative. Answer (A) **Miserē** is an adverb that might mislead you into thinking that the adjective **miser** must have the same ending as its noun, **Catulle**. Neither (B) **Miserī**, which is (genitive) singular, nominative, vocative plural, nor (D) **Miserō**, which is dative or ablative singular, agrees with **Catulle**.

8.   **(A)**
This quote from Martial asks the teacher to *spare the simple crowd*, that is, the students. The context requires a singular imperative, **parce**, because the person addressed (**magister**) is singular. Answer (B) **parcite** is a plural imperative, (C) **parcere** is a present active infinitive, and (D) **parsus** is a perfect passive participle, none of which fit the context here.

Stumper: (B)
Answer (A) mistranslates **relinquit** as *makes*, and (C) and (D) do not correctly translate the imperative **Crēde**. Nor do the remainder of the translations in (C) and (D) render the meaning of the original Latin correctly.

THE SAT SUBJECT TEST IN
LATIN

SECTION 7

Verbals

CHAPTER 24

Participles

Chapter 24

PARTICIPLES

VERBALS

Verbs that perform the functions of nouns or adjectives are known as "verbals." Verbal nouns consist of the gerund, the supine, and the infinitive. Verbal adjectives consist of participles, which include present and future active, perfect passive, and future passive forms. The future passive participle is also known as the gerundive. A review of verbals will be presented in the next three chapters, organized as follows: participles, then the gerund, gerundive, and supine, and finally, infinitives.

PARTICIPLES

Participles are so called because they "participate" in the functions of both verbs and adjectives. Because participles modify nouns or pronouns, they show gender, number, and case and follow the normal rules of agreement. Participles can also function independently as nouns or be combined with various forms of the verb **esse** to create new verb forms, such as **missus est** or **missūrus esse**. In Latin, participles often occur where English coordinates two clauses or uses a dependent clause introduced by a word such as *who*, *when*, or *since*:

> **Errōneus iēns ad thermās quadrantem āmīsit.**
> *Erroneus, who was going to the baths, lost his entry fee* (literally, *Erroneus going . . .*).

> **Quadrante āmissō, Errōneus īrātus erat.**
> *Because the entry fee had been lost, Erroneus was upset.*

There are three tenses and four forms of the Latin participle. The future passive participle functions more as a gerundive than as a participle, so this form will be reviewed in the next chapter. Note on the following chart that there is no perfect active (*having sent*) form and no present passive (*being sent*) participial form in Latin.

Quick Study of Participles

mittō, mittere, mīsī, missus

	Active	Passive
Present	**mittēns** (stem **mittent-**) *sending*	
Perfect		**missus, -a, -um,** *having been sent*
Future	**missūrus, -a, -um,** *about to send*	**mittendus, -a, -um,** *about to be sent* (also known as the gerundive)

The Present Active Participle

The present active participle is formed on the present stem, as in **mitte- + -ns** or **mitte- + -nt- +** endings of the single termination third declension adjective (see the chart in Chapter 16). The nominative singular of all three genders is therefore the same, **mittēns**, *sending*; the participial stem is **mittent-**:

> **Errōneus <u>dēmittēns</u> sē in labrum lapsus est.**
> <u>*Lowering himself into the tub*</u>, *Erroneus slipped.*

Use the letters **-ns (mittēns)** to recognize the form of the nominative singular of the present participle. The nominative singular lacks the **-nt-** of the remaining forms. Use the **-nt-** of the Latin form, as in **mittent-**, to identify the participle as pres<u>ent</u>. In the **-iō** conjugations, **-ie-** appears in the stem, for example **audiēns, audient-**.

Many adjectives are formed from the present active participle, such as **neglegēns** (gen., **neglegentis**), *careless*, as are substantive nouns, such as **amāns** (gen., **amantis**), *lover*.

The ablative singular of the present participle has alternative **-e** and **-ī** endings. Present participles usually have the ablative singular in **-e** (as with third declension nouns) when they function <u>verbally</u>, for instance, as a participle in an ablative absolute, as in **balneātōre laborante**, *(while) the bathman (is) working*. The **-e** ending is also found with present participles used as substantives, for example, **ā sapiente**, *by the wise man*. If the present participle is used as a descriptive <u>adjective</u> modifying an expressed noun, the **-ī** ending is commonly used (as with third declension adjectives), as in **cum laborantī balneātōre**, *with the working bathman*.

For greater clarity in English, translate the participle as a clause:

Exercēns in palaestrā, Errōneus sudat.

As a verbal adjective: *Exercising in the palaestra, Erroneus is sweating.*

As a clause: *While (he is) exercising in the palaestra, Erroneus is sweating.*

A participle, when translated as a clause, can have the same meaning as that of a relative clause with the indicative (see Chapter 12, "The Uses of the Relative Pronoun"):

Erroneus, who is exercising in the palaestra, is sweating.

Participle: **Errōneus exercēns in palaestrā sudat.**

Relative clause: **Errōneus quī in palaestrā exercet sudat.**

Because the participle may have the same meaning as the relative clause with the indicative, and vice versa, it is a candidate for the Syntax Substitution section of the SAT Latin Subject Test (Part E).

The action of the present participle takes place <u>continuously</u> and <u>at the same time as</u> the action of the main verb in a sentence. Therefore, if the main verb is found in the past tense, the present participle, in order to express contemporary action, must be translated *was -ing*, and not *is -ing*. Use the words *while* or *as* to translate the present participle:

present   present
Exercēns in palaestrā, Errōneus sudat.

present   present
While (he is) exercising in the palaestra, Erroneus is sweating.

present   past
Exercēns in palaestrā, Errōneus sudābat.

past   past
While (he was) exercising in the palaestra, Erroneus was sweating.

Here are additional examples of translating the present active participle as a clause:

Servīs in hypocaustō laborantibus balneātor aquam dat.
The attendant is giving water to the slaves who are working in the hypocaust.

Servī in hypocaustō laborantēs erant sitientēs.
While the slaves were working in the hypocaust, they were thirsty.

The Perfect Passive Participle

The perfect passive participle is the fourth principal part of the regular verb. We met this form in Chapter 19 when reviewing the perfect passive system of indicative verbs, such as **missus est**, *he has been sent*. As the perfect passive participle of the verb, **missus, -a, -um** is translated *having* (perfect) *been* (passive) *sent*. The participial stem, here **miss-**, will have a variety of spellings, but it will always have the endings of the first/second declension adjective (see Chapter 16):

> **Errōneus unctus ē palaestrā ēgressus est.**
> *Erroneus, having been oiled, left the exercise area.*

The perfect passive participle is also known as the "past participle," the "perfect participle," or the "PPP" (but <u>not</u> the supine). There is no perfect active participial form in Latin. Deponent participles, however, have active meanings (see below).

Unlike the action of the present participle, the action of the past participle is <u>completed</u> and takes place <u>prior</u> in time to the action of the main verb in the sentence. In the previous example, Erroneus was oiled down <u>before</u> he left the exercise area.

Here are some common ways to translate a perfect passive participle, using the sentence **Errōneus unctus ēgressus est**:

> *Erroneus, having been oiled, left.*
>
> *Erroneus left when he was* (or *had been*) *oiled.*
>
> *Erroneus left after he was* (or *had been*) *oiled.*
>
> *Erroneus left because he was* (or *had been*) *oiled.*
>
> *Erroneus, who was oiled, left.*
>
> *Erroneus was oiled and then left.*

Errōneus unctus, *Erroneus having been oiled* is not to be confused with **Errōneus unctus est**, *Erroneus has been oiled*, and so on. The latter is a form of the passive voice of finite verbs in the perfect system. Such forms, of course, do contain the past participle.

The Future Active Participle

The future active participle **missūrus, -a, -um** is formed by adding to the perfect passive stem **miss-** the letters **-ūr-** and the endings of the first/second declension adjective, **-us, -a, -um**:

Errōneus dīmissūrus servum plūs unguentī poposcit.
Erroneus, about to send away the slave, asked for more oil.

The future active participle, just as the past participle, has <u>a stem that is in the passive voice</u>, but just as the present participle, has <u>a meaning in the active voice</u>. With regard to the forms of Latin participles, the "future (**missūrus**) is built upon the past (**missus**)." Remember that a form such as **missūrus** is a participle in the future tense by noting that the **-ūr-** in the form reflects the -ur- in the English word "fut<u>ur</u>e." In fact, the English word derives from **futūrus**, *about to be*, which is the future active participle of the verb **esse**.

Here are some ways of expressing the future active participle in English:

About to . . .	*Intending to . . .*	*Planning to . . .*
Going to . . .	*On the point of . . .*	*Ready to . . .*

These sentences illustrate the translation of the future active participle as a clause:

Errōneus senātōrī in thermās ingressūrō occurrit.
Erroneus happened upon the senator <u>who was going to enter</u> the baths.

Errōneus senātōrem subsequēns, "Nōs lavātūrī tē salutāmus!" clāmāvit.
Erroneus, tagging along after the senator, proclaimed, "We <u>who are about to bathe</u> salute you!"

Participles of Deponent Verbs

Present participles of deponent verbs are formed on the present active stem (see Chapter 20), such as **hortālns (hortārī)**, **verēlns (verērī)**, **loquēlns (loquī)**, and **orilēns (orīrī)**. Thus, present participles of deponent verbs are formed in regular fashion. There is no perfect active participle in Latin; however, the past participles of deponent verbs have active meanings. For example, the past participle **locūtus** is translated *having spoken*.

Participles of Irregular Verbs

Present Active Participle of Irregular Verbs

ēō, īre	iēns, eunt–	*going*
ferō, ferre	ferēns, ferent–	*bringing*
volō, velle	volēns, volent–	*wishing*
nōlō, nōlle	nōlēns, nōlent–	*not wishing*

The irregular verb **esse** does not possess a present active participial form. **Potēns** (gen. **potentis**) serves only as an adjective, as in **rēx potēns**, *the powerful king*.

Perfect Passive Participle of Irregular Verbs

The only common irregular verb having a perfect passive participle is **ferō, ferre, tulī, lātus**.

Future Active Participle of Irregular Verbs

sum, esse	futūrus, -a, -um	*about to be*
eō, īre	itūrus, -a, -um	*intending to go*
ferō, ferre	lātūrus, -a, -um	*going to carry*

Special Uses of Participles

Participles as Nouns

In addition to serving as adjectives, present active and perfect passive participles may also serve as substantives, or nouns. When used in this way, these participles have an independent function in the sentence (see Chapter 16, "Adjectives as Substantives"):

Present participle:	**Natantēs in piscinā sē delectāvērunt.** *The swimmers* (i.e., *Those swimming*) *in the pool enjoyed themselves.*
Past participle:	**Errōneus spērat sē fāmam extentūrum esse factīs.** *Erroneus hopes that he will extend his reputation by deeds* (literally, *by things having been done*).

When a participle is used without a noun, generally a noun or pronoun must be provided during translation, such as **facta**, (*things*) *having been done*. Such verbal substantives often become nouns.

The Active Periphrastic

The future active participle is commonly used in combination with a form of **esse** that serves as an auxiliary or "helping" verb. The use of **missūrus est**, *he is about to send*, which is called the "active periphrastic," is a sort of roundabout equivalent to the regular use of the future tense form **mittet**, *he will send*. (In English, the periphrastic equivalent of the inflected form *he sent* is *he did send*.) The use of this alternative adds stylistic variety to the Latin.

> **Errōneus servum in apodytērium <u>missūrus erat</u>.**
> *Erroneus <u>was about to send</u> a slave into the changing room.*

The Ablative Absolute

The ablative absolute is a participial phrase that is <u>grammatically independent of the rest of the sentence</u> ("absolute," from **absolvere**, *to set free*, *separate*). It generally consists of a noun or pronoun that is accompanied by a present or past participle, with both forms found in the ablative case, as in this sentence:

> **<u>Thermīs aedificātīs</u>, Errōneus salūbritāte fruēbātur.**
> <u>*After the public baths were built*</u>, *Erroneus enjoyed good health.*

Compare the following sentence:

> **<u>Vīnum bibentēs</u>, virī inter sē colloquēbantur.**
> <u>*While drinking wine*</u>, *the men gossiped among themselves.*

How do these two sentences differ in structure? In the second example, the participial phrase is <u>not</u> an ablative absolute because there is a <u>direct connection</u> between the participial phrase **vīnum bibentēs** and **virī . . . colloquēbantur**, the main part of the sentence. That is, the participle **bibentēs** modifies the subject of the main clause, **virī**. This participial phrase is not "absolute" or separate from the main sentence. In the first sentence, the meaning of the ablative absolute **Thermīs aedificātīs** is separate from that of the main clause, **Errōneus salūbritāte fruēbātur**, that is, Erroneus did not build the baths (but he did enjoy them!). The ablative absolute is one of the most common constructions found in Latin and should be mastered thoroughly.

In Latin, the subject of the perfect passive participle in an ablative absolute is not the same as that of the main verb; however, in English it may be expressed as such if the identity of the two subjects is clearly the same, for example,

<u>Vestimentīs exūtīs</u>, Errōneus aliquid unguentī poscēbat.
>*<u>After he had taken off his clothes</u>, Erroneus asked for some oil.* (Literally, *After the clothes had been taken off, Erroneus . . .*)

In this sentence, the person who is disrobing and Erroneus are clearly the same, therefore the ablative absolute may be changed from the passive to the active voice in translation. When translating in such situations, be sure to express the action of the past participle as preceding that of the main verb.

Quick Study of the Ablative Absolute

Type 1*
(with the perfect passive participle, action precedes that of the main verb)

<u>Linteō ā balneātōre acceptō</u>, Errōneus sē ipsum strenuē defricābat.
>*<u>After the towel had been received from the attendant</u>* (literally, *The towel having been received from the attendant*), *Erroneus vigorously rubbed himself dry.*

Type 2
(with the present active participle, action contemporary with that of the main verb)

Errōneō in popīnā <u>bibente</u>, amīcus suus in caldāriō <u>madefacit</u>.
>*While Erroneus <u>is drinking</u> in the snack bar, his friend <u>is soaking</u> in the hot room.*

Errōneo in popīnā <u>bibente</u>, amīcus suus in caldāriō madefaciēbat.
>*While Erroneus <u>was drinking</u> in the snack bar, his friend <u>was soaking</u> in the hot room.*

Type 3
(with no participle)

<u>Errōneō balneātōre</u>, accipietne aliquis linteum?
>*<u>If Erroneus is the bath attendant</u>, will anyone receive a towel?*

<u>Aquā frīgidiōre</u>, Errōneus in frīgidārium intrāre nōn voluit.
>*<u>The water being too cold</u>, Erroneus did not wish to enter the cold room.* (Better English: *Because the water was too cold . . .*)

---

* The terms "Type 1," etc., are used for convenience.

Because the verb **esse** does not have a present or past participle in classical Latin, the ablative absolute can also consist of <u>two nouns</u>, a <u>noun and an adjective</u>, or a <u>noun and a pronoun</u>. The customary translation of this type contains the word *being* as the literal substitute for the missing participle of **esse**. Although English contains similar expressions, such as *all things being equal*, it is often better to rephrase ablatives absolute of this type to avoid this awkward word.

Tips on Recognizing an Ablative Absolute

- Every ablative absolute must contain at least <u>two</u> elements: the noun or pronoun and the participle or its substitute (a second noun, an adjective, or a pronoun).

- Often the noun or pronoun and participle are found in close proximity, but there may be additional, intervening words. The noun or pronoun regularly appears before the participle.

- The ablative absolute usually appears early in the sentence.

- As an independent thought unit in a sentence, the ablative absolute is usually (but not always) set off by commas from the rest of the sentence.

Translating the Ablative Absolute

The Type 1 ablative absolute (i.e., the ablative absolute containing a past participle) is by far the most common. When translating, begin by rendering the participle literally, as in **Thermīs aedificātīs**, *The baths having been built*. Use *having been* as your memorized or default translation of the past participle. Then move on to other possibilities that might better express the meaning in English. As with other participial constructions, the ablative absolute can be translated as a clause that expresses time (*after, when, since*) and cause (*because*), as well as condition (*if*), concession (*although*), or relation (*who*). The decision is up to you, the reader, to determine the best contextual sense of an ablative absolute:

> **Thermīs aedificātīs, cotidiē multī sē lavāre poterant.**

Temporal:	*After/When/the baths had been built, many people could bathe daily.*
Causal:	*Because the baths had been built, many people could bathe daily.*

The ablative absolute may also coordinate with the main clause and serve as a second main verb, such as *The baths had been built and* . . .

Here are some additional examples of ablatives absolute translated as clauses:

> **Errōneō morante, amīcī in apodytērium intrāvērunt.**
> *While Erroneus was loitering, his friends entered the dressing room.*

> **Vestimentīs exūtīs, Errōneus amīcōs dēridentēs eum audiēbat.**
> *After he had taken off his clothes, Erroneus heard his friends laughing at him.*

> **Hōc audītō, Errōneus linteō sē cēlāvit.**
> *When he (had) heard this, Erroneus hid himself with a towel.*

> **Amīcus molestus, Errōneō verēcundō, linteum surripuit.**
> *Because Erroneus was (being) bashful, his pesky friend stole away the towel.*

TIPS ON TRANSLATING PARTICIPLES

The following tips refer to this sentence:

> **Errōneus unguentum et strīgilem ferēns, in pavīmentō lapsus est.**
> *While Erroneus was carrying the oil and strigil, he slipped on the tiled floor.*

- Participles are verbal adjectives and must modify a noun or pronoun in the sentence. The participle follows the rules of noun–adjective agreement in Latin. When translating a participle, locate the participle (**ferēns**), and then link it with the pronoun or noun modified (**Errōneus**).

- The participle **ferēns** represents one of two actions in the sentence in which it appears. The expression in English of the time of the action of the participle depends upon the tense of the main verb of the sentence. **Ferēns** is expressed as *was carrying* because the main verb **lapsus est** is in the past tense.

- The participle as a verbal adjective is found in a participial phrase, which is a group of words without a subject or verb and containing a participle, as in **unguentum et strīgilem ferēns**.

In Latin, the participle is found at the end of the phrase (**unguentum et strīgilem <u>ferēns</u>**), whereas in English, the participle is found at the beginning, *<u>carrying</u> oil and a strigil*.

- Participial phrases are usually translated as subordinate clauses that express particular circumstances of time (*while, when, since*), cause (*because*), condition (*if*), concession (*although*), or relation (*who*). The phrase underlined above is expressed as a temporal clause, *<u>while</u> Erroneus was carrying*.

- Participial phrases can be found at the beginning, middle, or end of a Latin sentence.

- The word modified by the participle usually precedes it (**<u>Errōneus</u> . . . ferēns**).

- The phrase in which a participle is found is often framed by commas.

SAMPLE QUESTIONS

Part C: Translation

1. Servi Rōmānōs <u>venientēs</u> ad balneās saepe comitābantur.

   (A) who had come   (C) who were coming

   (B) who have come   (D) who will be coming

Part E: Syntax Substitution

2. Errōneus salūtat fēminās <u>quae</u> ad balneās <u>eunt</u>.

   (A) itūrae   (C) iērunt

   (B) iēns   (D) euntēs

Answers

1. (C)   2. (D)

PRACTICE QUESTIONS

Translation

1. Cīvēs, <u>fūribus vestēs surripientibus</u>, custodēs condūcēbant.

    (A) because the clothes had been stolen by the thieves

    (B) after the thieves had stolen the clothes

    (C) because the thieves were stealing the clothes

    (D) while the thieves are stealing the clothes

2. Cicero scrīpsit, "Sīgna rērum <u>futūrārum</u> mundō ā dīs ostenduntur."

    (A) having happened   (C) about to happen

    (B) happening   (D) had been happening

3. The voices of the men <u>singing</u> annoyed me <u>while I was soaking</u> in the hot bath.

    (A) cantantium; madefaciēns

    (B) cantantis; madefacientēs

    (C) cantantium; madefacientem

    (D) cantantēs; madefaciente

4. The girls <u>were going to hurry</u> into the changing room.

    (A) festīnātūrae erant   (C) festīnātūrae sunt

    (B) festīnātūrae fuerant   (D) festīnātūrī erant

5. Select the translation of the sentence that is <u>not</u> correct.

    <u>Servī strigilibus hominēs unctōs dēfricābant.</u>

    (A) While the men were being oiled down, the slaves were scraping them with strigils.

    (B) The slaves were scraping with strigils the men who had been oiled down.

    (C) The slaves are oiling down the men and then scraping them with strigils.

    (D) After the men had been oiled down, the slaves scraped them with strigils.

6. Hīs rēbus factīs, athlētae in palaestram iērunt.

    (A) While these things were being done

    (B) After these things were done

    (C) About to do these things

    (D) While doing these things

7. Exercēns athlēta plūs unguentī rogat.

    (A) While exercising   (C) Having exercised

    (B) About to exercise   (D) Who was exercising

8. "We who are about to bathe salute you!" the men proclaimed to the attendants.

    (A) lautantēs   (C) lavandī

    (B) lautūrī   (D) lautūrōs

9. Select the correct the translation of the underlined participial phrase.

    Illa, vix patiēns vapōrem, ē caldāriō ēgrediēbātur.

    (A) having scarcely endured the steam

    (B) who is barely enduring the steam

    (C) since she had barely endured the steam

    (D) who was scarcely enduring the steam

Syntax Substitution

Which of the following expressions best substitutes for the underlined construction?

10. Nōs pecūniam mendicīs morantibus extrā vestibulum dedimus.

    (A) quī morābantur   (C) cum morātī erant

    (B) morātūrīs   (D) quamquam morantur

11. <u>Postquam cīvēs dētersī erant</u>, balneātor lintea in ūnum locum contulit.

   (A) Cīvibus dētersīs

   (B) Ubi cīvēs dētergēbantur

   (C) Cum cīvēs dētergērentur

   (D) Dum cīvēs sē dētergēbant

SENTENTIAE ANTIQUAE

1. Quidquid id est, timeō Danaōs et dōna . . . ! (Vergil)

   (A) ferentia   (C) ferēns

   (B) ferentem   (D) ferentēs

2. Why are you laughing? <u>When the name has been changed</u>, the story is told about you. (Horace)

   (A) Mūtāns nōmen   (C) Mūtātīs nōminibus

   (B) Mūtātō nōmine   (D) Mūtātum nōmen

3. A word <u>to the wise</u> is sufficient. (Terence)

   (A) sapientī   (C) sapientēs

   (B) sapiēns   (D) sapientem

4. Ō vōs . . . graviōra, dābit deus hīs quoque fīnem. (Vergil)

   (A) passa   (C) passī

   (B) passus   (D) passōs

Stumper:

   The skill of an orator <u>about to recite</u> pleases those <u>who are going to listen</u>. (Quintilian)

   (A) dictūrī; audītūra   (C) dictī; audītōs

   (B) dīcentis; audientēs   (D) dictūrī; audītūrōs

Answers

Translation

1. Ablative absolute **(C)**
   This question tests your ability to translate an ablative absolute containing a present participle when the main verb is in a past tense. The present participle must be translated in the past because its action must be contemporary with that of the main verb, which is past. (See "The Present Active Participle" and "The Ablative Absolute.") The translations in (A) and (B) provide past actions that are completed, *had been stolen* and *had stolen*, which would require perfect passive participles. The translation in (D), *are stealing*, is not contemporary with the time of the main verb **condūcēbant**, which is in the imperfect tense. (See "The Ablative Absolute.")

2. Future participle **(C)**
   Answer (C) translates the underlined form **futūrārum** correctly as the future participle of the verb **esse**. The sentence reads *Indications of future events* (literally, *things about to be*) *are revealed to the world by the gods.* Answer (A) translates a perfect active participle, which doesn't exist as a form except in the case of deponent verbs. Answer (B) *happening* is a present active participle, and (D) *had been happening* does not exist as a participle in Latin. (See "The Future Active Participle.")

3. Present participle **(C)**
   Of the men singing requires a form that is genitive plural and *annoyed me (while I was) soaking* requires a form that is accusative singular to modify **mē**, leading to **cantantium; madefacientem**. Although the verbs may be unfamiliar, their forms should not. **Madefaciēns** in (A) is nominative singular and does not agree with **mē**, the direct object of the verb *annoyed* in the sentence. Answer (B) contains forms that are genitive singular and nominative/accusative plural, which are incorrect. Answer (D) contains forms that are also in the incorrect case and number (nominative/accusative plural and ablative singular). (See "The Present Active Participle.")

4. Active periphrastic **(A)**
   This question tests your familiarity with the active periphrastic. *(They) were going to hurry* requires a future active participle (i.e., *going to hurry*) and the auxiliary verb *(they) were*, which is **erant**. Answer (B) is translated as *had been about to hurry*, and (C) is *are about to hurry*. Answer

(D) *were about to hurry* provides the correct translation, but the participle **festīnatūrī** has a masculine ending where a feminine ending, modifying *the girls*, is required. (See "The Active Periphrastic.")

5.   Perfect passive participle **(A)**
     This sentence reads literally *The slaves were scraping with strigils the men having been oiled down*. The participle is **unctōs**, the perfect passive participle of **unguere** modifying **hominēs**, which is the direct object of the verb **dēfricābant**. Answer (A) requires a present participle to render the meaning *while*, which is an action contemporary with that of the main verb, rather than prior to it, as required by the perfect passive participle **unctōs**. (See "The Perfect Passive Participle.")

6.   Ablative absolute **(B)**
     After these things were done is a condensation of *these things having been done*, a more literal translation of the ablative absolute **Hīs rēbus factīs**. Answer (D) requires the present participle *while doing* (**facientēs**), and (C) requires the future participle *about to do* (**factūrī**), both directly modifying **athlētae** and thus not ablatives absolute. Answer (A) renders a present passive participial form (*were being done*), which is inexpressible in Latin.

7.   Present participle **(A)**
     Exercēns is the nominative singular form of the present participle modifying **athlēta**, the subject of the sentence. Answer (B) *about to exercise* translates the future participle **exercitūrus**, (C) *having exercised* gives an impossible meaning of **exercēns**, and (D) *was exercising* requires that the main verb be **rogābant**, a past tense. The sentence reads *While exercising, the athlete is requesting more oil*. Note the appearance of the partitive genitive.

8.   Future participle **(B)**
     This sentence requires a future participle, *about to bathe*, modifying the subject *we*, which is the form **lautūrī** (remember that the masculine ending is preferred when the gender is not specified). Answer (A) **lavantēs** is a present participle, *bathing*, and (C) **lavandī** is a gerund or gerundive form that is not appropriate in this context. Answer (D) **lautūrōs** is a future participle, but it has an accusative ending rather than the necessary nominative. (See "The Future Active Participle.")

9. Present participle **(C)**

Vix patiēns vāpōrem is a present participial phrase that must be rendered as continuous action in the past tense in order to be contemporary with the time of the main verb **ēgrediēbātur**, which is in the imperfect tense. Answers (A) and (C) contain translations of actions that have already taken place to the main verb and therefore do not correctly render the present participle **patiēns**.

Syntax Substitution

10. **(A)**

This question tests your awareness that participles may be translated as clauses. The meaning of the present participle **morantibus**, *lingering* can also be rendered as **quī morābantur**, *who were lingering*. The sentence reads *We gave money to the beggars (who were)* <u>*lingering in the entryway*</u>. Answer (B) **morātūrīs** is translated *about to linger*, (C) **cum morātī erant** is translated *when* (or *since*) *they had lingered*, and (D) **quamquam morantur** is translated *although they are lingering*. (See "The Present Active Participle.")

11. **(A)**

Postquam cīvēs dētersī erant, *After the citizens had been dried off*, can also be rendered in Latin by the ablative absolute as a temporal clause, **cīvibus dētersīs**. The sentence reads <u>*After the citizens had been dried off,*</u> *the bathman gathered the towels into one place*. Answers (B), (C), and (D) all express continuous action in past time (**dētergēbantur**, **dētergērentur**, and **dētergēbant** are all in the imperfect tense), whereas the verb **dētersī erant** expresses completed action in past time.

Sententiae Antiquae Answers

1. Present participle **(D)**

The missing participle, which must be in the present tense, given the possible answers, agrees with the direct object **Danaōs**, according to the sense required by the context. Answer (A) is misleading because it tempts you to use **ferentia** to modify **dōna**. But the *gifts* are not doing the *bringing*! Answer (B) **ferentem** is a singular form where a plural is required, and (C) **ferēns** is a nominative singular form where an accusative plural is required. The sentence reads *Whatever it is* (i.e., *the wooden horse*), *I fear Greeks even* <u>*bearing*</u> (or <u>*when they bear*</u>) *gifts*.

2.   Ablative absolute **(B)**
   The ablative absolute **mūtātō nōmine** correctly translates the time clause *When the name has been changed.* Answer (A) **mūtāns nōmen** contains a present participle, which does not correctly render the meaning. Answer (C) **mūtātīs nōminibus** is an ablative absolute, but it has forms in the plural, whereas the singular is required. Answer (D) **mūtātum nōmen** is a phrase with the past participle, but it does not make sense in the context.

3.   Present participle, substantive **(A)**
   This question presents the participle **sapiēns** as a substantive, that is, *the one being wise, the wise.* Because the English requires a dative form, *to the wise,* **sapientī** is the correct answer. Answer (B) is nominative, (C) is nominative/accusative plural, and (D) is accusative singular, none of which fit the context.

4.   Past participle, deponent **(C)**
   All answers are in the perfect passive participial form of the deponent verb **patior, patī, passus sum**. This participle, when translated in the active voice, means *having suffered.* All that's left to do is to determine the function, or case, of the missing participle. The form modifies the subject **vōs**, given the sense, so it must be nominative plural, ergo **passī**. Answer (A) tempts you to use the participle to modify **graviōra**, but this word serves as the (neuter plural substantive) direct object. Answer (B) **passus** is singular, not plural, and (D) **passōs** is accusative, not nominative, as required by the context. The sentence reads *O you <u>having suffered</u> (who have suffered) rather serious trials, god will make an end to these, too.* (See "Participles of Deponent Verbs.")

Stumper: Future participle **(D)**
   About to recite and *going to listen* both require future active participles. The first participle modifies *of an orator*, which requires a form in the genitive case. The clause *who are going to listen* modifies *those*, which serves as the accusative direct object. (There are no dative forms offered as answers, so a verb other than **placēre** for *please* must be assumed.) The forms in (D) **dictūrī; auditūrōs** fulfill all the requirements and provide the correct answer. Answer (A) **dictūrī; auditūra** contains future participles, but **auditūra** does not modify *those* (*people*), which is personal and not neuter. Answers (B) and (C) contain participles other than those in the future tense; **dīcentis** is present, and **dictī** and **audītōs** are past.

CHAPTER 25

The Gerund,
the Gerundive,
and the Supine

Chapter 25

THE GERUND,
THE GERUNDIVE,
AND THE SUPINE

THE GERUND

The gerund is a verbal noun that has characteristics of both a verb and a noun, as in the following sentence:

Possumus discere multa dē deīs Rōmānīs <u>legendō</u>.
We can learn much about the Roman gods <u>by reading</u>.

The gerund is formed by adding **-nd-** to the present stem of the verb, together with the endings of the second declension singular noun in all cases but the nominative. The gerund serves the functions of a noun in these cases and is translated with *-ing*, such as *reading*.

	Forms	Common Uses
Nominative		
Genitive	**legendī**, *of reading*	purpose with **causā** or **grātiā**
Dative	**legendō**, *to, for reading*	indirect object or with special adjectives
Accusative	**legendum**, *reading*	purpose with **ad**
Ablative	**legendō**, *by, with reading*	means/instrument or with **dē**, **ē/ex**, or **in**

There is no nominative form of the gerund. The subjective infinitive **legere**, *reading*, is substituted. (For this type of infinitive, see the next chapter.)

Avoid confusing the gerund with the present participle used as a substantive, which is also translated as *-ing*:

Gerund: **Narcissus timet <u>nātandum</u>.**
                              Narcissus fears <u>swimming</u> (that is, *the act of swimming*).

Present participle: **Narcissus timet <u>nātantem</u>.**
                                Narcissus fears <u>the swimmer</u> (that is, *the one swimming*).

Some Latin expressions that contain the gerund appear in English, such as **modus operandī**, *method of operating,* and **onus probandī**, *burden of proof* (literally, *of proving*). Use these examples to help you recall how to translate the gerund.

THE GERUNDIVE (FUTURE PASSIVE PARTICIPLE)

The gerundive is a verbal adjective formed by adding **-ndus, -a, -um** to the present stem of the verb, as in **legendus, -a, -um**. As a verbal adjective, the gerundive agrees with a noun:

> **Possumus discere dē deīs Rōmānīs <u>fābulīs legendīs</u>.**
> *We can learn about the Roman gods <u>by reading stories</u>* (literally, *by stories about to be read*).

In the preceding example, note that the gerundive **legendīs** is attracted into the ablative case in agreement with the noun **fābulīs**, *by (means of) stories.* You would normally expect the accusative form **fābulās** to serve as the direct object of **legendīs**, but the Romans preferred to use a gerundive, **fābulīs legendīs**, instead of a gerund, **fābulās legendō**, when a direct object was involved.

The form of both the gerund and gerundive may be recognized by the **-nd-**, deriving from **gerendus, -a, -um**, *about to be done,* which is the gerundive form of the Latin verb **gerere**. You can remember that the gerundive serves as a verbal adjective by learning the phrase "the gerundive is an adjective."

The gerundive forms of deponent verbs are formed on the present active stem (see Chapter 20). Thus, the gerundive of the verb **loquī** is **loquendus, -a, -um**.

The gerund and gerundive forms of irregular verbs are as follows:

	Gerund	Gerundive
eō, **īre**	**eundī**, etc.	**eundus**, -a, -um
ferō, **ferre**	**ferendī**, etc.	**ferendus**, -a, -um
fīō, **fierī**	**faciendī**, etc.	**faciendus**, -a, -um

Simple Gerundive

The gerundive is found in all noun cases, as in the following examples:

Dative: **Orpheus apud īnferōs lyram modulātus est <u>acquīrendae</u> uxorī.**
Orpheus played his lyre in the underworld <u>to gain possession of</u> his wife.

Ablative: **Orpheus uxōrem amīsit eā <u>respiciendā</u>.**
Orpheus lost his wife <u>by looking back</u> at her.

When translating gerundives, it is important to avoid misplaced or dangling modifiers:

<u>Orpheus cupidus uxōris acquīrendae</u> Plūtōnem implōrābat.

Wrong: *Orpheus pleaded with Pluto desirous of gaining possession of his wife.*
(Pluto is <u>not</u> the one pleading for his wife.)

Right: *Orpheus, desirous of gaining possession of his wife, pleaded with Pluto.*

Gerundive of Purpose (with ad, causā, or grātiā)

The gerundive accompanying **ad** (+ accusative), *to, in order to,* **causā** (+ genitive) or **grātiā** (+ genitive), *for the purpose of, for the sake of,* indicates purpose or intent, as in:

Īcarus altē volābat <u>caelī tangendī causā</u>.
Icarus flew high <u>for the sake of touching</u> the sky.

> **Daedalus mare investīgābat <u>ad fīlium mortuum inveniendum</u>.**
> *Daedalus searched the sea <u>in order to find his dead son</u>.*

With the gerundive of purpose, note that the ending will either be accusative or genitive singular or plural. **Causā** or **grātiā** typically follow the gerund or gerundive.

Passive Periphrastic (Gerundive of Obligation)

The gerundive is commonly used with a form of the verb **esse** to express necessity or obligation. When the gerundive has this function, it has meanings such as *must be*, *ought to be*, or *should be*. This use is known either as the "passive periphrastic" (a time-honored Greek term that roughly means "roundabout") or the "gerundive of obligation." (See Chapter 24, "The Active Periphrastic.") Any tense of the verb **esse** may be used, as in the following sentences:

> **Medūsa necanda est.** *Medusa has to be (must be) killed.*
>
> **Medūsa necanda erat.** *Medusa had to be killed.*
>
> **Medūsa necanda erit.** *Medusa will have to be killed,* etc.

Note that the gerundive of obligation is frequently used in indirect statements and indirect questions:

Indirect statement:	**Persēus scit Medūsam <u>necandam esse</u>.** *Perseus knows that Medusa <u>must be killed</u>.*
Indirect question:	**Persēus nōn rogāvit cur Medūsa <u>necanda esset</u>.** *Perseus did not ask why Medusa <u>had to be killed</u>.*

When an intransitive verb (a verb that does not take a direct object) appears in the passive periphrastic, the gerundive is translated <u>impersonally</u>, which means that the verb has "it" as its subject. For better English, transform the passive voice to the active, as in the following example:

> **Ad Graiās Persēō eundum est.**
> *Perseus must go to the Graiae* (literally, *It must be gone by Perseus to the Graiae*).

You will note in the previous example that **Perseō** is expressed in the <u>dative</u> case. In the passive periphrastic, the person who must perform the obligation expressed in the verb is found in the dative case, a use known as the dative of agent. (The ablative of personal agent with **ā/ab** is <u>not</u> used with this construction. For this usage, see Chapter 10, "Ablative of Personal Agent.")

Obligation may also be expressed in Latin by use of the verb **debēre** + the present passive infinitive:

> **Medūsa necārī debet.**
> *Medusa ought to be killed* or *should be killed.*

Quick Study of the Gerund and the Gerundive

The Gerund . . .	The Gerundive . . .
is a verbal noun	is a verbal adjective
corresponds to the English verbal noun in *-ing*, e.g., **mittendum**, *sending*	agrees with a noun or pronoun, e.g., **ad epistulam mittendam**, *for the purpose of sending the letter*
is present and active in meaning	is future and passive in meaning
is found only in the gen., dat., acc., and abl. sing. forms of the second declension	is found in all case forms of the first/second declension adjective

THE SUPINE

Just like the gerund, the supine is a verbal noun. It is formed from the fourth principal part of the verb, but it has a different meaning from that of the perfect passive participle. Only two cases invite review: the accusative, for example **narrātum**, and the ablative, **narrātū**. Note that the endings of the supine are those of the fourth declension noun. The supine is used with the accusative to express purpose, as in **narrātum**, *to tell*, and with the ablative to express respect or specification, as in **narrātū**, *with respect to telling*. Use the context to distinguish between **narrātum** as a supine, *to tell*, and **narrātum** as a perfect passive participle, *having been told*.

Purpose: **Hercules ad īnferōs Cerberum <u>captum</u> iit.**
Hercules went to the underworld <u>to capture</u> Cerberus.

(Note that translating **captum** as *having been captured* would not make sense here.)

Respect: **Cerberus tria capita habēbat (horribile <u>vīsū</u>!)**
Cerberus had three heads (horrible <u>to see</u>!)

The supine can take its own object. Verbs that govern the accusative supine usually express motion, as in the preceding example.

The supine as ablative of respect is found with certain neuter adjectives, such as **facile/difficile**, *easy/difficult*, **horribile**, *dreadful*, **mīrābile**, *remarkable*, **miserābile**, *wretched*, and **optimum**, *best*. (See Chapter 10, "Ablative of Respect or Specification.")

SAMPLE QUESTION

Part E: Syntax Substitution

Thēsēus ad Crētam Mīnōtaurī occīdendī causā nāvigāvit.

(A) quī Mīnōtaurum occīdit

(B) Mīnōtaurō occīsō

(C) cum Mīnōtaurum occīdisset

(D) Mīnōtaurum occīsum

Answer: (D)

PRACTICE QUESTIONS

1. <u>Quod erat dēmonstrandum</u>

 (A) What was being shown

 (B) What has to be shown

 (C) What had to be shown

 (D) What is being shown

2.   Prōmēthēus ignem surripuit hominis . . . causā.

   (A)   adiuvandus (adjuvandus)

   (B)   adiuvandī (adjuvandī)

   (C)   adiuvandīs (adjuvandīs)

   (D)   adiuvandum (adjuvandum)

3.   Mīnōtaurō necātō, . . . domum redeundum est.

   (A)   Thēsēus   (C)   Thēseō

   (B)   Thēsēum   (D)   Thēseī

4.   Thēsēus nāvigāvit ad Crētam <u>ut Mīnōtaurum necāret</u>.
     The best substitute for this clause is

   (A)   necāre Mīnōtaurum

   (B)   ad Mīnōtaurum necandum

   (C)   quod Mīnōtaurus necābitur

   (D)   Mīnōtaurō necātō

5.   <u>Sīsyphus scīvit saxum sibi semper volvendum esse</u>.

   (A)   Sisyphus knows that he will always roll the stone.

   (B)   Sisyphus knew that he must roll the stone forever.

   (C)   Sisyphus knew that the stone had always been rolled by him.

   (D)   Sisyphus knew that he was going to roll the stone forever.

6.   Ārachne melius Minervā . . . texere poterat.

   (A)   mīrābilis dictū   (C)   mīrābile dictū

   (B)   mīrābile dictum   (D)   mīrābilis dictum

7.   Multī vēnērunt <u>ad videndum Pēgasum</u>.
     The construction that has the same basic meaning is

   (A)   Pēgasum vīsum

   (B)   quod Pēgasum vidēbant

   (C)   Pēgasō vīsō

   (D)   videntēs Pēgasum

8. <u>Daphnē fugiente, Apollinī celerrimē currendum erat</u>.

   The basic meaning of this sentence is that

   (A) Daphne had to run after Apollo

   (B) Apollo had to run after Daphne

   (C) Apollo has to run after Daphne

   (D) Apollo was running from Daphne

9. Hercules duodecīm laborēs complevit <u>laborandō</u> dīligenter.

   (A) for working   (C) about to work

   (B) by working   (D) having worked

10. <u>Pyramus Thisbēn vīsam amāvit</u>.

    Which of the following is <u>not</u> correct?

    (A) Pyramus loved to look at Thisbe.

    (B) Pyramus saw Thisbe and fell in love with her.

    (C) Pyramus loved Thisbe after seeing her.

    (D) When he had seen her, Pyramus loved Thisbe.

SENTENTIAE ANTIQUAE

1. Wise thinking is the source <u>of writing</u> well. (Horace)

   (A) scrībendum   (C) scrībendī

   (B) scrībendae   (D) scrībendōrum

2. Gossip gains strength <u>by going</u> (as it goes). (Vergil)

   (A) iēns   (C) eundō

   (B) eundum   (D) euntem

3. <u>Caesarī omnia ūnō tempore erant agenda</u>. (Caesar)

   (A) Everything was being done by Caesar at the same time.

   (B) Caesar had to do everything at the same time.

   (C) Caesar was about to do everything at the same time.

   (D) Everything was done to Caesar at the same time.

4. <u>Mea Mūsa ā compōnendō carmine tenērī nōn potest</u>.

   In this sentence, Ovid says that

   (A) creating his verse cannot be kept from the Muse.

   (B) his Muse keeps him from creating verse.

   (C) his Muse cannot keep him from creating verse.

   (D) his Muse cannot be kept from creating verse.

Stumper:

   <u>Rēgulus laudandus est in conservandō iūre iūrandō</u> (jūre jūrandō).
   (Cicero)

   (A) Regulus ought to be praised for keeping his oath.

   (B) Regulus is praising those who keep their oath.

   (C) Regulus had to be praised for keeping his oath.

   (D) Regulus is being praised for keeping his oath.

Answers

1. Passive periphrastic **(C)**
   Dēmonstrandum is a gerundive modifying the relative pronoun **quod**, whose antecedent is the unstated pronoun **id**. The appearance of the verb **erat** defines the construction **erat demonstrandum** as a gerundive in a passive periphrastic, meaning (*that*) *which had to be demonstrated* (*was, in fact, demonstrated*). This Latin phrase, abbreviated QED, is often found at the end of mathematical proofs. (See "Passive Periphrastic.")

2. Gerundive of purpose **(B)**
   This question evaluates your knowledge of the gerundive of purpose with **causā**. The sentence reads *Prometheus stole fire <u>for the sake of helping mankind</u>*. Because **causā** takes the genitive case, its object is **hominis**, to be modified by the gerundive **adiuvandī**. Answer (A) is nominative singular, (B) is dative/ablative plural, and (D) is accusative singular; all are designed to prompt consideration because of the similarity of their endings to those already found in the sentence. (See "Gerundive of Purpose.")

3. Dative of agent **(C)**

The periphrastic **redeundum est** in this sentence requires that *Theseus* be a dative of agent, **Thēsēō**. The sentence reads *After the Minotaur was killed, Theseus was obliged to return home.* **Thēsēō** . . . **redeundum est**, which is an example of the passive periphrastic used with an intransitive verb, reads literally *It must be returned home by Theseus* . . . . Answer (B) might seem to be a good choice because **Thēseum** appears to agree with **redeundum est**, but the accusative case is not justifiable. Answers (A) and (B), which are nominative and genitive singular, respectively, make no sense here. (For the dative of agent, see "Passive Periphrastic.")

4. Gerundive of purpose **(B)**

The gerundive of purpose, **ad Mīnōtaurum necandum**, *for the purpose of killing the Minotaur*, may be substituted for **ut Mīnōtaurum necāret**, which is an **ut** clause of purpose with the subjunctive. The infinitive in (A) is not generally used to express purpose. Answer (C) is a causal clause, *because the Minotaur will be killed*, which changes the meaning, and the ablative absolute in (D) expresses that the Minotaur had already been killed. (See "Gerundive of Purpose.")

5. Passive periphrastic **(B)**

The periphrastic **volvendum esse** is found in the context of an indirect statement following the verb **scīvit**. This construction requires the use of an infinitive. The sentence reads *Sisyphus knew that he must roll the stone forever* (literally, *that the stone must always be rolled by him*). Note that **sibi**, the dative of agent, replaces the accusative form **sē**, which would ordinarily be the subject accusative of the infinitive. (For the use of the infinitive and the dative of agent, see "Passive Periphrastic.")

6. Supine **(C)**

The supine phrase **mīrābile dictū**, a favorite of Vergil, here completes the sentence *Arachne was able to weave better than Minerva* (*remarkable to say!*). The supine as ablative of respect (*remarkable with respect to saying so*) is found with the neuter form of **mīrābilis**, hence (A) and (D) must be omitted because **mīrābilis** is masculine/feminine. (See "The Supine.") Because the meaning of this sentence does not require a supine of purpose, (B) **mīrābile dictum** may be eliminated.

7. Gerundive of purpose; supine **(A)**

The acceptable substitute for the gerundive of purpose, **ad videndum Pēgasum**, is the supine phrase **Pēgasum vīsum**. The sentence reads *Many came to see Pegasus*. Neither the causal clause in (B) nor the participial phrases in (C) and (D) express purpose.

8.   Passive periphrastic **(B)**
      The sentence reads *Because Daphne was fleeing, Apollo had to run very quickly*. The passive periphrastic construction with an intransitive verb, **currendum erat**, expresses necessity in past time. **Apollinī** is dative of agent. Answers (A) and (D) reverse the meaning, and Answer (C), which is not in past time, requires the form **currendum est**. (See "Passive Periphrastic.")

9.   Gerund **(B)**
      Because **laborandō** serves the function of a noun in this sentence, (B) *by working*, which serves as an ablative of means, is correct. If **laborandō** were a gerundive, it would modify another word. The sentence reads *Hercules completed the twelve labors by working tirelessly*. Answer (C) *about to work* translates a future active participle, and (D) *having worked* translates a perfect active participle, which has no form in Latin. Answer (A) is a potential translation of **laborandō**, but it has no contextual meaning in this sentence. (See "The Gerund.")

10.   Perfect passive participle **(A)**
      To look at incorrectly translates the perfect passive participle **vīsam** as a supine. The accusative form of the supine ends in -**um**, giving **vīsum**. Answers (B), (C), and (D) are acceptable ways of translating **vīsam** as a past participle. (See "The Supine.")

Sententiae Antiquae Answers

1.   Gerund **(C)**
      Of writing is a noun, therefore requiring that the gerund **scrībendī** have its ending in the genitive case. Answer (A) **scrībendum** could be a gerund, but it is not in the genitive case. Answers (B) **scrībendae** and (D) **scrībendōrum** must be gerundives because of their adjectival endings.

2.   Gerund **(C)**
      By going is a gerund, here serving the function of the ablative of means. This quote from Vergil's *Aeneid* is the source of the motto of the State of New Mexico, **Crescit eundō**. All answers are forms of the irregular verb **īre**: (A) **iēns** is a present participle in its nominative singular form, and (D) **euntem** is an accusative singular form of the present active

participle, neither of which may be translated as *by going.* Answer (B) **eundum** may be seen as a gerund, but the accusative case is not justified by the context. (For gerunds and gerundives of irregular verbs, see "The Gerundive.")

3.   Passive periphrastic **(B)**
     This sentence contains the passive periphrastic **erant agenda**, with **Caesarī** serving as dative of agent. Answers (A), (C), and (D) do not express the idea of necessity or obligation, but of past continuous action (*was being done*), future action (*was about to do*), or past completed action (*was done*), respectively. Note the word order of **erant agenda**.

4.   Gerundive **(D)**
     The core of the meaning of this sentence is the prepositional phrase that includes a gerundive, **ā compōnendō carmine**, *from composing verse.* The use of the ablative here contains the idea of separation. Answer (A) is incorrect because the prepositional phrase does not serve as the subject of the sentence. In (B) and (C), the Muse is not *keeping him from creating verse* because there is no Latin pronoun *him* in the original sentence. This sentence translates *However, my Muse cannot be kept from creating verse.*

Stumper: Passive periphrastic **(A)**
     The correct answer to this question centers on the expression of the meaning of the periphrastic, **laudandus est**. Answers (B) *is praising* and (D) *is being praised* can be eliminated because they do not express obligation. Answer (C) *had to be praised* can be eliminated because it expresses past time.

CHAPTER 26

Infinitives

Chapter 26

INFINITIVES

TO BE OR NOT TO BE

As a verb form, the infinitive (**in** + **finis**, *without an ending*) is "infinite" with regard to person and number, that is, a form such as **mittere** is without limit and unchangeable. Verb forms that do change with respect to person and number, such as **mittō** or **mittunt**, are said to be finite, or limited. Both finite verbs and infinitives show variations in tense and voice.

The infinitive can serve as a verbal noun that can be used as a subject or object. For example, **mittere**, *to send*, can also mean *sending*. The infinitive can also complement or extend the meaning of another verb, such as in the following example:

> **Epistulam mittere vult.**
> *He wishes to send a letter.*

Furthermore, it can also be used to restate or report what someone says, thinks, or knows, as in the following sentence:

> **Scit sē epistulam mīsisse.**
> *He knows that he has sent the letter.*

As you will remember, it is the present active infinitive (the second principal part) that determines the conjugation of the verb and provides the stem of the present, imperfect, and future tenses of all indicative verbs, active and passive. Infinitives also provide the stems of the active and passive forms of the imperfect and pluperfect subjunctive, such as **mitteret**, **mitterētur**, **mīsisset**, and **missus esset**. (These forms will be reviewed in Chapter 27.)

Quick Study of Infinitives

mittō, mittere, mīsī, missus

	Active	Passive
Present	**mittere**, *to send*	**mittī**, *to be sent*
Perfect	**mīsisse**, *to have sent*	**missus esse**, *to have been sent*
Future	**missūrus esse**, *to be about to send*	**missus īrī**, *to be about to be sent* (rare)

THE INFINITIVES OF REGULAR VERBS

For the importance of the present active infinitive in the formation of the tenses of the present system of a verb, return to Chapter 19.

With one exception, the formation of the present <u>passive</u> infinitive includes the same stem vowel as the active:

	Active	Passive
1st	**spectāre**, *to see*	**spectārī**, *to be seen*
2nd	**favēre**, *to favor*	**favērī**, *to be favored*
3rd	**mittere**, *to send*	**mittī**, *to be sent*
4th	**finīre**, *to finish*	**finīrī**, *to be finished*

Note that the present stem vowel -**e**- is dropped from the present passive infinitive of verbs of the third conjugation, such as **mittī**.

The perfect active infinitive is formed from the perfect active stem + -**esse**, so **mīs**- + -**esse** = **mīsisse**. (The spelling of -**esse** becomes -**isse** for pronunciation reasons.) As you can see in the "Quick Study of Infinitives" chart, the perfect passive and future active infinitives have compound forms that include the perfect passive participle **missus, -a, -um** and future active participle **missūrus, -a, -um**, respectively, such as **missus esse**, *to <u>have been sent</u>* and **missūrus esse**, *to be <u>about to send</u>*. The future passive infinitive is extremely rare.

The infinitives of deponent verbs are formed as regular passive infinitives, for example **hortārī**, *to encourage*, **verērī**, *to fear*, **loquī**, *to talk*, and **orīrī**, *to rise*.

THE INFINITIVES OF IRREGULAR VERBS

Ferō is the only irregular verb with passive infinitive forms: **ferrī**, *to be brought,* and **lātus esse**, *to have been brought*. The word **fore** is often used as a substitute for **futūrum esse**.

The Infinitives of Irregular Verbs

Present	Perfect	Future
esse, *to be*	**fuisse**, *to have been*	**futūrus esse**, *to be about to be*
posse, *to be able*	**potuisse**, *to have been able*	
īre, *to go*	**iisse**, *to have gone*	**itūrus esse**, *to be about to go*
ferre, *to bring*	**tulisse**, *to have brought*	**latūrus esse**, *to be about to bring*
velle, *to wish*	**voluisse**, *to have wished*	
nōlle, *to be unwilling*	**nōluisse**, *to have been unwilling*	
mālle, *to prefer*	**māluisse**, *to have preferred*	
fierī, *to become*	**factus esse**, *to have become*	

USES OF THE INFINITIVE

In Chapter 23, we met the infinitive in a negative command or prohibition, for example, **Nōlī/Nōlīte oblīviscī!** *Don't forget!* The most common additional uses of the infinitive are (1) as a subject or direct object, (2) as a complement to another verb, and (3) as the verb in an indirect statement. Less common uses, such as the exclamatory infinitive and the historical infinitive, are not covered by this book.

Subjective Infinitive and Objective Infinitive

The infinitive—usually the present active infinitive—may be used as a subject or object of the main verb. Subjective infinitives are considered neuter singular nouns:

subjective

Dulce et decōrum est prō factiōne mori.*
It is sweet and glorious to die for one's racing team (i.e., *Dying is sweet . . .*).

The subjective infinitive serves as the "nominative" of the gerund (see Chapter 25). A famous example of this use is **Esse quam vidērī**, *Being rather than seeming* (literally, *To be rather than to seem*).

The infinitive may also serve as the direct object of a verb:

objective
Vincere quam vincī aurīga māvult.
A charioteer prefers victory to defeat (literally, *to win rather than to be defeated*).

Complementary Infinitive

The complementary (not complimentary!) infinitive (from **complēre**, *to fill up*) completes the meaning of another verb. The other verb is often irregular, such as in the following examples:

Potestne Līmax hoc certāmen vincere?
Is Limax able to win this race?

Nōnne Līmax metam vītāre vult? Eheu!
Surely Limax wants to avoid the turning post? Oops!

Quadrīgās frēgisse vidētur.
He seems to have broken his chariot.

TIPS ON TRANSLATING INFINITIVES

- When translating, consider the context of the sentence in which the infinitive is found. Look for a controlling verb in the case of a complementary infinitive.

---

* After the famous saying by Horace, **Dulce et decōrum est prō patriā mori**, *It is sweet and glorious to die for one's country.*

- The literal translation of an infinitive, *to*, will not always be appropriate to the context in which the infinitive is found, for example, as a subject or object or in indirect statement.

- Be alert for the use of an adjective + **esse** that may appear to be a perfect passive infinitive, such as the following:

  Adjective + **esse**:   **Aurīga putat sē <u>optimum</u> esse.**
  The charioteer thinks that he (himself) <u>is the best</u>.

  Perfect passive infinitive: **Aurīga putat sē victōrem prōnuntiātum esse.**
  The charioteer thinks that he (himself) <u>was declared</u> the winner.

- The literal translation of an infinitive rarely shows or expresses purpose, that is, *in order to*. For the latter, a gerund or gerundive of purpose (**ad** or **causā/grātiā** + the gerund or gerundive) or a clause of purpose (**ut** + subjunctive) is used.

- It is important to stay alert for Latin words that appear to be infinitives but are not, such as the ablative singular of some third declension nouns and adjectives like **genere** (from **genus, generis,** *birth, type*) and **consulāre** (from **consulāris, -is, -e,** *pertaining to a consul*).

- Especially in poetry, an alternative form of the perfect tense, such as **sumpsēre,** may fool you into thinking that it is the present infinitive **sūmere.** Closer inspection reveals that it is the perfect stem, **sumps-,** that precedes what appears to be an infinitive ending. The form **sumpsēre** is, in fact, an alternative to the third person plural of the perfect tense, **sumpsērunt,** *they have obtained,* and not the present active infinitive **sūmere,** *to obtain.*

- Subjunctive verbs formed from the present and perfect active infinitives are not to be confused with the infinitives themselves; for example, **esse** is a present infinitive whereas **essem** is an imperfect subjunctive, and **ēgisse** is a perfect infinitive whereas **ēgisset** is a pluperfect subjunctive.

INDIRECT STATEMENT

The infinitive may be used to report what someone hears, says, thinks, and so on. This grammatical construction is known as "indirect statement," "indirect discourse," or "accusative and infinitive." The following sentences illustrate the grammatical differences between direct and indirect statement:

Direct statement: **Aurīga quadrīgās magnā arte agit.**
The charioteer drives the chariot with great skill.

Indirect statement: **Dīcit aurīgam quadrīgās magnā arte agere.**
He says that the charioteer drives the chariot with great skill.

Verbs of mental or verbal action, such as **dīcit** above, are followed by a subject accusative, as **aurīgam**, and an infinitive, as **agere**, unless they introduce a direct quotation. Such verbs should be remembered because of the frequency in which the indirect statement occurs in Latin. (This might lead you to think that the ancient Romans were gossipy!) A memory device such as "M and M (mind and mouth) verbs" may help you to remember the following verbs that commonly introduce indirect statements in Latin:

arbitrāri, *to think*   **negāre**, *to deny*

audīre, *to hear*   **putāre**, *to think*

cognoscere, *to recognize*   **scīre**, *to know*

crēdere, *to believe*   **sentīre**, *to feel, perceive*

dīcere, *to say*   **sperāre**, *to hope*

intellegere, *to know, understand*   **vidēre**, *to see*

An infinitive shows the same time relationship to the main verb of mental action as a participle does to its main verb (see Chapter 24, "The Perfect Passive Participle" and "The Future Active Participle"). For instance, the present tenses of both the participle and the infinitive in the sentences below are translated in the past tense, because the tense of the main verb is past:

Participle: **Līmācem equōs <u>pascentem</u> cōnspeximus.**
We spotted Limax, <u>who was feeding</u> his horses.

Infinitive: **Līmax pūtābat Vēlōcem optimum equum <u>esse</u>.**
Limax thought that Velox <u>was</u> the best horse.

In the following table, note that infinitives in the <u>present</u> tense are translated <u>at the same time</u> as the main verb, those in the <u>perfect</u> tense are translated at a time <u>before</u> the main verb, and those in the <u>future</u> tense at a time <u>after</u> the main verb.

Quick Study of Indirect Statement

Tense of Main Verb	The Active Infinitive in Indirect Statement	Tense of Infinitive
Present	**Līmax <u>dīcit</u> sē quadrīgās <u>agere</u>.** *Limax <u>says</u> that he <u>drives</u> (is driving) the chariot.*	Present
Present	**Līmax <u>dīcit</u> sē quadrīgās <u>ēgisse</u>.** *Limax <u>says</u> that he <u>drove</u> (has driven) the chariot.*	Past
Present	**Līmax <u>dīcit</u> sē quadrīgās <u>actūrum esse</u>.** *Limax <u>says</u> that he <u>will drive</u> the chariot.*	Future
Past	**Līmax <u>dīcēbat</u> sē quadrīgās <u>agere</u>.** *Limax <u>said</u> that he <u>was driving</u> the chariot* (i.e., he said this at the same time as he was driving).	Present
Past	**Līmax <u>dīcēbat</u> sē quadrīgās <u>ēgisse</u>.** *Limax <u>said</u> that he <u>had driven</u> the chariot* (i.e., he drove before he spoke about it).	Past

Past	**Līmax dīcēbat sē quadrīgās actūrum esse.** *Līmax said that he would drive the chariot.*	Future

	The Passive Infinitive in Indirect Statement	
Present	**Līmax dīcit quadrīgās ā sē agī.** *Līmax says that the chariot is (being) driven by him.*	Present
Present	**Līmax dīcit quadrīgās ā sē actās esse.** *Līmax says that the chariot has been driven by him.*	Past
Past	**Līmax dīcēbat quadrīgās ā sē agī.** *Līmax said that the chariot was (being) driven by him* (i.e., he said this at the same time that he was driving).	Present
Past	**Līmax dīcēbat quadrīgās ā sē actās esse.** *Līmax said that the chariot had been driven by him* (i.e., he drove before he spoke about it).	Past

TIPS ON TRANSLATING INDIRECT STATEMENT

- Look for a verb of mental or verbal action that introduces an infinitive with a subject accusative.

- Distinguish between reflexive and nonreflexive subjects of the infinitive, such as **sē**, *himself*, and **eum**, *him*, that is, someone other than the subject of the main verb. (For reflexive pronouns, see Chapter 15.)

- In indirect statement, when the infinitive has a compound or two-part form, as in the perfect passive or future active, the participial portion of the infinitive agrees in gender and number with its subject, which will be accusative. For example,

Perfect passive:	**Aurīga vīdit mapp<u>am</u> dēmiss<u>am</u> esse.**
	The charioteer saw that the white starting cloth had been dropped.
Future active:	**Spērābat <u>sē</u> metam prīmum circumitūr<u>um</u> esse.**
	He was hoping that he (himself) would go around the turning post first.

- The indirect statement will <u>never</u> have quotes around it.

- For the best sense, insert the word *that* after the main verb in the English translation, even though this word does not appear in the Latin. Do not use the word *to* when translating an infinitive in an indirect statement:

Līmax dīcit sē victōrem <u>esse</u>.

Incorrect:	*Limax says he (himself) <u>to be</u> the winner.*
Correct:	*Limax says <u>that</u> he (himself) <u>is</u> the winner.*

- Remember that it is the time relationship between the main verb and the infinitive that you are translating; it is the tense of the infinitive relative to that of the main verb that determines the meaning of the indirect statement. Take special care with sentences containing a main verb in the past tense, such as **dīcēbat**, *he was saying*, when found with an infinitive either in the present tense, such as **esse**, *was*, or the past tense, such as **fuisse**, *had been*. When faced with an example of the latter, where the tenses of both the main verb and the infinitive are past, remember the acronym PPH, "past-past-*had*." If you are uncertain about how to express the time relationship, turn the indirect statement into a direct statement:

Indirect:	**Līmax <u>dīcēbat</u> sē quadrīgās <u>ēgisse</u>.** (Note that the infinitive is in the past tense.)
	Limax <u>said</u> that he . . . the chariot.
Direct:	*Limax said, "I drove the chariot."* (That is, he had already driven the chariot at the time he spoke)
Therefore:	*Limax said that he had driven the chariot.*

- The form **esse** is often omitted from the perfect or future active infinitive, as in **missum (esse)** and **missūrum (esse)**, and their meanings assumed or understood from context.

SAMPLE QUESTIONS

Part C: Translation

1. Ovidius scrībit fēminās ad circum <u>vidērī</u> velle.

   (A) to see   (C) to be seeing

   (B) to have been seen   (D) to be seen

Part D: Sentence Completion

2. Putantne spectātōrēs Līmacem crās . . . ?

   (A) victūrum esse   (C) vīcit

   (B) victum esse   (D) vīcisse

Answers

1. (D)   2. (A)

PRACTICE QUESTIONS

1. "<u>Don't fall</u> out of your chariot, Limax!" laughed the spectators.

   (A) Nōn cadere   (C) Nōlī cadere

   (B) Nōlīte cadere   (D) Nōn licet cadere

2. Fīnīre *is to* fīnīrī *as* vincere *is to*

   (A) vincī   (C) vince

   (B) vicī   (D) victī

3. Spectātor animadvertit *that charioteer* ē quadrīgīs cecidisse.

   (A) ille aurīga   (C) illī aurīgae

   (B) illum aurīgam   (D) illōs aurīgās

4. Līmax putāvit sē ā multīs nōn <u>fautum esse</u>.

   (A) has not been favored

   (B) is not favored

   (C) was not favored

   (D) had not been favored

5. Infēlix aurīga semper sperat crās melius. . . .

   (A) fuisse   (C) fuerat

   (B) fore   (D) erit

6. Līmax dixit sē scīre <u>velle</u> quot factiōnēs contenderent.

   (A) has wanted   (C) wants

   (B) was wanting   (D) will want

7. <u>Making an effort is noble</u>.

   (A) Conāns est nōbilis.   (C) Conātus est nōbiliter.

   (B) Conārī est nōbile.   (D) Nōbiliter conātur.

8. "Mīror tot mīlia virōrum cupere equōs vidēre," inquit Plinius.

   (A) Pliny doesn't understand why so many people like chariot racing.

   (B) Pliny wonders what it would be like to be a charioteer.

   (C) Pliny thinks that everyone should experience chariot racing.

   (D) Pliny says that many people want to ride horses.

9. Līmax scīvit <u>sibi carcerēs purgandōs esse</u>.

   (A) that he is going to clean out the stalls

   (B) that he must have the stalls cleaned out

   (C) that he had to clean out the stalls

   (D) that he will be invited to clean out the stalls

10. <u>Spērat aurīga sē diū victūrum.</u>

   (A) The charioteer, who is going to live for a long time, is hopeful.

   (B) The charioteer hoped that he would live for a long time.

   (C) He hopes that the charioteer will live for a long time.

   (D) The charioteer hopes that he will live for a long time.

SENTENTIAE ANTIQUAE

1. Identify the item that is <u>not</u> one of the three components necessary for an indirect statement.

   <u>Ait omnia pecūniā efficī posse.</u> (Cicero)

   (A) Ait   (C) omnia

   (B) posse   (D) efficī

2. We often see that the victor <u>has been overcome</u> by the vanquished. (Dionysius Cato)

   (A) superāvisse   (C) superāre

   (B) superātum esse   (D) superātūrum esse

3. <u>If you wish to be loved, love</u>! (Seneca)

   (A) Sī vīs amārī, amā!   (C) Sī vīs amārī, amāte!

   (B) Sī vīs amāre, amā!   (D) Sī vīs amātus esse, amā!

4. He preferred <u>to be</u> good rather than <u>to seem</u> good. (Sallust)

   (A) esse ... vidēre   (C) fuisse ... vīsus esse

   (B) esse ... vidērī   (D) esse ... vīdisse

5. ... quid antequam nātus sīs acciderit id est semper esse puer. (Cicero)

   (A) Nōlī nescīre   (C) Nesciendus

   (B) Nescīre   (D) Nescīrī

6. Pudor docērī nōn potest, nascī potest. (Publilius Syrus)

   (A) Modesty cannot be learned, it can be obtained.

   (B) One cannot be taught modesty, one is born with it.

   (C) Teaching is not shameful, it can be a product of birth.

   (D) He cannot teach modesty, but he can obtain it.

7. He is ungrateful who denies that <u>he has received</u> a kindness that he has received. (Cicero)

   (A) accipī   (C) accipere

   (B) acceptum esse   (D) accēpisse

8. Ego vērum amō; vērum volō mihi <u>dīcī</u>. (Plautus)

   (A) to be spoken   (C) to speak

   (B) to have spoken   (D) to have been spoken

Stumper:

   <u>Making a mistake is human</u>. (Seneca)

   (A) Errāns est hūmānus.

   (B) Esse hūmānus est error.

   (C) Errāre hūmānum est.

   (D) Errāns est hūmānus.

Answers

1. Prohibition **(C)**
   The negative command *Don't fall*, **Nōlī cadere**, represents one of the varied uses of the infinitive. Answer (A) is not a negative command; (B) is plural (Limax is being addressed in the original sentence); and (D) is not a command but an infinitive phrase with an impersonal verb. (For the infinitive in the negative command, see Chapter 23, "Negative Imperatives.")

2. Present passive infinitive **(A)**
   The present active infinitive of **fīniō** is to the present passive as the present active infinitive of **vincō** is to the present passive, which is **vincī**. Answer (B) **vīcī** is the third principal part or perfect tense, first person

singular. Answer (C) **vince** is the present imperative, and (D) **victī** is a form of the perfect passive participle.

3.   Subject accusative **(B)**
     The subject of an infinitive in an indirect statement is in the accusative case. Of the choices provided, **illum aurīgam** is in the accusative case and in the singular, as required by *that charioteer*. Answer (A) **ille aurīga** presents what would have been the subject of the direct statement. Answer (C) **illī aurīgae** is nominative plural or dative singular, and (D) **illōs aurīgās** is plural. (See "Indirect Statement.")

4.   Indirect statement **(D)**
     This sentence contains an example of "past-past-*had*," that is, both the main verb **putāvit** and the infinitive **fautum esse** are in the past tense, resulting in the translation *had been favored*. Answers (A) *has been favored* and (C) *was favored* are only possible if the main verb is in the present tense. Answer (B) *is favored* is **favērī**, which is a present passive infinitive. The sentence reads *Limax knew that he <u>had not been favored</u> by many*.

5.   Indirect statement with **fore (B)**
     In this sentence, the verb **spērat** is a verb of mental action, which prompts an indirect statement, of which **crās** is the subject and **fore** (= **futūrum esse**) the infinitive. The sentence reads *The unsuccessful charioteer always hopes that tomorrow <u>will be</u> better*. Answer (A) **fuisse** translates as *has been*, and (C) and (D) are not infinitives but pluperfect and future tense forms of the verb **esse**.

6.   Indirect statement **(B)**
     The main verb **dixit** in this sentence keys an indirect statement, the subject of which is **sē** and the infinitive **velle**. The combination of the main verb in the past tense and the infinitive in the present tense leads to the translation *was wanting*. (See "Indirect Statement.") Answer (A) *has wanted* is **voluisse**. Answer (C) *wants* is a literal translation of the infinitive **velle**, but given the context, the infinitive cannot have this meaning. Answer (D) *will want* cannot translate the present active infinitive **velle**. The sentence reads *Limax said that he <u>was wanting</u> to know how many racing teams were in contention*.

7.   Subjective infinitive **(B)**
     This sentence contains the subjective infinitive of the deponent verb **conārī**, *to try* = *trying*. Therefore **Conārī est nōbile** is the correct an-

swer. Because a subjective infinitive is considered equivalent to a neuter noun, the adjective **nōbile**, which is neuter, is correct. The obvious but incorrect answer is (A), whereas (C) **Conātus est nōbiliter** expresses the action in past time. Answer (D) **Nōbiliter conātur**, meaning *He is trying nobly*, is also incorrect. (See "The Infinitives of Regular Verbs.")

8. Indirect statement **(A)**
    Pliny said, *I wonder that so many thousands of men want to watch horses.* Answers (B), (C), and (D) contain various inaccuracies in their translations.

9. Indirect statement with passive periphrastic **(C)**
    This sentence contains an indirect statement in which the infinitive consists of **purgandōs esse**, a gerundive in the passive periphrastic construction, which expresses necessity. The subject of the infinitive has reverted from accusative to dative as the agent of the necessary action. Therefore **sē** becomes **sibi**. Answer (A) *is going to clean out* is (**sē**) . . . **purgātūrum esse**. Answer (B) *must have the stalls cleaned out* is in colloquial English and cannot express the Latin in the original sentence. In (D), the Latin for *he will be invited* is not found in the original. Poor Limax, who even has to clean out the stalls!

10. Indirect statement **(D)**
    The sentence reads *The* (or *A*) *charioteer hopes that he will live for a long time.* The subject of the sentence, **aurīga**, is put in a secondary position to tempt you into thinking that it is the subject of the infinitive, which is **sē**. Note the ellipsis of the future infinitive **victūrum (esse)**. Answer (A) requires a future participle in the nominative case, (**aurīga**) **victūrus**. Answer (B) requires a main verb that is in the past tense and not the present. Answer (C) requires that **aurīga** be **aurīgam** in order to serve as the accusative subject of the infinitive **victūrum (esse)**. Remember that **aurīga** is masculine.

Sententiae Antiquae Answers

1. **(D)**
    Efficī is a complementary infinitive dependent upon **posse** in this sentence. **Posse**, the subject of which is **omnia**, is the infinitive in the indirect statement following **ait**. The sentence reads *He says that all things can be accomplished with money.*

2. Indirect statement **(B)**
    The underlined phrase *has been overcome* requires an infinitive that is perfect and passive, such as **superātum esse**. Answer (A) **superāvisse** is active; (C) **superāre** and (D) **superātūrum esse** are in the wrong tenses and voices (present and future active).

3. Complementary infinitive **(A)**
    Answer (B) is incorrect because the infinitive **amāre** is active and does not correctly express *to be loved*. In (C), the imperative is plural, whereas the singular is required, as indicated by the second person singular form **vīs**. Answer (D) offers an incorrect translation in the past tense, *If you wish to have been loved, love!* (See "Complementary Infinitive.")

4. Complementary infinitive **(B)**
    In (A), **docērī** is incorrectly translated as *learned* (this is **discī**). Answer (C) *Teaching is not shameful* reverses the thought of the original sentence, *Shame cannot be taught*. Answer (D) incorrectly translates the passive infinitive **docērī** as active and misreads **nascī** as the infinitive of **nanciscor**, *obtain*, rather than **nascor**, *be born*.

5. Subjective infinitive **(B)**
    Cicero's famous thought contains a subjective infinitive, **nescīre**, *not knowing*. The sentence reads <u>*Being unaware*</u> *of what happened before you were born is always to be a child*. The infinitive acts as the antecedent of the pronoun **id**. Note the two subjunctive clauses within this sentence: **quid . . . acciderit** and **antequam nātus sīs**. (For the subjective infinitive, see "The Infinitives of Irregular Verbs.")

6. Complementary infinitive **(B)**
    Answer (C) is immediately rejected because **fuisse**, *to have been*, does not correctly translate the infinitive *to be*, as required in the original sentence. Answers (A) and (D) have the incorrect form of the infinitive because **vidēre** means *to see* and **vīdisse** means *to have seen*. *To seem* requires the present passive infinitive, which is **vidērī**, *to be seen* = *to seem*. (See Chapter 20, "Deponent Verbs with Additional Meanings.")

7. Indirect statement **(D)**
    The verb *denies*, which introduces the indirect statement *that he has received*, is in the present tense and active voice. The corresponding form of the infinitive *he has received* is the perfect active form **accēpisse**. Answer (A) **accipī** is present passive, which has a contextual meaning *he is*

received. Answer (B) **acceptum esse** is perfect passive, *he has been received*, and (C) **accipere** is present active, *he is receiving*.

8.   Complementary infinitive **(A)**

Dīcī is the present passive infinitive of the verb **dīcere**. The sentence reads *I love (what is) true* (i.e., *the truth*); *I wish the truth to be spoken to me*. Answer (B) *to have spoken* is the perfect active infinitive **dīxisse**; (B) *to speak* is the present active form **dīcere**; and (D) *to have been spoken* is the perfect passive form **dictum esse**. Note the substantive adjective **vērum**.

Stumper: Subjective infinitive **(C)**

This famous saying contains the subjective infinitive **errāre** modified by the neuter adjective **hūmānum**, a gender required by the use of the infinitive as a noun.

THE SAT SUBJECT TEST IN
LATIN

SECTION 8

Subjunctive Verbs

CHAPTER 27
Forms of the Subjunctive

Chapter 27

FORMS OF THE SUBJUNCTIVE

THE SUBJUNCTIVE MOOD

The subjunctive is the third of the three moods of finite verbs.* Remember from your review of the indicative and imperative moods that mood indicates the function of a verb in a sentence. We have met the indicative mood, which indicates a statement of fact or an assertion, as well as a direct question. We have also reviewed the imperative mood, which expresses a command. The third mood, the subjunctive, is used to express a nonfactual or hypothetical action, such as a possibility or wish, often requiring in English an auxiliary or helping verb such as *might*, *should*, or *would*:

Indicative: **Lībertus gladiātor esse volēbat.**
The freedman wanted to be a gladiator.

Imperative: **"Nōlī esse gladiātor!" dīcēbat amīcus.**
"Don't be a gladiator!" his friend said.

Subjunctive: **Amīcus mīrābātur cur lībertus gladiātor esse vellet.**
The friend wondered why the freedman wished to be a gladiator.

The use of the subjunctive, such as *I wish I were in Rome now* (not *was!*) or *be it ever so humble*, has virtually disappeared from English. In Latin, verbs found in the subjunctive mood have a variety of uses, including serving as the verb with independent meaning found in a main clause or as the verb in a variety of subordinate or dependent clauses. The subjunctive appears most commonly as the verb of a dependent clause, as in the third

---

* For an excellent presentation of the subjunctive mood, see Greta Ham, "The Subjunctive in Latin: Some Basic Functions," http://www.facstaff.bucknell.edu/gretaham/Teaching/latin102/latin/subjunctive_main.html.

example. This is evident from the meaning of its Latin root **subiungere** (**subjungere**), *to subjoin, subordinate*. It has been observed that the subordinating nature of the Latin language, that is, the fact that a single main idea can establish control or priority over secondary or dependent thoughts in a sentence, reflects the martial character of the Romans and the direct authority that they established over other peoples.*

There are four tenses of the subjunctive, with no forms in the future or future perfect tenses. The expression of the tense of a subjunctive verb is the same as its indicative equivalent; for example, the imperfect subjunctive **mitteret**, *he was sending*, translates just as the imperfect indicative **mittēbat**, *he was sending*. The meaning of a subjunctive verb is dependent upon and derived from its context. This chapter will also help you to review the sequence of tenses, which outlines the rules for correlating the tense of the subjunctive verb with that of the indicative verb in a sentence. In the synopses of the four tenses of the subjunctive mood, the following verbs are used:

1st conjugation:	**pugnō, pugnāre, pugnāvī, pugnātus**
2nd conjugation:	**deleō, delēre, delēvī, delētus**
3rd conjugation:	**mittō, mittere, mīsī, missus**
4th conjugation:	**custodiō, custodīre, custodīvī, custodītus**

You will recall that the imperfect and pluperfect tenses of the subjunctive (provided in the following charts) are based on forms of the infinitive, and that the present and perfect subjunctives have forms similar to those of the present and future perfect tenses of the indicative mood. During your review, focus on distinguishing between forms in the indicative mood and those in the subjunctive.

Present Subjunctive: Active and Passive

	1st Conjugation	2nd Conjugation	3rd Conjugation	4th Conjugation
Present active	**pugnet**	**deleat**	**mittat**	**custodiat**
Present passive	**pugnētur**	**deleātur**	**mittātur**	**custodiātur**

---

* Carl R. Trahman, "What Does Latin Tell Us about the Romans?" *Classical Journal*, February 1972: 240–250.

- Formation: the vowel that marks the present subjunctive of the second, third, and fourth conjugations is -**a**-, as in **deleat**, **mittat**, and **custodiat**. Because the stem vowel of the first conjugation in the indicative is already -**a**-, the present subjunctive of that conjugation is formed using the vowel -**e**-, for example **pugnet**. "Let's eat caviar" and "we hear a liar" are memory devices that might help you remember the stem vowels of the four conjugations that are found in the present subjunctive.*

- The first person singular, or "I" form, of each tense in the active voice ends in -**m**, as in **mittam**, **mitterem**, **miserim**, **misissem**. The remaining personal endings for all tenses of the subjunctive are the same as those of indicative verbs. (For these forms, see Chapter 19).

- The present subjunctive is most often found by itself in a main clause and also in "should . . . would" conditional clauses.

Imperfect Subjunctive: Active and Passive

	1st Conjugation	2nd Conjugation	3rd Conjugation	4th Conjugation
Imperfect active	**pugnāret**	**delēret**	**mitteret**	**custodīret**
Imperfect passive	**pugnārētur**	**delērētur**	**mitterētur**	**custodīrētur**

- Formation: present active infinitive + regular personal active and passive endings, for example **mittere** + -**t** = **mitteret** and **mittere** + **tur** = **mitterētur**.

- The imperfect subjunctive is regularly used in purpose, result, and **cum** clauses, present contrary to fact conditions, and optative subjunctive expressions with **utinam**. It is perhaps the most commonly used of subjunctive forms.

---

* David Pellegrino, http://latinteach.com/verbmnemonics.html.

Perfect Subjunctive: Active and Passive

	1st Conjugation	2nd Conjugation	3rd Conjugation	4th Conjugation
Perfect active	**pugnāverit**	**delēverit**	**mīserit**	**custodīverit**
Perfect passive	**pugnātus sit**	**delētus sit**	**missus sit**	**custodītus sit**

- Active formation: perfect active stem + active forms of the future tense of the verb **esse**, for example **mīs** + **erit** = **mīserit**.

- Passive formation: perfect passive stem **miss-** + first/second declension adjective endings -**us**, -**a**, -**um** + detached present subjunctive of **esse**, such as **missus sim**, **missus sīs**, **missus sit**, and so on.

- The perfect tense active gives the appearance of the future perfect tense active (see Chapter 19, "Future Perfect Indicative: Active and Passive"). Note, however, that the first person singular of the perfect active subjunctive is **mīserim**, whereas that of the future perfect indicative is **mīserō**. All other forms are the same.

- The perfect tense appears the least often of the four tenses of the subjunctive. It occurs independently as a potential subjunctive, and in conditional, result, and indirect question clauses.

Pluperfect Subjunctive: Active and Passive

	1st Conjugation	2nd Conjugation	3rd Conjugation	4th Conjugation
Pluperfect active	**pugnāvisset**	**dēlēvisset**	**mīsisset**	**custodīvisset**
Pluperfect passive	**pugnātus esset**	**delētus esset**	**missus esset**	**custodītus esset**

- Active formation: perfect active infinitive + regular personal endings, for example **mīsisse** + -**t** = **mīsisset**.

- Passive formation: perfect passive stem **miss-** + first/second declension adjective endings **-us**, **-a**, **-um** + detached imperfect subjunctive of **esse**, as in **missus essem**, **missus essēs**, **missus esset**, and so on.

- The pluperfect tense of the subjunctive appears frequently in past contrary to fact conditions, in **cum** clauses, and as an optative subjunctive expressing an unfulfilled wish in past time.

Quick Study Synopsis of Subjunctive Verbs

	Active	Passive
Present	**mittat**	**mittatur**
Imperfect	**mitteret**	**mitterētur**
Perfect	**mīserit**	**missus sit**
Pluperfect	**mīsisset**	**missus esset**

Synopses of Deponent Verbs in the Subjunctive

1st conjugation:	**hortor, hortārī, hortātus sum**
2nd conjugation:	**vereor, verērī, veritus sum**
3rd conjugation:	**loquor, loquī, locūtus sum**
4th conjugation:	**orior, orīrī, ortus sum**

	1st Conjugation	2nd Conjugation	3rd Conjugation	4th Conjugation
Present	**hortētur**	**vereātur**	**loquātur**	**oriātur**
Imperfect	**hortārētur**	**verērētur**	**loquerētur**	**orīrētur**
Perfect	**hortātus sit**	**veritus sit**	**locūtus sit**	**ortus sit**
Pluperfect	**hortātus esset**	**veritus esset**	**locūtus esset**	**ortus esset**

Synopses of Irregular Verbs in the Subjunctive

Except for the present tense, the rules for the formation of the subjunctive of irregular verbs are the same as those for regular verbs. (For forms of irregular verbs in the indicative, see Chapter 21.)

	sum, esse, fuī	possum, posse, potuī	eō, īre, iī/īvī	ferō, ferre, tulī, lātus	volō, velle, voluī	fiō, fierī,[†] factus sum
Present	sit	possit	eat	ferat	velit	fīat
Imperfect	esset	posset	īret	ferret	vellet	fieret
Perfect	fuerit	potuerit	ierit/ iverit	tulerit	voluerit	factus sit
Pluperfect	fuisset	potuisset	īsset/ ivisset*	tulisset	voluisset	factus esset

* Be reminded that the perfect stem of the verb **īre** is found variously as **i-** and **īv-**. Thus, both **īsset** and **īvisset** are correct.

† In addition to the passive forms of **fierī**, the verb **ferre** contains passive forms of the subjunctive: present tense, **ferātur**; imperfect tense, **ferrētur**; perfect tense, **lātus sit**; and pluperfect tense, **lātus esset**.

SEQUENCE OF TENSES

In a Latin sentence, the time relationship between the indicative verb of the main clause and the subjunctive verb of the dependent or subordinate clause is called sequence of tenses. The tense of the dependent or subjunctive verb "follows" upon that of the main verb.

Primary Sequence

The verb in the <u>main</u> clause in what is known as "primary sequence" must refer to present or future time; that is, it must be in the <u>present</u>, <u>future</u>, or <u>future perfect</u> tense. The verb in the <u>dependent</u> clause indicates that the action of the subordinate clause is happening before, during, or after that of the main verb.

        main clause   subordinate clause

1. Gladiātor Anxius nōn **intellegit** [cūr Maximum **pugnet**].
                present   present

> *The gladiator Anxius doesn't understand <u>now</u> why he is fighting Maximus <u>now</u>.*

main clause   subordinate clause
2. Gladiātor Anxius nōn **intellegit** [cūr Maximum **pugnāverit**].
                         present   perfect

> *The gladiator Anxius doesn't understand <u>now</u> why he fought Maximus <u>previously</u>.*

main clause   subordinate clause
3. Gladiātor Anxius nōn **intellegit** [cūr Maximum **pugnatūrus sit**].
                         present active   periphrastic

> *The gladiator Anxius doesn't understand <u>now</u> why he is going to fight Maximus <u>in the future</u>.*

Secondary Sequence

The verb in the <u>main</u> clause in secondary sequence must refer to past or "historic" time; that is, it must be in the <u>imperfect</u>, <u>perfect</u>, or <u>pluperfect</u> tense. In secondary sequence, the relationships between the indicative verb of the main clause and the subjunctive verb of the dependent clause are the same as those for primary sequence.

main clause   subordinate clause
4. Gladiātor Anxius nōn **intellēxit** [cūr Maximum **pugnāret**].
                         perfect   imperfect

> *The gladiator Anxius didn't understand <u>then</u> why he was fighting Maximus <u>then</u>.*

main clause   subordinate clause
5. Gladiātor Anxius nōn **intellēxit** [cūr Maximum **pugnāvisset**].
                         perfect   pluperfect

> *The gladiator Anxius didn't understand <u>then</u> why he had fought Maximus <u>previously</u>.*

main clause   subordinate clause
6. Gladiātor Anxius nōn **intellēxit** [cūr Maximum **pugnatūrus esset**].
                         perfect active   periphrastic

> *The gladiator Anxius didn't understand <u>then</u> why he would fight Maximus <u>in the future</u>.*

The following table extends the preceding examples and summarizes the various possible combinations of indicative and subjunctive verb tenses. In a Latin sentence, any indicative verb in the second column may be found, with regard to tense, with any subjunctive verb in the third column, as long as the line between primary and secondary sequence is not crossed. With a few exceptions, the appropriate sequence must be maintained; for example, a main verb in the present tense (primary sequence), such as **intellegit**, cannot be followed by a dependent verb in the imperfect tense (secondary sequence), such as **pugnāret**.

Quick Study of Sequence of Tenses

Tense of Indicative (time of action of main clause)	Main Clause	Dependent Clause	Tense of Subjunctive (time of action relative to main clause)
Primary Sequence			
Present	**intellegit,** *he understands*	**pugnet,** *he is fighting*	Present
Future	**intelleget,** *he will understand*	**pugnāverit,** *he has fought*	Perfect
Future perfect	**intellēxerit,** *he will have understood*	**pugnatūrūs sit,** *he will fight*	Active periphrastic
Secondary Sequence			
Imperfect	**intellegēbat,** *he was understanding*	**pugnāret,** *he was fighting*	Imperfect
Perfect	**intellēxit,** *he understood*	**pugnāvisset,** *he had fought*	Pluperfect
Pluperfect	**intellēxerat,** *he had understood*	**pugnātūrus esset,** *he would fight*	Active periphrastic

Future time is expressed in the subjunctive with the active periphrastic = future participle + the present subjunctive of **esse** (**sim, sīs, sit,** etc.) in the primary sequence and imperfect subjunctive of **esse** in the secondary (**essem, essēs, esset,** etc.), as illustrated in the preceding chart.

As with verbs in the indicative mood, subjunctive verbs in the present and imperfect tenses show action that is ongoing or not completed, whereas those in the perfect and pluperfect tenses show action that is completed.

TIPS ON MASTERING FORMS OF THE SUBJUNCTIVE

- The present and perfect subjunctive forms are sometimes mistaken for their present, future, and future perfect indicative counterparts; for example, the present subjunctive **mittat** can be mistaken for the present or future indicative, **mittit** or **mittet**. You should assume that a verb form containing the ending vowel -**a**- is in the present subjunctive because this vowel characterizes the present subjunctive of three conjugations (second, third, and fourth), whereas it characterizes the indicative of only one, the first. Therefore, such a verb form has a much greater chance of being subjunctive than indicative.

- Use context to distinguish the perfect subjunctive **mīserit** from the future perfect indicative form **mīserit**. (Remember, however, that the first person singular of the perfect subjunctive is -**erim**, e.g, **mīserim**, whereas the future perfect indicative form is -**erō**, e.g., **mīserō**.) To differentiate between ambiguous forms, know principal parts and use contextual clues.

- As was mentioned in the previous chapter on infinitives, the imperfect and pluperfect tenses of the subjunctive, both active and passive, are formed from the present and perfect infinitives. Avoid confusing forms of the subjunctive with those of the infinitive.

- Remember that a verb in the subjunctive mood can be found both independently, as a main verb, and in a clause that is dependent on the main verb.

- The tenses of the subjunctive are rendered in the same manner as those of the indicative. In a clause, the subjunctive verb depends on the tense of the main verb for its meaning.

- Subjunctive verbs, whether independent or dependent, express nonfactual or hypothetical situations. Use words such as *can*, *could*, *may*, *might*, *should*, or *would* when translating.

CHAPTER 28

The Subjunctive
Used Independently

Chapter 28

THE SUBJUNCTIVE USED INDEPENDENTLY

A subjunctive verb may be found independently in a sentence, that is, by itself in a main clause as opposed to serving as the verb in a dependent clause:

Independent (main clause): **Omnēs gladiātōrēs fortiter pugnent!**
Let all gladiators fight bravely!

Dependent (subordinate clause): **Gladiātōrēs pugnant ut vīvant.**
Gladiators fight in order to live.

The presentation in this chapter is limited to independent uses of the subjunctive, which include polite command and encouragement (jussive and hortatory), questions in which the speaker or writer expresses doubt or disbelief by "thinking aloud" (deliberative), wishes that cannot or may not be fulfilled (optative), and the possibility that something may happen or might have happened (potential). The actions of such verbs in the subjunctive, as opposed to those in the indicative, may not actually take place or have taken place, and they are therefore to be considered hypothetical.

English words such as *can, could, may, might, should,* and *would* best express the meaning of the various uses of the independent subjunctive. You should concentrate on determining the suitable English meaning from context. For example, **nē pugnent** has meanings such as *let them not fight, if only they wouldn't fight,* or *they should not fight,* depending upon the circumstances. For the forms of the independent subjunctive, which are found most often in the present tense, see Chapter 27.

On the SAT Latin Subject Test, the meaning of the independent subjunctive is tested in context, that is, in Latin-to-English questions (Part C: Translation) and in Latin-to-Latin questions (Part D: Sentence Completion and Part E: Syntax Substitution).

USES OF THE INDEPENDENT SUBJUNCTIVE

Jussive and Hortatory Subjunctives

Perhaps the most common uses of the independent subjunctive are the jussive and the hortatory:

Jussive:
> **"Cēdant togae armīs!" exclāmābant gladiātōrēs.**
> *"Let the togas yield to arms!" yelled the gladiators.*

Hortatory:
> **Nē pugnēmus, mī Maxime, atque vīvāmus.**
> *Let us not fight, my Maximus, and let us live.*

Descriptive Label	Function	Tense Used	Negative
Jussive (**iubēre/jubēre**, *to order*)	polite command	present (*Let him/them . . .*)	**nē**
Hortatory (**hortārī**, *to urge*)	encouragement	Present (*Let us . . .*)	**nē**

Because the uses and meanings of the jussive and hortatory are substantially identical (distinguished by whether the first or third person is being addressed), the forms are often combined into a single category and translated *Let . . .* You may enjoy remembering this usage as the "Caesar salad" subjunctive:

> *Lettuce do this, lettuce do that.**

For an example of the jussive subjunctive, keep in mind the well-known saying **Caveat emptor**, *Let the buyer beware* (i.e., be an informed consumer).

---

* From a roundtable sharing session, Oklahoma Classics Association workshop, 1996.

When the second person (*you*) is required in the expression of a command, Latin prefers the imperative mood of the verb, as in the following saying:

> **<u>Cape</u> cōnsilium in arēnā!**
> (<u>*You*</u>) <u>*make*</u> *your plan in the arena!**

The perfect tense of the subjunctive is sometimes used to express a negative command or prohibition:

> **Nē <u>cēperis</u> cōnsilium in arēnā.**
> <u>*Don't make*</u> *your plan in the arena.*

This is an alternative to the more common **nōlī/nōlīte** + infinitive (see Chapter 23, "Negative Imperatives").

Deliberative Subjunctive

Unlike the direct question, which is found with the indicative mood (see Chapter 23), the deliberative question with the subjunctive is expressed as a question to oneself, with no answer expected. This type of question can imply doubt, indignation, surprise, or confusion, as in the following example:

> **Āndroclēs leōnī sē oppositūrus erat. "<u>Quid faciam</u>?" gemuit.**
> *Androcles was about to face the lion. "<u>What should I do?</u>" he groaned.*

Descriptive Label	Function	Tenses Used	Negative
Deliberative (**dēlīberāre**, *to consider*)	self-question	present (*Am I to? Should I?*)	**nōn**
		imperfect (*Was I to?*)	

The difference between a direct question with the indicative and a deliberative question is that the former expresses a fact and the latter a nonfact:

Direct question: **Quod cōnsilium in arēnā <u>capis</u>?**
                                   What plan <u>are you making</u> in the arena?

Deliberative question: **Quod cōnsilium in arēnā <u>capiās</u>?**
                                     What plan <u>should you make</u> in the arena?

---

*   The example sentences in this section derive from Roman *sententiae*: **Cēdant arma tōgae**, *Let arms yield to the toga* (Cicero), i.e., the military should be subordinate to the government; **Vīvāmus, mea Lesbia, atque amēmus**, *Let us live, my Lesbia, and let us love* (Catullus); **Gladiātor in arēnā cōnsilium capit**, *The gladiator makes his plan in the arena* (Seneca), i.e., the gladiator must be able to think on his feet and adjust to circumstances.

Optative Subjunctive

The optative subjunctive expresses a wish felt or spoken by the speaker or writer. It is found either independently or as a clause, and most often with the particle **utinam** (negative **utinam nē**), which has the meanings *if only*, *would that*, *I wish (that)*, *may*. A clause introduced by **utinam** usually expresses a wish incapable of fulfillment or a regret. It is most often found with the imperfect or pluperfect tense:

Imperfect tense:

Lanista cogitābat, "Utinam meliōrēs gladiātōrēs habērem."
> *The trainer was thinking, "I wish that I had better gladiators (but I do not)"* (or *"I regret that I do not have . . .").*

Pluperfect tense:

Utinam naumachiam in amphitheātrō vīdissēmus.
> *If only we had seen a sea battle in the amphitheater (but we did not)* (or *"I regret that we did not see . . .").*

Descriptive Label	Function	Tenses Used	Negative
Optative (**optāre**, *to choose*)	wish	present (*if only*, *may*, *hope*, possible future)	**nē**
		imperfect (*if only . . . were*, unaccomplished present)	
		pluperfect (*if only . . . had*, unaccomplished past)	

The present tense is used when the wish is conceived of as possibly coming true in the future:

Utinam sīs victor, Anxī.
> *If only you would be the victor, Anxius* (or *May you be the victor, Anxius [and you very well may be]*).

For testing purposes, the optative subjunctive is usually found with **utinam**. However, the optative may also appear independently of this particle when its meaning has the effect of a jussive/hortatory or a conditional, as in a prayer, for example,

> **Dī mē <u>adiuvent</u>.**
> <u>*May*</u> *the gods <u>help</u> me* (or *If only the gods would help me*).

The imperfect tense is used when the wish is not capable of fulfillment now:

> **Utinam victor <u>essēs</u>, Anxī.**
> *If only <u>you were</u>* (or <u>*might be*</u>) *the victor, Anxius* (*but you aren't*).

The pluperfect tense is used when the wish was not capable of fulfillment in the past:

> **Utinam victor <u>fuissēs</u>, Anxī.**
> *If only <u>you had been</u> the victor, Anxius* (*but you weren't*).

Potential Subjunctive

The potential subjunctive is an independent subjunctive that expresses an action as possible or conceivable in past, present, or future time. It is translated as *can, could, may, might, should,* or *would* in the present (and occasionally the perfect) tense when referring to present or future time and as *could have, might have,* or *would have* in the imperfect tense when referring to past time.

> Present or future time: **Spartacus Rōmānōs <u>superet</u>.**
> *Spartacus <u>may defeat</u> the Romans* (*and there is the possibility that he might*).

> Past time: **Nēmo hoc <u>crederet</u>.**
> *No one <u>would have believed</u> this* (*but there is the possibility that they might have*).

Descriptive Label	Function	Tenses Used	Negative
Potential (**posse**, *to be able*)	possibility	present (*may, could, would, should,* present or future)	**nōn**
		imperfect (*might have, could have, would have,* past)	

Quick Study of Independent Subjunctives

Context	Translation(s)	Type	Function
Present Time			
Rōmae vīvam.	*Let me live in Rome.*	hortatory	exhortation
(Utinam) Rōmae vīvam.	*May I live in Rome.* *I wish I could live in Rome.* *If only I might live in Rome.*	optative	wish
Rōmam vīvam.	*I could live in Rome.*	potential	possibility
Rōmam vīvam.	*I may or might live in Rome.*	potential	possibility
Rōmae vīvat.	*Let him live in Rome.*	jussive	polite command
Vīvamne Rōmae?	*Should I live in Rome?*	deliberative	self question
Past Time			
Vīveremne Rōmae?	*Was I to live in Rome?*	deliberative	self question
Utinam Rōmae vīverem.	*If only I were to live in Rome.*	optative	wish
Utinam Rōmae vīxissem.	*If only I had lived in Rome.*	optative	wish
Rōmae vīverem.	*I might have/could have/would have lived in Rome.*	potential	possibility

TIPS ON TRANSLATING INDEPENDENT SUBJUNCTIVES

- The present tense is the tense most often found in the various uses of the independent subjunctive.

- When in the process of identifying and translating a subjunctive verb as independent, look carefully at the environment of the verb. When translating, observe the context to help you to make an educated guess about whether or not the verb is sub-junctive. For instance, consider this sentence from Horace:

Nōn omnis <u>moriar</u>, multaque pars meī vitābit Libitīnam.
I will not perish altogether, and indeed a great part of me will elude Libitina (goddess of the dead).

The verb **moriar** could mean either *I will die* (future indica-tive) or *Let me die* (present subjunctive). The context of this verb, which includes the more obvious future form **vitābit**, will help you to determine that the best meaning is *I will die*. (Of course, you've probably already decided this because you know that **nōn** negates **moriar** here, whereas **moriar** as a hor-tatory subjunctive would be negated by **nē**!)

• Translation of the present subjunctive can be confusing, be-cause of the variety of its functions (exhortation, wish, pos-sibility, etc.) Similar blurring of intent or tone has taken place in English, for example, *I would be careful* could be conceived of as advice (hortatory), a wish (optative), the main clause of a condition (*if I were you*), and so on. It is important to let the context of the sentence dictate how you express the meaning of the present subjunctive. Use words such as *can, could, may, might, should,* and *would,* as well as *let.*

PRACTICE QUESTIONS

1. <u>May she rest</u> in peace.

    (A) Requiescit

    (B) Requiescēns

    (C) Requiesce

    (D) Requiescat

2. <u>Sit tibi terra levis</u>. (i.e., STTL, often inscribed on Roman tombstones)

    (A) The earth is gentle upon you.

    (B) Be gentle upon the earth.

    (C) You are resting gently in the earth.

    (D) May the earth be gentle upon you.

3. <u>Palmam quī meruit, ferat</u>. (Lord Nelson)

   (A) Whoever deserves the palm will display it.

   (B) He who has earned the palm, let him display it.

   (C) He is displaying the palm which he earned.

   (D) Whoever wants the palm should display it.

4. Would that <u>we had been</u> less desirous of life. (Cicero)

   (A) fuissēmus   (C) fuerāmus

   (B) essēmus   (D) fuerimus

5. <u>Sit</u>. (The Beatles)

   (A) It is.   (C) Let it be.

   (B) He can.   (D) Would that it were.

6. <u>Quid agam</u>? (Cicero)

   (A) What should I do?   (C) What have I done?

   (B) What was I to do?   (D) What had I done?

7. <u>Dum inter hominēs sumus, colāmus hūmānitātem</u>. (Seneca)

   (A) While we are among men, let us cherish humanity.

   (B) We must cherish humanity while we are among men.

   (C) We do cherish humanity as long as we are among men.

   (D) While we were among men, we should have cherished humanity.

8. <u>Let us hope</u> for what we want, but <u>let us endure</u> whatever happens. (Cicero)

   (A) Spērāmus; ferimus   (C) Spērāmus; ferāmus

   (B) Spērēmus; ferēmus   (D) Spērēmus; ferāmus

9. Utinam populus Romānus ūnam cervīcem . . . ! (Suetonius, quoting Caligula)

   (A) habet   (C) habēret

   (B) habuerat   (D) habēbat

10. Quod sentimus loquāmur; quod loquimur sentiāmus. (Seneca)

    If we were to negate the subjunctive verbs in this sentence, we would use the word . . .

    (A) nōn

    (B) nē

    (C) nihil

    (D) nōnne

11. Utinam ratiō <u>duxisset</u>, nōn fortūna. (*pace* Livy)

    (A) might guide

    (B) would guide

    (C) had guided

    (D) was guiding

12. <u>Utinam liberōrum nostrōrum mōrēs nōn ipsī perderēmus</u>. (Quintilian)

    (A) Would that we might not ruin our children's character.

    (B) I wish that we will not ruin our children's character.

    (C) If only we had not ruined our children's character.

    (D) We were not ruining our children's character.

13. <u>Let us rejoice</u>, therefore, while we are young! (medieval song)

    (A) Gaudēmus

    (B) Gaudēbimus

    (C) Gaudēte

    (D) Gaudeāmus

14. Which word is <u>not</u> appropriate for translating the independent subjunctive?

    (A) should

    (B) might

    (C) may

    (D) will

Stumper:

Fortūnam citius <u>inveniās</u> quam retineās. (Publilius Syrus)

(A) you will find

(B) you find

(C) you may find

(D) you might have found

Answers

1. Jussive **(D)**
    The epitaph RIP, **Requiescat in pāce**, is an example of the jussive subjunctive in the present tense. Answer (A) **Requiescit** is in the present indicative form, (B) **Requiescēns** is the present participle, and (C) **Requiesce** is the singular form of the present imperative. (See "Jussive and Hortatory Subjunctives.")

2. Jussive **(D)**
    The verb **sit** in this epitaph is also a jussive subjunctive. Answer (A) requires a verb that is present indicative, and (B) requires a present imperative. Answer (C) also requires a present indicative and mistranslates the other words in the epitaph.

3. Jussive **(B)**
    Because **ferat** is a form of the present subjunctive, (B) ... *let him display it* is the best translation. Answer (A) requires the future tense **feret**, and (C) requires the present tense **fert**. Answer (D) translates **meruit** incorrectly.

4. Optative **(A)**
    Would that introduces the subjunctive of a wish, therefore *we had been* must be a subjunctive form in the pluperfect tense. This is **fuissēmus**. Answer (B) **essēmus** is in the wrong tense (imperfect); (C) **fuerāmus** is in the correct tense (pluperfect) but wrong mood (indicative); and (D) **fuerimus** is in the wrong tense and mood (future perfect indicative, *we will have been*) or simply the incorrect tense (perfect subjunctive, *we have been*). (See "Optative Subjunctive.")

5. Jussive **(C)**
    Let it be is an obvious answer if you're a Beatles fan! Answers (A) and (B) call for the indicative mood, and (D) is optative in past time.

6. Deliberative **(A)**
    Quid agam? is a classic example of the use of the subjunctive mood in a deliberative question. The real question here is, "What is the tense of the verb **agam**?" Well, the answer is the present tense, leading to (A) *What am I to do?* Answers (B) *What was I to do?*, (C) *What have I done?*, and (D) *What had I done?* all have incorrect verb tenses. (See "Deliberative Subjunctive.")

7. Hortatory **(A)**

In this sentence, focus your thinking on the mood and tense of the main verb **colāmus**. Because the verb **colō**, **colere** belongs to the third conjugation, this form is a hortatory subjunctive in the present tense, that is, *Let us cherish*. Answer (B) *We must cherish (humanity)* requires a construction that expresses necessity or obligation, such as (**hūmānitās**) **nōbīs colenda est**. Answer (C) *We do cherish* is **colimus**, and (D) *We should have cherished* is **coluerimus**. (The verb sequence here is primary; see Chapter 27.)

8. Hortatory **(D)**

Determining the correct answer to this question requires familiarity with the principal parts or forms of the regular verb **spērō**, **spērāre** and the irregular verb **ferō**, **ferre**. (These may be deduced from the answers provided.) **Spērāre** belongs to the first conjugation, so (A) and (C) are incorrect because **spērāmus** is in the present indicative and the hortatory or present subjunctive is required by the English meaning. Answer (B) **ferēmus** is in the future tense, leaving **ferāmus** as the correct answer.

9. Optative **(C)**

The appearance of the particle **utinam** defines this sentence as a wish, which requires a subjunctive verb. Because **habēret** is the only subjunctive appearing among the choices, it is the correct answer. Answer (A) is present indicative, (B) is pluperfect indicative, and (D) is imperfect indicative. In this wish, Caligula wanted the people to have one head so he could decapitate them all at once.

10. Hortatory **(B)**

The hortatory subjunctive forms **loquāmur** and **sentiāmus** require the negative **nē**. Answers (C) and (D) do not require the subjunctive, and (B), when found with the subjunctive, is most commonly used in the context of the result clause (i.e., **ut nōn**).

11. Optative **(C)**

The subjunctive verb **duxisset** in this wish is in the pluperfect tense, hence *had guided* is the correct response. (Note that all forms in the answers appear in the active voice.) Answers (A) *might guide* and (B) *would guide* are in the present tense (**dūcat**), whereas (D) *was guiding* is in the imperfect tense (**dūceret**).

12. Optative **(A)**

The tense of the verb **perderēmus** in this wish introduced by **uti-nam** is imperfect, which nullifies the translations in (B) and (C). These contain verbs in the future and pluperfect tenses, respectively. Answer (D) is not possible because the translation is phrased as a (factual) assertion, not a wish, therefore requiring the indicative mood.

13. Hortatory **(D)**

This famous song, often sung or played at graduations, is an encouragement to celebrate. Therefore, the hortatory subjunctive **Gaudeāmus**, *Let us rejoice*, is correct. Answer (A) **Gaudēmus**, *We are rejoicing*, is in the present indicative; (B) **Gaudēbimus**, *We shall rejoice*, is in the future indicative; and (C) **Gaudēte**, *Rejoice!* is a plural imperative.

14. **(D)**

The word *will* is only used in the indicative mood because it implies a statement that is going to come true. The words *should, might,* and *may* are all used to express meanings that are only potentially true, and are thus subjunctive.

Stumper: Potential **(C)**

This sentence, which reads *You <u>may come upon</u> fortune sooner than (you may) hold onto it*, contains two potential subjunctives, **inveniās** and **retineās**, expressing possibilities capable of realization. Answers (A) and (B) are in the future and present tenses of the indicative, respectively, and as such make assertions of fact rather than possibility. Answer (D) *you might have found* translates a potential subjunctive in the imperfect tense (**invenīrēs**) rather than in the present (**inveniās**), and expresses past time.

CHAPTER 29
Conditional Sentences

Chapter 29

CONDITIONAL SENTENCES

Conditional, or "if . . . then," sentences in Latin are complex in that they really express two ideas, one in a main or independent clause, the other in a subordinate or dependent clause, for example,

If you understand this, then you understand conditional sentences.

A conditional sentence contains a conditional clause, or condition, which consists of the if-clause introduced by **sī** (or its negative equivalent **nisi**, *if . . . not, unless*) and ending with a verb. In our example conditional sentence, the conditional clause is *If you understand this*. The then-clause serves as the main or independent clause, also known as the conclusion. In the example sentence, the main clause is *then you understand conditional sentences*. The if-clause is traditionally known as the protasis (Greek for "premise"), and the then-clause as the apodosis (Greek for "outcome"). Note that the word *then* is not necessarily expressed in the English translation.

condition/subordinate or
dependent clause/protasis

[**Sī Lesbia Catullum amābit**], **ipse laetus erit.**

conclusion/main or
independent clause/apodosis

[*If Lesbia loves Catullus*], (*then*) *he will be happy.*

The clauses in conditional sentences may be found with verbs in either the indicative or the subjunctive mood, and in any tense. There are three main types of conditional sentences, which are classified as simple, future less vivid (or "should . . . would"), and contrary to fact. Simple conditionals have the indicative in both clauses, the future less vivid conditional has the present subjunctive in both clauses, and contrary to fact conditionals have a past tense of the subjunctive in both clauses. In this chapter, you will read about the Roman poet Catullus, who had a love affair with a woman to whom he gave the name "Lesbia."

TYPES OF CONDITIONAL SENTENCES

Conditionals with the Indicative Mood (Simple and Future More Vivid)

This type of conditional sentence, also known as a "factual" or "open" condition, makes a simple statement. Simple conditionals have verbs in the <u>indicative mood in both clauses</u>. Use of the indicative implies that the condition is happening or is likely to happen. Any tense may be used.

If the tense used is future or future perfect in the if-clause and future in the then-clause, then the sentence is classified as a future more vivid conditional.

Here are some examples:

Simple conditions:	**Sī Lesbia Catullum <u>amat</u>, ipse laetus est.** *If Lesbia <u>loves</u> Catullus (and very possibly she does), (then) <u>he is</u> happy.*
	Sī Lesbia Catullum <u>amābat</u>, ipse laetus erat. *If Lesbia <u>loved</u> Catullus (and very possibly she did), <u>he was</u> happy.*
Future more vivid conditions:	**Sī Lesbia Catullum <u>amābit</u>, ipse laetus <u>erit</u>.** *If Lesbia <u>will love</u> Catullus, (and very possibly she will), <u>he will be</u> happy.*
	Sī Lesbia Catullum <u>amāverit</u>, ipse laetus <u>erit</u>. *If Lesbia <u>will have loved</u> Catullus (and very possibly she will have), <u>he will be</u> happy.*

In future more vivid conditional clauses, it is better to translate verbs in the future and future perfect tenses as present tenses in English, as in the following:

Sī Lesbia Catullum <u>amāverit</u>, ipse laetus erit.
*If Lesbia <u>loves</u> (literally, *will have loved*) Catullus, he will be happy.*

Conditionals with the Subjunctive Mood

Future Less Vivid Conditional Sentences

This type of conditional, sometimes called "ideal," expresses a remote future possibility, that is, a condition that may possibly (but improbably) be true or realized in the future. These appear with the <u>present subjunctive in both clauses</u>. They may be translated traditionally, if somewhat archaically, by *should* in the if-clause and *would* in the then-clause, as in this example:

> **Sī Lesbia Catullum <u>amet</u>, ipse laetus <u>sit</u>.**
> *If Lesbia <u>should love</u> Catullus (and it is possible but unlikely that she does), <u>he would be</u> happy.*

This type of conditional sentence is found less frequently than the other two types.

Contrary to Fact Conditional Sentences

Such conditionals express conditions and conclusions that could not possibly happen or be true.

The verbs of these conditionals, which are also known as "contra-factual," "imaginary," or "unreal," are both subjunctive. In present time, or present contrary to fact, the <u>imperfect subjunctive</u> appears in both clauses; in past time, or past contrary to fact, Latin uses the <u>pluperfect subjunctive</u> in both clauses:

> **Sī Lesbia Catullum <u>amāret</u>, ipse laetus <u>esset</u>.**
> *If Lesbia <u>were to love</u> Catullus (but she does not), <u>he would be</u> happy (but he is not).*

> **Sī Lesbia Catullum <u>amāvisset</u>, ipse laetus <u>fuisset</u>.**
> *If Lesbia <u>had loved</u> Catullus (but she did not), he <u>would have been</u> happy (but he was not).*

Mixed Conditions

The tenses or moods of both clauses in a conditional sentence need not be the same. Mixed conditionals may be found containing clauses (1) with different tenses of the subjunctive, (2) with an indicative paired with an independent subjunctive, and (3) with a subjunctive if-clause paired with an imperative, or with various other combinations. The meaning of such sentences is usually apparent from the sense implied by the context, as in these examples:

(1) Mixed tenses: **<u>Essetne Catullus laetus, sī Lesbia eum amāvisset?</u>**
<u>*Would Catullus be* happy (*now*), *if Lesbia had loved* him (*previously*)?</u>

(2) Mixed moods: **Sī Lesbia Catullum <u>amat, gaudeāmus</u>.**
If Lesbia <u>does love</u> Catullus, <u>let us be delighted</u>.

(3) Mixed moods: **Sī <u>putātis</u> Lesbiam Catullum amāre, <u>gaudēte</u>!**
If <u>you think</u> that Lesbia does love Catullus, <u>be glad</u>!

Quick Study of Conditional Sentences

Type	Verbs in Clauses	Meanings of Verbs	
		Dependent Clause	**Main Clause**
Simple (likely to happen)	indicative	*If he does . . . ,* *If he did, . . .*	*then he is. . . . ,* *then he was . . .*
Future more vivid (likely to happen)	future, future perfect indicative	*If he will (have) . . . ,*	*then he will. . . .* (best translated in the present)
Future less vivid (possible, but unlikely)	present subjunctive	*If he should . . . ,*	*then he would . . .*
Present contrary to fact (impossible or unreal)	imperfect subjunctive	*If he were to . . . ,*	*then he would . . .*
Past contrary to fact (impossible or unreal)	pluperfect subjunctive	*If he had . . . ,*	*then he would have . . .*

TIPS ON TRANSLATING CONDITIONAL SENTENCES

- Conditional sentences present few problems in translation because they are very similar to English.

- The conclusion (then-clause) may precede the condition (if-clause) in the word order of a Latin sentence for emphasis or other considerations. Always read through in Latin the entirety of a Latin sentence before determining its meaning.

- In the if-clause, translate future and future perfect tenses in the present tense.

- Note that all three types of conditional sentences in Latin reveal something about the truth of what is being said or written, that is, simple conditions reveal that it is likely that the condition is true, future less vivid conditions reveal the possibility that the condition may be true, and contrary to fact conditions express that it is impossible that the condition is true.

SAMPLE QUESTIONS

Part C: Translation

1. Nisi Catullus poeta fuisset, Lesbia eum <u>nōn amāvisset</u>.

   (A) had not loved   (C) would not love

   (B) would not have loved (D) did not love

Part D: Sentence Completion

2. Sī Lesbia discēdat, Catullus maximē . . .

   (A) doleat   (C) dolēret

   (B) dolet   (D) doluit

Answers

1. (B)   2. (A)

PRACTICE QUESTIONS

Catullus is to be imagined as speaking in many of these sentences.*

1. <u>Sī valēs, Lesbia, gaudeō</u>.

    (A) If you are well, Lesbia, I am happy.

    (B) If you should be well, Lesbia, then I would be happy.

    (C) If you were well, Lesbia, then I would be happy.

    (D) If you will be well, Lesbia, then I am happy.

2. Sī pulchram Lesbiam vīdissēs, certē eam <u>amāvissēs</u>.

    (A) you would love   (C) you would have loved

    (B) you had loved   (D) you were loving

3. Ō dī, <u>sī vītam puriter agam</u>, <u>ēripiātis</u> hanc pestem perniciemque mihi.

    (A) If I will lead an upright life, you will take away . . .

    (B) If I should lead an upright life, you would take away . . .

    (C) If I were to lead an upright life, you would take away . . .

    (D) If I am leading an upright life, you should take away . . .

4. <u>Sī cum passere lūdere possem</u>, tristēs cūrās animī levārem.

    (A) If I can play with the sparrow

    (B) If I am able to play with the sparrow

    (C) If I were able to play with the sparrow

    (D) If I should be able to play with the sparrow

5. Sī Lesbiam in matrīmōnium ducere <u>velim</u>, dīcatne "Ita vērō"?

    (A) should wish   (C) am wishing

    (B) will wish   (D) was wishing

---

* Several questions in this practice exercise are derived directly from the poems of Catullus: question 3, Poem 76.19–20; question 4, Poem 2.9–10; question 6, Poems 5 and 7; question 7, Poem 77.3–4; question 10, Poem 13.4–7.

6. <u>Mortuus essem, nisi mea puella mihi mille bāsia daret</u>.

    (A) I would die if I gave my girl a thousand kisses.

    (B) Unless I were to give my girl a thousand kisses, I would die.

    (C) If I would not have given my girl a thousand kisses, I would die.

    (D) I would die unless my girl were to give me a thousand kisses.

7. <u>Sī meam Lesbiam amēs, Rūfe, miserō mihi intestīna erīpiās</u>.

    This sentence tells us that

    (A) There is no information as to whether or not Rufus loves Lesbia.

    (B) It is possible, but unlikely, that Rufus loves Lesbia.

    (C) Rufus could not, in any way, love Lesbia.

    (D) It is a fact that Rufus loves Lesbia.

8. Sepulcrum meī frātris vīsam, <u>sī ego ipse ad Bīthȳniam ierō</u>.

    (A) if I go to Bithynia

    (B) if I had gone to Bithynia

    (C) if I would have gone to Bithynia

    (D) if I were going to Bithynia

9. Sī nāvis mihi nōn fuisset, ad Sirmiōnem nāvigāre nōn . . . .

    (A) potero   (C) potuissem

    (B) possem   (D) poteram

10. Sī candidam puellam et vīnum <u>attuleris</u>, mī Fābulle, bene cēnābis.

    Which of the following is <u>not</u> an acceptable translation of <u>attuleris</u>?

    (A) you will have brought

    (B) you bring

    (C) you will bring

    (D) you brought

SENTENTIAE ANTIQUAE

1. Discere <u>sī quaeris</u>, docē. Sīc ipse docēris. (medieval)

    (A) if you will seek   (C) if you will be sought

    (B) if you are sought   (D) if you seek

2. If anyone <u>should violate</u> this, I wish that he would live for a long time in pain. (from a tombstone)

    (A) violāverit   (C) violāvisset

    (B) violāverat   (D) violābat

3. <u>Sī ea defendēs quae ipse recta esse sentiēs</u>. (Cicero)

    (A) If only you will stand by what you feel to be correct.

    (B) If only you should stand by what you would feel to be correct.

    (C) If only you had stood by what you would have felt to be correct.

    (D) If only you were standing by what you saw to be correct.

4. The whole world <u>would perish</u> if compassion <u>were</u> not <u>to end</u> bad feelings. (Seneca the Elder)

    (A) pereat; fīniat   (C) perīret; fīnīret

    (B) periet; fīniet   (D) perēbat; fīniēbat

5. Salus omnium ūnā nocte āmissa esset, nisi Catilīna captus esset. (Cicero)

    The tense and voice of the subjunctive verbs in this sentence are

    (A) imperfect passive   (C) pluperfect passive

    (B) imperfect active   (D) present passive

6. Minus saepe errēs, <u>sī sciās quid nesciās</u>. (Publilius Syrus)

    (A) If you knew what you did not know

    (B) If you know what you did not know

    (C) If you should know what you do not know

    (D) If you knew what you do not know

Stumper:

Which of the following conditional sentences contains a future more vivid condition?

(A) Dīcēs "heu" sī tē in speculō vīderis. (Horace)

(B) Sī tū eō diē fuissēs, tē certō vīdissem. (Cicero)

(C) Laus nova nisi oritur, etiam vetus āmittitur. (Publilius Syrus)

(D) Sī quiētem māvis, dūc uxōrem parem. (Quintilian)

Answers

1. Simple **(A)**
    This is a simple conditional sentence with the indicative, stating as a fact that if Lesbia is well, then Catullus is happy. Answer (B) *If you should be well* contains a translation that requires a "should . . . would" condition; (C) *If you were well* has a present contrary to fact condition; and (D) *If you will be well* has a future more vivid condition with the future tense. This sentence greets Lesbia as if in a letter or note. (See "Conditionals with the Indicative Mood.")

2. Past contrary to fact **(C)**
    This condition is revealed by the appearance of the pluperfect subjunctive form **amāvissēs**. The sentence reads *If you had seen the gorgeous Lesbia, you would have loved her*. Answer (A) requires the imperfect subjunctive form **amārēs** in a present contrary to fact condition. Answer (B) *you had loved*, although in the proper tense, is a statement requiring the indicative mood (**amāverās**), as is (D) *you were loving* (requiring **amābās**). (See "Contrary to Fact Conditional Sentences.")

3. Future less vivid **(B)**
    That this sentence is a "should . . . would" conditional is indicated by the present subjunctive form **ēripiātis**. The verb **agam** could, of course, be a form of the future indicative, but this possibility is negated by the appearance of **ēripiātis**. This sentence, taken from Catullus's Poem 76, reads *O gods, if I should lead an upright life, you would snatch away from me this plague and pestilence* (i.e., Lesbia). Answers (A) and (D) require the indicative mood. Answer (C) is phrased as a present contrary to fact clause, *If I were to lead . . .* , which would require a verb in the imperfect subjunctive (i.e., **agerem**). (See "Contrary to Fact Conditional Sentences.")

4.   Present contrary to fact **(C)**
     The underlined clause is part of a present contrary to fact conditional sentence. The appearance of the verb **possem** in the imperfect tense of the subjunctive leads to the translation *If I were able*. Answers (A) and (B) express the same thing in different ways, both requiring the indicative, since they are assertions. Answer (D) *If I should be able* . . . translates a future less vivid clause, which is **Sī . . . possim**. This sentence, from Catullus's Poem 2, reads *If I were able to* (i.e., *If I could*) *play with the songbird, I would relieve the sad cares of my heart*. (See "Contrary to Fact Conditional Sentences.")

5.   Future less vivid **(A)**
     This condition sentence contains a "should . . . would" conditional, requiring the present subjunctive in the protasis, or if-clause, **(velim)**, and in the apodosis, or then-clause, **(dīcat)**. Answer (B) *will* requires the future indicative **(volam)**, (C) requires the present indicative **(volō)**, and (D) requires the imperfect indicative or subjunctive **(volēbat** or **vellet)**.

6.   Present contrary to fact **(D)**
     This sentence is a present contrary to fact condition, containing the verbs **essem** and **darem**, both in the imperfect tense: *Unless Lesbia were to give Catullus a thousand kisses (which she will not), he would die (but he will not)*. Answer (A) does not translate **nisi** correctly, (B) turns the thought around and has Catullus giving Lesbia the kisses, and (C) translates the tense of the verb **darem** incorrectly as *would have given*. (See "Contrary to Fact Conditional Sentences.")

7.   Future less vivid **(B)**
     This is a "should . . . would" conditional sentence, expressing the fact that it is possible, but unlikely, that if Rufus should love Lesbia, he would tear out Catullus's guts. Answer (C) requires a contrary to fact condition, which is impossible, given the present tenses of the verbs, and (D) requires that the Latin express a simple factual condition, but the verbs are subjunctive. (See "Future Less Vivid Conditional Sentences.")

8.   Future more vivid **(A)**
     This sentence reads *If Catullus goes to Bithynia, he will visit his brother's grave*. The use of the future and future perfect tenses **vīsam** and **ierō** reveal this sentence to be a future more vivid conditional. Remember that in English the present tense may be used to express future time in such a context. Answers (B) and (D) are past contrary to fact conditions requiring the pluperfect subjunctive and (C) is a present contrary to fact

condition, which requires the imperfect subjunctive. The verb **ierit** in the if-clause is a future perfect indicative form (or a perfect subjunctive, which doesn't fit the context). (See "Conditionals with the Indicative Mood.")

9. Past contrary to fact **(C)**
    This sentence reads *If I had not had a ship, I would not have been able to sail to Sirmio.* This is a past contrary to fact condition, which requires the pluperfect subjunctive in both the protasis and apodosis of the sentence. Answer (A) **poterō** is future indicative, (B) **possem** is imperfect subjunctive, and (D) **poteram** is imperfect indicative.

10. Future more vivid **(D)**
    The future indicative verb form **cenābis** reveals that **attuleris** is in the future perfect tense in a sentence that expresses a future more vivid condition. As a past tense, (D) *you brought* is the only translation that does not have an acceptable meaning of the future perfect tense. (See "Conditionals with the Indicative Mood.")

Sententiae Antiquae Answers

1. Simple **(D)**
    This simple conditional sentence reads, *If you seek to learn, teach. And so you yourself are taught.* The verb **quaeris** is present active indicative. Answer (A) requires the future tense (**quaerēs**), (B) requires the present passive (**quaereris**), and (C) requires the future passive (**quaerēris**). (See "Conditionals with the Indicative Mood.")

2. Future less vivid **(A)**
    The perfect subjunctive may appear in "should...would" conditions such as this. The nonfactual nature of the statement removes (B) and (D), which are indicative, from consideration. Answer (C) **violāvisset**, which is in the pluperfect tense, cannot produce the translation *should violate*, which expresses a meaning that derives from the present system of verbs. (See "Future Less Vivid Conditional Sentences.")

3. Future more vivid **(A)**
    This sentence expresses the future more vivid condition **Si** . . . **defendēs**, *If you (will) defend* . . . , **sentiēs**, *(then) you will feel.* The translation in (B) *If you should stand* requires a "should . . . would" condition with the present subjunctive; (C) *If you had stood* requires a past contrary to fact condition with the pluperfect subjunctive; and (D) *If you were*

standing requires a present contrary to fact condition with the imperfect subjunctive. (See "Conditionals with the Indicative Mood.")

4.   Present contrary to fact **(C)**
    Seneca's thought expresses a contrary to fact condition in present time, as the imperfect subjunctive is suggested by the translation *were to end*. Thus the forms **perīret** and **finīret** are correct. Answer (A) contains verbs in the present subjunctive, (B) in the future indicative, and (D) in the imperfect indicative, none of which fit the sense required. (See "Contrary to Fact Conditional Sentences.")

5.   Past contrary to fact **(C)**
    Āmissa esset and **captus esset** are forms of the pluperfect passive subjunctive in a past contrary to fact conditional sentence. (See Chapter 27 for charts of verbs in the subjunctive mood.) The sentence reads *The safety of everyone would have been lost in a single night, if Catiline had not been captured.*

6.   Future less vivid **(C)**
    This sentence reads *You would be wrong less often, if you (should) know (that) which you do not know.* The main clause of this future less vivid condition contains the indirect question **quid nesciās**. The translations in (A) and (D) contain verbs in the past tense, which the original sentence does not contain. The meaning of the sentence in (B) is rendered by the indicative in a simple condition. (See "Future Less Vivid Conditional Sentences.")

Stumper: **(A)**
    The correct answer reads *You will say "Ugh!" if you see yourself in the mirror.* This sentence contains verbs in the future (**Dīcēs**) and future perfect (**vīderis**) tenses. Answer (B) reads *If you had been (there) on that day, I surely would have seen you*, a past contrary to fact condition. Answer (B) reads *Unless brand new praise is forthcoming, even the previous (praise) is lost*, a simple condition. Answer (D) reads *If you prefer peace, marry a wife of equal (station)* is another simple condition with the indicative. (See "Conditionals with the Indicative Mood.")

CHAPTER 30

Subordinate Clauses with *Ut*

Chapter 30

SUBORDINATE CLAUSES WITH *UT*

SUBORDINATE CLAUSES WITH THE SUBJUNCTIVE

As you have been reminded in the past two chapters, subjunctive verbs are found both independently in main clauses and as verbs in dependent clauses, which are also known as secondary or subordinate clauses. In Chapter 12, we reviewed dependent clauses with the indicative, introduced by the relative pronoun **quī**, **quae**, **quod**. Dependent clauses with the subjunctive are usually introduced by words such as **sī**, **quis**, **cum**, or, as presented in this chapter, the adverb **ut**. For example,

main/independent clause   subordinate/dependent clause

Omnēs militēs ferōciter pugnant [ut hostēs superent].

All soldiers fight hard [in order to defeat the enemy].

In the preceding sentence, the main thought is *all soldiers fight hard*. Secondary to this thought and dependent on it is the purpose clause *in order to defeat the enemy*, which gives additional information about the main thought. Such clauses can be "triggered" or set off by a word in the main clause that provides a context for the dependent clause, such as **tam** with this result clause:

Mīlitēs <u>tam</u> ferōciter pugnābant [ut hostēs superārentur].

The soldiers fought <u>so hard</u> [that the enemy was defeated].

Subjunctive verbs, whether in independent or in dependent clauses, express wishes, possibilities, doubts, opinions, and so forth, whereas indicative verbs express statements of fact. In this and the next two chapters, we will review the ways to identify various subjunctive clauses, as well as the ways in which they differ in meaning. Only the most common subordinate clauses with the subjunctive are presented in these chapters, because these types appear most frequently in Latin literature. Our review is organized according to the word that introduces the dependent clause, such as **ut**, **quid**, or **cum**. In this chapter, we will review four clauses introduced by the adverb **ut**: purpose, result, indirect command, and fear. Square brackets [ ] will be used to designate the subordinate clause.

TYPES OF UT CLAUSES WITH THE SUBJUNCTIVE

The adverb **ut** introduces several different types of subjunctive clauses, and it is also found in one type of clause with the indicative. The negative of these clauses varies with the type of clause. The terms used to identify **ut** clauses, such as purpose or result, give insight into their meanings.

Purpose Clause with Ut

Although there are several different ways to express in Latin the idea of the purpose or intent of an action, the **ut** clause is perhaps the most common. This clause is also known as a "final" clause. The negative is **nē**. When translating, use wording such as *to*, *in order to*, *so that*, or *for the purpose of*, and render the verb by using the helping verbs *may* or *might*. Most often, the present or imperfect tense is found in a purpose clause, as in these examples:

> **Glōriōsus mīlēs esse vult [ut ipse praeclarissimus fīat].**
> *Gloriosus wants to be a soldier [in order to become famous].*

> **Glōriōsus praeclarissimus esse volēbat [ut puellae eum amārent].**
> *Gloriosus wanted to be famous [so that girls might like him].*

Whereas the infinitive is used in English to express purpose, this use appears rarely in Latin, and then only in poetry. (For the relative purpose clause and a summary of purpose constructions in Latin, see Chapter 31.)

Result Clause with Ut

The result clause, also called a "consecutive" clause, begins with **ut** (negative **ut nōn**) and ends with a subjunctive verb, usually in the present or imperfect tense. This clause, however, is set up by a trigger word, such as **adeō**, **ita**, **sīc**, or **tam**, which mean *so*, *to such an extent*, **tālis, -is, -e**, *of such a kind*, **tantus, -a, -um**, *of such a size*, or **tot**, *so many*. Such words appear outside of and preceding the **ut** clause. When translating **ut** in a result clause, use the word *that* (= *with the result that*):

> **Glōriōsus <u>tam</u> defessus est [ut Rubicōnem transīre nōn possit].**
> *Gloriosus is <u>so</u> weary [that he cannot cross the Rubicon River].*

> **Rubicō flūmen <u>ita</u> vīvum fluēbat [ut Glōriōsus lapsus in aquam caderet].**
> *The Rubicon River was running <u>so</u> fast [that Gloriosus slipped and fell in].*

Sometimes the perfect subjunctive, instead of the imperfect, is found in the result clause if the past event whose action is being described <u>actually occurred</u>:

> **Glōriōsus tālis <u>conspiciēbātur</u> [ut aliī mīlitēs rīserint].**
> *Gloriosus was such a sight [that the other soldiers (in fact) laughed].*

A variation of the result clause, often referred to as a substantive (noun) clause of result, appears with verbs of causing or happening, such as **facere ut**, *to bring it about that*, or with several impersonal verbs, such as **accīdit ut**, **ēvenit ut**, or **fit/fiēbat ut**, *it happens/happened that*, or **fīerī potest ut**, *it may be that, it is possible that*. For example,

> **Caesar <u>faciēbat</u> [ut Rōmānī urbem Rōmam oppugnārent].**
> *Caesar <u>was bringing it about</u> [that Romans were attacking Rome].*

Indirect Command

You might expect a highly structured and militaristic society such as that of the Romans to have several different ways to express the idea of command. We have reviewed the direct command (imperative mood, Chapter 23) and the independent subjunctive with the force of a gentle command (jussive and hortatory, Chapter 28). The indirect command expresses or reports a command as second-hand communication, by stating what the original command was. Also known as the "jussive clause," "jussive noun clause," or "substantive noun clause of purpose," the indirect command is a substantive or noun clause that consists of **ut** (or **nē**) + the subjunctive and answers the implied question "What is commanded?" A substantive is anything that takes the place of a noun, including a verbal clause:

> **Centuriō Glōriōsō imperat.**
> *The centurion gives an order to Gloriosus.*

What order does the centurion give?

> **"Dēsilī dē nāve."**

The order *Jump down from the ship* becomes the direct object of the verb **imperat** (i.e., that which was ordered). The direct command "**Dēsilī dē nāve**" now becomes the substantive clause, or indirect command, **ut dē nāve dēsilīret.** The translation of **ut** in this type of subjunctive clause is *to . . .* or *that . . .* , as in the following:

Direct command: **"Dēsilī dē nāve, Glōriōse!" centuriō imperat.**
The centurion commands, "Jump down from the ship, Gloriosus!"

Indirect command: **Centuriō Glōriōsō imperat** [**ut dē nāve dēsiliat**].
The centurion commands Gloriosus [*to jump down from the ship*].

The indirect command could be written alternatively as:

Centuriō imperat [**ut Glōriōsus dē nāve dēsiliat**].
The centurion orders [*that Gloriosus jump down from the ship*].

In this sentence, Glorious is not the direct recipient of the centurion's command (the word **Glōriōsus** is found inside the dependent clause), but receives the command through another.

For the Romans, the use of verbs that mean *bid, order, request,* as well as *invite, persuade, beg,* or *pray,* carried weight and required a response. The following verbs introduce an indirect command:

hortārī, *to encourage, urge*   **orāre**, *to plead, pray*

imperāre (+ dative), *to order*   **persuādēre** (+ dative), *to convince*

invītāre, *to invite*   **petere**, *to ask*

mandāre, *to command*   **praecīpere** (+ dative), *to instruct*

monēre, *to advise, warn*   **rogāre**, *to ask*

obsecrāre, *to beg, beseech*

You can remember these verbs by using the convenient, if goofy, acronym HIPPIPROMMO.

Most of the verbs in the list take a direct object in the accusative case. The verbs **imperāre**, **persuadēre**, and **praecipere**, however, take the <u>dative</u> case (see Chapter 8, "Dative with Certain Types of Verbs").

The verb **iubēre (jubēre)**, which also has the meaning *order*, is not followed by the indirect command but takes the infinitive with subject accusative, for example,

> **Centuriō Glōriōsum <u>dēsilīre</u> iubēbat (jubēbat).**
> *The centurion <u>was ordering</u> Gloriosus to jump down.*

Fear Clauses

Fear clauses are structured like other **ut** clauses with the subjunctive, except that the meanings of **ut** and **nē** are unique. Their meanings are reversed, that is, **ut** and **nē** have meanings that are the opposite of those found in other **ut** clauses. They express in a different way what was originally an independent jussive clause in the context of the emotion of fear or apprehension. For example, **Vereor. Nē cadās!** *I'm scared. May you not fall!* became **Vereor nē cadās**, *I'm scared that you may fall.* Thus **nē** expresses the positive, *that . . .* , and **ut** expresses the negative, *that . . . not*, following words that suggest or mean fear or apprehension. That which is feared is expressed in the fear clause. The fear clause, like the indirect command, is a noun or substantive clause, in that it serves as the direct object of the main verb and answers the implied question "What is feared?"

Verbs that introduce a fear clause include **metuere**, **pāvēre**, **timēre**, and the deponent **verērī**, as in the following sentences:

> **Glōriōsus <u>verētur</u> [ut scūtō defendātur].**
> *Gloriosus <u>fears</u> [that he may not be protected by his shield].*

> **<u>Timēbātne</u> Glōriōsus [nē in testūdine nigresceret]?**
> *<u>Was</u> Gloriosus <u>afraid</u> [that it would be dark inside the "tortoise"]?*

Alternatively, the verbs of fearing listed above may be accompanied by an infinitive, as in this example:

> **Glōriōsus metuēbat ē castrīs <u>discēdere</u>.**
> *Gloriosus was afraid <u>to leave</u> camp.*

Quick Study of Ut Clauses with the Subjunctive

Type of Clause	Main Clause Cue	Introductory Word	Meaning of Clause	Subjunctive
Purpose	[none]	**ut**	*to, in order that, so that*	present, imperfect
		nē	*so that . . . not, not to . . .*	
Example:	**Glōriōsus sē cēlābat ut diū dormīret.** *Gloriosus was hiding in order to sleep for awhile.*			
Result	**adeō, ita, sīc, tam,** etc.	**ut**	*that, with the result that*	present, imperfect, perfect
		ut nōn	*that . . . not*	
Example:	**Iste tam bene sē cēlāverat ut centuriō eum invenīre nōn posset.** *He had hidden so successfully that the centurion couldn't find him.*			
Indirect Command	verb of command or persuasion	**ut**	*that*	present, imperfect
		nē	*that . . . not*	
Example:	**Scelestō inventō, centuriō eī imperāvit ut matellās vacuēfaceret.** *When the rascal had been found, the centurion ordered him to empty the chamber pots.*			
Fear	word of fearing	**nē**	*that*	present, imperfect
		ut	*that . . . not*	
Example:	**Glōriōsus timuerat nē centuriō eī nocēret.** *Gloriosus had feared that the centurion might harm him.*			

TIPS ON TRANSLATING UT CLAUSES

- When translating **ut** clauses, look for a prejudicial word in the main clause that may trigger the specific meaning of the subordinate clause, such as **ita** or **tam** (result), **hortārī** or **imperāre** or (indirect command), or **timēre** or **verērī** (fear). Remember that trigger words are found outside of and preceding the subjunctive clause. It is helpful to bracket the subjunctive clause in order to indicate that it contains information that is separate from that of the main clause of the sentence.

- **Ut** clauses are generally found with the present or imperfect subjunctive and follow the rules of sequence of tenses.

- Most **ut** clauses are best translated using the words *that . . .* or *to. . . .*

- The adverb **ut** may also be found with a verb in the indicative, in which case it has the meaning of *as* or *when*, such as the following:

    Glōriōsus, <u>ut</u> centuriō <u>imperāverat</u>, dē nāve dēsiluit.
    Gloriosus, <u>as</u> the centurion <u>had ordered</u>, jumped down from the ship.

SAMPLE QUESTIONS

Part C: Translation

1. Glōriōsus <u>amīcōs hortābātur nē mīlitēs fīerent</u>.

    (A) was urging his friends to become soldiers.

    (B) urged that the soldiers become his friends.

    (C) was urging his friends not to become soldiers.

    (D) was urged by his friends not to become a soldier.

Part D: Sentence Completion

2. Glōriōsus perterritus est . . . in proeliō moriātur.

    (A) ut   (C) ut . . . nōn

    (B) nē   (D) quīn

Part E: Syntax Substitution

3. Centuriō clāmābat <u>ad Glōriōsum ē somnō excitandum</u>.

    (A) Glōriōsō ē somnō excitātō

    (B) ut Glōriōsum ē somnō excitāret

    (C) postquam Glōriōsus ē somnō excitābatur

    (D) quod Glōriōsus ē somnō excitātus erat

Answers

   1.   (C)   2.   (B)   3.   (B)

PRACTICE QUESTIONS

1. Admonēbitne Caesar suōs <u>ut Britannī suās faciēs tingant</u>?

    (A) that the Britons dye their faces

    (B) to dye his own face like the Britons

    (C) that his men will dye the faces of the Britons

    (D) that the Britons will dye the faces of his men

2. Suntne tot barbarī in Galliā . . . Caesar eōs vincere . . . ?

    (A) nōn; potest   (C) nē; potest

    (B) ut; nōn possit   (D) nē; possit

3. Are soldiers afraid <u>to die</u>?

    (A) ut moriantur   (C) ut morerentur

    (B) nē moriuntur   (D) nē moriantur

4. Traiānō imperātōre, accidit ut Daciī. . . .

    (A) victī sunt   (C) vincerentur

    (B) victūrī sint   (D) vincēbantur

5. Mīlēs bibēbat <u>ad bellum oblīviscendum</u>.

   Which answer provides the closest substitute?

   (A) ut bellum oblīvisceretur

   (B) bellō oblītō

   (C) quia bellum oblīviscēbatur

   (D) oblīviscēns bellum

6. . . . superbus Glōriōsus erat ut multōs amīcōs nōn habēret.

   (A) Tamen   (C) Tandem

   (B) Tam   (D) Tunc

7. Glōriōsus, <u>ut hostēs cōnspexit</u>, arborem ascendit.

   (A) in order to see the enemy

   (B) to see the enemy

   (C) with the result that he saw the enemy

   (D) when he saw the enemy

SENTENTIAE ANTIQUAE

1. <u>Nōn ut edam vīvō sed ut vīvam edō</u>. (Quintilian)

   (A) I do not eat to live, but I live to eat.

   (B) I should not live to eat, but I should eat to live.

   (C) I do not live to eat, but I eat to live.

   (D) I will not live so that I may eat, but I will eat so that I may live.

2. The fruit vendors ask <u>that you make</u> M. Holconius Priscus aedile. (from a Pompeiian election poster)

   (A) ut vōs facitis   (C) nē vōs faciātis

   (B) ut vōs facerētis   (D) ut vōs faciātis

3. Fēminae spectātum veniunt et veniunt ut ipsae. . . . (Ovid)

   (A) spectentur   (C) spectent

   (B) spectārentur   (D) spectantur

4. Ōrandum est <u>ut sit</u> mens sāna in corpore sānō. (Juvenal)

    (A) that there will be   (C) that there be

    (B) that there was   (D) that there must be

5. Nēmo adeō ferus est ut mītēscere <u>nōn possit</u>. (Horace)

    (A) was not able   (C) has not been able

    (B) will not be able   (D) is not able

6. Cito scrībendō nōn fit <u>ut bene scrībātur</u>; bene scribendō fit ut cito. (Quintilian)

    (A) that it is written well

    (B) as it should be well written

    (C) in order to write well

    (D) that it was written well

Stumper:

Hortātur eōs <u>nē anīmō deficiant</u>.

Caesar's direct command would have been:

(A) Nōlī dēficere!   (C) Dēficite!

(B) Nōlite dēficere!   (D) Nōn dēficere!

Answers

1. Indirect command **(A)**
    The appearance of the verb **Admonēbit** defines the clause **ut . . . tingant** as an indirect command with its subjunctive verb in primary sequence. The sentence reads *Will Caesar advise his men <u>that the Britons dye their faces?</u>* For various reasons, the remaining answers do not translate the Latin correctly. Answers (C) and (D) translate as part of the subordinate clause elements that are really part of the main clause. (See "Indirect Command.")

2. Result clause **(B)**
    The word **tot** preceding the clause cues this as a result clause. The sentence reads *Are there so many barbarians in Gaul <u>that</u> Caesar <u>cannot</u> defeat them?* This **ut** result clause requires a subjunctive verb in primary

sequence because the main verb is in the present tense, which removes (A) and (C) from consideration. The negative of a result clause is not **nē**, as in (D), but **ut nōn**. (See "Result Clause with Ut" and Chapter 27, "Sequence of Tenses".)

3. Fear clause **(D)**
     This fear clause is in primary sequence, which requires that the subjunctive be in the present tense, as in the clause **nē . . . moriātur**. Remember that the meanings of **ut** and **nē** are reversed in fear clauses! Answer (A) disregards this fact, (B) does not contain a subjunctive verb, and in (C), the tense of the verb **morerētur** is not justifiable, given the present tense of the main verb. (See "Fear Clauses".)

4. Substantive result clause **(C)**
     This sentence reads *While Trajan was emperor, it came to pass* (i.e., *happened*) *that the Dacians were conquered*. The appearance of **accidit** sets up a result clause requiring a subjunctive verb, which eliminates (A) **victī sunt** and (D) **vincēbantur**. Answer (B) **victūrī sint** is subjunctive, but it has a meaning in the active voice (i.e., *about to conquer*), which does not fit the context. Therefore (C) **vincerentur** is correct.

5. Purpose clause **(A)**
     The purpose clause **ut . . . oblīviscerētur**, (*in order*) *to forget the war*, is the best substitution for the underlined gerundive of purpose **ad bellum oblīviscendum**. The original sentence reads *The soldier drank for the purpose of forgetting the war*. Answer (B) is an ablative absolute, (C) is a causal clause, and (D) is a present participial phrase, none of which fit the context. (See Chapter 25, "Gerundive of Purpose".)

6. Result clause **(B)**
     The sense of the thought here, *Gloriosus was so arrogant that he did not have many friends*, leads to the conclusion that this sentence contains a result clause. Of the choices, the word **tam**, *so . . .*, introduces the result clause **nē . . . habēret** in secondary sequence. None of the adverbs in (A), (B), and (C) are relevant to defining an **ut** clause with the subjunctive.

7. Ut + indicative **(D)**
     This sentence reads *When he saw the enemy, Gloriosus climbed a tree*. Because the verb **cōnspexit** is indicative, **ut** must be translated *as* or *when*. Answers (A) and (B) call for purposes clauses, and (C) calls for a result clause, all requiring subjunctive verbs.

Sententiae Antiquae Answers

1. Purpose clause **(C)**
   Quintilian's sentence contains two purpose clauses, **ut . . . edam** and **ut vīvam**. Answer (A) reverses the two clauses, (B) requires independent subjunctives in the present tense, and (D) mistranslates the tenses of the verbs **vīvere** and **edere**.

2. Indirect command **(D)**
   Ut vōs faciātis idiomatically translates *that you vote*. This clause is an indirect command introduced by the verb *ask* in the main clause of the English sentence and requiring a subjunctive verb in primary sequence. Answer (A) is not a subjunctive clause, (B) has the verb in the wrong tense, and (C) **nē vōs faciātis** incorrectly negates the original positive statement.

3. Purpose clause **(A)**
   This sentence, which reads *They come to see (and) to be seen themselves*, referring to women at the races, contains a purpose clause with its verb in primary sequence (**spectentur**, after **veniunt**). Answer (B) **spectārentur** is in the imperfect tense in secondary sequence, (C) **spectent** is active and doesn't fit the context, and (D) **spectantur** is in the indicative mood. Note the supine of purpose, **spectātum** (see Chapter 25, "The Supine").

4. Indirect command **(C)**
   Ut sit is an indirect command after the verb **orāre** in the periphrastic **orandum est**. Juvenal's famous statement says (*We*) *must maintain that there be a sound mind in a sound body*. Answer (A) requires the "future subjunctive" form (**futūra sit**), (B) requires the imperfect tense (**esset**), and (D) requires an expression of necessity in the clause.

5. Result clause **(D)**
   The appearance of **adeō** keys the result clause **ut nōn mītēscere possit**. The present tense of the subjunctive verb **possit** is correctly translated *is not able* or *cannot*. The sentence reads *No one is so fierce that he cannot be tamed.*

6. Substantive result clause **(A)**
   The underlined clause is a substantive result clause following the verb **fit**. Quintilian's thought reads *Not by writing quickly does it come about*

that it is written well; *by writing well, it comes about that* (*it is written*) *quickly.* Note the condensation of the Latin, with the omission of **scrībātur** in the second half of the sentence. In (B), the translation *as* for **ut** requires an indicative verb, whereas **scrībātur** is subjunctive. Answer (C) *in order to* is phrased as a purpose clause and has the verb in the active voice, and (D) incorrectly translates the tense of **scrībātur** as imperfect. (See "Result Clause with Ut".)

Stumper: Indirect command **(B)**

The particle **nē** negates the indirect command in the sentence *He is urging them not to lose heart* (literally, *that they not be lacking in spirit*). Because Caesar is urging **eōs**, *them*, the command must be plural as well as negative, giving the answer **Nōlīte dēficere** as the original direct command in Latin. Answer (A) **Nōlī dēficere** is singular, (C) **Dēficite** is a positive rather than negative command, and (D) is an improperly constructed prohibition.

CHAPTER 31

Subordinate Clauses with Q-Words

Chapter 31

SUBORDINATE CLAUSES WITH Q-WORDS

During your review, you have met the relative, or **quī**, clause with the indicative, as in **Cicerō quī consul erat**, *Cicero, who was a consul* (Chapter 12), and the deliberative question with the independent subjunctive, as in **Quid agam**? *What should I do?* (Chapter 28). There are several different types of subjunctive clauses that are introduced in Latin by question words or by a word that begins with the letter **q**. Because of the similarity in the appearance of these clauses, it is appropriate to consider them together. The most common subjunctive clauses introduced by a **q**-word are the indirect question, relative clause of characteristic, and causal clause.

SUBJUNCTIVE CLAUSES INTRODUCED BY Q-WORDS

Indirect Questions

Indirect questions are to direct questions as indirect commands are to direct commands. They express the fact that someone is reporting a direct question, for example,

Direct question: **"Quid agis?" Cicerō rogābat.**
         "How are you doing?" Cicero asked.

Indirect question: **Cicero rogābat [quid agerem].**
         Cicero asked [how I was doing].

An indirect question consists of a dependent subjunctive clause that is introduced by a "question word" such as **cūr, quid, quis, quōmodō, ubi,** or **unde** (see Chapter 23, "Direct Questions"). Such clauses are triggered by an indicative verb of asking, wondering, or knowing, such as **quaerere, mirārī,** or **scīre**. In this respect, the indicative verb of the main clause is the same type of verb as that which introduces an indirect statement (see Chapter 26, "Indirect Statement"). When working out the meaning of a Latin sentence containing an indirect question, look for the following components: a verb of verbal or mental action, a question word, and a subjunctive verb, as in the following example:

Indirect question:

verb of verbal action	question word	subjunctive verb

Atticus <u>rogat</u> Scribācem [<u>cur</u> epistulās nōndum <u>scrīpserit</u>].
Atticus is asking (his scribe) Scribax [why he has not yet written the letters].

Indirect statement:

verb of mental action	subject acc.	infinitive

Atticus <u>nescīvit</u> <u>Scribācem</u> stilum suum <u>amīsisse</u>.
Atticus did not know that Scribax had lost his pen.

The subjunctive verb in an indirect question is translated in the same tense as it would be if it were an indicative verb. Remember that indirect questions in Latin will never contain question or quotation marks. Use your **IQ**! Take care to distinguish the indirect question clause from other types of **q**-clauses, such as the relative clause found with the indicative (see Chapter 12, "The Uses of the Relative Pronoun").

In an indirect question, the Romans often preferred to emphasize the question by placing it first in the sentence:

> **[Quid sit futūrum crās] fuge quaerere.** (Horace)
> *Stop asking [what may happen tomorrow].*

Because a direct question may be expressed by using a verb in the future tense, it should be remembered that, in an indirect question, the <u>active periphrastic</u> (future participle + form of **esse**) may be used to express future time, for example,

> **Scrībax scīre voluit [quot epistulās ipse <u>scriptūrus esset</u>].**
> *Scribax wanted to know [how many letters <u>he was about to transcribe</u>].*

Indirect questions can be alternative or double; that is, more than a single question may be asked in a sentence, such as the following questions introduced by **utrum . . . an**, *whether . . . or*:

> **Atticus mīrābātur [<u>utrum</u> Scrībax ignāvus <u>an</u> strenuus esset].**
> *Atticus was wondering [<u>whether</u> Scribax was lazy <u>or</u> energetic].*

An indirect question may express <u>doubt</u> in the following ways:

1. The subjunctive clause of doubt is introduced by the words **num** or **an**, *whether*, preceded by a verb of questioning or doubting, such as a form of the verb **dubitāre,** *to doubt*, or the phrase **dubium est**, *there is doubt that*, as in the following:

   Aliquī dubitant [<u>num</u> Cicerō carmina scrīpserit].
   Some people doubt [<u>whether</u> Cicero wrote poetry].

   Note that the interrogative particle **num** can also introduce a direct question with the indicative, to which a negative answer is expected. (See Chapter 23, "Direct Questions.")

2. The negative subjunctive clause of doubt is introduced by the word **quīn** (*that*) preceded by the stated or implied <u>negative</u> of the doubting word or expression, for example **nōn dubitāre** or **nōn dubium est** (= **sine dubiō**):

   Est nōn dubium [<u>quīn</u> Caesar ad Cicerōnem epistulās scrīpserit].
   There is no doubt (i.e., *It is doubtless*) [<u>that</u> *Caesar wrote letters to Cicero*].

Relative Clause of Characteristic

This type of subjunctive clause, which is introduced by a relative pronoun, describes a type of person or thing rather than one that is actual or specific. This type of relative clause describes a general quality or characteristic of the antecedent. Such clauses follow indefinite words or phrases such as **nēmō est quī** (*there is no one who . . .*), **is est quī** (*he is the type* or *kind of person who . . .*), and **sunt quī** (*there are those of the sort who . . .*). The relative clause of characteristic is generally found with the present subjunctive. Be especially careful to distinguish the relative characteristic clause with the subjunctive from the explanatory relative clause with the indicative. The explanatory clause provides (more) factual information about the antecedent:

Relative clause with the indicative:	**Tīrō est scrība [quī dīligēns <u>est</u>].** *Tiro is the (<u>particular</u>) scribe [who is careful].*
Relative clause with the subjunctive:	**Tīrō est scrība [quī dīligēns <u>sit</u>].** *Tiro is the (<u>type of</u>) scribe [who is careful].*

Additional examples of relative clauses of characteristic:

Nēmō est [quī omnēs epistulās Cicerōnis lēgerit].
There is no one (in the opinion of the writer) [*who has read all of Cicero's letters*].

Erant [quī dīcerent] Tīrōnem scrībam optimum omnium esse.
There were those [who said] that Tiro was the best secretary of all.

The relative, or **quī**, clause with the subjunctive can also be used to express purpose:

Cicerō Terentiae dedit epistulam [quam legeret].
Cicero gave Terentia a letter [to read (i.e., that she was to read)].

In such situations, the relative pronoun (**quam**), refers back to a particular antecedent (**epistulam**), and at the same time indicates purpose or intent (**quam legeret**).

When translating a relative clause, identify the antecedent of the relative pronoun, determine if the verb of the clause is indicative or subjunctive, and then consider the contextual sense of the **quī** clause carefully before deciding upon its meaning.

Causal Clauses

Causal clauses are dependent clauses introduced by explanatory words such as **quod, quia,** or **quoniam**, all meaning *because, since*. Such clauses are found with either the indicative or the subjunctive. When the indicative is used, the writer or speaker is taking responsibility for the reason: the explanation is viewed by the writer as a known fact. When the subjunctive is found in the dependent clause, the reason is viewed as that of someone other than the speaker: it is alleged.

Indicative (fact):	**Cicerō ōrātiōnēs Philippicās habēbat [quod Antōnius tyrannus erat].** *Cicero delivered the Philippics [because Antony was a tyrant, (as far as the writer of the sentence is concerned)].*
Subjunctive (allegation):	**[Quia Cicerō rem publicam servāvisset], "Pāter Patriae" salūtābātur.** [*Because Cicero had saved the state, in the opinion of someone other than the writer], he was saluted as "Father of his Country."*

When **quod** is found in a clause with its verb in the indicative mood, be careful to use context in order to determine whether **quod** has the meaning *because* (causal) or *which, that* (relative).

Quod causal (indicative-factual):	**Cicerō scrīpsit Dē Natūrā Deōrum [quod crēdit] deōs esse.** *Cicero wrote* On the Nature of the Gods [*because he believes that the gods exist*].
Quod relative (indicative-factual):	**Placēbatne Cicerōnī nōmen [quod eī datum erat]?** *Was Cicero pleased with the name [that had been given to him]?*

Quick Study of Q-Clauses

Type of Clause	Introductory Word	Meaning	Function
Indicative (factual)			
Relative	**quī, quae, quod**	*who, which, that*	explains, describes
Causal	**quod, quia, quoniam**	*because*	gives a reason as a fact
Subjunctive (nonfactual)			
Indirect question	**cūr, quid, quis, quōmodō, ubi,** etc.	*why, what, who, how, when,* etc.	restates a question
Double indirect question	**utrum . . . an**	*whether . . . or*	restates more than one question
Doubt clauses	**num**	*whether*	expresses uncertainty (**dubitāre, dubium est**)
	quīn	*that*	expresses certainty (**nōn dubitāre**)

Quick Study of Q-Clauses (*cont'd*)

Type of Clause	Introductory Word	Meaning	Function
Relative characteristic	**quī, quae, quod**	*the type who* . . .	describes a type
Relative purpose	**quī, quae, quod**	*to, in order to*	indicates purpose (relates to antecedent)
Causal	**quod, quia, quoniam**	*because*	gives a reason as an allegation

PRACTICE WITH Q-CLAUSES

Look carefully at the prior and succeeding context of a **q**-word in the clause in order to determine its meaning. Is there a word in the main clause that sets up the meaning expressed in the subordinate clause? Does an indicative or subjunctive verb appear in the dependent clause? Now review what you know about **q**-word clauses by bracketing the clause in each of the following sentences and then inspecting its context. Finally, translate the entire sentence:

1. Antōnius quī inimīcus Cicerōnis erat illum necāre voluit.

2. Quot senēs libellum Dē Senectūte lēgerint, Cicerō scīre vult.

3. Estne Cicerō quī virtūtem optimam esse crēdat?

4. Cicerō dē philosophiā scrīpsit quod cāra Tūllia mortua esset.

5. Cicerō ōrātiōnem habēbat quae Milōnem defenderet.

6. Legimus ōrātiōnēs Cicerōnis quod dē Rōmānīs nōs certiōrēs faciunt.

Answers

1. [**Quī . . . erat**]
Antony, who was a personal enemy of Cicero, wished to kill him.

This sentence contains a relative clause of fact with the indicative (see Chapter 12).

2. [**Quot . . . lēgerint**]
Cicero wants to know how many elderly men have read his treatise On Old Age.

Remember that subjunctive verbs are used in clauses that express hypothetical or incomplete actions. Here, a subjunctive verb is used because Cicero does not yet know for a fact how many men have read his essay (see "Indirect Questions").

3. [**quī . . . crēdat**]
Is Cicero the type of man who believes that virtue is the greatest (good)?

This sentence contains a relative clause of characteristic, which uses a subjunctive verb because it describes the type of man Cicero might be (see "Causal Clauses").

4. [**quod . . . mortua esset**]
Cicero wrote about philosophy because his dear Tullia had died.

A subjunctive verb is used here because it is the opinion of someone other than the writer that Cicero wrote philosophy because his daughter had died (causal clause with the subjunctive; see "Causal Clauses").

5. [**quae . . . defenderet**]
Cicero gave a speech to defend Milo.

The use of the subjunctive in the clause in this sentence tells us that Cicero gave the speech in order to defend Milo (see "Relative Clause of Characteristic").

6. [**quod . . . faciunt**]
We read the speeches of Cicero because they inform us about the Romans.

This sentence contains a **quod** causal clause with the indicative, which indicates a factual statement (see "Causal Clauses").

PRACTICE WITH INDIRECT EXPRESSIONS

You have now met three different types of expressions that are "indirect": an infinitive clause and two subjunctive clauses. Each reports in second-hand fashion an original statement, command, or question. To test your command of indirect expressions, translate the following sentences and then create in English the original direct expression:

Indirect statement: **Multī sciunt Cicerōnem Arpīnī natum esse.**

Indirect command: **Aliquis Cicerōnī persuāsit ut Tusculī habitāret.**

Indirect question: **Scitne quisquam in quō locō Cicerō mortuus sit?**

Answers

Indirect statement: *Many know that Cicero was born at Arpinum.*

Direct statement: *"Cicero was born at Arpinum."*

Indirect command: *Someone persuaded Cicero to live in Tusculum.*

Direct command: *"Live in Tusculum, Cicero!"*

Indirect question: *Does anyone know where Cicero died?*

Direct question: *"Where did Cicero die?"*

EXPRESSIONS OF PURPOSE

We have now met several different types of verbal constructions that express purpose or intent in Latin. Expressions of purpose appear frequently on the SAT Latin Subject Test.

Quick Study of Expressions of Purpose

Gerundive of purpose:	**Cicerō iter facit <u>ad</u> amīcum <u>vīsendum</u>.** *Cicero is traveling <u>to visit</u> a friend.*	Chapter 25, "Simple Gerundive"
Supine:	**Cicerō iter facit <u>vīsum</u> amīcum.** *Cicero is traveling <u>to visit</u> a friend.*	Chapter 25, "The Supine"
Ut purpose clause:	**Cicerō iter facit <u>ut</u> amīcum <u>vīsat</u>.** *Cicero is traveling <u>to visit</u> a friend.*	Chapter 30, "Purpose Clause with **Ut**"
Relative purpose clause:	**Cicerō epistulam mittet <u>quae dīcat</u> sē venīre.** *Cicero will send a letter <u>to say</u> that he is coming.*	"Relative Clause of Characteristic"

SAMPLE QUESTIONS

Part C: Translation

1. Atticus rogābat Cicerōnem <u>cur</u> tot multās epistulās ad Quintum <u>scrīpsisset</u>.

    (A) whether he would write

    (B) why he had written

    (C) why he was writing

    (D) to whom he had written

Part D: Sentence Completion

2. Cicerō nōn dubitāvit . . . Catilīnāriī inter sē coniurāvissent.

    (A) utinam   (C) ut

    (B) sē   (D) quīn

Part E: Syntax Substitution

3. Cicerō fīlium suum Athēnās mittet <u>quī artem dīcendī discat</u>.

    (A) arte dīcendī doctā

    (B) ubi artem dīcendī discēbat

    (C) ut artem dīcendī discat

    (D) discere artem dīcendī

Answers

1. (B)   2. (D)   3. (C)

PRACTICE QUESTIONS

1. Cicerō scīre vult <u>quis</u> sibi nōmen "Tully" <u>dederit</u>.

   (A) who will have given   (C) who had given

   (B) who was giving   (D) who has given

2. Cicerō Milōnem . . . quia Clōdium per Viam Appiam occīdisset.

   (A) defendēbat   (C) defenderet

   (B) defendet   (D) defenditur

3. Nōn dubium erat . . . Cicerō clēmentiam Caesaris. . . .

   (A) quī; colat   (C) quīn; coleret

   (B) nē; coleret   (D) quīn; colēbat

4. Quid agās, cūrā ut sciam.

   (A) Take care that I know where you are going.

   (B) Take care to know who you are.

   (C) Take care that I know how you are doing.

   (D) Take care to know what you are doing.

5. Cicero mīrābātur quōmodō cum senātōribus <u>grātiam habitūrus esset</u>.

   (A) has gained favor

   (B) was going to gain favor

   (C) is going to gain favor

   (D) will be able to gain favor

6. <u>Erant quī nōn crēdidit Cicerōnem mīlitem fuisse.</u>

   (A) There are those who do not believe that Cicero was a soldier.

   (B) There were those who believe that Cicero was not a soldier.

   (C) There were those who did not believe that Cicero had been a soldier.

   (D) There were those who did not believe that Cicero was a soldier.

7. Nēmō scīvit utrum Hortensius an Cicerō optimus ōrātor <u>factus</u>
   <u>esset</u>.

   (A) has become   (C) had become

   (B) was becoming   (D) was about to become

8. <u>Nēmo est quī dubitet quīn Cicerō bonus consul fuerit</u>.

   (A) There is no one who will doubt that Cicero would have been
   a good consul.

   (B) There is no one who does not doubt that Cicero was a good
   consul.

   (C) There is no one who doubts that Cicero was a good consul.

   (D) There is no one who doubts that Cicero was not a good
   consul.

SENTENTIAE ANTIQUAE

1. Vidētis quantum scelus contrā rem publicam vōbīs <u>nuntiātum sit</u>.
   (Cicero, on Catiline)

   (A) has been reported   (C) was being reported

   (B) had been reported   (D) is reported

2. Scīre ubi aliquid invenīre . . . , ea maxima pars erudītiōnis est.
   (anonymous)

   (A) possēs   (C) potuerās

   (B) potēs   (D) possīs

3. <u>Quod</u> cum animadvertisset Caesar nāvēs mīlitibus complērī iussit.
   (Caesar)

   (A) Because   (C) The fact that

   (B) What   (D) This

4. Malum est consilium quod mutārī nōn. . . . (Publilius Syrus)

   (A) potuerit   (C) potuisset

   (B) posset   (D) potest

5. Ōdī et amō. <u>Quārē id faciam</u>, fortasse requīris. (Catullus)

    (A) Why I have done this

    (B) Why I will do this

    (C) Why I do this

    (D) Why I will have done this

6. Multī cīvēs ea perīcula <u>quae imminent</u> neglegunt. (Cicero)

    (A) which might be imminent

    (B) which are imminent

    (C) which were imminent

    (D) which will be imminent

7. <u>Quis dubitet num in vīrtūte fēlīcitās sit</u>? (Cicero)

    (A) Who would doubt whether there is happiness in virtue?

    (B) Who would doubt whether or not there is happiness in virtue?

    (C) Who doubts whether virtue is happiness?

    (D) Who will doubt whether he is happy in his virtue?

8. Caesar mīlitēs reprehendit <u>quod sibi ipsi iūdicāvissent (jūdicāvissent)</u> <u>quid agendum esset</u>. (Caesar)

    (A) because they had (in fact) decided for themselves what had to be done.

    (B) because they were deciding for themselves what he must do.

    (C) because they did the thing which they had decided.

    (D) because they had (according to others) decided for themselves what had to be done

Stumper:

Do both of the following have the same meaning?

Exēgī monumentum aere perennius. (Horace)

Nihil est manū factum quod tempus nōn consūmat. (Cicero)

(A) Yes   (B) No

Answers

1. Indirect question **(D)**
    This sentence contains an indirect question in primary sequence, with the main verb in the present tense and the subjunctive verb **dederit** in the perfect tense. The sentence reads *Cicero wants to know <u>who has given</u> him the name "Tully."* **Dederit** could be identified as a future perfect tense, as is suggested in (A) *who will have given*, but the question word **quis** requires that the verb be subjunctive in an indirect question. Answers (B) and (C) require verbs in secondary sequence, which do not correlate with the tense of the main verb. (See Chapter 28.)

2. Causal clause **(A)**
    A main verb in the past tense is required because the subjunctive verb of the causal clause, **quia . . . occīdisset**, is in the pluperfect tense. Answers (B) and (D) are in the future and present tenses, respectively, and (C) is in the imperfect tense, but it is subjunctive, which does not fit the context of the main or independent clause. The sentence reads *Cicero <u>was defending</u> Milo because he had killed Clodius along the Appian Way.* (See "Causal Clauses.")

3. Doubt clause **(C)**
    The words **nōn dubium** introduce a doubt clause with its verb in secondary sequence after **erat**. This sentence reads *There was no doubt <u>that</u> Cicero <u>respected</u> Caesar's clemency.* The verb in (A) is in the wrong tense of the subjunctive; (B) contains **nē**, an incorrect particle for a doubt clause; and (D) **quīn . . . gaudēbat** is a clause with a verb in the indicative rather than the required subjunctive. (See "Indirect Questions.")

4. Indirect question and indirect command **(C)**
    This sentence, which contains two subjunctive clauses, reads *Take care that I know how you're doing.* **Quid agās** is an indirect question following the verb **sciam. Ut sciam**, after **cūrā**, has the force of an indirect command. Answer (A) mistranslates the indirect question that contains the idiomatic expression **Quid agis?** *How are you?* Answers (B) and (D) imply that the subject of the verb **sciam** is in the second person rather than the first. (See Chapter 28.)

5. Indirect question **(B)**
    This sentence contains an example of the "future subjunctive," that is, the use of the future active participle with a subjunctive form

of the verb **esse** as an active periphrastic (see Chapter 24.) The **q**-word **quōmodō** introduces the indirect question clause. The sentence reads *Cicero was wondering how <u>he was going to gain favor</u> with the senators*. Answers (B) and (C) incorrectly translate **esset** in the perfect and present tenses, respectively, and the translation in (D) assumes the future tense of the verb **posse**, which does not appear in the sentence. (See Chapters 19, "Future Indicative"; 24, "The Active Periphrastic"; and 27, "Quick Study of Sequence of Tenses" chart.)

6.　Relative clause with the indicative **(C)**

The accuracy of the translation of this sentence depends upon the correct rendering of the tenses of the three verbs: **erant**, **crēdidit**, and **fuisse**. **Quī nōn crēdidit** is a relative clause with the indicative, indicating that it was considered a fact that some did not believe that Cicero had been a soldier. The verb **erant** is in the imperfect tense, eliminating (A). In (B), **nōn** incorrectly negates **esse**. In (D), the infinitive is translated incorrectly; that is, *was a soldier* requires the infinitive **esse** instead of **fuisse**. (See Chapter 12.)

7.　Indirect question **(C)**

This sentence reads *No one knew whether Hortensius or Cicero <u>had become</u> the best orator*. **Factus esset** is the subjunctive of the verb **fierī** in the pluperfect tense, completing the double indirect question **utrum . . . an . . . factus esset**. Answer (A) *has become* requires the perfect tense, which would be in the incorrect time sequence. Answer (B) *was becoming* requires the form **fieret** rather than **factus esset**, and (D) *was about to become* requires the active periphrastic **factūrus esset**. (See "Indirect Questions.")

8.　Relative clause of characteristic and doubt clause **(C)**

The correct translation is *There is no one who doubts that Cicero was a good consul*. This sentence contains two subordinate clauses with the subjunctive. **Quī dubitet** is a relative clause of characteristic with a verb in the present subjunctive in primary sequence, describing a type of person who doubts. The appearance of **dubitet** in this clause introduces a clause of doubt, **quīn . . . fuerit**. Answer (A) incorrectly translates **dubitet** as a future tense, therefore making the original characteristic clause an explanatory relative clause. The translation in (B) *does not doubt* incorrectly negates the verb **dubitet**, creating a meaning that is the opposite of that of the original sentence. In the same way, (D) incorrectly negates the subordinate verb **fuerit**. (See "Relative Clause of Characteristic" and "Indirect Questions.")

Sententiae Antiquae Answers

1. Indirect question **(A)**

   Nuntiātum sit is a form of the perfect passive subjunctive (see Chapter 27), here found in an indirect question introduced by **quantum**. The sentence reads *You see how much evil against the State* (i.e., by the Catilinarian conspirators) <u>*has been reported*</u> *to you all*. The remaining answers translate the verb **nuntiātum sit** in the incorrect tense: (B) is pluperfect (**nuntiātum esset**), (C) is imperfect (**nuntiārētur**), and (D) is present (**nuntiātur**).

2. Indirect question **(D)**

   As all the verbs in this sentence are found in the present tense, the primary sequence is used, eliminating (A), which is in the imperfect tense. The subjunctive mood is required because the missing form completes an indirect question introduced by **ubi**, thereby eliminating (B) **potes** and (C) **potuerās**, which are both indicative. The sentence reads *Knowing* (*To know*) *where* <u>*you can*</u> *find something, that is the most important part of being educated.*

3. (Ambush!) **(D)**

   The form **quod** is a relative pronoun referring to some previous antecedent that is neuter singular. Answers (A), (B), and (C) do not fit the context of the meaning, which is, *When Caesar had noticed* <u>*this,*</u> *he ordered the ships to be filled up with soldiers.* It is tempting to connect **quod** with the following subjunctive verb **animadvertisset**, but this verb follows **cum** in a circumstantial clause. (See Chapter 12.)

4. Relative clause with the indicative **(D)**

   Quod . . . potest is a simple relative clause, describing **malum consilium**. An indicative verb is therefore required in the subordinate clause, hence **potest**. The sentence reads *It is a bad plan that* <u>*cannot*</u> *be changed.* Answer (A), when read as a form of the future perfect indicative, does not make sense, and when read as a form of the perfect subjunctive, is out of place in an explanatory relative clause. Answers (B) and (C) are subjunctive, which is not justifiable in the context of this sentence. (See Chapter 12.)

5. Indirect question **(C)**

   The indirect question **quārē id faciam**, dependent upon **requīris**, is found in Catullus's Poem 85. This sentence reads *I hate and I love.* <u>*Why*</u>

I do this, perhaps you ask. Because the verbs are all in the present tense, the sequence is primary. Answer (A) mistranslates the tense of **faciam** as perfect, (B) as a future indicative, and (D) as a future perfect indicative.

6.   Relative clause with the indicative **(B)**
     The relative clause **quae imminent** describes its antecedent **ea perīcula,** and it thus requires the indicative mood. The sentence reads *Many citizens disregard those dangers which are imminent.* Answer (A) *might be imminent,* as a nonfact, requires the subjunctive. Answers (C) and (D) translate the tense of **imminent** incorrectly as imperfect and future. (See Chapter 12.)

7.   Doubt clause **(A)**
     The doubt clause **num . . . sit** is introduced by the deliberative question **Quis dubitet?** *Who would doubt?* Answers (B) and (C) incorrectly negate the verb **sit** and (D) contains two errors: the verb **dubitet** is not in the future tense and **fēlīcitās** is not an adjective, but a noun. (See "Indirect Questions.")

8.   Causal clause and indirect question **(D)**
     This sentence contains two subjunctive clauses, a causal clause with the subjunctive, **quod . . . iūdicāvissent (jūdicāvissent)**, indicating that the speaker is doubtful of the reason given by Caesar, and an indirect question, **quid agendum esset**, whose verb is a passive periphrastic. Answer (A) is incorrect because it suggests that the statement is factual, which would require the verb **iūdicāverit**, in the indicative mood. The verb tense of **iūdicāvissent** in (B) is translated incorrectly, and (D) gives a wholesale mistranslation of the Latin.

Stumper: (B)
     Horace's line reads *I have built a monument more lasting than bronze* (i.e., something timeless). Cicero says, *There is nothing made by (man's) hand that time does not consume* (i.e., all things are transitory). These statements oppose one another in meaning.

CHAPTER 32

Subordinate Clauses with *Cum*

Chapter 32

SUBORDINATE CLAUSES WITH *CUM*

The word **cum** has two basic functions in Latin: as a preposition governing an object in the ablative case, as in **cum laude**, *with praise*, and as a conjunction that joins a dependent clause to a main clause, for example,

[**<u>Cum</u> strenuissimē <u>laborāvisset</u>**], **summam laudem recēpit.**
[<u>*Because he had worked*</u> *the hardest*], *he received the greatest praise.*

There are three major types of **cum** clauses found with the subjunctive: causal, circumstantial, and concessive (the "three Cs"). In such clauses, the word **cum** means *because, when,* or *although,* depending upon the context. A variation of the circumstantial clause that expresses action at a specific time appears with its verb in the indicative mood. **Cum** clauses with verbs in the subjunctive are found in the imperfect and pluperfect tenses and follow the rules for sequence of tenses.

TYPES OF CUM CLAUSES

Cum Causal Clause (*because, since*)

When the **cum** clause expresses the reason why the action of the main clause occurred, **cum** means *because* or *since* and is followed by a subjunctive verb, as in these examples:

[**Cum Trōianōs (Trōjanōs) superāre nōn possent**], **Graecī equum ligneum aedificāvērunt.**
[*Because they were unable to defeat the Trojans*], *the Greeks constructed a wooden horse.*

Laōcoōn [**cum hastā equum percussisset**] **ā serpentibus necātus est.**
Laocoon, [*because he had struck the horse with a spear*], *was killed by serpents.*

Cum clauses are generally located close to the front of the sentence.

The clause **quae cum ita sint**, *because these things are so*, appears often in prose.

For causal clauses introduced by **q**-words, see Chapter 31, "Causal Clauses."

Cum Time Clauses (*when*)

Circumstantial and Temporal Clauses

When a dependent **cum** clause expresses the general <u>circumstances</u>, <u>situation</u>, or <u>conditions</u> in which the action of the clause occurs, a <u>subjunctive</u> verb is used, and **cum** means *when*. The circumstantial clause is found with the imperfect or pluperfect subjunctive and refers to past time. **Cum** meaning *when* may also be found with a past tense of the <u>indicative</u>, but in this case, the **cum** clause indicates or dates a <u>specific or precise point in time</u>, and it is sometimes accompanied by a clarifying phrase or word, such as **eō tempore**, *at that time*, or **tum**, *then*. When the clause has this meaning, it is generally referred to as a temporal clause.

Circumstantial (+ subjunctive):	[**Cum mānēs ad Acherontem flūmen <u>pervēnissent</u>**], **Charon eōs scaphā transportāvit.** [*When souls had reached the river Acheron*], *Charon carried them across in a boat.*
Temporal (+ indicative):	[**Cum ad Acherontem <u>pervēnerat</u>**], **tenuitne Aenēās obolum?** [*(At the time) when he had reached the Acheron*], *did Aeneas have the fare?*

A famous example of the **cum** temporal clause is Cicero's saying, **Cum tacent, clāmant**, *When they are silent, they cry aloud*, meaning that they (i.e., the senators) have made their feelings clear without having to express them.

In **cum** clauses, the appearance of **cum** with the indicative is much less frequent than with the subjunctive.

Other Types of Time Clauses

1. Time clauses with the indicative (*when, as soon as*)

   Temporal or time clauses introduced by words such as **ubi,** *when,* and **simul atque** or **simul ac,** *as soon as,* are found with the indicative and express pure time.

2. Clause of anticipation (*before*)

   Time clauses introduced by anticipatory words such as **antequam** and **priusquam,** *before,* are found with both indicative and subjunctive verbs. In indicative clauses, which refer strictly to the time of something that has actually occurred, the present, perfect, and future perfect tenses are used. In subjunctive clauses, when expectancy or action that did not actually occur is expressed in past time, the imperfect tense is used:

Indicative (actually happens/ happened):	[**Priusquam Aenēas ad Ītaliam pervēnit**], **magna tempestās coorta est.** [*Before Aeneas <u>reached</u> Italy*], *a great storm arose.*
Subjunctive (anticipated as happening):	[**Antequam omnēs nāvēs dēlērentur**], **vīs tempestātis cecidit.** [*Before all the ships <u>were destroyed</u>*], *the force of the storm weakened.*

3. **Dum** clauses

   The adverbs **dum** or **dōnec** + the <u>indicative</u> express an actual fact in pure time and mean *while* or *as long as,* depending on the context:

   [**Dum Trōianī (Trōjanī) ad Ītaliam navigābant**], **Palinūrus in mare cecidit.**
   [*While the Trojans were sailing to Italy*], *Palinurus fell overboard.*

   Dum or **donec** also can have the meaning *until* when expressing expectancy or anticipation. In this case, the verb of the dependent clause is <u>subjunctive</u>:

   Aenēas multa passus est [**dum conderet urbem**]. (Vergil)
   Aeneas endured many things [*until he could found the city*].

Dum (often strengthened by **modo** = **dummodo**) + the present or imperfect <u>subjunctive</u> can also be translated *provided that, if only*, in which case the clause is known as a "clause of proviso":

Ōderint [**dum metuant**]. (attributed to Caligula by Suetonius)
Let them hate me [*provided that they fear me*].

Cum Concessive Clauses (*although*)

The word "concessive" implies that the statement within the **cum** clause is granted or assumed as true by the speaker or writer. In this context, **cum** means *although* and introduces a clause with its verb in the subjunctive mood. The concessive **cum** clause is often (but not always) accompanied by the word **tamen**, *nevertheless*, in the main clause:

[**Cum Vergilius dē armīs virōque caneret**], **(tamen) dē fēminā optimē scrīpsit.**
[*Although* (or *Granted that*) *Vergil sang about arms and a man*], *(nevertheless) he did his best writing about a woman.*

The words **quamquam** and **etsi**, meaning *although*, also introduce concessive clauses, either with the indicative or the subjunctive, depending on whether the clause contains a statement of fact.

TIPS ON TRANSLATING CUM CLAUSES

When translating **cum** clauses, which are almost all grammatically identical, try one meaning of **cum**, then another, and so on, to see which meaning makes the best sense in context. **Cum** clauses are regularly found with subjunctive verbs in either the imperfect or pluperfect tense. Be especially alert for the appearance of **cum** as a preposition. Questions on the SAT Latin Subject Test are not designed to be misleading, so they will rarely present you with a grammatical decision that is not clearly defined. Because of its ambiguity, the **cum** clause is often tested in the Reading Comprehension passages, where more context is available. A question might read:

In line such and so, **cum** is translated

(A) when   (C) although

(B) with   (D) since

Another possible question might read "The first sentence (**Cum . . . esset**) tells us that . . ."

Quick Study of Cum Clauses

Type of Clause	Cue in Main Clause	Meaning of Clause	Function
Indicative			
Temporal	**eō tempore, tum**	*when, whenever*	specific time
Subjunctive			
Causal		*because, since*	gives a reason
Circumstantial		*when*	general circumstance
Concessive	**tamen**	*although*	truth granted by writer

Quick Study of Time Clauses

Type of Clause	Introductory Word	Meaning of Clause	Function
Indicative			
Temporal	**ubi**	*when*	pure time
	simul atque/ac	*as soon as*	
	dum*	*while, until*	fact in real time
	donec*	*as long as*	
	cum	*when*	specific time
Subjunctive			
Circumstantial	**cum**	*when*	general circumstance
Anticipatory	**antequam**[†] **priusquam**[†]	*before*	anticipation
	dum	*until*	intention, expectancy
Provisonal	**dum(modo)**	*provided that*	conditional wish

* These clauses are also found with their verbs in the subjunctive.
† These clauses are also found with their verbs in the indicative.

SAMPLE QUESTIONS

Because of the variety of ways in which the Romans expressed cause, time, and other ideas that can be both factual and nonfactual, **cum** clauses and their alternatives, such as participles, are good candidates for the syntax substitution section of the SAT Latin Subject Test.

Cum Vergilius mortuus est, eōdem annō quoque Tibullus poeta.

(A) Vergiliō mortuō

(B) Quod Vergilius moriēbātur

(C) Postquam Vergilius mortuus erat

(D) Sī Vergilius mortuus esset

Answer: (A)

PRACTICE QUESTIONS

1. Cum Augustus novam Rōmam aedificāre vellet, tamen dīcēbat "Ō fortūnātī, quōrum iam (jam) moenia surgunt!"

   (A) When　　　　　　　(C) Provided that

   (B) Because　　　　　　(D) Although

2. Cum Aeneās Carthāgine excessisset, Didō sē necāre constituit.

   (A) Because Aeneas left Carthage

   (B) When Aeneas leaves Carthage

   (C) When Aeneas had left Carthage

   (D) Because Aeneas was leaving Carthage

3. When Troy had been captured, it was burned.

   (A) Trōia (Trōja) cum capta esset, incensa est.

   (B) Trōia (Trōja) dum capiēbātur, incensa est.

   (C) Trōiā (Trōjā) captā, incensa erat.

   (D) Trōia (Trōja) cum caperētur, incendēbātur.

4. Vergilius <u>cum</u> apibus avibusque rurī lībēnter habitābat.

   (A) when   (C) because

   (B) with   (D) although

5. <u>Cum Vergilius mortuus sit</u>, *Aeneïs* nōn complēta est.

   (A) While Vergil was dying

   (B) After Vergil died

   (C) When Vergil dies

   (D) Because Vergil died

6. When Aeneas <u>heard</u> Cerberus barking, the Sibyl said, "Cavē canem, cavē canem, cavē canem!"

   (A) audīret   (C) audīvisset

   (B) audītus erat   (D) audit

7. Eōdem tempore cum Vergilius dē Marcellō . . . , Augustus lacrimāvit.

   (A) lēgit   (C) legat

   (B) legeret   (D) lēgisset

8. Rōmānī, <u>cum crēderent</u> Aenēam gentem togātam condidisse, Aeneidem legēbant.

   (A) because they believed

   (B) whenever they believe

   (C) after they believed

   (D) although they believe

9. Trōiānīs (Trōjānīs) fugientibus, cum Creūsa ē conspectū . . . tum Aeneas ad urbem rediit.

   (A) abiisset   (C) abit

   (B) abeat   (D) abierat

10. <u>Cum Augustus dē Līviā certior factus esset</u>, cōgitāvit, "Dux fēminā factī."

 (A) Because Augustus is informed about Livia

 (B) When Augustus was informed about Livia

 (C) When Augustus had been informed about Livia

 (D) Because Augustus was being informed about Livia

SENTENTIAE ANTIQUAE

1. A man is outside of his body at that very moment <u>when he is angry</u>. (Publilius Syrus)

 (A) cum īrātus est   (C) cum īrātus sit

 (B) cum īrātus esset   (D) cum īrātus esse potest

2. <u>Satis est beātus quī potest cum vult morī</u>. (Publilius Syrus)

 (A) He is happy enough who wants to die when he can.

 (B) Happy enough is the one who can die when he wants.

 (C) He who dies can be happy enough whenever he wants.

 (D) Because he wants to die, he who is happy enough can.

3. <u>Quae cum ita sint</u>, Catilīna, ... (Cicero)

 (A) Because these things are this way

 (B) Whenever this is true

 (C) Although this was the case

 (D) Whatever things are so

4. Quod bellum ōdērunt, cum fīde dē pāce . . . . (Livy)

 (A) agerent   (C) ēgissent

 (B) agēbant   (D) aguntur

5. You hope (to see) a fox's tail at the very moment <u>when you see</u> his ears. (medieval)

(A) cum vidīstī   (C) cum videās

(B) cum vidēs   (D) cum visūrus es

Stumper:

<u>Cum essent</u> cīvium dominī, libertōrum erant servī. (Pliny the Younger)

(A) Seeing that they were (C) Since they had been

(B) Although they were (D) Provided they are

Answers

1. Concessive **(D)**
The appearance of the word **tamen** in the main clause cues the **cum** clause in this sentence as concessive. The sentence, which contains a quote from Book 2 of the *Aeneid*, reads *Although Augustus wished to build a new Rome, nevertheless he said, "O fortunate are they whose walls are already rising!"* The translations in (A) *When* and (B) *Because* are possible grammatically, but less likely than *Although* because of **tamen**. Answer (B) *Provided that*, which is a provisional clause, does not fit the context. (See "**Cum** Concessive Clauses.")

2. Circumstantial **(C)**
This sentence requires decisions about the type of clause and the tense of the verb. Because the verb **excessisset** is in the pluperfect tense, (A), (B), and (D) are incorrect because they offer translations in the simple past, present, and imperfect tenses, respectively. The clause is translated as circumstantial because the only answer with the subordinate verb in the correct tense is introduced by the word *when*. The sentence reads *When Aeneas had left Carthage, Dido decided to kill herself.* (For the forms of the various tenses of the subjunctive, see Chapter 27.)

3. Circumstantial **(A)**
The subordinate clause in this sentence can be found with either an indicative or a subjunctive verb. Answer (B) provides Latin that does not give the translation *When Troy had been captured*. Answer (C) is incorrect because the verb of the main clause, the pluperfect form **incensa erat**, does not translate *it was burned* correctly. Answers (A) and (D) contain

subjunctive verbs, so the decision becomes one of tense. The original sentence reads *had been captured*, which requires a pluperfect passive verb form in the subordinate clause. This is **capta esset**. Answer (D) gives the verb **caperētur** in the imperfect tense. (See "**Cum** Time Clauses.")

4.   Prepositional phrase **(B)**
      This question is included to keep you honest about the possibility that **cum** can be a preposition followed by a noun in the ablative case, as here: **cum apibus avibusque**. The sentence reads *Vergil gladly lived in the country <u>with</u> the birds and bees.*

5.   Causal **(D)**
      The **cum** clause in this sentence makes the best sense as a causal clause, *Because Vergil died, the* Aeneid *was not completed*. Answers (A) *While Vergil was dying* and (C) *When Vergil dies* do not translate the perfect subjunctive form **mortuus sit** correctly. Answer (B) *After Vergil died* does not give an appropriate rendering of the conjunction **cum**.

6.   Circumstantial **(A)**
      The choices of answers provide two verbs in the indicative and two in the subjunctive, so the decision must be made on the basis of tense. Answers (B) and (C) are incorrect because they are pluperfect and the imperfect or perfect is required to translate *When Aeneas heard . . .* Answer (C) **audit** is in the present tense, leaving **audīret**, an imperfect subjunctive form in secondary sequence, as the correct answer. Hopefully, you enjoyed the humor of this sentence!

7.   Temporal **(A)**
      The time phrase *at the moment* specifies the time of the action of the verb in the **cum** clause, thus requiring an indicative verb in a temporal clause. Because (B) **legeret**, (C) **legat**, and (D) **lēgisset** are all forms of the subjunctive, (A) **lēgit** is correct. (See "**Cum** Time Clauses.")

8.   Causal **(A)**
      This sentence reads <u>*Because*</u> *the Romans believed that Aeneas had founded the toga-ed race, they read the* Aeneid. Answers (B) and (C) do not correctly translate the **cum** of the subordinate clause in this sentence. Answer (D) *although* is possible grammatically, but even if the clause **cum crēderent** were concessive (note that the trigger word **tamen** is missing), this clause does not make sense when translated as concessive. (See "**Cum** Concessive Clauses.")

9. Temporal **(D)**

The correlative time words, **tum** . . . **cum**, *at the time when* . . . specify the time of the action of the clause, thereby establishing it as a temporal clause with the indicative. The correct answer is therefore **abierat.** Answers (B) and (C) are in the present tense, which is incorrect in a sentence that contains **rediit**, a verb that requires the secondary sequence in the subordinate clause. Answer (A) **abiisset** would make the clause circumstantial and the time element more generalized. The sentence reads *While the Trojans were fleeing, Aeneas returned to the city at the time when Creusa had vanished.* (See Chapter 35 for correlatives.)

10. Circumstantial **(C)**

The tense of the verb in the subordinate clause determines which answer is correct. As **factus esset** is a form of the pluperfect passive, Answer (C) is correct. Answer (A) requires the present tense, and (B) *was informed* and (D) *was being informed* require the imperfect tense.

Sententiae Antiquae Answers

1. Temporal **(A)**

The appearance of *at that very moment* in the sentence creates a specific time frame for the action of the subordinate clause, which is a temporal clause with the indicative. Answers (B) and (C) contain subjunctive clauses with subjunctive verbs in the imperfect and present tenses, respectively, and (D) is not a correct translation because the verb **potest** does not appear in the original sentence.

2. Temporal **(B)**

The use of the indicative in the subordinate clause **cum vult** means that Publilius Syrus is saying that he who dies at the very moment that he wishes is happy. Answers (A), (C), and (D) all change the meaning of the original statement by altering the elements contained in the **cum** clause.

3. Causal **(A)**

Answer (C) contains a mistranslation of the present subjunctive verb **sint,** and (D) contains a mistransltion of the relative pronoun **quae**, which refers to some antecedent that is unidentified here. (See Chapter 12, "The Uses of the Relative Pronoun.") When **cum** means *whenever*, the indicative mood is used, eliminating (B).

4. Prepositional phrase **(B)**
    Cum fide is a prepositional phrase, which removes from consideration the use of **cum** in a subordinate clause and any need for the subjunctive, eliminating (A) and (C). The present passive form in (D) does not make sense in the context here. The sentence reads *Because they hated war, they were acting with reliability concerning peace.*

5. Temporal **(B)**
    Answer (B) **cum vidēs** is the only choice that contains a verb in the correct tense. Answers (A) and (D) both contain verbs in incorrect tenses (i.e., perfect indicative and the future tense in an active periphrastic construction). Answer (C) is incorrect because **cum** circumstantial clauses are found with verbs in the imperfect or pluperfect tenses, and **videās** is in the present tense. This sentence indicates that at the specific time when you see the ears (i.e., the head) of a fox, then it probably sees you, and you may be in danger. But when you see the tail (i.e., its back), it has passed by, so you are safe.

Stumper:　　**(B)**
    Answers (C) and (D) are incorrect because they contain incorrect translations of the underlined verb **essent**, which is in the imperfect tense. Answer (A) contains a verb that is correctly translated (*they were*) but has a less acceptable meaning than that of (B) in its context. The sentence reads *Although they were the masters of the citizens, they were the slaves of freedmen.* Note the omission of **tamen.**

Quick Study of Dependent Clauses*

Indicative (factual)

Type of Clause	Meaning of Clause	Example	Review
1. Relative	*who, which, that*	**Plinius homō erat** [<u>**cui**</u> **imperātor crēdidit**]. *Pliny was a person* [<u>*whom*</u> *the emperor trusted*].	Chapter 12, "Uses of the Relative Pronoun"; see also 11 and 12 in this chart
2. **Quod** causal	*because, since*	**Plinius praefectus creātus est** [<u>**quod**</u> **officiōsus erat**]. *Pliny was appointed an official* [<u>*because*</u> *(it was a fact that) he was dutiful*].	Chapter 31, "Causal Clauses"; see also 13
3. **Cum** temporal	*when*	[**Eōdem tempore** <u>**cum**</u> **natus est**], **Plinī pater Cōmī habitābat.** [*At the time* <u>*when*</u> *he was born*], *Pliny's father was living at Comum.*	"**Dum** Clauses"; see also 14–16
Dum temporal	*while, as long as, until*	[<u>**Dum**</u> **in Bīthȳnia erat**], **Plinius multās epistulās ad imperātōrem mīsit.** [<u>*While*</u> *he was in Bithynia*], *Pliny sent many letters to the emperor.*	"Other Types of Time Clauses"; see also 19

Quick Study of Dependent Clauses* (continued)

Anticipatory	before	**Plinius consul Rōmae erat [priusquam prōconsul in Bīthȳniā fuit].** *Pliny was a consul in Rome [(in fact) before he was governor in Bithynia].*	"Clause of Anticipation"; see also 18

Subjunctive (nonfactual)

4. Conditional	*if*	**[Nisi Mons Vesūvius ērupuisset], urbs Pompēī mansisset.** *[If Mount Vesuvius had not erupted], the city of Pompeii would have remained.*	Chapter 29, "Contrary to Fact Conditional Sentences"
5. **Ut** purpose	*to, in order that*	**Quintiliānus Plinium docēbat [ut melius scrīberet].** *Quintilian taught Pliny [to write better].*	Chapter 30, "Purpose Clause with **Ut**"; see also 12
6. **Ut** result	*that*	**Tantum perīculum erat [ut multī Pompēiānī fūgerent].** *The danger was so great [that many Pompeians fled].*	Chapter 30, "Result Clause with **Ut**"; see also 7
7. Substantive result	*that*	**Plinius effēcit [ut complūrēs prōconsulēs damnārentur].** *Pliny brought it about [that several governors were condemned].*	Chapter 30, "Result Clause with **Ut**"; see also 6

#	Construction	Keyword(s)	Example	Reference
8.	Indirect command	*that*	**Plinius Christiānīs imperābat [nē in unum locum congregārent].** *Pliny ordered the Christians [not to gather together in one place].*	Chapter 30, "Indirect Command"
9.	Fear	*that*	**Hodiē multī timent [nē Vesūvius iterum ēruptūrus sit].** *Today many are afraid [that Vesuvius is going to erupt again].*	Chapter 30, "Fear Clauses"
10.	Indirect question	*who, what, why*	**Secundus cognoscere voluit [cūr amīcus Tacitus Annālēs scrīpsisset].** *Secundus wanted to know [why his friend Tacitus had written the Annals].*	Chapter 31, "Indirect Questions"; see also 17
11.	Relative characteristic	*the type who*	**Secundus homō erat [quī ēruditiōnem magnī aestimāret].** *Secundus was the type of person [who thought highly of education].*	Chapter 31, "Relative Clause of Characteristic"; see also 1, 12
12.	Relative purpose	*to, in order to*	**Plinius legatum mīsit [quī imperātōrem dē Christiānīs certiōrem faceret].** *Pliny sent an envoy [to inform the emperor about the Christians].*	Chapter 31, "Relative Clause of Characteristic"; see also 1, 11

Quick Study of Dependent Clauses* (continued)

13.	**Quod** causal	*since, because*	[**Quod multī Christiānī essent**], **multī dēlātōrēs erant.**	Chapter 31, "Causal Clauses"; see also 2, 14
			[*Because there were many Christians*], *there were many informers.*	
14.	**Cum** causal	*because, since*	[**Cum Christiānī in prōvinciā essent**], **Plīnius cōnsilium Traiānī (Trajānī) petēbat.**	"**Cum** Causal Clause"; see also 1, 13
			[*Because there were Christians in the province*], *Pliny sought the advice of Trajan.*	
15.	**Cum** Circumstantial	*when*	[**Cum Plīnius prōcōnsul in Bīthȳniā esset**], **cīvēs flōrēbant.**	"**Cum** Time Clauses"; see also 3, 14, 16
			[*When Pliny was proconsul in Bithynia*], *the citizens were prosperous.*	
16.	**Cum** concessive	*although*	[**Cum Bīthȳnia prōvincia Rōmāna esset**], **tamen cīvēs Graecē loquēbantur.**	"**Cum** Concessive Clauses"; see also 3, 14, 15
			[*Although Bithynia was a Roman province*], *nevertheless the citizens spoke Greek.*	
17.	Doubt	*doubt that*	**Est nōn dubium** [**quīn Plīnius suum patruum dīlexerit**].	Chapter 31, "Causal Clauses"; see also 10
			There is no doubt [*that Pliny held his uncle in high regard*].	

18.	Anticipatory	*before*	[**Priusquam dē Vesuviō scrībere posset**], **patruus Plīniī mortuus est.**	"Clause of Anticipation"; see also 3
			[*Before be could write about Vesuvius*], *Pliny's uncle died.*	
19.	Anticipatory	*until*	**Plīnius exspectābat** [**dum audīret**] **nūntium ex imperātōre.**	"**Dum** Clauses"; see also 3, 18
			Pliny was waiting [*to bear* (literally, *until be should bear*)] *news from the emperor.*	
20.	Proviso	*provided that, if only*	**Licēbat servīs custodēs in Bīthȳniā esse** [**dummodo fidelēs essent**].	"**Dum** Clauses"; see also 3
			Slaves were allowed to be guards in Bithynia, [*provided that they were trustworthy*].	

* The sentences in this quick study portray the life and times of Pliny the Younger.

THE SAT SUBJECT TEST IN
LATIN

SECTION 9

Special Aspects of the SAT Latin Subject Test

CHAPTER 33

Syntax Substitution

Chapter 33

SYNTAX SUBSTITUTION

In this chapter, you will learn more about perhaps the most difficult of
the six parts of the SAT Latin Subject Test, Syntax Substitution. In the
following two chapters, you will be provided with opportunities to practice for the Translation and Reading Comprehension sections, which together make up 65 percent of the content of the exam. This section will
end with two complete (simulated) Latin Subject Tests.

The practice questions provided in this chapter will assist in your
preparation for Syntax Substitution, which evaluates your familiarity
with the variety of expression that can occur in Latin. The directions
for this part call for you to choose the answer that most closely approximates the designated Latin.

SAMPLE QUESTION

Part E: Syntax Substitution

<u>Quod elephantī vīsī erant</u>, equitēs Rōmānī perterritī erant.

(A) <u>Elephantīs videntibus</u>

(B) <u>Elephantīs vīsīs</u>

(C) <u>Elephantōs videntēs</u>

(D) <u>Elephantī vīsī</u>

The appropriate substitution is (B), which is an ablative absolute that,
when translated as a causal clause, expresses the same meaning as the
quod-causal clause in the original sentence, which reads *Because elephants
had been seen, the Roman cavalry was completely terrified.*

Some substitutions, such as **ille** for **hic**, may have lexical differences
that exist in Latin but have meanings that are close enough in English to
serve as alternatives.

Syntax Substitution on the SAT Latin Subject Test

Expressions of Purpose

dative of purpose	Chapter 8
ad + accusative of gerund or gerundive	Chapter 25
causa or **grātiā** + accusative of gerund or gerundive	Chapter 25
supine	Chapter 25
ut purpose clause	Chapter 31
relative (**quī**) purpose clause	Chapter 31

Expressions of Necessity or Obligation

necesse est or **oportet** + infinitive or subjunctive	Chapter 22
debet + infinitive	Chapter 22
passive periphrastic	Chapter 25

Variety of Meanings of Participles

participial phrase = relative (**quī**) explanatory	Chapter 12
participial phrase = relative (**quī**) characteristic	Chapter 31
active periphrastic = future tense	Chapter 19
ablative absolute = **quod** causal	Chapter 31
ablative absolute = **cum** temporal	Chapter 32

Variety of Expression of Certain Words and Constructions

active verb = passive verb with ablative of agent	Chapters 10, 19
habēre + accusative = dative of possession	Chapter 8
rogāre + accusative = **petere** + ablative	Chapter 10
ablative of comparison = **quam** + comparative adjective or adverb	Chapters 16, 17
genitive of description = ablative of description	Chapters 7, 11
hic = **ille** (or other demonstrative pronoun)	Chapter 11
iubēre (jubēre) + accusative + infinitive = **imperāre** + dative + subjunctive	Chapter 30

PRACTICE QUESTIONS

Directions: Select from the choices the form or expression that **best** approximates the meaning of the underlined portion of the sentence provided.*

1. Caesar Helvētiōs <u>captūrus est</u>.

    (A) <u>capiētur</u>   (C) <u>capiendus est</u>

    (B) <u>capiet</u>   (D) <u>cēperit</u>

2. Rōmānī Rēgulum ad Āfricam <u>redeuntem</u> laudāvērunt.

    (A) <u>ut redīret</u>   (C) <u>ad redeundum</u>

    (B) <u>cum rediisset</u>   (D) <u>quī redibat</u>

3. <u>Augustō principe</u>, multī poetae Rōmae habitābant.

    (A) <u>Dum Augustus princeps erat</u>

    (B) <u>Augustus princeps</u>

    (C) <u>Ut Augustus princeps fiēret</u>

    (D) <u>Cum Augustus princeps fuisset</u>

4. Poteratne Mercurius celerius <u>Pēgasō</u> volāre?

    (A) <u>Pēgasus</u>   (C) <u>quam Pēgasō</u>

    (B) <u>quam Pēgasus</u>   (D) <u>Pēgasum</u>

5. <u>Sī multa pecūnia tibi est</u>, esne dīvitior quam Croesus?

    (A) <u>Sī multā pecūniā potīris</u>

    (B) <u>Multam pecūniam tribuens</u>

    (C) <u>Sī multam pecūniam habēre velīs</u>

    (D) <u>Sī multam pecūniam habēbās</u>

6. <u>Huic</u> miserō dēnārium dedit, illī nihil.

    (A) <u>Cui</u>   (C) <u>Eī</u>

    (B) <u>Istum</u>   (D) <u>Ipsius</u>

---

*   The relevant Latin in the questions and answers of this section is underlined, as you will find on the actual SAT Latin Subject Test.

7. Fortēs fortūna adiuvat (adjuvat).

   (A) Fortēs ā fortūnā adiuvantur (adjuvantur).

   (B) Fortūna adiuvatur (adjuvatur) ā fortibus.

   (C) Fortēs fortūnam adiuvant (adjuvant).

   (D) Fortis fortūnam adiuvat (adjuvat).

8. Scīpio ad Āfricam profectus est ut Hannibalem vinceret.

   (A) sī Hannibal vincerētur

   (B) quod Hannibal vincendum est

   (C) cum Hannibalem vīcisset

   (D) ad Hannibalem vincendum

9. Sunt quī putent discessum animī ā corpore esse mortem.

   (A) putātī   (C) putātūrī

   (B) putantēs   (D) putantem

10. Ēgistī quod tibi agendum erat.

    (A) necesse erat tē agere (C) tibi agere licēbat

    (B) tū actūrus erās   (D) ā tē actum erat

11. Cum Caesar dictātor erat, Romānī putāvērunt istum regem fīerī velle.

    (A) Postquam Caesar dictātor erat

    (B) Sī Caesar dictātor esset

    (C) Dum Caesar dictātor est

    (D) Caesare dictātōre

12. Cicerō ab Antōniō petīvit ut iste Rōmā discēderet.

    (A) Cicerō rogāvit Antōnium cūr iste Rōmā discēderet.

    (B) Cicerō dīxit Rōmā ab Antōniō discēdendum esse.

    (C) Cicerō Antōnium ut Rōmā discēderet rogāvit.

    (D) Antōnius rogāvit Cicerōnem Rōmae ut manēret.

13. <u>Quibus verbīs dictīs</u>, Cicerō ē Forō discessit.

    (A) <u>Ad haec verba dīcenda</u>

    (B) <u>Quae verba cum dicta erant</u>

    (C) <u>Haec verba dīcentis causā</u>

    (D) <u>Quae verba dictūrus</u>

14. Spartacus Capuā <u>ēgressus</u> ad Montem Vesūvium iter fēcit.

    (A) <u>ubi discēdēbat</u>   (C) <u>cum discesserat</u>

    (B) <u>discēdēns</u>   (D) <u>ut discēderet</u>

15. <u>Exeāmus</u> ē thermīs.

    (A) <u>Discēdēmus</u>   (C) <u>Proficiscimur</u>

    (B) <u>Ēgrediāmur</u>   (D) <u>Migrāmus</u>

16. Caesar mīlitēs hortābātur <u>quī proelium committerent</u>.

    (A) <u>ut proelium committerent</u>

    (B) <u>cum proelium committēbant</u>

    (C) <u>quod proelium committendum erat</u>

    (D) <u>proeliō commissō</u>

17. Hercules vir <u>exīmiae fortitūdinis</u> fuisse dīcitur.

    (A) <u>exīmia fortitūdō</u>   (C) <u>exīmiam fortitūdinem</u>

    (B) <u>exīmiae fortitūdinī</u>   (D) <u>exīmiā fortitūdine</u>

18. <u>Mē labōris taedet</u>.

    (A) <u>Labor mē defessum facit.</u>

    (B) <u>Ego laborāns defessus erō.</u>

    (C) <u>Labor omnia vincit.</u>

    (D) <u>Dum labōrabam, defessus eram.</u>

19. Cum hostēs superātī essent, dux triumphum celebrāvit.

    (A) Postquam hostēs superat

    (B) Quod hostēs superatūrus erat

    (C) Hostēs superāns

    (D) Hostibus superātīs

20. Pater fīlium matrī parēre iussit (jussit).

    (A) Pater fīliō praecipit ut matrī pareat.

    (B) Pater imperāvit ut mater fīliō parēret.

    (C) Pater fīliō imperāvit ut matrī parēret.

    (D) Fīlius ā patre imperātus matrī parēbat.

Answers

1. **(B)** future tense substitutes for active periphrastic

2. **(D)** relative clause for present participle

3. **(A)** temporal clause for ablative absolute

4. **(B) quam** + comparative for ablative of comparison

5. **(A)** verb of possession for dative of possession

6. **(C)** one demonstrative pronoun (**is**) for another (**hic**)

7. **(A)** passive voice for active

8. **(D)** gerundive of purpose for **ut** purpose clause

9. **(B)** present participle for relative characteristic clause

10. **(A) necesse erat** for passive periphrastic

11. **(D)** ablative absolute for **cum** temporal clause

12. **(C) rogāre** + accusative for **petere** + ablative

13. **(B) cum** temporal clause for ablative absolute

14. **(C) cum** temporal clause for past participle

15. **(B)** hortatory subjunctive, deponent verb for irregular verb

16. **(A)** **ut** purpose clause for **quī** purpose clause

17. **(D)** ablative of description for genitive of description

18. **(A)** regular verb phrase for impersonal verb

19. **(D)** ablative absolute for **cum** circumstantial clause

20. **(C)** indirect command for **iubēre (jubēre)** + infinitive

CHAPTER 34

Translation

Chapter 34

TRANSLATION

TRANSLATING LATIN

Translation (**trans + ferre**, *to carry across*) is essentially an exercise that asks you to account for the meaning of every word and every form as you recreate in English a sentence written in Latin. Your ability to translate all or part of a Latin sentence is evaluated explicitly on the Translation portion of the SAT Latin Subject Test (20 percent), and implicitly on the Sentence Completion, Syntax Substitution, and Reading Comprehension sections. There is much difference of opinion about the importance of transferring a Latin sentence word for word into English, and the debate continues.* For many, "reading" Latin means translating. Whatever your background, the SAT Latin Subject Test evaluates both your ability to translate and your ability to read comprehensively (see Chapter 35). The way <u>not</u> to translate is to hop, skip, and jump around the sentence, randomly searching for the subject, verb, object, and so on. Another way <u>not</u> to translate is to write down the lexical meaning of each word above the Latin and then scramble until done. However, before you review some suggestions that <u>will</u> help you produce, and therefore recognize and select, an effective translation on the SAT Latin Subject Test, consider the following points.

SOME OBSERVATIONS ABOUT THE STRUCTURE OF A LATIN SENTENCE

Remember that Latin, when expressing a thought, makes use of participles and dependent clauses more often than English does. When in Rome, do as the Romans do. Think like a Roman!

Latin: <u>After this was done</u>, he did that.

English: He did this <u>and then</u> he did that.

---

* Translators have been referred to as "traitors." **Dē gustibus nōn disputandum est**. For an excellent discussion of translation vs. reading for comprehension, see B. D. Hoyos, *Latin: How to Read it Fluently*, Amherst, MA: Classical Association of New England (CANE), 1997.

Latin regularly (but not always!) places the most emphatic words at the beginning and end of a clause or sentence. The intervening words contribute to the overall sense. The words within word groups or "sense units" in a Latin sentence are never mixed together:

> **Urbe Rōmā condītā, multī mīrābantur num Rōmulus deus factūrus esset.**
>
> *After Rome had been founded, many wondered whether Romulus would become a god.*

Words from the main clause **multī mīrābantur** may not intrude upon or interject themselves into the ablative absolute **urbe Rōmā condītā**. No elements from either of these constructions may intrude upon the dependent clause **num . . . factūrus esset**, and so forth. However, one word group may contain another.

Patterns of word order do appear in Latin sentence structure (more on this topic follows). "Normal" word order in a Latin sentence consists of subject + indirect object + direct object + adverb and prepositions + verb, with the result that the subject and verb bookend the thought. Remember that such a pattern is common but not obligatory.

Be aware that the functional meaning of a Latin word derives from its ending, which forces your mind's eye to work from right to left, or backwards, through a word; for example, in translating **mittēbat**, you read -**t**, *he*, -**ba**-, *was*, **mittē**-, *sending*. This puts your mind, which is trained to read English from left to right, at odds with itself and creates a sort of mental tension that must be reduced through practice in translation.

No doubt you have observed that Latin can express the same thought in fewer words than English. Because the Romans, at least early in their history, were spare and economical by nature, their language is often condensed or elliptical, leaving out verbal elements whose meaning is understood (i.e., must be deduced from context):

> **Quī nōn est hodiē, crās minus aptus erit.**
>
> *He who is not (ready) today will be less ready tomorrow.*

If the Latin were expanded, it would read:

> **(Is) quī nōn (aptus) est hodiē, crās (ille) minus aptus erit.**

STEPS TO USE WHEN TRANSLATING A LATIN SENTENCE

The effective use of your time during the test is critical to achieving success on the SAT Latin Subject Test, so apply the following steps during the exam as time allows. Consistent practice is, of course, the key to developing facility in translating. **Repetītiō est māter studiōrum.**

1. Read for Context

Read through the entire sentence to see all of its words in context. Get a feel for the meaning from the particular vocabulary used and from the way in which the forms associate with one another. Warning: do not use derivatives as meanings when rendering a Latin word in English because the meaning of the Latin root and its English derivative often vary, as in **tradere**, *to hand over*, not *to trade*.

2. Read for Structure

Take the words in the order in which they were written and develop the sense as you proceed. Focus on recognizing the way the sentence is structured: take the main clause/s, dependent clause/s, and phrase/s in the sequence in which they are found. As you move through the sentence, divide it into "sense" units by placing real or imagined brackets around word groups, for example,

ablative absolute   main clause   dependent clause (indirect question)

[**Urbe Rōmā condītā**], [**multī mīrābantur**] [**num Rōmulus deus factūrus esset**].

[*After Rome had been founded*], [*many wondered*] [*whether Romulus would become a god*].

It is most important that you understand the meaning of the thought in the Latin sentence before expressing it in English.

3. Read for Relationships

Much of how Latin expresses meaning depends on the relationship of dependent clauses to main clauses, as well as to other dependent clauses, so you must be familiar with how these interact:

- The main subject or object of a sentence is found in the main clause, not the dependent clause. Avoid identifying the verb of the dependent clause as the main verb.

Commovēbāturne Remus quod paucās avēs modo vīderat?
Was Remus upset because he had seen only a few birds?

Note that the verb **vīderat,** while found in the slot normally occupied by the main verb, actually serves as the verb of the dependent **quod** clause.

- Think of the words in a clause as a self-contained unit of thought. Don't pull words out of a main clause or a dependent clause and place them somewhere else in the sentence (see step 2, "Read for Structure"). Use brackets to contain or hold together the words in a clause:

[**Cum Remus moenia urbis Rōmae dēridēret], Rōmulus īrātus factus est.**
[*Because Remus was mocking the city walls of Rome*], *Romulus became angry.*

Once you have begun to articulate the meaning of a dependent clause, complete the meaning of that clause before moving further into the sentence.

- The meaning of a dependent clause usually relates to a specific word or phrase in the main clause, which regularly precedes the dependent clause. Continue to look backward as you move forward through the sentence and try your best to retain what has come before. Use graphic symbols such as arrows to link one part of a sentence to another, for example,

Rōmulus frāter <u>Remī</u> erat [<u>quem ipse occidit</u>].
Romulus was the brother of <u>Remus,</u> [<u>whom he killed</u>].

- The emphatic words in both main and dependent clauses are usually found at the beginning and end of their sense units. Look for additional "directional signals" provided by the placement of important words or word groups as you proceed through the sentence. In the following sentence, note how the word **hominem** is common to two different grammatical constructions:

Nōnne nēmō crēdit [hominem (quī suum frātrem occiderit) deum fierī posse]?
Surely no one believes [that a man (who has killed his own brother) can become a god]?

This sentence contains the dependent clause **quī . . . occiderit** within the indirect statement (**crēdit**) **hominem . . . posse**. The relative clause describes its antecedent **hominem,** which also serves as the subject of the infinitive in indirect statement and therefore binds together the two constructions.

4. Rephrase into Idiomatic English

Your initial translation may result in a sort of "translationese," which will require further exploration of the possible meaning through the juggling of words, phrases, and clauses. Rephrasing and the application of English idiom are often required to make the sense clear.

Some Observations about Word Order

Here are some important observations regarding word order in a Latin sentence:

- The first position in a sentence is emphatic.

- The more unusual the position of a word, the more emphatic its meaning.

- A name or a personal pronoun often stands in an emphatic place.

- Demonstrative, interrogative, and possessive adjectives regularly precede their nouns, as in **hic pater**, **quae māter?** and **mea culpa**.

- The adjective precedes the noun modified, just as the adverb precedes the verb. Adjectives used as attributes are usually placed after the noun modified, such as **senātor prudēns** and **servus ignāvissimus**.

- Certain common conjunctions, such as **itaque**, regularly come first in a sentence, whereas words such as **autem, enim, igitur, quidem, quoque**, and **vērō** are never found first. **Quidem** and **quoque** immediately follow the words they emphasize.

- A preposition regularly precedes its noun, as in **in hōc signō vincēs**; a prepositional phrase often immediately precedes the verb to which it is connected.

- When a form of **esse** is used as the main verb, it regularly stands first, before its subject; for example, **Est prudēns**, *He is wise*.

- A negative, such as **haud, nōn**, or **neque**, precedes the word it affects.

CONJUNCTIONS

Although conjunctions are not tested specifically on the SAT Latin Subject Test, they are the "connective tissue" of a Latin sentence and therefore are important for translation and comprehension. Conjunctions are indeclinable words that join together words, phrases, clauses, and sentences. They are used either to connect two ideas of equal importance (coordinating) or to attach a dependent or secondary idea to a main thought (subordinating). As has been noted, because dependent clauses appear frequently in Latin, subordinating conjunctions are most important for understanding the relationship between the dependent clause and the main clause:

Coordinating conjunction: **Cicerō in rostra ascendit <u>et</u> ōrātiōnem habuit.**
Cicero mounted the Rostra <u>and</u> gave a speech.

Subordinating conjunction: **Ōrātiōnem habuit <u>ut</u> Pompēium laudāret**.
He gave the speech <u>to</u> praise Pompey.

Important Coordinating Conjunctions

et **-que** **atque** **ac**	*and*	**neque** **nec**	*nor, and not*
aut **vel** **-ve**	*or, either*	**sīve** **seu**	*whether, or*
sed **at**	*but*	**autem**	*however*
nam **enim**	*for*	**quārē (quā rē)** **quamobrem** **(quam ob rem)**	*wherefore, for* *which reason*
ergō **itaque** **igitur**	*therefore*		

Latin has lots of dinky words, doesn't it?

Important Subordinating Conjunctions

Causal:	**cum**	*because, since*
	quod	
	quia	
	quandō	
	quoniam	
Conditional:	**sī**	*if*
	nisi	*if not, unless*
Concessive:	**cum**	*although*
	etsi	
	quamquam	
Interrogative:	**num**	*whether*
	utrum	
Purpose/Result:	**ut**	*to, in order to, that, so that*
	nē	*that . . . not, lest*
	ut . . . nōn	*so that . . . not* (result)
Temporal:	**cum**	*when*

The conjunction -**que**, which means *and*, is usually joined to the second of a combination of two words that are closely connected in meaning, such as **terrā marīque**, *land and sea*, or **Senātus Populusque Rōmānus** (**SPQR**), *the Senate and People of Rome*. Here is an example in context:

> **Servī Cicerōnis eī <u>fortiter fidēliterque</u> serviēbant.**
> *Cicero's slaves served him <u>bravely and faithfully</u>.*

When connecting clauses, -**que** is usually attached to the first word of the connected clause. The conjunction does not always connect the word to which it is attached with the word or those words immediately preceding it, but may be separated by intervening words:

> **Atticus Cicerōnī [<u>discedentī</u>] ē cūriā [<u>procedentīque</u>] ad bibliopōlam occurrit.**
> *Atticus happened upon Cicero, [<u>who was leaving</u>] the Senate House [<u>and proceeding</u>] to the bookseller.*

> **[Epistula ā Tīrōne <u>scripta est</u>], [iussūque Cicerōnis ad Atticum <u>missa est</u>].**
> *[The letter <u>was transcribed</u> by Tiro] [<u>and was sent</u> to Atticus at Cicero's bidding].*

WORDS THAT CORRELATE AND COORDINATE

Latin sentences often contain words that correlate, that is, ones that have partners or are paired. Such words are known as "correlatives." These words are usually separated within the sentence, so, as you begin to comprehend the meaning, be alert to the possibility that their partners may appear further along. Here are some common examples of correlatives:

ibi . . . ubi; *there . . . where*

nōn solum . . . sed etiam; *not only . . . but also*

tālis . . . quālis; *such . . . as*

tantus . . . quantus; *so great . . . as (great)*

tot. . . . quot; *so many . . . as (many)*

tum . . . cum; *then . . . when*

Some adverbs also coordinate with one another, that is, they are found in pairs:

aut . . . aut (or **vel . . . vel**); *either . . . or*

cum . . . tum; *while . . . so also* or *at the same time*

et . . . et (or **-que . . . -que**); *both . . . and*

modo . . . modo; *now . . . now*

neque . . . neque (**nec . . . nec**); *neither . . . nor*

nunc . . . nunc (or **iam . . . iam**); *now . . . now*

sīve (**seu** or enclitic **-ve**) . . . **sīve** (**seu** or enclitic **-ve**); *whether . . . or, if . . . if*

tam . . . quam; *so (as) . . . as*

The following pairs of indefinite pronouns are also used in this way:

alius . . . alius; *one . . . another* (plural **aliī . . . aliī;** *some . . . others*)

alter . . . alter; *the one . . . the other*

In the following example of the use of correlatives, **quam** correlates with **tam**:

> **Ea tam antīqua est quam amphitheātrum Flāvium!**
> *She is so (or as) old as the Colosseum!*

Such sentences are often condensed. The expanded original reads:

> **Ea tam antīqua est quam amphitheātrum Flāvium (antīquum est).**
> *She is so (or as) old as the Colosseum (is old).*

In the following sentence, note the relationship between **tantam** and **quanta**:

> **Dīves tantam pecūniam habēbat quanta erat numquam satis.**
> *The rich man had so (or as) much money as was never enough (literally, so much money as much [as] was never enough).*

The relative adjective **quanta** must agree in gender and number (feminine singular) with that of its correlative antecedent **tantam**, but observe also that its case (nominative) is determined by how it functions within its clause. That is, in the preceding example, **quanta (pecūnia)** serves as the subject of its clause, whereas **tantam pecūniam** serves as the direct object of the main clause.

IDIOMS

An idiom (from Greek, "one's own," "personal") is an expression in one language that cannot be expressed precisely in another or one that has a meaning that requires familiarity with the cultural context of the language, such as the English "to bum a ride." Idioms are found regularly in Latin and should be considered in any thorough review of the language. Here are some common Latin idioms:

bellum gerere, *to wage war*

certior facere, *to inform*

consilium capere, *to make a plan*

grātiās agere, *to thank*

in animō habēre, *to intend*

in mātrimōnium dūcere, *to marry*

in memoriam habēre, *to remember*

iter facere, *to make a journey, travel*

ōrātiōnem habēre, *to deliver a speech*

proelium committere, *to begin battle*

vītam agere, *to live one's life*

TRANSLATION ON THE SAT LATIN SUBJECT TEST

In this section of the SAT Latin Subject Test, you are asked to choose the best translation of part of a sentence or an entire sentence. This part of the exam evaluates your ability to recognize, rather than produce, the precise meaning of the Latin indicated. If the question presents a portion of a sentence, place the answer you select in the context of the entire sentence and then read it back to yourself to confirm that it makes sense. Avoid choosing an answer simply because it makes sense in English, because often more than one answer will do so.

PRACTICE SENTENCES

1. Augustus dīxit trēs legiōnēs <u>captōs esse</u>.

    (A) are being captured   (C) have captured

    (B) have been captured   (D) had been captured

2. <u>Sī carmina scrīberēs</u>, ea legerem.

    (A) If you had written poems

    (B) If you were to write poems

    (C) If you are writing poems

    (D) If you will write poems

3. <u>Servī auxiliō dominō sunt</u>.

    (A) The slaves helped the master.

    (B) The slaves seek help from the master.

    (C) The master is helping the slaves.

    (D) The slaves are helping the master.

4. Horātius mīrātur cur mors <u>verenda sit</u>.

    (A) must be feared   (C) has been feared

    (B) will be feared   (D) is feared

5. <u>Claudiō occīsō</u>, Nero imperātor factus est.

    (A) After Claudius was killed

    (B) While Claudius was being killed

    (C) Having killed Claudius

    (D) Because he was about to kill Claudius

6. Epistula Rōmam <u>quinque diēbus</u> adveniet.

    (A) for five days   (C) within five days

    (B) on the fifth day   (D) after five days

7. Caligula putābat <u>sē</u> deum esse.

    (A) he (someone else)   (C) he (himself)

    (B) they   (D) no one

8. <u>Exeāmus Rōmā</u>.

    (A) We are leaving Rome.

    (B) Let us leave Rome.

    (C) We must leave Rome.

    (D) We will leave Rome.

9. <u>Nāvibus nāvigantibus, tempestās coorta est</u>.

    (A) While the ships were sailing, a storm struck.

    (B) As the ships sail, a storm is striking.

    (C) After the ships had sailed, a storm struck.

    (D) Before the ships sailed, a storm struck.

10. <u>Vir timēbat nē uxor quid accidisset scīret</u>.

    (A) The husband feared that his wife did not know what had happened.

    (B) The husband feared that his wife did not know what was happening.

    (C) The husband fears that his wife knows what happened.

    (D) The husband was afraid that his wife knew what had happened.

11. Possumusne vōbīs persuādēre ut nōbīscum veniātis?

    (A) Can you convince us to come with you?

    (B) Can we convince you to come with us?

    (C) Can we convince you not to come with us?

    (D) Are we convincing you to come with us?

12. Complūrēs basilicae in forō Rōmānō aedificātae erant.

    (A) must be built   (C) have been built

    (B) had been built   (D) were about to build

13. Mea villa magnam piscīnam habet. Vīdistīne eam?

    (A) her   (C) him

    (B) them   (D) it

14. Omnēs volēbant cōgnoscere ā quibus cūria incensa esset.

    (A) Everyone wanted to know by whom the Senate House had been burned.

    (B) Everyones want to know by whom the Senate House was burned.

    (C) Everyone wanted to know when the Senate House had been burned.

    (D) Everyone wanted to know by whom the Senate House was being burned.

15. Utinam ego plūs tempōris habērem.

    (A) If only I had had more time.

    (B) I must have more time.

    (C) If only I had more time

    (D) Let me have more time.

16. Nōlī dīvitī pecūniam dare.

    (A) I don't wish to give   (C) I did not wish to give

    (B) Do not give   (D) Give nothing

17. Dīcuntur multa mīraque <u>vīdisse</u>.

    (A) to see   (C) to be seen

    (B) to have been seen   (D) to have seen

18. Equī <u>multō celeriōrēs canibus</u> currere possunt.

    (A) much faster than dogs

    (B) much faster with dogs

    (C) a little faster than dogs

    (D) as fast as dogs

19. Nāvēs <u>quās</u> Cleopātra Antōniō dederat dēlētae sunt.

    (A) whose   (C) that

    (B) whom   (D) to whom

20. Caesar ducī Gallōrum dīxit, "Nunc ā Rōmānīs <u>regēris</u>."

    (A) you are being ruled   (C) you will have ruled

    (B) you will be ruled   (D) be ruled

Answers

1. Indirect statement **(D)**

    This sentence contains an indirect statement following **dīxit**, with an infinitive in the past tense of the passive, **captōs esse**. It is therefore translated as a PPH, or "past-past-had." The sentence reads *Augustus said that three legions <u>had been captured</u>*. Answer (A) *are being captured* is an obvious but incorrect translation of the infinitive. Don't be misled because the infinitive contains a form of **esse**. Answer (B) *have been captured* is in the incorrect tense (the main verb is in past tense), and (C) *have captured* is in the incorrect voice (active). (See Chapter 26, "Tips on Translating Infinitives.")

2. Present contrary to fact condition **(B)**

    This sentence reads <u>*If you were to write poems*</u>, *I would read them*, an example of a present contrary to fact condition with the subjunctive verb in the imperfect tense. This condition is not possible; it implies that you are not likely to write poems. Answer (A) translates a past contrary to fact condition, and (C) and (D) mistake the imperfect subjunctive **scrīberēs** for the present and future indicative, respectively. (See Chapter 29, "Contrary to Fact Conditional Sentences.")

3.   Double dative **(D)**
      This sentence reads *The slaves help (their) master* (literally, *The slaves were for a help to/for their master*), an example of a double dative. Answer (A) contains the incorrect verb tense, (B) contains the verb *seek*, which is not found in the original, and (C) turns the meaning around. (See Chapter 8, "Datives of Reference and Purpose.")

4.   Indirect question in passive periphrastic **(A)**
      The verb **mīrātur** sets up the indirect question **cur . . . verenda sit**. The verb **verenda** is a gerundive modifying **mors**, and it is accompanied by the present subjunctive of the verb **esse** in a passive periphrastic. The sentence reads *Horace wonders why death must be feared*. Only (A) expresses a sense of obligation or necessity. (See Chapter 31, "Indirect Questions," and Chapter 25, "Passive Periphrastic.")

5.   Ablative absolute **(A)**
      This sentence contains a "Type 1" ablative absolute, with the participle in the past tense. The sentence reads *After Claudius was killed*, Nero *became emperor* (literally, *Claudius having been killed . . .*). Answers (B) and (C) cannot be expressed directly with a Latin form, and (D) *Because he was about to kill Claudius* expresses the future active participle **occīsūrus**, modifying **Nero**, thus linking the participial phrase with the main clause and invalidating it as an ablative absolute. (See Chapter 24, "The Ablative Absolute.")

6.   Ablative of time within which **(C)**
      The sentence translates *The letter will arrive in Rome (with)in five days*. Answer (A) expresses extent of time with the accusative (**quinque diēs**); (B) expresses a point in time, but with the ordinal number *fifth* (**quintō diē**) instead of *five*; and (D) *after five days* may be expressed with either the ablative or accusative (**quinque post diēbus** or **post quinque diēs**, respectively), but both require the word **post**. (See Chapter 10, "Ablative of Time.")

7. Reflexive pronoun **(C)**

The pronoun **sē** refers back to the subject, here **Caligula**, and itself serves as the accusative subject of the indirect statement (**putābat) sē . . . esse**. And so, the sentence translates *Caligula thought that he (himself) was becoming a god.* Answer (A) **eum** is not reflexive; (B) *them* cannot be reflexive because the subject **Caligula** is singular; and (D) *no one* translates the original incorrectly. (See Chapter 15.)

8. Hortatory subjunctive; ablative of place from which with the name of a city **(B)**

Answer (B) is correct, <u>*Let us leave Rome*</u>. The answer options reveal that the decision to be made concerns the form of the verb **Exeāmus**, which is present subjunctive of the irregular verb **exīre**. Answer (A) is present indicative (**eximus**); (C) a passive periphrastic (**nōbīs exeundum est**); and (D) future indicative (**exibimus**). (See Chapter 28, "Jussive and Hortatory Subjunctives," and Chapter 10, "Ablative of Place from Which.")

9. Ablative absolute **(A)**

This sentence translates *While the ships were sailing, a storm struck.* The appearance of the present participle **navigantibus** means that the action of that participle is happening at the same time as that of the main verb, which is in past tense (**coorta est**), therefore requiring a translation such as *was/were sailing*. In (B), the verb sequence in the translation is incorrect. Answer (B) requires a past participle, and (D) requires a dependent clause introduced by a conjunction such as **priusquam**. (See Chapter 24, "The Ablative Absolute.")

10. Fear clause and indirect question **(D)**

This sentence reads *The husband was afraid* (**timēbat**) *that* (**nē**) *(his) wife knew* (**scīret**) *what had happened* (**quid accidisset**). The verbs in both the dependent clauses (**timēbat) nē . . . scīret** and **quid accidisset** found in this sentence are in the secondary sequence of the subjunctive. Answer (A) ambushes you into thinking that **nē** expresses a negative thought in a fear clause, but it does not. The verb tenses in (B) and (C) are incorrect. (See Chapter 30, "Fear Clauses," and Chapter 31, "Indirect Questions." See also Chapter 27, "Sequence of Tenses.")

11. Dative with special verb; indirect command **(B)**

This sentence reads *Can we convince you to come with us?* The verbs in this sentence are in primary sequence. The personal pronoun **vōbīs** is dative after the verb **persuādēre**, which also introduces the indirect command clause **ut . . . veniātis**. Answer (A) turns the meaning of the sentence around, (C) incorrectly negates the dependent clause, and (D) omits the main verb **Possumus**. (See Chapter 8, "Dative with Certain Types of Verbs," and Chapter 30, "Indirect Command.")

12. Pluperfect passive verb **(B)**
    The verb **aedificātae erant** is translated *had been built*, giving the sentence the meaning *Several basilicas had been built in the Roman Forum*. Answer (A) *must be built* requires a periphrastic construction (**aedificandae sunt**); (C) *have been built* requires the perfect passive (**aedificātae sunt**); and (D) *were about to build* requires the active periphrastic (**aedificātūrae erant**). (See Chapter 19.)

13. Demonstrative/personal pronoun **(D)**
    This question is designed to prompt you to think about the connection of a pronoun with its antecedent. **Eam** refers to and replaces **piscīnam** in the previous sentence (both serve as direct objects). Because a fish pool is a thing, the meaning *it* is required, despite the tempting fact that the gender of **eam** is feminine, suggesting a meaning of *she* or *her*, as in (A). Answer (B) is incorrect because it is plural, and (C) is incorrect because the gender *him* is not appropriate to the meaning of this sentence. (See Chapters 11 and 14.)

14. Indirect question **(A)**
    This sentence translates *Everyone wanted to know by whom the Senate House had been burned*. The indirect question clause **ā quibus . . . incensa esset** is in secondary sequence and follows the verb **cōgnoscere**. The translation in (B) contains an incorrect translation of **volēbant**; (C) gives an incorrect reading of **ā quibus**; and (D) uses the incorrect tense of the subjunctive verb, *was being burned*, which requires the imperfect tense form **incenderētur**. (See Chapter 31, "Indirect Questions.")

15. Optative subjunctive **(C)**
    This sentence, introduced by **Utinam** and containing a subjunctive verb (**habērem**), is translated as *If only I had more time*. This use of the subjunctive expresses a wish incapable of fulfillment. Answer (A) requires the verb form **habuissem**; (B) requires the periphrastic expression **mihi habendum est**; and (D) requires the hortatory subjunctive **habeam**. (See Chapter 28, "Optative Subjunctive.")

16. Negative imperative (prohibition) **(B)**

This sentence commands someone not to do something: *Do not give a rich man money*. Answers (A) and (C) are common mistakes made in translating the negative imperative, in which the meaning of **nōlī** or **nōlīte** is not rendered literally. Answer (D) requires that the Latin be **Da nihil**, which is incorrect. (See Chapter 23, "Negative Imperatives.")

17. Perfect active infinitive **(D)**

This sentence translates, *They are said to have seen many (and) wonderful things*. The infinitive, in the perfect tense and active voice, completes the meaning of the main verb **dīcuntur**. Answer (A) requires the present tense (**vidēre**); (B) requires the passive voice (**vīsōs esse**); and (C) requires the present passive form (**vidērī**). Note the appearance of the substantives **multa** and **mīra**. (See Chapter 26.)

18. Ablative of degree of difference with ablative of comparison **(A)**

This sentence reads *Horses can run much faster than dogs*. **Multō celeriōrēs** means, literally, *faster by much*, and modifies **Equī**. **Canibus** is one of the two options for expressing the comparison of two persons or things, the ablative or the use of **quam**. The former appears here. Answer (B) requires the preposition **cum** and (C) the adverb **paulō** as a substitute for **multō**. Answer (D) requires a correlative such as **tam . . . quam**. (See Chapter 10, "Ablatives of Comparison and Degree of Difference"; see Chapter 16, "Comparative Adjectives," for the **quam** comparative construction; see also "Words that Correlate and Coordinate" in this chapter.)

19. Relative pronoun **(C)**

This sentence translates *The ships that Cleopatra had given Antony were destroyed*. **Quās** is a relative pronoun in the feminine accusative plural. The form is the accusative object of the verb **dederat** in its clause (**quās . . . dederat**). Answer (A) requires a genitive form; (B) requires an accusative, but with a personal antecedent; and (D) requires a dative. (See Chapter 12.)

20. Future passive **(B)**

The second singular future passive (**regēris**) is often confused with the second singular present passive (**regeris**) and with the second singular future perfect active (**rexeris**). The macron is "functional" and characteristic of the future passive form. The sentence reads *Caesar said to the leader of the Gauls, "Now you will be ruled by Romans."* Answer (A) requires the present tense; (C) requires the future perfect active; and (D) requires the present passive singular imperative (**regere**). (See Chapter 19.)

CHAPTER 35

Reading Comprehension

Chapter 35

READING COMPREHENSION

The final section of the SAT Latin Subject Test, which evaluates reading comprehension, is the most important of the six parts of the test (45 percent). Although it is the last section of the exam, you should plan to spend the greatest share of your hour on these questions. If you cannot answer a question immediately, move on, because questions that you omit are not counted. This part consists of three to five sight-reading passages, one of which is poetry, averaging about eight lines in length. There are between five and fifteen multiple choice questions on each passage, for a total of 30 to 35 questions out of the 70 or so on the exam.

The content of the reading passages is derived from passages of authentic Latin literature that have been "adapted," that is, edited for the purposes of the exam. There is some glossing of vocabulary (i.e., words deemed unfamiliar are provided), and each passage is given a title. Exploit this information to help you understand the passage. Some questions in the following practice section will ask you for a judgment or interpretive decision about the Latin you are reading. Although this is not the type of question that is customarily found on the SAT Latin Subject Test, it is included here to make your review more interesting and more challenging. For the same reason, the practice passages from Caesar, Catullus, Pliny, and Vergil provided in this chapter have had very little adaptation. If you can be successful with these reading passages, you can handle anything on the SAT Latin Subject Test!

To enhance your reading skills further, practice sight reading by using the resources provided in the online archives of the National Latin Exam.*

---

* National Latin Exam, http://www.nle.org/exams.html#exams_previous. Answers are provided.

TYPES OF QUESTIONS ON THE READING COMPREHENSION SECTION

The Reading Comprehension section presents multiple-choice questions that evaluate your ability to understand the meaning of what you read. This section includes questions of the following types:

- determination of the meaning of a particular word in context

- identification of the antecedent of a pronoun or the subject of a verb

- identification of the case and number of a noun or the tense and voice of a verb

- location of the particular noun or pronoun modified by an adjective (i.e., agreement)

- designation of the words connected by the enclitic **-que**

- translation of a phrase or clause

- summary of content

- scansion of the first four feet of a line of verse composed in dactylic hexameter (see Chapter 36)

TIPS ON READING FOR COMPREHENSION

- On the SAT Latin Subject Test, do not attempt to <u>translate</u> the reading passages. You are directed to "read the following texts carefully." It is intended that you read for the general sense, that is, for comprehension rather than word-for-word translation. Scan the Latin text to understand the general meaning, reading in the order in which the Latin is given. Pay attention to the clues given in the English title and in the vocabulary help.

- Work from each question back to the text, trying to locate the specific answer. Note that the questions are asked in the sequence of the sentences in the passage. If you are stumped and cannot eliminate one or two answers as incorrect, move on.

- Remember that Latin prefers to use subordinate clauses and participles whose meaning is equivalent to subordinate clauses.

- As you read, focus on groups of words that go together. Pay particular attention to noun–adjective agreement; antecedents and references of pronouns; tense, voice, and mood of verbs; and boundaries of phrases and clauses.

READING COMPREHENSION PRACTICE

<u>Directions</u>: Select the correct answer to each question, basing your choice on the reading passage provided.

Passage A

The Britons prevent Caesar's invading troops from disembarking

1   At barbarī, consiliō Rōmānōrum cognitō, praemissō equitātū, cum reliquīs cōpiīs subsecūtī nostrōs laborantēs ē nāvibus ēgredī prohibēbant. Erat ob hās causās summa difficultās: nāvēs propter magnitūdinem nisi in altō constituī[1] nōn poterant. Mīlitibus
5   autem, ignōtīs locīs, impedītīs manibus, magnō onere armōrum oppressīs, simul dēsilientibus[2] dē nāvibus cum hostibus erat pugnandum. Illī aut ex āridō aut paulum in aquam progressī, omnibus membrīs expedītīs,[3] nōtissimīs locīs, audacter tēla coniciēbant.

1.   constituī: *to be anchored*
2.   dēsiliō, dēsilīre: *to jump down*
3.   expedītus, -a, -um: *unimpeded*

1.   The best translation of <u>consiliō Rōmānōrum cognitō</u> (line 1) is

   (A)   while learning of the Roman plan

   (B)   the plan about to be learned by the Romans

   (C)   when they had learned of the Roman plan

   (D)   the Romans having learned of the plan

2.   In lines 2–3, Caesar's troops

   (A)   hindered the Britons from boarding

   (B)   struggled with the support troops

   (C)   were unable to leave the ships

   (D)   pursued the ships of the Britons

3.   <u>Subsecūtī</u> (line 2) is best translated

   (A)   having been pursued (C)   pursuing

   (B)   having pursued   (D)   about to pursue

4. As we learn from <u>At</u> . . . <u>prohibēbant</u> (lines 1–3), which of the following was <u>not</u> one of the reasons the Romans stayed on board their ships?

   (A) the Britons had learned the Roman plan

   (B) the Britons had sent ahead cavalry

   (C) the Britons had followed up with support troops

   (D) the Britons had boarded the Roman ships

5. The Roman ships were unable to draw close to the shore (lines 3–4) because of the

   (A) weather   (C) rocks

   (B) size of the ships (D) number of the ships

6. <u>Dēsilientibus</u> (line 6) means

   (A) having jumped   (C) when they had jumped

   (B) while jumping   (D) about to jump

7. The phrase <u>Mīlitibus</u> . . . <u>erat pugnandum</u> (lines 4–7) means

   (A) The soldiers had to fight

   (B) The soldiers were about to fight

   (C) He was about to attack the soldiers

   (D) There was fighting among the soldiers

8. <u>Cum</u> (line 6) means

   (A) with   (C) while

   (B) although   (D) because

9. As described in <u>Mīlitibus</u> . . . <u>pugnandum</u> (lines 4–7), which of the following was a reason why the Roman soldiers were at a disadvantage in the battle?

   (A) the weight of their weapons

   (B) loss of control of the ships

   (C) lack of leadership

   (D) seasickness

10. <u>Illī</u> (line 7) refers to:

    (A) Britons

    (B) ships

    (C) Roman soldiers

    (D) cavalry and charioteers

11. As described in <u>Illī</u> . . . <u>coniciēbant</u> (lines 7–8), the Britons were successful partly because

    (A) they had more men

    (B) they fought in shallow water

    (C) their weapons were superior

    (D) their horses were well trained

Passage B

Catullus takes exception to an offense

1   Alfēne immemor atque ūnanimīs false sodālibus,[1]

    iam tē nīl misēret, dūre, tuī dulcis amīculī?

    Iam mē prōdere, iam nōn dubitās fallere[2], perfīde?

    Num facta impia fallācum hominum caelicolīs[3] placent?

5   Quae tū neglegis, ac mē miserum dēseris in malīs;

    eheu quid faciant, dīc, hominēs, cuīve[4] habeant fīdem?

1. sodālis, sodālis, m.: *friend*
2. fallō, fallere: *to betray, deceive*
3. caelicola, caelicolae, f.: *a god*
4. cuīve: *"or in whom"*

12. In lines 1–2 of this poem, we learn that Catullus is addressing

    (A) himself

    (B) some unnamed friend

    (C) Alfenus

    (D) a girlfriend

13. In line 2, <u>iam tē nīl misēret</u> . . . <u>tūi dulcis amīculī</u> is translated

    (A) do you no longer take pity on your dear friend

    (B) does your dear friend not take pity on you now

    (C) was your dear friend unhappy with you now

    (D) does nothing about your dear friend cause you pity

14. Which of the following does <u>not</u> contribute to the tone of lines 1–2?

    (A) falsē   (C) dūre

    (B) nīl misēret   (D) dulcis amīculī

15. The repetition of <u>iam</u> in lines 3–4 suggests that Catullus is being

    (A) forgetful   (C) emphatic

    (B) careful   (D) wary

16. The case of <u>perfīde</u> (line 3) is

    (A) nominative   (C) dative

    (B) ablative   (D) vocative

17. It seems from line 3 that the offense being addressed by Catullus is:

    (A) anger   (C) envy

    (B) betrayal   (D) greed

18. According to Catullus, the addressee's answer to the question <u>Num</u> . . . <u>placent?</u> (line 4) should be

    (A) Minimē vērō   (C) Ita vērō

    (B) Nōn sciō   (D) Fortasse

19. In line 5, <u>Quae</u> refers to

    (A) the addressee

    (B) the entire content of line 4

    (C) disloyal actions

    (D) deceitful people

20. <u>Ac mē miserum dēseris in malīs</u> (line 5) tells us that Catullus

    (A) wants his friend to leave him alone

    (B) will desert his friend when he is in trouble

    (C) is deserting his friend who was in trouble

    (D) is feeling ignored while in some difficulty

21. The word <u>eheu</u> (line 6) reveals Catullus to be

    (A) hopeless   (C) confident

    (B) angry   (D) impatient

22. In line 6, <u>quid faciant</u> . . . <u>hominēs</u> is translated

    (A) what should men do   (C) what will men do

    (B) what are men doing   (D) what must men do

23. In line 6, the tense and mood of <u>habeant</u> are

    (A) present indicative   (C) imperfect subjunctive

    (B) present subjunctive   (D) future indicative

Passage C

Pliny the Younger describes his uncle's activities during the eruption of Vesuvius

1   Plinius Maior erat Mīsenī classemque imperiō praesēns regēbat. Nonum Kal. Septembrēs hōrā ferē septimā māter mea indicat eī apparēre nūbem inūsitātā[1] et magnitūdine et speciē . . . Magnum[2] propiusque noscendum[3] est ut ērudītissimō virō vīsum est. Iubet
5   (Iubet) liburnicam[4] aptārī[5] et me rogat sī venīre sēcum vellem. Respondī studēre mē mālle, et forte ipse quod scrīberem dederat. Ēgrediēbātur domō.

1. inūsitātus, -a, -um: *unusual, extraordinary*
2. Magnum: *modifies what was described previously*
3. noscō, noscere: *investigate, observe*
4. liburnica, liburnicae, f.: *light vessel, galley*
5. aptō, aptāre: *to outfit, equip*

24. In line 1, we learn that

    (A) Pliny the Elder was ruling the empire

    (B) the fleet was arriving at Misenum

    (C) the Emperor was present

    (D) Pliny the Elder was in charge of the fleet

25. The pronoun <u>eī</u> (line 2) refers to

    (A) Pliny the Elder

    (B) Pliny the Younger's mother

    (C) the fleet

    (D) the cloud

26. <u>Inūsitātā</u> (line 3) describes

    (A) hōrā . . . septimā (line 2)

    (B) māter mea (line 2)

    (C) nūbem (line 3)

    (D) et magnitūdine et speciē (line 3)

27. In <u>Nōnum</u> . . . <u>speciē</u> (lines 2–3), the mother of Pliny the Younger pointed out to him that

    (A) it was September 24

    (B) his uncle was commanding the fleet at Misenum

    (C) there was an unusual cloud

    (D) it was nearly noon

28. The fact that is <u>not</u> supported by <u>Magnum</u> . . . <u>vīsum est</u> (lines 3–4) is

    (A) Pliny's uncle was a learned man

    (B) Pliny's uncle thought that the appearance of the cloud was important

    (C) Pliny's uncle wanted to inspect the cloud more closely

    (D) Pliny's uncle planned to consult an educated man to learn more

29. In line 4, <u>ut</u> means

    (A) as   (C) with the result that

    (B) so that   (D) because

30. The word <u>eruditissimō</u> (line 4) means

    (A) very educated   (C) too educated

    (B) rather educated   (D) educated

31. <u>Sī</u> . . . <u>vellem</u> (line 6) means

    (A) if I wished   (C) if I had wished

    (B) if I will wish   (D) if I wish

32. To his uncle's invitation to accompany him, as expressed in line 6, Pliny the Younger says

    (A) I reply that I prefer to study

    (B) I replied that I preferred to study

    (C) I reply that I preferred to study

    (D) I replied that I prefer to study

33. In line 6, <u>ipse</u> refers to

    (A) the cloud   (C) Pliny the Younger

    (B) Pliny's studies   (D) Pliny the Elder

34. <u>Quod scrīberem</u> (line 6) means

    (A) because I was writing

    (B) what I was writing

    (C) so that I might write

    (D) what I was going to write

35. <u>Ēgrediēbātur domō</u> (line 7) means

    (A) He left home   (C) He will leave home

    (B) He left for home   (D) He had left home

Passage D

Aeneas awakens to find Troy under attack

1   Dīversō intereā miscentur moenia dolōre,

     et magis atque magis, quamquam sēcrēta[1] parentis

     Anchīsae domus arboribusque obtecta[2] recessit,

     clārēscunt sonitūs armorumque advenit horror.

5   Excutior somnō et summī fastīgia[3] tectī

     ascēnsū superō atque arrēctīs auribus adstō.

1.   sēcrētus, -a, -um: *set apart, screened*
2.   obtēgō, obtēgere, obtēxī, obtectus: *cover up, protect*
3.   fastīgium, fastīgī, n.: *gable end or pediment of a roof*

36. Dīversō (line 1) modifies

    (A) miscentur   (C) dolōre

    (B) moenia   (D) the city of Troy (understood)

37. As described in line 1, the general situation in Troy is that

    (A) in the city, hatred has turned to grief

    (B) the Trojans are winning the battle

    (C) the walls are collapsing on the hopeless

    (D) there is confusion and pain everywhere

38. Magis atque magis (line 2) means

    (A) bigger and better   (C) the more . . . the more

    (B) great, then greater   (D) more and more

39. Sēcrēta (line 2) modifies

    (A) moenia (line 1)   (C) parentis (line 2)

    (B) dolōre (line 1)   (D) domus (line 3)

40. Obtecta (line 3) means

    (A) covering   (C) having been covered

    (B) having covered   (D) she has been covered

41. We learn from <u>quamquam</u> . . . <u>recessit</u> (lines 2–3) that Anchises's house was

    (A) protected by trees and the guardian of the secrets of his ancestors

    (B) set apart and screened by trees and off in the distance

    (C) in the trees and set apart from the house of his parents

    (D) remote and hidden from the trees of his forefathers

42. In the parallel wording in line 4, <u>clārēscunt</u> *is to* <u>sonitūs</u> as

    (A) advenit *is to* horror   (C) advenit *is to* armōrum

    (B) sonitūs *is to* horror   (D) clarescunt *is to* advenit

43. The case and number of <u>sonitūs</u> (line 4) is

    (A) nominative singular   (C) accusative plural

    (B) nominative plural   (D) genitive singular

44. The enclitic <u>-que</u> (line 4) connects

    (A) clārēscunt sonitūs *with* armōrum advenit horror

    (B) armōrum *with* advenit

    (C) clārēscunt sonitūs *with* armōrum horror

    (D) sonitūs armōrum *with* advenit horror

45. From <u>Excutior somnō</u> (line 5), we learn that during the early stages of the sack of Troy, Aeneas was

    (A) drunk   (C) daydreaming

    (B) asleep   (D) unable to sleep

46. From <u>summī</u> . . . <u>adstō</u> (lines 5–6), we learn that Aeneas

    (A) climbed onto the roof to hide his gold

    (B) listened carefully and then climbed onto the roof

    (C) heard the gable of the roof fall down from on high

    (D) climbed onto the rooftop and listened intently

47. The metrical pattern of the first four feet of line 6 is

   (A) − − |−∪∪|− − |− −
   (B) −∪∪|− − |− − |− −
   (C) − − |− − |−∪∪|− −
   (D) − − |− − |− − |−∪∪

48. In this passage, the writer is most likely attempting to

   (A) emphasize the size of the city of Troy
   (B) find fault with Aeneas for being inattentive to his duties
   (C) dramatize how loud and dreadful were the sounds of war
   (D) demonstrate the reverence Aeneas had for his ancestral home

Answers

Passage A	Passage B	Passage C	Passage D
1. (C)	12. (C)	24. (D)	36. (C)
2. (C)	13. (A)	25. (A)	37. (D)
3. (B)	14. (D)	26. (D)	38. (D)
4. (D)	15. (C)	27. (C)	39. (D)
5. (B)	16. (D)	28. (D)	40. (C)
6. (B)	17. (B)	29. (A)	41. (B)
7. (A)	18. (A)	30. (A)	42. (A)
8. (A)	19. (C)	31. (A)	43. (B)
9. (A)	20. (D)	32. (B)	44. (A)
10. (A)	21. (A)	33. (D)	45. (B)
11. (B)	22. (A)	34. (B)	46. (D)
	23. (B)	35. (A)	47. (A)
			48. (C)

Translations of Passages

Passage A

But the barbarians, when they had learned the plan of the Romans, (their) cavalry having been sent ahead, followed after with their remaining forces and kept our struggling men from leaving the ships. There was very great hardship for these reasons: because of their size, the ships could not be anchored except in deep (water). (And there was great hardship) for the soldiers, moreover, because the place was unfamiliar and because their hands were hindered, burdened by the great weight of their weapons, and because those leaping down at the same time from the ships had to engage the enemy. Those (Britons), having moved forward either from dry land or a little into the water, because all their limbs were unimpeded and the place was familiar, boldly cast their spears. (Caesar)

Passage B

Alfenus, forgetful of and untrue to your soulmate companions, do you no longer take pity on your dear friend, cruel one? Do you not now hesitate to betray me, do you not now hesitate to deceive me, faithless one? Surely the disloyal actions of false men do not please the gods? Why do you ignore (me) and leave me to my misery in bad times? Alas, tell me what men should do, or in whom they should put their trust? (Catullus)

Passage C

Pliny the Elder was at Misenum and, (because he was) holding the command (i.e., the imperium), he was in charge of the fleet. On the ninth day before the Kalends of September (i.e., the 24th of August), at about the seventh hour (i.e., between 12:00 and 1:00 pm), my mother pointed out to him that a cloud of unusual size and shape was visible. As it seemed to this learned man, (this) great (event) must be investigated more closely. He ordered a galley to be outfitted, and he gave me the chance to go along with him if I wished. I replied that I preferred to study, and as it happened, he himself had assigned (me that) which I was writing. (And so) he left the house. (Pliny the Younger)

Passage D

Meanwhile, the walls (of Troy) are mingled with the different (sounds of) pain and, although the house of my father Anchises lie set apart in the distance and screened by trees, more and more the sounds grow distinct and the dreadful noise of the weapons reaches (me). I am shaken from sleep, reach the pediment of the lofty roof by climbing up, and stand there with ears alert. (Vergil)

CHAPTER 36

Scansion

Chapter 36

SCANSION

The SAT Latin Subject Test presumes knowledge of the scansion of dactylic hexameter, which is the meter of Ovid, Vergil, and other poets. Scansion is tested in the context of the poetry passage found in the Reading Comprehension section, and it usually consists of one or two questions of the type found below. Because you must complete at least one question every minute on this exam, do not spend extra time working out the scansion if the answer is not immediately apparent. If you are unfamiliar with scanning Latin verse, it is hoped that you will find the following summary useful.

THE LANGUAGE OF METER

- **dactyl**: one long syllable followed by two short syllables, $-\smile\smile$.

- **diphthong**: a double vowel with a single sound, e.g., **ae** (**aes**-tas), **au** (**Pl<u>au</u>tus**), **eu** (**eh<u>eu</u>**), or **oe** (**c<u>oe</u>pit**). Double vowels that have two sounds are not diphthongs, e.g., **filia**. The vowel combination **ei** also consists of two syllables, e.g., **deinde** = **de** + **inde**.

- **elision** (verb, *elide*): to slur an end vowel with an initial vowel (**quaeque ipse**), an end vowel with an initial **h** (**meminisse horret**), or a final -**m** with an initial vowel (**quamquam animus**).

- **foot**: a metrical unit consisting of a dactyl or spondee in a hexameter line.

- **hexameter**: a line of verse containing six (hexa-) metrical units.

- **scansion** (verb, *scan*): to determine the long or short length of each syllable in a line of verse.

- **spondee**: two long syllables, $-\ -$.

- **syllable**: a vowel, diphthong, or elision.

Reminder: Macrons (long marks) are provided on the SAT Latin Subject Test.

SCANSION

In scansion, every syllable of a Latin word, that is, every vowel, diphthong, or elision, is assigned a long or short sound. Whether the sound is long or short reflects the length of time the sound was held when spoken.

Each line of hexameter verse contains six feet. The basic metrical unit of a line of dactylic hexameter is the dactyl (Greek for "finger," i.e., one long knuckle and two short ones). A spondee may be substituted for a dactyl in any of the first four feet. For the purposes of the SAT Latin Subject Test, as permitted by the College Board, the **final two feet** are **always** to be considered **a dactyl and a spondee in succession**, that is, —∪∪ | — —. Thus, the quantities found in the first four feet of a hexameter line are available for testing, for example, "The metrical pattern of the first four feet of line so and so is . . ." or "How many elisions occur in the first three feet of line such and so?"

The detailed rules for the assignment of long and short values to syllables lie outside the scope of this book. To review these, ask your teacher, consult your textbook or reader, or go online (some Web sites are suggested at the end of this chapter). In general, sounds are long if they are long by nature (i.e., have a naturally long sound when pronounced), such as the ablative singular (**servō**) and plural (**servīs**) and accusative plural (**servōs**) of some nouns. You may know these simply by having learned the correct pronunciation of Latin. Also long are diphthongs and vowels followed by two or more consonants in the same or different words; for example, the -**o**- in **p̲o̲ssumus** is long by position because it is followed by two consonants, -**ss**, as is the second -**u**- in **possum̲u̲s legere,** which is followed by **s** and **l**. In general, if there is no reason for a syllable to be long, it is to be considered short. Logic and deduction are also useful strategies to apply when determining the length of a syllable in Latin, e.g., a single short syllable cannot be found between two long syllables in a hexameter line, which consists of units of —∪∪ and — —. You are not required to designate foot-breaks in your scansion of a line on the exam, but it helps to do so in order to determine whether or not you have completed scansion of each of the first four feet. The following is an example of the scansion of a hexameter line. Note that the first syllable is always long, and remember that no substitutions are allowed in the fifth and sixth feet:

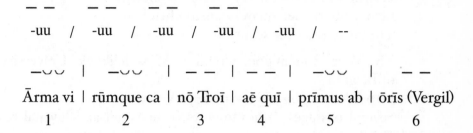

$$-uu \quad / \quad -uu \quad / \quad -uu \quad / \quad -uu \quad / \quad -uu \quad / \quad --$$

Ārma vi | rūmque ca | nō Troī | aē quī | prīmus ab | ōrīs (Vergil)

    1   2   3   4   5   6

TIPS ON SCANSION

- The enclitic **-que** is not a diphthong. Its quantity is determined by its position in the line, as in the following:

  frāctī bellō fātīs<u>que</u> repulsī (short)
  aedificant sectā<u>que</u> <u>in</u>texunt abiete costās (long by position)

- A word ending in a vowel or diphthong preceding a word beginning with **m-**, such as **puellae māter**, does <u>not</u> create an elision!

- An **x** makes a short vowel long by position because it gave the sound of a double consonant (= **ks**).

ONLINE RESOURCES FOR METER AND SCANSION

- Examples of Greek and Latin Meters in English Verse (Rosemary Wright), http://www.cornellcollege.edu/classicalstudies/meters.shtml An example of dactylic hexameter from English verse.

- Hexametrica: an introduction to Latin hexameter verse (Skidmore College), http://www.skidmore.edu/academics/classics/courses/metrica/scansion.html Thoroughgoing presentation of all aspects of the hexameter line.

- Scansion (Kentucky Educational Television), http://www.dl.ket.org/latinlit/carmina/scansion/index.htm Good for rules about elision and for poetic terms.

- Scansion of Latin Poetry (Marc Moskowitz),
  http://suberic.net/~marc/scansion.html
  The basic rules for scansion.

- Viva Voce: Roman poetry recited (V. Nedeljkovic, University
  of Belgrade),
  http://dekart.f.bg.ac.yu/~vnedeljk/VV
  Several passages of hexameters from Vergil and Juvenal read
  aloud.

PRACTICE QUESTIONS ON SCANSION

1. The metrical pattern of the first four feet of this line is

    hūc sē prōvectī dēsertō in lītore condunt

    (A) $- \cup \cup \, | - \cup \cup \, | - - | - -$

    (B) $- - | - - | - - | - -$

    (C) $- - | - - | - - | - \cup \cup$

    (D) $- - | - \cup \cup | - - | - \cup \cup$

2. How many elisions occur in this passage?

    Aut hōc inclūsī lignō occultantur Achīvī,
    aut haec in nostrōs fabricata est māchina mūrōs,
    īnspectūra domōs ventūraque dēsuper urbī,
    aut aliquis latet error; equō nē crēdite, Teucrī.

    (A) 0   (C) 2

    (B) 1   (D) 3

3. The metrical pattern of the first four feet of this line is

    panduntur portae iuvat (juvat) īre et Dōrica castra

    (A) S S D S   (C) S D S S

    (B) S S S D   (D) D S D S

4. How many elisions occur in this line?

   fēcissentque utinam saepe illōs aspera pontī

   (A) 0   (C) 2

   (B) 1   (D) 3

5. The metrical pattern of the first four feet of this line is

   idque audīre sat est, iamdūdum (jamdūdum) sūmite poenās

   (A) $-\ -\ |-\cup\cup|-\cup\cup|-\ -$

   (B) $-\cup\cup|-\cup\cup|-\ -\ |-\ -$

   (C) $-\ -\ |-\ -\ |-\cup\cup|-\cup\cup$

   (D) $-\ -\ |-\cup\cup|-\ -\ |-\ -$

Answers

1. (B)   2. (C)   3. (A)   4. (C)   5. (D)

THE SAT SUBJECT TEST IN
LATIN

SECTION 10

Practice Tests

PRACTICE TEST 1

This test is also on CD-ROM in our special interactive SAT Latin TEST*ware*®. It is highly recommended that you first take this exam on computer. You will then have the additional study features and benefits of timed conditions and instantaneous, accurate scoring. See page 9 for guidance on how to get the most out of our SAT Latin software.

SAT Latin Subject Test
Practice Test 1

(Answer sheets appear in the back of this book.)

PART A

8:55

> **DIRECTIONS**: In each of the following statements, you are to recognize the specified form of the underlined word. Choose the correct form and fill in the corresponding oval on your answer sheet.

1. The comparative of <u>miserum</u> is
   (A) <u>miserior</u>   (C) <u>miserius</u>
   (B) <u>miserē</u>   (D) <u>miserrimus</u>

2. The accusative plural of <u>nōmen</u> is
   (A) <u>nōminī</u>   (C) <u>nōminum</u>
   (B) <u>nōminibus</u>   (D) <u>nōmina</u>

3. The vocative singular of <u>Cornēlius</u> is
   (A) <u>Cornēliī</u>   (C) <u>Cornēlius</u>
   (B) <u>Cornēlī</u>   (D) <u>Cornēliō</u>

4. The perfect of <u>custodimur</u> is
   (A) <u>custodīvimus</u>   (C) <u>custodiendī sumus</u>
   (B) <u>custodītī sumus</u> (D) <u>custodītī erāmus</u>

5. The accusative plural of <u>hic</u> is
   (A) <u>hunc</u>   (C) <u>hōs</u>
   (B) <u>haec</u>   (D) <u>hīs</u>

517

6. The pluperfect subjunctive of <u>patiuntur</u> is *pass. 3rd person pl*

    (A) <u>passī sint</u>   (C) <u>passī essent</u>

    (B) <u>paterentur</u>   (D) <u>passī erant</u>

7. The perfect indicative of <u>eunt</u> is

    (A) <u>iērunt</u>   (C) <u>ierant</u>

    (B) <u>eant</u>   (D) <u>ierint</u>

8. The future of <u>quaereris</u> is

    (A) <u>quaesīveris</u>   (C) <u>quaerēminī</u>

    (B) <u>quaesītus eris</u>   (D) <u>quaerēris</u>

PART B

DIRECTIONS: Decide which of the following answers provides the Latin word that is related by derivation to the underlined English word. Then fill in the corresponding oval.

---

9. Members of Mensa are famous for their <u>cognitive</u> abilities.

    (A) <u>cognoscō</u>   (C) <u>coniciō</u>

    (B) <u>cogō</u>   (D) <u>congregō</u>

10. Romulus was guilty of <u>fratricide</u>.

    (A) <u>cadō</u>   (C) <u>caedō</u>

    (B) <u>currō</u>   (D) <u>cēdō</u>

11. <u>Pensive</u> people often prop their chins on their hands.

    (A) <u>pendō</u>   (C) <u>perdō</u>

    (B) <u>pellō</u>   (D) <u>pereō</u>

12. The attorney attempted to <u>mollify</u> the outraged judge.

(A) <u>molēs</u>   (C) <u>mōlior</u>

(B) <u>mollis</u>   (D) <u>molestus</u>

PART C

DIRECTIONS: In each sentence given below, part or all of the sentence is underlined. Select the best translation of the underlined word or words and fill in the appropriate oval on your answer sheet.

---

13. Brūtus negāvit sē Caesarem <u>necāvisse</u>.

(A) has killed   (C) was killing

(B) had killed   (D) had been killed

14. <u>Lūdī incipiant</u>.

(A) The games are beginning.

(B) The games must begin.

(C) The games will begin.

(D) Let the games begin.

15. Cicerō <u>Athēnās</u> iter fēcit.

(A) to Athens   (C) in Athens

(B) from Athens   (D) at Athens

16. <u>Hannibale victō</u>, Scīpiō Rōmam rediit.

(A) While Hannibal was being defeated

(B) Hannibal having won

(C) After Hannibal had been defeated

(D) Because Hannibal was winning

17. Canēbatne Nerō <u>cum Rōma incenderet</u>?

    (A) after Rome had burned

    (B) when Rome was burning

    (C) while Rome is burning

    (D) since Rome had burned

18. Multa senātōribus <u>agenda erant</u>.

    (A) were being done   (C) had been done

    (B) had done   (D) had to be done

19. Dīxit <u>sē haec factūrum esse</u>.

    (A) that they would do these things.

    (B) that he would have done these things.

    (C) that he would do these things.

    (D) that he must do these things.

20. <u>Aliī</u> equō iter faciēbant, <u>aliī</u> nāve.

    (A) Some; others   (C) These; those

    (B) One; another   (D) Several; few

21. Sī Rōmae habitāvissēs, <u>fuissēsne laetī</u>?

    (A) were you being happy

    (B) would you have been happy

    (C) will you be happy

    (D) have you been happy

22. Senātōrēs <u>quibus</u> Cicerō persuāsit inimīcī fuerant.

    (A) who   (C) whom

    (B) whose   (D) by whom

23. <u>Medūsā moriente</u>, Pēgasus ē sanguine ēmergēbat.

    (A) While Medusa is dying
    (B) Because Medusa is dead
    (C) While Medusa was dying
    (D) After Medusa died

24. Erantne thermae maiōrēs <u>amphitheātrīs</u>?

    (A) in amphitheaters
    (B) near amphitheaters
    (C) away from amphitheaters
    (D) than amphitheaters

25. Polyphēmus <u>plūs vīnī</u> semper volēbat.

    (A) much wine
    (C) more wine
    (B) better wine
    (D) very much wine

26. Pyrāmus Thisbēn <u>vīsam</u> statim amābat.

    (A) after he saw
    (B) at the time when he sees
    (C) while he was seeing
    (D) who was about to be seen

PART D

27. Mīnōtaurus, . . . Thēsēus necāverat, mortālis erat.

    (A) quī   (C) quod

    (B) cui   (D) quem

28. Gladiātor nesciēbat utrum . . .

    g in, not case (case from use!)

    (A) moritūrus esset

    (B) moritur

    (C) moriturus esse

    (D) mortuus erat

29. Ūna fīlia . . . erat.

    (A) Cicerōnis   (C) Cicerōnī

    (B) Cicerōnem   (D) Cicerō

30. . . . imperātōrem, mīlitēs!

    (A) Nōlī necāre   (C) Necāre

    (B) Necā   (D) Nōlīte necāre

31. Spartacus scīvit omnēs servōs . . . .

    (A) līberāre   (C) līberātī essent

    (B) līberandōs esse   (D) līberantur

32. Crede . . . , vērē dīcō.

    (A) sē   (C) mihi

    (B) mē   (D) meī

33. ... , omnēs imperātōrem laudābant.

   (A) Thermīs confectīs

   (B) Thermae conficientēs

   (C) Thermae confectae

   (D) Thermīs conficientibus

PART E

DIRECTIONS: In each of the following sentences, part or all of the sentence is underlined. Select the expression that <u>best</u> substitutes for the underlined word or words, that is, the expression that changes the meaning of the sentence least. Then fill in the corresponding oval.

---

34. Magister docēbat <u>haec</u> illīs discipulīs.

   (A) <u>illa</u>   (C) <u>eandem</u>

   (B) <u>id</u>   (D) <u>sua</u>

35. Octāvia fēmina <u>magnā virtūte</u> erat.

   (A) <u>magna virtūs</u>   (C) <u>magnam virtūtem</u>

   (B) <u>magnae virtūtis</u>   (D) <u>magnae virtūtī</u>

36. <u>Prūdentia ā bonīs semper petitur.</u>

   (A) <u>Prūdentia bonōrum semper petitur.</u>

   (B) <u>Prūdentia bonōs semper petit.</u>

   (C) <u>Bonī ā prūdentibus semper petuntur.</u>

   (D) <u>Bonī prūdentiam semper petunt.</u>

37. Brutus Rōmā exiit <u>ut ē Caesariānīs effugeret</u>.

   (A) <u>Caesariānī effugientēs</u>

   (B) <u>ad Caesariānōs effugiendōs</u>

   (C) <u>effugere ē Caesariānīs</u>

   (D) <u>quod ē Caesariānīs effugerant</u>

38. <u>Dum Cicerō consul erat</u>, Catilīna mortuus est.

   (A) <u>Sī Cicerō consul est</u>

   (B) <u>Postquam Cicerō consul est</u>

   (C) <u>Cicerōne consule</u>

   (D) <u>Quod Cicerō consul futūrus est</u>

PART F

DIRECTIONS: Look over each of the following passages of prose and poetry to understand the meaning. Then, relying on the context of the reading passage, answer each question or complete each statement, as directed. Choose the answer that best expresses your understanding of the meaning of any form, clause, sentence, or lines specified. Then fill in the corresponding oval.

Passage A

The poet Martial laments the young slave girl Erotion

    Hanc tibi, Fronto pater, genetrīx[1] Flaccilla, puellam   1
      oscula commendō dēliciāsque meās,   2
    parvula nē nigrās horrescat Erōtion umbrās   3
      ōraque Tartareī prodigiōsa canis.[2]   4
    Mollia nōn rigidus caespēs[3] tegat[4] ossa; nec illī,   5
      terra, gravis fuerīs;[5] nōn fuit illa tibi.

1.   genetrīx, genetricis, f.: *mother*
2.   Tartareī . . . canis: *hound of Tartarus, Cerberus*
3.   caespēs, caespitis, m.: *turf, sod*
4.   tegō, tegere: *cover*
5.   nec . . . fuerīs: = *don't be . . .*

39. In lines 1–2 (<u>Hanc</u> . . . <u>meās</u>), Martial entrusts

    (A) his mother to his father

    (B) his father to his mother

    (C) his mother and a little girl to his father

    (D) a little girl to his father and mother

40. The enclitic -<u>que</u> (line 2) joins together

    (A) <u>oscula</u> *and* <u>dēliciās meās</u>

    (B) <u>commendō</u> *and* <u>dēliciās meās</u>

    (C) <u>dēliciās</u> *and* <u>meās</u>

    (D) <u>oscula commendō</u> *and* <u>meās</u>

41. The meaning of <u>nē</u> . . . <u>horrescat</u> (line 3) is

    (A) she will not shudder at

    (B) so that she does not shudder at

    (C) do not shudder at

    (D) may she not shudder at

42. The word <u>parvula</u> (line 3) contrasts in meaning with

    (A) <u>nigrās</u> (line 3)   (C) <u>prodigiōsa</u> (line 4)

    (B) <u>ōra</u> (line 4)   (D) <u>canis</u> (line 4)

43. What does the language of lines <u>parvula</u> . . . <u>canis</u> (lines 3–4) suggest that Erotion is doing now?

    (A) avoiding death

    (B) awaiting burial

    (C) accompanying her pet dog

    (D) entering the underworld

44. The verb <u>tegat</u> (line 5) is translated

    (A) it is covering   (C) it will cover

    (B) let it cover   (D) it must cover

45. Line 5 (<u>Mollia</u> . . . <u>ossa</u>) speaks of

    (A) the act of dying

    (B) conditions in the underworld

    (C) life after death

    (D) the burial ground

46. What is the metrical pattern of the first four feet of line 5?

    (A) − − |−∪∪ |− − |−∪∪

    (B) −∪∪ |−∪∪ |− − |− − |

    (C) − − |− − |−∪∪ |− − |

    (D) −∪∪ |−∪∪ |− − |−∪∪ |

47. In line 6, <u>tibi</u> refers to

    (A) the sod   (C) Erotion

    (B) the bones   (D) the earth

48. In the final two lines (<u>nec</u> . . . <u>tibi</u>), Martial is

    (A) asking the earth to grieve for Erotion

    (B) cursing the earth for being so heavy on tiny Erotion

    (C) describing Erotion in the grave

    (D) bidding the earth to rest gently on Erotion

Passage B

Why the palm branch became a symbol of victory

1   Per hercle rem mīrandam Plutarchus dīcit. Sī super palmae arboris
    lignum magna pondera[1] imponās ac tam graviter urgeās onerēsque,
    ut magnitūdō oneris sustinērī nōn queat,[2] nōn deorsum[3] palma
    cēdit nec intrā flectitur, sed adversus pondus resurgit et sursum[4]
5   nītitur[5] recurvāturque; proptereā, in certāminibus palmam signum
    esse placuit vīctoriae, quoniam ingenium lignī eiusmodī (ejusmodī)[6]
    est, ut urgentibus opprimentibusque nōn cēdat.

1. pondus, ponderis, n.: *weight*
2. queō, quīre, quiī, quitum: *to be able*
3. deorsum: *downward*
4. sursum: *upward*
5. nītor, nītī, nīxus sum: *strive, make an effort*
6. eiusmodī (ejusmodī): *of this kind, such*

49. <u>Sī</u> . . . <u>impōnās</u> (lines 1–2) is translated

    (A) If you are placing

    (B) If you will place

    (C) If you should place

    (D) If you are about to place

50. The case and number of <u>pondera</u> (line 2) is

    (A) nominative singular

    (B) accusative plural

    (C) ablative singular

    (D) nominative plural

51. The word <u>ac</u> (line 2) means

    (A) and   (C) nor

    (B) but   (D) or

52. The clause <u>Sī super palmae</u> . . . <u>urgeās onerēsque</u> (lines 1–2), describes an experiment in which

    (A) heavy weights are attached to a palm tree

    (B) the wood of the palm tree is weighed

    (C) a great weight of palm tree wood is stacked up

    (D) someone is attempting to lift a load of palm wood

53. The subject of the verb <u>queat</u> (line 3) is

    (A) the size (of the weight)

    (B) the weight

    (C) the support of the weight

    (D) the palm tree (understood)

54. <u>Flectitur</u> (line 4) is translated

    (A) is bending   (C) will bend

    (B) has bent   (D) is bent

55. In lines 3–5 (<u>nōn deorsum</u> . . . <u>recurvāturque</u>), what do we learn?

    (A) The wood of the palm yields a great deal before it eventually breaks.

    (B) The weight of the palm tree eventually causes it to bend and break.

    (C) The wood of the palm is flexible and will bend without breaking.

    (D) When pushed upright, the palm tree can be made to stand straight.

56. The word <u>vīctoriae</u> (line 6) is

    (A) dative singular   (C) genitive singular

    (B) nominative plural   (D) vocative plural

57. What is the meaning of the clause <u>proptereā</u> . . . <u>vīctoriae</u> (line 5–6)?

    (A) It is acceptable to raise your palm when a victory is won.

    (B) In competitions, it has become acceptable that the palm be a symbol of victory.

    (C) In contests, the sign of the palm branch means the victor is pleased.

    (D) When a palm appears during contests, it is an omen of potential victory.

58. The word <u>ut</u> (line 7) is translated

    (A) as   (C) in order to

    (B) when   (D) that

59. In the last clause, <u>quoniam</u> . . . <u>nōn cēdat</u> (line 6–7), for what reason is the palm a symbol of victory?

    (A) It does not yield to pressure or force.

    (B) The wood is considered magical.

    (C) Weapons were originally made of wood.

    (D) It stands straight and tall, like the victor.

Passage C

Cicero describes a public meeting during the late Republic

1 Pompēius ut perōrāvit,[1] surrēxit Clōdius. Eī tantus clāmor ā
nostrīs[2] (placuerat enim referre grātiam), ut neque mente neque
linguā neque ōre cōnsisteret. Ea rēs acta est, cum hōrā sextā vix
Pompēius perōrāvisset, usque ad hōram octāvam, cum omnia
5 maledicta, versūs etiam obscēnissimī in Clōdium et Clōdiam
dīcerentur. Hōrā ferē nōnā, quasī signō datō, Clōdiānī nostrōs
cōnspūtāre[3] coepērunt. Exarsit dolor. Ursērunt illī, ut ē locō nōs
movērent. Factus est ā nostrīs impetus; fuga operārum.[4] Ēiectus
est dē rostrīs Clōdius ac nōs quoque tum fūgimus, nē aliquid
10 accīderet in turbā.

1. perōrō, perōrāre: *finish a speech*
2. nostrīs: *Cicero associates himself with supporters of Pompey*
3. cōnspūtō, cōnspūtāre: *spit on in contempt*
4. opera, operae, f.: *thug, operative*

60. Pompēius ut perōrāvit (line 1) is translated

    (A) So that Pompey might finish speaking

    (B) When Pompey finished speaking

    (C) Although Pompey completed his speech

    (D) In order that Pompey should finish speaking

61. As a result of the uproar mentioned in lines 1–2, who could neither
    think nor speak?

    (A) Cicero

    (B) Pompey

    (C) Cicero and his supporters

    (D) Clodius

62. The subjunctive verb cōnsisteret (line 3) is in the same tense as
    which of the following indicative forms?

    (A) consīstit   (C) consistēbat

    (B) constiterat   (D) constitit

63. <u>Ea rēs acta est</u> (line 3) refers to

    (A) Pompey's speech

    (B) The shouting of Pompey's supporters

    (C) The shouting of Clodius's supporters

    (D) The general unrest in the Forum

64. In line 3, <u>hōrā sextā</u> means

    (A) at the sixth hour

    (B) in six hours

    (C) after the sixth hour

    (D) for six hours

65. The clause <u>cum</u> . . . <u>perōrāvisset</u> (lines 3–4) is translated

    (A) when he had finished speaking

    (B) since he was finished speaking

    (C) when he was finished speaking

    (D) although he is finished speaking

66. What happened at the eighth hour as described in <u>cum</u> . . . <u>dīcerentur</u> (lines 4–6)?

    (A) Clodius and his sister Clodia cursed Cicero.

    (B) Clodius and his sister Clodia were cursed.

    (C) Clodia cursed her brother Clodius.

    (D) Clodius was cursing everyone.

67. <u>Quasī signō datō</u> (line 6) is translated

    (A) as if a signal was being given

    (B) as if giving a signal

    (C) as if a signal is being given

    (D) as if a signal had been given

68. What happened approximately one hour later, as indicated in the sentence H̄orā . . . coeperunt (lines 6–7)?

    (A) Cicero's people began to spit on Clodius.

    (B) The Clodians in Cicero's group began to spit.

    (C) The Clodians began to spit on Cicero's people.

    (D) Everyone was spitting on everyone else.

69. Given the context, the best meaning of Exarsit dolor (line 7) is

    (A) He broke down in grief.

    (B) Resentment flared up.

    (C) Anxiety arose.

    (D) Regret took over.

70. What did not happen after Clodius's men started pushing (lines 7–8)?

    (A) Cicero's men were driven back.

    (B) The thugs ran off.

    (C) Clodius was thrown down from the Rostra.

    (D) Cicero's men made a counterattack.

71. In lines 9–10 (nē . . . turbā), Cicero relates that he and his followers ran off because

    (A) something had happened

    (B) something is happening

    (C) nothing was happening

    (D) something might happen

SAT Latin Subject Test
Practice Test 1

ANSWER KEY

1.	(C)	21.	(B)	41.	(B)	61.	(D)
2.	(D)	22.	(C)	42.	(C)	62.	(C)
3.	(B)	23.	(C)	43.	(D)	63.	(B)
4.	(B)	24.	(D)	44.	(B)	64.	(A)
5.	(C)	25.	(C)	45.	(D)	65.	(A)
6.	(C)	26.	(A)	46.	(B)	66.	(B)
7.	(A)	27.	(D)	47.	(D)	67.	(D)
8.	(D)	28.	(A)	48.	(D)	68.	(C)
9.	(A)	29.	(C)	49.	(C)	69.	(B)
10.	(C)	30.	(D)	50.	(B)	70.	(A)
11.	(A)	31.	(B)	51.	(A)	71.	(D)
12.	(B)	32.	(C)	52.	(A)		
13.	(B)	33.	(A)	53.	(A)		
14.	(D)	34.	(A)	54.	(D)		
15.	(A)	35.	(B)	55.	(C)		
16.	(C)	36.	(D)	56.	(C)		
17.	(B)	37.	(B)	57.	(B)		
18.	(D)	38.	(C)	58.	(D)		
19.	(C)	39.	(D)	59.	(A)		
20.	(A)	40.	(A)	60.	(B)		

DETAILED EXPLANATIONS
OF ANSWERS

PRACTICE TEST 1

PART A

1. **(C)**
The neuter form of the comparative corresponding with **miserum** is **miserius**. Answer (A) **miserior** is a comparative adjective, but masculine/feminine; (B) **miserē** is a positive adverb; and (D) **miserrimus** a superlative form. (See Chapter 16.)

2. **(D)**
Nōmina is the correct form because **nōmen** is a neuter noun, so the nominative and accusative singular and plural are the same. Answer (A) **nōminī** is dative singular; (B) **nōminibus** is dative/ablative plural; and (C) **nōminum** is genitive plural (See Chapter 5.)

3. **(B)**
Cōrnelī is correct because the rule requires that for a noun ending in **-ius**, the **-us** is dropped to create the vocative. Answer (A) **Cōrneliī** is nominative plural; (C) **Cōrnelius** is nominative singular; and (D) **Cōrneliō** is dative/ablative singular (See Chapter 23.)

4. **(B)**
Custodītī sumus is the correct form. It is important to note that the verb to be transformed is in the present passive form and that the perfect passive equivalent in person and number is requested. Thus, **custodītī sumus**, *we have been guarded* is the perfect tense equivalent of **custodimur**, *we are being guarded*. Answer (A) is perfect active; (C) is a passive periphrastic; and (D) the pluperfect passive. (See Chapter 19.)

5. **(C)**
Hōs is the accusative plural masculine of **hic**, which is nominative singular masculine. Answer (A) **hunc** is accusative singular masculine; (B)

haec is feminine nominative singular or neuter nominative/accusative plural; and (D) **hīs** is ablative/dative plural of all genders. (See Chapter 11.)

6. **(C)**
   Passī essent: this is the pluperfect subjunctive of the deponent verb **patior, passī, passus sum.** Answer (A) **passī sint** is perfect subjunctive; (B) **paterentur** is imperfect subjunctive; and (D) **passī erant** is pluperfect indicative. (See Chapter 20 for deponent verbs and Chapter 27 for forms of the subjunctive.)

7. **(A)**
   Iērunt is the perfect indicative form of **eunt.** All choices are various tenses and moods of the irregular verb **īre,** in the third person plural. Answer (B) **eant** is a form of the present subjunctive; (C) **ierant** is in the pluperfect indicative; and (D) **ierint** is in the future perfect indicative or perfect subjunctive form. (See Chapter 21.)

8. **(D)**
   This question tests knowledge of the functional use of the macron, which distinguishes the present passive form **quaereris,** *you are being sought* from the future passive form **quaerēris,** *you will be sought.* Answer (A) **quaesīveris** is in the future perfect active indicative form; (B) **quaesītus eris** is the passive equivalent of (A); and (C) **quaerēminī** is the plural equivalent of **quaerēris.** (See Chapter 19.)

PART B

9. **(A)**
   The stem of <u>cognitive</u>, **cognīt-**, comes from the fourth principal part of **cognoscō, cognoscere, cognōvī, cognitus,** *to recognize, know.* Answer (B) **cogō** means *to collect, compel;* (C) **coniciō,** *to throw together, guess;* and (D) **congregō,** *to gather together.*

10. **(C)**
    Answers (A) and (D) are tempting alternatives to the correct answer, **caedō,** as the root of the English word <u>fratricide</u>. The principal parts are **caedō, caedere, cecīdī,** *to kill.* Answer (B) **cadō, cadere, cecīdī** means *to fall;* (B) **currō, currere, cucurrī** means *to run;* and (D) **cēdō, cēdere, cessī** means *to go or yield.*

11. **(A)**

The word <u>pensive</u> derives from the fourth principal part of the verb **pendō, pendere, pependī, pensus**, *to weigh, consider, judge*. Answer (B) is **pellō, pellere, pepulī, pulsus**, *to drive*; (B) **perdō, perdere, perdidī, perditus**, *to destroy*; and (D) **pereō, perīre, periī, peritus**, *to perish*.

12. **(B)**

<u>Mollify</u> derives from the adjective **mollis, -is, -e**, *soft, gentle, tender*. Answer (A) **molēs, mōlis**, means *mass or bulk*; (C) **mōlior, mōlīrī, mōlitus sum**, *to set in motion or work*; and (D) **molestus, -a, -um**, *troublesome or annoying*.

PART C

13. **(B)**

The perfect active infinitive **necāvisse** is found in an indirect statement after **negāvit**, the main verb, which is in the past tense. The action of the infinitive is thus prior in time to a past tense, or past-past—*had*. Answers (A) *has killed* and (C) *was killing* both require **necāre**, and (D) *had been killed*, requires the passive form **necātum esse**. (For indirect statement, see Chapter 26.)

14. **(D)**

Incipiant is an example of the jussive subjunctive (see Chapter 28). Answers (A) and (C) require verbs in the indicative, as *are* and *will* are assertions or statements. Answer (B) *The games must begin* requires a construction that expresses necessity, such as the passive periphrastic or the phrase **necesse est** + infinitive.

15. **(A)**

Athēnās is in the accusative plural form, thus requiring the understood preposition **ad**, *to Athens*. Answers (B) *from Athens*, (C) *in Athens*, and (D) *at Athens* require the ablative or locative form **Athēnīs**. Note that the city name of Athens is found in the plural. (See Chapter 10.)

16. **(C)**

The sentence reads <u>*After Hannibal had been defeated*</u>, *Scipio returned to Rome*. **Hannibale victō** is an ablative absolute with the perfect passive participle. More literally, the sentence reads *Hannibal having been defeated*, that is, he was defeated before Scipio returned to Rome. Answers (A) and (D) require a present participle in the ablative absolute, such as **Hannibale vincente**, because the translations *being defeated* and *winning* are in the present tense. Answer (B) *Hannibal having won* not only changes the meaning, but also expresses the participle as a perfect active participle, which does not exist in Latin. (See Chapter 24.)

17. **(B)**
The sentence reads *Was Nero singing when Rome was burning?* This sentence contains a circumstantial clause, **cum . . . incenderet**, with its verb in the imperfect subjunctive. Answers (A) and (D) require a subjunctive verb in the pluperfect tense, namely, **incendisset**, and (C) needs a verb in the present tense, **incendat**. (See Chapters 27 and 32.)

18. **(D)**
This sentence, which contains a passive periphrastic in the past tense (**agenda erant**) with a dative of agent (**senātōribus**) reads *Many things had to be done by the senators*. None of the other answers has the sense of necessity or obligation. Answer (A) requires that the verb be **agēbantur**, (B) **ēgerant**, and (C) **acta erant**. (See Chapter 25.)

19. **(C)**
This sentence, which contains an indirect statement with the introductory verb in the past tense and the infinitive in the future, reads *He said that he himself would do these things*. Answer (A) does not correctly translate the reflexive pronoun **sē**, and it is plural, whereas the infinitive **factūrum esse** requires a singular subject. The meaning in (B), *that he would have done these things*, cannot be expressed in Latin by an infinitive; and (D) requires a periphrastic infinitive, **faciendum esse**. (See Chapter 26 for infinitives and indirect statement.)

20. **(A)**
Aliī . . . aliī are correlating indefinite pronouns meaning *some . . . others*, leading to the meaning *Some journeyed by coach, others by ship*. Answer (B) requires the singular, **alius . . . alius**; (C) the demonstratives **hī** and **illī**; and (D) **complūrēs** and **paucī**, which are not parallel. (For correlatives, see Chapter 34.)

21. **(B)**
The sentence reads *If you had lived in Rome, would you have been happy?* In this sentence, you are asked to translate the conclusion of a past contrary to

fact conditional sentence. Answer (A) *were you being* requires a subjunctive verb in the imperfect tense in a present contrary to fact condition, **essēs**. Answer (C) *will you be* requires a verb in the future indicative in a future more vivid condition, **eris**, which would not combine with **habitāvissēs**, the verb of the main clause, which is in the pluperfect subjunctive. Answer (D) *have you been* requires a subjunctive verb in the perfect tense, **fueris**, in a mixed condition. (See Chapter 27 for forms of the subjunctive and Chapter 29 for conditional sentences.)

22. **(C)**

   The sentence reads *The senators <u>whom</u> Cicero persuaded had been (his) personal enemies*. The relative pronoun **quibus** must be in the dative case, because it serves as the object of the verb **persuāsit**. Answer (A) requires the nominative form **quī**; (B) the genitive form **cuius**; and (D) the ablative form **ā quibus**. (See Chapter 12.)

23. **(C)**

   Medusā moriente is an ablative absolute that contains a present participle. The action of the participle is happening at the same time as that of the main verb, which is in the past tense. Therefore, the sentence reads *<u>While Medusa was dying</u>, Pegasus was emerging from (her) blood*. Answers (A) and (D) give incorrect translations of the participles. Answer (A) requires a verb in the main clause that is in the present tense, and (D) *after Medusa died*, needs a participle that is both perfect and passive, because the *dying* would have happened prior in time to the *emerging*. Answer (B) expresses the same basic meaning as (D), that Pegasus emerged after Medusa died. (See Chapter 24.)

24. **(D)**

   The sentence reads *Were Roman baths bigger <u>than</u> (the) <u>amphitheaters</u>?* This sentence contains an example of the ablative of comparison. Answers (A) and (B) contain prepositional phrases expressing place, **in amphitheātrīs** and **prope amphitheātra**, respectively. Answer (C) *with the amphitheaters* suggests that **amphitheātrīs** might be an ablative of means. (For the ablative of comparison, see Chapter 10.)

25. **(C)**

   Plūs vīnī is a partitive genitive, giving this sentence the meaning *Polyphemus always wanted <u>more wine</u>*. Answer (A) requires **multum vīnī**, (B) **melius vīnum**, and (D) **plurimum vīnī**. (See Chapter 7.)

26. **(A)**

The sentence reads *After Pyramus saw Thisbe, he immediately loved her.* This sentence evaluates your command of the perfect passive participle. **Vīsam** is a past participle modifying **Thisbēn** (a Greek accusative form). The past participle must express action that happened prior to that of the main verb, eliminating (B) and (C), which express action contemporary with that of the verb in the main clause. Answer (D) requires a future active participle, **visūram**. (See Chapter 24.)

PART D

27. **(D)**

The sentence reads *The Minotaur, which Theseus had killed, was mortal.* The relative pronoun must be in the accusative case as the direct object of **necāverat** in its clause, thus the correct answer is **quem**. Answer (A) **quī** is nominative, (B) **cui** is dative, and (C) **quod** is nominative or accusative but neuter (**Mīnōtaurus** is masculine). (See Chapter 12 for relative clauses.)

28. **(A)**

The sentence reads *The gladiator did not know whether he was about to die.* The word **utrum** introduces an indirect question clause with a subjunctive verb, triggered by the verb **nesciēbat** in the main clause. The correct answer, **moritūrus esset**, is an example of the active periphrastic with the future infinitive (see Chapter 24). Answers (B) and (D) are in the indicative mood, and (C) is a (future) infinitive, which does not meet the grammatical requirements of the context. (See Chapter 31 for indirect questions.)

29. **(C)**

The sentence reads *Cicero had one daughter* (literally, *There was one daughter to Cicero*). This sentence contains a dative of possession (see Chapter 8). The other answers are in cases that are unjustified by the context: (A) is genitive, (B) is accusative, and (D) is nominative.

30. **(D)**

The exclamation point signals the appearance of an imperative. Because the vocative form **mīlitēs** is plural, a plural imperative is needed, eliminating (A) and (B), which are singular. Answer (C) is an infinitive.

The correct answer, **Nōlīte necāre**, is a plural form of the negative imperative. (See Chapter 23.)

31. **(B)**

Liberandōs esse is the correct answer. The verb **scīvit** introduces an indirect statement with an infinitive, thus eliminating (C) and (D), which have pluperfect passive subjunctive and present passive indicative forms, respectively. Answer (A) is not possible grammatically, because **liberāre** requires a meaning that is both present and active, namely, *were freeing* (remember that the verb is in the past tense). The sentence must therefore read *Spartacus knew that all slaves <u>must be set free</u>*.

32. **(C)**

Mihi is the correct form because the verb **crēdere** takes a dative object. Thus, **Crēde mihi, vērē dīcō** means *Trust <u>me</u>, I speak the truth*. Answers (A) **sē** and (B) **mē** are accusative or ablative, and (D) **meī** is genitive singular of the personal pronoun **ego**. (See Chapter 8 for the dative and Chapter 14 for personal pronouns.)

33. **(A)**

The choice that makes the best sense is the ablative absolute, **Thermīs confectīs**, *The baths having been completed*. The ablative absolute, remember, stands alone and its meaning is separate from that of the main clause. Answers (B) and (C) do not make sense in the context of the main clause. Answer (D) contains the present active participle **conficientibus**, which gives the impossible meaning *while the baths were completing*. The sentence reads *<u>After the baths were</u>* (or *<u>had been</u>*) *<u>completed</u>, everyone praised the emperor*.

PART E

34. **(A)**

Although there is a distinction in meaning between **haec** and **illa**, for the purposes of this question, they are to be taken as having the same meaning. The original sentence reads *The teacher was teaching those students <u>these things</u>*. Thus, both **haec** and **illa** are accusative plural neuter forms of demonstrative pronouns. Answer (B) is incorrect because **id** is singular and **haec** plural; (C) does not work because **eandem** is feminine and **haec** neuter; and (D) cannot be the answer because **sua**, a reflexive adjective, does not make sense. (See Chapter 11 for demonstratives.)

35. **(B)**

The best substitution for the ablative of description **magnā virtūte** is the genitive of description, **magnae virtūtis**. The sentence reads *Octavia was a woman of great virtue*. Answer (A) is nominative, (C) is accusative, and (D) is dative, none of which is an adequate substitute for the ablative of description. (For the ablative of description, see Chapter 10; for the genitive of description, Chapter 7.)

36. **(D)**

This question asks for the transformation of a sentence containing a passive verb to one containing its active equivalent. The original says *Wisdom is always sought by good men*. Answer (D) reads *Good men always seek wisdom*. Answer (A) reads *The wisdom of good men is always sought*. Answer (B) is translated *Wisdom always seeks good men*, and (C) *Good men are always sought by the wise* (*men*). (For active and passive voices, see Chapter 19.)

37. **(B)**

The sentence reads *Brutus left Rome in order to escape from Caesar's men*. The best substitution for this **ut** purpose clause is the gerundive of purpose found in (B). Answers (A) and (C) are participial and infinitive phrases, respectively, neither of which expresses purpose. Answer (D) **quod ē Caesariānīs effugerant** is a causal clause with the indicative, which expresses a statement of fact, not purpose or intent. (See Chapter 30 for the purpose clause and Chapter 25 for the gerundive of purpose.)

38. **(C)**

The temporal clause **Dum Cicerō consul erat**, *While Cicero was consul* is best approximated by the ablative absolute **Cicerōne consule**. Answer (A) states a simple condition and (B), which contains **postquam**, *after*, is inconsistent with the time of the original clause, introduced by **dum**, *while*. Answer (D) is a causal clause in the future tense, which is also inconsistent with the time expressed in the original. The sentence reads *While Cicero was consul* (literally, *Cicero being consul*), *Catiline died*.

PART F

Passage A

39. **(D)**
The Latin reads *I entrust this girl to you, father Fronto and mother Flaccilla . . . .* The pronoun **tibi** is singular for poetic reasons.

40. **(A)**
The enclitic -**que** connects **oscula** with **dēliciās meās**, both of which characterize the young girl, whose name, Erotion, is mentioned.

41. **(B)**
The sense requires that **nē . . . horrescat** be a purpose clause, indicating the reason for which Martial is entrusting the little girl to his parents. Answer (D) *may she not shudder at* is grammatically possible, but the meaning is not as contextually appropriate as that of a purpose clause.

42. **(C)**
The word **parvula**, *tiny* (referring to Erotion) contrasts with **prodigiōsa**, *enormous* (referring to the jaws of Cerberus).

43. **(D)**
Lines 3–4 read *so that tiny Erotion may not shudder at the dark shadows and monstrous jaws of the dog of Tartarus.* Tartarus is a region of the underworld, and **Tartareī . . . canis** refers to Cerberus, who guards the gates.

44. **(B)**
Tegat is an example of a jussive subjunctive. (See Chapter 28.)

45. **(D)**
Line 5 reads *May the gentle earth cover her tender bones.* Thus, Martial is describing the circumstances of Erotion's burial and his hope that she will rest in peace. The phrase **nōn rigidus** modifies **caespēs**, and **mollia** modifies **ossa**.

46. **(B)**
This line requires two dactyls, followed by a spondee and a dactyl. (See Chapter 36.)

47. **(D)**

Tibi is a dative of reference that refers to the earth, here addressed by Martial in a prayer. (See Chapter 8.)

48. **(D)**

The final two lines read *Earth, be not heavy upon her; she was not (heavy) on you.* The pronouns **illī** and **illa** refer to Erotion. **Nec . . . fuerīs** is an example of the perfect subjunctive used in place of a negative command. (For this use, see Chapter 23.)

Passage B

49. **(C)**

Sī . . . imponās is a "should-would" or future-less-vivid conditional clause with the present subjunctive. Answer (A) requires a simple condition with the indicative verb **imponis**; (B) a future more vivid condition with the indicative verb **imponēs**; and (D) a future more vivid condition with the active periphrastic, **impositūrus es**. (For conditional sentences, see Chapter 29.)

50. **(B)**

Pondera is the accusative plural direct object of **imponās**. Note from the vocabulary help that **pondus** is a neuter noun. (For noun forms, see Chapter 5.)

51. **(A)**

Ac is a conjunction meaning *and*, equivalent to **atque**. It is usually found preceding a word beginning with a consonant, as here, **tam**.

52. **(A)**

This clause reads *If you should place a great weight on top of the wood of the palm tree and press on it and weigh it down . . .* **Super palmae arboris lignum** is a prepositional phrase, **pondera** the direct object of **imponās**, and **imponās** and **urgeās onerēsque** the verbs of a two-part conditional clause.

53. **(A)**

The result clause reads *(With the result that) the size of the load cannot be sustained . . .* The subject of this subordinate clause is the word **magnitūdō**.

54. **(D)**

Flectitur is present passive and translates *is being bent* or *is bent*. Answer (A) is active, (B) is past tense, and (C) future tense.

55. **(C)**

Lines 3–5 read *the palm does not give way downward nor is it bent from within, but rises back up against the weight and strives upward and bends back again.* Answers (A) and (B) are eliminated because nothing in the passage suggests that the palm wood breaks. Answer (D) is logical but not supported by the Latin.

56. **(C)**

Palmam is the subject of the infinitive **esse** after the verb **placuit**.

57. **(B)**

Lines 5–6 read *therefore, in competitions it has been acceptable that the palm be a symbol of victory . . . .*

58. **(D)**

Urgentibus opprimentibusque are participles used as substantives, and they are translated *to (those) pressing and forcing*. (For substantives, see Chapter 16.)

59. **(A)**

Lines 6–7 read *because the nature of this kind of wood is such that it does not yield to pressure or force.*

Passage C

60. **(B)**

Ut perōrāvit is an **ut** clause with an indicative verb, thus **ut** means *as* or *when*. Answers (A) and (D) suggest that this is a purpose clause, and (C) suggest a concessive clause, all of which are found with subjunctive verbs.

61. **(D)**

Clodius is the antecedent of the pronoun **eī** (line 1), so it serves as the subject of the subordinate clause **ut . . . cōnsisteret** (lines 2–3).

62. **(C)**

Cōnsisteret is in the imperfect tense of the subjunctive, thus matching with **cōnsistēbat**, the imperfect tense of the indicative. (For subjunctive forms, see Chapter 27; for the indicative, see Chapter 19.)

63. **(B)**

Ea rēs acta est means *This activity was carried out*, referring to **tantus clāmor** (line 1), the shouting of Pompey's supporters, as implied in the information provided in the parentheses. The **clāmor** was apparently in retaliation for the way in which Clodius's people had behaved during Pompey's speech.

64. **(A)**

Horā sextā is an example of the ablative of time, *at the sixth hour*. Answer (B) *in six hours* is **sex hōrīs**, an ablative of time within which; (C) *after the sixth hour*, could be **sextā post hōrā** or **post sextam hōram**, a prepositional phrase; and (D) *for six hours* is **sex hōrās**, an accusative extent of time. (For time expressions, see Chapters 9 and 10.)

65. **(A)**

Cum perōrāvisset is a **cum** circumstantial clause with the subjunctive verb in the pluperfect tense. Answers (B) and (C) require the imperfect tense (**perōrāret**) and (D) the present tense (**perōret**). (For **cum** clauses, see Chapter 32.)

66. **(B)**

Lines 4–6 of the passage reads *when all (sorts of) curses, (and) even the most scurrilous verses, were spoken to Clodius and Clodia.* **Cum . . . dīcerentur** is another **cum** circumstantial clause.

67. **(D)**

Signō datō is an ablative absolute with a past participle, literally *the signal having been given*. Cicero qualifies his statement with the word **quasī**, *as if*.

68. **(C)**

Lines 6–7 read *At nearly the ninth hour, as if a signal had been given, the Clodians began to spit on our people.*

69. **(B)**

Answer (A) is unacceptable because *in grief* does not correctly translate **dolor**, which is nominative. The translations of **exarsit** (from **exardescere**, *to blaze up, become hot*) in (C) and (D) do not do justice to the implications of the metaphor present in the verb here.

70. **(A)**

Cicero's men were not driven back. There is no information in the passage regarding this event. On the contrary, Cicero's men counterattacked (**factus est ā nostrīs impetus**, line 8).

71. **(D)**

Nē aliquid accīderet in turbā reads *lest something (else) happen in the mob.* This is a negative purpose clause.

Translations of Passages

Passage A

To you, father Fronto and mother Flaccilla, I entrust this girl, my pet ("little kiss") and my darling, so that tiny Erotion may not be frightened by the dark shadows and monstrous jaws of the hellhound, Cerberus. May the gentle turf cover her tender bones; and earth, be not heavy on her; she was not (heavy) on you. (Martial)

Passage B

By Hercules, Plutarch makes a wonderful observation. If you should place a great weight on top of the wood of the palm tree and press on it and weigh it down so heavily that the size of the load cannot be sustained, the palm neither gives way downward nor is bent from within, but rises back up against the weight and strives upward and bends back again; therefore, in competitions it has been accepted that the palm be the symbol of victory, because the nature of this kind of wood is such that it does not yield to pressure or force. (Aulus Gellius)

Passage C

When Pompey finished his speech, Clodius stood up. Such a great uproar (arose) from our people (for it had been a pleasure to return the favor), that he could control neither his thoughts nor his tongue nor his mouth. This went on, (from) when Pompey had barely finished speaking at the sixth hour, until the eighth hour, when all (manner of) curses, and even the most repulsive doggerel, were hurled at Clodius and Clodia. At nearly the ninth hour, as if a signal had been given, the Clodians began to spit on our people. (Our) resentment flared up. They pressed us hard, to move us out of there. A rush was made by us and the thugs ran off. Clodius was thrown down from the Rostra, and then we also took off, lest something (else) happen in the mob. (Cicero)

PRACTICE TEST 2

This test is also on CD-ROM in our special interactive SAT Latin TEST*ware*®. It is highly recommended that you first take this exam on computer. You will then have the additional study features and benefits of timed conditions and instantaneous, accurate scoring. See page 9 for guidance on how to get the most out of our SAT Latin software.

PRACTICE TEST 2

SAT Latin Subject Test Practice Test 2

(Answer sheets appear in the back of this book.)

PART A

DIRECTIONS: In each of the following statements, you are to recognize the specified form of the underlined word. Choose the correct form and fill in the corresponding oval on your answer sheet.

---

1. The comparative of <u>fortiter</u> is
   - (A) <u>fortissimē</u>
   - (B) <u>fortius</u>
   - (C) <u>fortior</u>
   - (D) <u>fortis</u>

2. The genitive singular of <u>ea</u> is
   - (A) <u>eī</u>
   - (B) <u>eae</u>
   - (C) <u>eīs</u>
   - (D) <u>eius (ejus)</u>

3. The future tense of <u>sunt</u> is
   - (A) <u>erunt</u>
   - (B) <u>fuerint</u>
   - (C) <u>fuērunt</u>
   - (D) <u>fuerant</u>

4. The accusative plural of <u>vīs</u> is
   - (A) <u>virōs</u>
   - (B) <u>vīrēs</u>
   - (C) <u>vim</u>
   - (D) <u>vīribus</u>

5. The imperative singular of <u>dīcō</u> is
   - (A) <u>dic</u>
   - (B) <u>dīcite</u>
   - (C) <u>dīcī</u>
   - (D) <u>dīcere</u>

6. The dative singular of <u>quae</u> is

   (A) <u>quibus</u>   (C) <u>cuius (cujus)</u>

   (B) <u>cui</u>   (D) <u>quae</u>

7. The perfect passive infinitive of <u>audiō</u> is

   (A) <u>audīvisse</u>   (C) <u>audītūrus esse</u>

   (B) <u>audīrī</u>   (D) <u>audītus esse</u>

8. The present participle of <u>ēgredior</u> is

   (A) <u>ēgressūrus</u>   (C) <u>ēgrediēns</u>

   (B) <u>ēgressus</u>   (D) <u>ēgrediendus</u>

PART B

DIRECTIONS: Decide which of the following answers provides the Latin word that is related by derivation to the underlined English word. Then fill in the corresponding oval.

---

9. Teenagers sometimes exhibit <u>regressive</u> behavior.

   (A) <u>regnō</u>   (C) <u>regredior</u>

   (B) <u>redeō</u>   (D) <u>referō</u>

10. That metal has great <u>tensile</u> strength.

   (A) <u>tendō</u>   (C) <u>teneō</u>

   (B) <u>tenebrae</u>   (D) <u>tenuis</u>

11. Criminals habitually <u>circumvent</u> the law.

   (A) <u>venēnum</u>   (C) <u>vendō</u>

   (B) <u>veniō</u>   (D) <u>ventus</u>

12. Baseball umpires shouldn't be <u>ambivalent</u>.

    (A) <u>amābilis</u>   (C) <u>ambulō</u>

    (B) <u>ambrosia</u>   (D) <u>ambō</u>

PART C

> **DIRECTIONS**: In each sentence given below, a portion or all of the sentence is underlined. Select the best translation of the underlined word or words and fill in the appropriate oval on your answer sheet.

13. Gladiātōrēs <u>audācissimī</u> sunt.

    (A) rather daring   (C) daring

    (B) very daring   (D) somewhat daring

14. <u>Trēs uxōrēs Caesarī erant</u>.

    (A) Three Caesars have wives.

    (B) Caesar had three wives.

    (C) Caesar has three wives.

    (D) They are the three wives of Caesar.

15. Sextā hōrā Mons Vesūvius <u>ēruptūrus erat</u>.

    (A) had erupted   (C) had to erupt

    (B) was erupting   (D) was about to erupt

16. <u>Pūniantur malī</u>.

    (A) The wicked are being punished.

    (B) The wicked will be punished.

    (C) They are punishing the wicked.

    (D) Let the wicked be punished.

17. Sāturnālia <u>complūrēs diēs</u> habēbantur.

    (A) for several days   (C) several days ago

    (B) in several days   (D) after several days

18. Omnēs sciēbant Hannibālem <u>superātum esse</u>.

    (A) has been conquered (C) had to be conquered

    (B) had been conquered (D) is conquered

19. Occurrēmus vōbīs <u>Athēnīs</u>.

    (A) from Athens   (C) in Athens

    (B) to Athens   (D) near Athens

20. Suntne fēlēs fēlīciōrēs <u>canibus</u>?

    (A) with dogs   (C) by dogs

    (B) than dogs   (D) as dogs

21. <u>Haec</u> quam vidēs pulchra est.

    (A) This woman   (C) These women

    (B) These things   (D) That thing

22. <u>Ōrātiōne habītā</u>, omnēs "Mīrābile audītū!"

    (A) While the speech was being delivered

    (B) As the speech was about to be delivered

    (C) After the speech had been delivered

    (D) Having delivered the speech

23. <u>Ille timuit nē fratrem suum necāvisset</u>.

    (A) He was afraid that he had not killed his brother.

    (B) He feared that his brother would kill him.

    (C) He was afraid that he had killed his own brother.

    (D) His brother was afraid that he had killed him.

24. Tacitus scīre voluit quālis vir Nerō esset.

    (A) what type of person Nero is

    (B) what sort of man Nero had been

    (C) who Nero was

    (D) what kind of man Nero was

25. Nōbīs domum redeundum est.

    (A) He must return to us at home.

    (B) We must return home.

    (C) We are going to return home.

    (D) He must return the house to us.

26. Nisi Caesar occīsus esset, imperātor fuisset.

    (A) he would have been emperor

    (B) he had been emperor

    (C) he would be emperor

    (D) he was about to become emperor

PART D

DIRECTIONS: In each of the following sentences, you will find a blank, indicated by the ellipsis points (. . .). From the choices provided, select the word or phrase that best completes the sentence, then fill in the corresponding oval.

---

27. Fugitīvus scīvit . . . ipsum vīsum esse.

    (A) sē   (C) eam

    (B) quem   (D) nōs

28. Rōma est . . . .

    (A) aeternam urbem   (C) aeternā urbe

    (B) aeterna urbs   (D) aeternae urbis

29. Mīlēs hostem . . . vulnerāvit.

    (A) gladiī   (C) gladiōs

    (B) gladiō   (D) gladium

30. . . . , discipulī!

    (A) Tacēte   (C) Tacēns

    (B) Tacē   (D) Tacēre

31. Herculēs vir . . . erat.

    (A) magnae fortitūdinī   (C) magna fortitūdo

    (B) magnā fortitūdine   (D) magnam fortitūdinem

32. Rōmulus scit sē frātrem . . . .

    (A) necārī   (C) necāvisse

    (B) necāvit   (D) necātum esse

33. Tam frigidus erat ut aqua . . . glaciēs.

    (A) fīēbat   (C) fīat

    (B) factus erat   (D) fieret

PART E

DIRECTIONS: In each of the following sentences, part or all of the sentence is underlined. Select the expression that best substitutes for the underlined word or words, that is, the expression that changes the meaning of the sentence least. Then fill in the corresponding oval.

34. Illa puella erat multō altior <u>quam haec</u>.

    (A) <u>haec</u>

    (B) <u>hāc</u>

    (C) <u>hanc</u>

    (D) <u>huic</u>

35. Centuriō <u>mīlitem iubet aquam invenīre</u>.

    (A) <u>mīlitī imperat aquam invenīre</u>.

    (B) <u>mīlitem imperat ut aquam invenīret</u>.

    (C) <u>mīlitī imperat ut aquam inveniat</u>.

    (D) <u>mīlitī imperat ut sibi aqua invenienda sit</u>.

36. <u>Necesse erat simul omnia agere</u>.

    (A) <u>Omnia simul agentur</u>.

    (B) <u>Omnia simul agenda sunt</u>.

    (C) <u>Omnia simul actūra sunt</u>.

    (D) <u>Omnia simul agenda erant</u>.

37. <u>Hōc factō</u>, sē quiētī dedit.

    (A) <u>Cum hoc factum erat</u>

    (B) <u>Ubi hoc faciēbātur</u>

    (C) <u>Quod hoc faciēbat</u>

    (D) <u>Sī hoc fēcerat</u>

38. Dominus duōs servōs mīsit <u>quī onera ferrent</u>.

    (A) <u>onere ferre</u>

    (B) <u>ut onera ferat</u>

    (C) <u>ad onera ferenda</u>

    (D) <u>oneribus latīs</u>

PART F

DIRECTIONS: Look over each of the following passages of prose and poetry to understand the meaning. Then, relying on the context of the reading passage, answer each question or complete each statement, as directed. Choose the answer that best expresses your understanding of the meaning of any form, clause, sentence, or lines specified. Then fill in the corresponding oval.

Passage A

A boy and a dolphin

1   Est in Africā colōnia marī proxima. Quō locō puerīs glōria et virtūs
altissimē[1] provehī[2] est: victor ille, quī longissimē nōn sōlum lītus
sed etiam simul natantēs relīquit. Hōc certāmine puer quīdam
audentior cēterīs in ulteriōra tendēbat. Delphīnus occurrit, et
5   nunc praecēdere[3] puerum nunc sequī nunc circumīre, postrēmō
subīre dēpōnere iterum subīre, trepidantemque perferre prīmum
in altum, mox flectit ad lītus, redditque terrae et aequālibus.[4]

1. altissimē: *very far out on the deep*
2. prōvehō, prōvehere, prōvexī, prōvectus: *carry forth; to swim out*
3. praecēdere: historical infinitive = praecēdēbat
4. aequālis, -is, -e: *equal (in age), companion*

39. The appropriate translation of <u>marī</u> (line 1) is

    (A) from the sea   (C) to the sea

    (B) on the sea   (D) in the sea

40. The form <u>prōvehī</u> (line 2) means

    (A) carry forth   (C) I have carried forth

    (B) to carry forth   (D) to be carried forth

41. The translation of <u>natantēs</u> (line 3) that is <u>not</u> acceptable is

    (A) those swimming   (C) those who were swimming

    (B) those having swum   (D) the swimmers

42. In lines 2–3 (quī . . . relīquit), we learn that the winner of the contest is the one who

    (A) swims farthest from shore

    (B) swims farther than the others

    (C) swims farthest from shore and farther than the others

    (D) swims for the longest time

43. Audentior cēterīs (line 4) is translated

    (A) more daring than the rest

    (B) rather daring because of the others

    (C) most daring of all

    (D) as daring as the rest

44. The words in ulteriōra tendēbat (line 4) tell us that

    (A) the others went farther out

    (B) the finish line was extended

    (C) the contest lasted longer than expected

    (D) the boy went farther out

45. In line 4 (Delphīnus occurrit), what happened while the boy was swimming?

    (A) he headed toward a dolphin

    (B) a dolphin came to meet him

    (C) he saw a dolphin

    (D) a dolphin attacked him

46. Which of the following things did the dolphin not do, as described in lines 4–5 (et nunc . . . circumīre)?

    (A) went ahead of the boy

    (B) circled the boy

    (C) swam next to the boy

    (D) followed the boy

47. What do we learn from <u>postrēmō subīre dēpōnere iterum subīre</u> (lines 5–6)?

    (A) The boy swam toward the dolphin and dove beneath it

    (B) The dolphin repeatedly came up from beneath the boy

    (C) The boy placed himself on top of the dolphin for a ride

    (D) The dolphin dove deep, then leaped from the water

48. The form <u>trepidantem</u> (line 6) modifies

    (A) <u>puerum</u> (line 5)   (C) <u>delphīnum</u> (understood)

    (B) <u>altum</u> (line 7)   (D) <u>prīmum</u> (line 6)

49. In lines 7–8 (<u>trepidantem</u> . . . <u>aequālibus</u>), the dolphin

    (A) headed for shore, then turned out to sea

    (B) was scared away and then came back

    (C) made for the sea, then turned toward shore

    (D) returned to land for the boy's companions

Passage B

A thirsty boy finds more than water

1   Hīc puer et studiō vēnandī[1] fessus et aestū
    procūbuit speciēque locī fonteque mōtus,
    dumque sitim[2] exstinguere cupit, sitis altera crēvit[3]
    dumque bibit, visā correptus imāgine formam
5   sine corpore amat et corpus putat esse quod umbra est.
    Adstupet ipse sibi vultūque immōtus eōdem
    haeret ut ē Pariō[4] formāta marmore statua.

1. vēnor, vēnārī, venātus sum: *hunt*
2. sitis, sitis, f.: *thirst*
3. sitis altera crēvit: *this second type of "thirst" is described in the passage*
4. Parius, -a, -um: *Parian* (Greek)

50. The form <u>vēnandī</u> (line 1) is translated as

    (A) of hunting   (C) going to hunt

    (B) having been hunted (D) by hunting

51. In line 2, the boy was attracted to the place partly because of its

    (A) wildlife   (C) remoteness

    (B) shade   (D) beauty

52. In line 2, -que . . . -que means

    (A) either . . . or   (C) the one . . . the other

    (B) whether . . . or   (D) both . . . and

53. Vīsā . . . imāgine (line 4) translates

    (A) by the image that he had seen

    (B) while seeing the image

    (C) the image having seen him

    (D) having been visited by an image

54. The pronoun quod (line 5) refers to

    (A) imāgine (line 4)   (C) corpus (line 5)

    (B) formam (line 4)   (D) umbra (line 5)

55. We learn from lines 4–5 (formam . . . est) that the boy

    (A) thinks that the shape is but a shadow

    (B) believes the vision is real

    (C) is loved by the unbodied image

    (D) is dreaming

56. How many elisions are there in lines 6 and 7?

    (A) 0   (C) 2

    (B) 1   (D) 3

57. The form sibi (line 6) tells us that the verb Adstupet (line 6) takes what case?

    (A) nominative   (C) dative

    (B) genitive   (D) ablative

58. Line 6 (<u>vultū</u> . . . <u>eōdem</u>) refers to

    (A) the face that the boy wanted

    (B) the face of the statue

    (C) the reflection of the boy's face

    (D) the boy's actual face

59. The word <u>ut</u> (line 7) has the meaning

    (A) as   (C) when

    (B) in order that   (D) that

60. Line 7 (<u>haeret</u> . . . <u>statua</u>) tells us that

    (A) the vision became a marble statue

    (B) the boy turned into a marble statue

    (C) a marble statue stood nearby

    (D) the boy was as still as a marble statue

Passage C

The murder of Cicero

1   Cicerō, regressus ad villam, "Moriar," inquit, "in patriā saepe ā
    mē servātā!" Satis cōnstat servōs fortiter fidēliterque parātōs
    fuisse ad dīmicandum;[1] ipsum dēpōnī lectīcam, et quiētōs patī,
    quod sors inīqua cōgeret, iūssisse (jūssisse). Prōminentī ex lectīcā
5   praebentīque[2] immōtam cervīcem caput praecīsum est. Nec id sa-
    tis stolidae[3] crūdēlitātī mīlitum fuit: manūs quoque, scrīpsisse in
    Antōnium aliquid exprobantēs,[4] praecīdērunt. Ita relātum est ca-
    put ad Antōnium, iūssūque (jūssūque) eius (ejus) inter duās manūs
    in rostrīs[5] positum.

1. dīmicō, dīmicāre: *fight, struggle*
2. praebeō, praebēre: *offer*
3. stolidus, -a, -um: *unfeeling*
4. exprobō, exprobāre: *reproach, charge*
5. rostra, rostrōrum, n. pl.: *Rostra, speaker's platform*

61. In lines 1–2 (<u>Moriar</u> . . . <u>servātā</u>), Cicero asks to die

    (A) in the land often served by him

    (B) in the land that he has often preserved

    (C) so that he may serve his country

    (D) in the land that has often saved him

62. <u>Parātōs fuisse</u> (lines 2–3) is translated as

    (A) had been prepared   (C) have been prepared

    (B) have prepared   (D) were being prepared

63. The translation of <u>ad dīmicandum</u> (line 3) is

    (A) to fight

    (B) with the result that they fought

    (C) because they were fighting

    (D) so that they must fight

64. In lines 3–4 (<u>ipsum</u> . . . <u>iūssisse</u>), Cicero ordered his slaves to cooperate because

    (A) he thought that fate was against him

    (B) he did not want his slaves killed

    (C) he wanted to make his own fight

    (D) he wanted to die in peace

65. The <u>-que</u> in line 5 connects

    (A) <u>lectīca</u> with <u>praebentī</u>

    (B) <u>praebentī</u> with the understood pronoun <u>eī</u>

    (C) <u>Prōminentī</u> with <u>praebentī</u>

    (D) <u>immōtam cervicem</u> with <u>caput</u>

66. In line 5, <u>cervīcem</u> is the direct object of

    (A) <u>iūssisse</u> (<u>jūssisse</u>) (line 4)

    (B) <u>praebentī</u> (line 5)

    (C) <u>immōtam</u> (line 5)

    (D) <u>praecīsum est</u> (line 5)

67. In lines 5–6 (<u>Nec</u> ... <u>fuit</u>), the author says that the soldier–assassins were

    (A) merciful   (C) hesitant

    (B) quick   (D) cruel

68. During the murder, <u>Prōminentī</u> ... <u>praecīdērunt</u> (lines 4–7), which of the following occurred?

    (A) Cicero left the lectica and died fighting

    (B) Cicero's slaves came to his rescue

    (C) Cicero's head and hands were cut off

    (D) Cicero attempted to hide in the lectica

69. We learn in <u>manūs</u> ... <u>praecīdērunt</u> (lines 6–7) that Cicero's hands were removed because

    (A) Antony had approved of his writing

    (B) Cicero had approved of what Antony had written

    (C) a separate written charge had been made by Antony

    (D) they had written something against Antony

70. The word <u>eius</u> (<u>ejus</u>) in line 8 refers to

    (A) Cicero   (C) an assassin

    (B) Antony   (D) an unnamed participant

71. In <u>Ita</u> ... <u>positum</u> (lines 7–9), Antony ordered

    (A) that Cicero's head and hands be placed on the Rostra

    (B) that Cicero's head be brought to him

    (C) that the head be placed on the Rostra by his own two hands

    (D) that the story of Cicero's murder be told from the Rostra

SAT Latin Subject Test
Practice Test 2

$$\boxed{\textbf{ANSWER KEY}}$$

1. (B)	21. (A)	41. (B)	61. (B)
2. (D)	22. (C)	42. (C)	62. (C)
3. (A)	23. (C)	43. (A)	63. (A)
4. (B)	24. (D)	44. (D)	64. (A)
5. (A)	25. (B)	45. (B)	65. (C)
6. (B)	26. (A)	46. (C)	66. (B)
7. (D)	27. (A)	47. (B)	67. (D)
8. (C)	28. (B)	48. (A)	68. (C)
9. (C)	29. (B)	49. (C)	69. (D)
10. (A)	30. (A)	50. (A)	70. (B)
11. (B)	31. (B)	51. (D)	71. (A)
12. (D)	32. (C)	52. (D)	
13. (B)	33. (D)	53. (A)	
14. (B)	34. (B)	54. (C)	
15. (D)	35. (C)	55. (B)	
16. (D)	36. (D)	56. (B)	
17. (A)	37. (A)	57. (C)	
18. (B)	38. (C)	58. (C)	
19. (C)	39. (C)	59. (A)	
20. (B)	40. (D)	60. (D)	

DETAILED EXPLANATIONS
OF ANSWERS

PRACTICE TEST 2

PART A

1. **(B) fortius**
   The comparative adverb has the same form as the neuter comparative adjective. Answer (A) is the superlative adverb, (C) is a comparative adjective, and (D) is a positive adjective. (See Chapter 17 for comparison of adverbs.)

2. **(D) eius (ejus)**
   This is the genitive singular of all genders of the demonstrative pronoun **is, ea, id**. Answer (A) is dative singular, all genders, and nominative plural masculine; (B) is nominative plural; and (C) is dative/ablative plural. (See Chapter 11 for demonstratives.)

3. **(A) erunt**
   Be careful to distinguish the freestanding future form **erunt** from that of the perfect, **fuērunt**. Answer (B) is future perfect, (C) is perfect, and (D) is pluperfect. (See Chapter 21.)

4. **(B) vīrēs**
   The irregular noun **vīs** is often confused with **vir**. Answer (A) is accusative plural of **vir**; (C) is accusative singular of **vīs** (cf. **virum**); and (D) is dative/ablative plural of **vīs** (cf. **virīs**). (See Chapter 5 for this noun.)

5. **(A) dīc**
   This verb has an irregular imperative, as do **dūcō**, **faciō**, and **ferō**. Answer (B) **dīcite** is the plural imperative, (C) **dīcī** is the present passive infinitive, and (D) **dīcere** is the present active infinitive. (See Chapter 23 for irregular imperatives.)

6. **(B) cui**

This is the dative singular form of all genders of the relative pronoun **quī, quae, quod**. Answer (A) is dative/ablative plural, (C) is genitive singular, and (D) is nominative plural, feminine, and nominative/accusative plural, neuter. (See Chapter 12 for forms of the relative pronoun.)

7. **(D) audītus esse**

The perfect passive infinitive is a compound form. Answer (A) **audivisse** is the perfect active infinitive, (B) **audīrī** is the present passive, and (C) **audītūrus esse** is the future active. (See Chapter 26 for infinitives.)

8. **(C) ēgrediēns**

This is the nominative singular form of the present participle of a deponent third **-iō** verb. Answer (A) **ēgressūrus** is the future active participle, (B) **ēgressus** is the past participle, and (D) **ēgrediendus** is the future passive participle or gerundive. (See Chapter 20 for deponent verbs and Chapter 24 for present participles.)

PART B

9. **(C) regredior**

Regressive derives from the last principal part of **regredior, regredī, regressus sum**, *to go back*. The other choices are (A) **regnō, regnāre, regnāvī, regnātus**, *to rule*, (B) **redeō, redīre, rediī, reditus**, *to go back*, and (D) **referō, referre, rettulī, relātus**, *to bring back*.

10. **(A) tendō**

Tensile, which means capable of being stretched or extended (cf. *tension*), comes from **tendō, tendere, tetendī, tensus**, *to stretch* or *extend*. Answer (B) **tenebrae, -ārum** means *darkness* or *blackness*; (C) **teneō, tenēre, tenuī, tentus** means *to hold*; and (D) **tenuis, -is, -e** means *slender, thin*.

11. **(B) veniō**

Circumvent is a compound form of **veniō, venīre, vēnī, ventus**, *to come*. The other answers are (A) **venēnum**, *poison*; (C) **vēndō, vēndere, vēndidī, vēnditus**, *to sell*; and (D) **ventus**, *wind*.

12. **(D) ambō**

Ambivalent is a compound form of **valeō, valēre, valuī** with the adjective **ambō, -ae, -o** serving as its prefix. The other Latin words are (A) **amābilis**, *lovable*; (B) **ambrosia** (the food of the gods); and (C) **ambulō, ambulāre, ambulāvī, ambulātus**, *to walk*.

PART C

13. **(B)**

Very daring, **audacissīmi,** is a superlative adjective, modifying **gladiātōrēs**. Answers (A) and (D) require **audāciōrēs**, and (C) requires **audācēs**. (See Chapter 16 for comparison of adjectives.)

14. **(B)**

Caesar had three wives is an example of the dative of possession. Answers (A), (C), and (D) do not translate the Latin correctly. In (A), **trēs** does not modify **Caesarī**; (C) gives the wrong tense; and (D) **Caesarī** is in the dative case, not the genitive. (See Chapter 8 for dative of possession.)

15. **(D)**

Was about to erupt correctly translates the underlined active periphrastic, **ēruptūrus erat**. Answer (A) requires **ērupuerat**, (B) requires **ērumpēbat**, and (C) requires **ērumpendus erat**. (See Chapter 24.)

16. **(D)**

Let the wicked be punished correctly expresses the adjective **malī** as a substantive and the jussive use of the present subjunctive, **puniantur**. Answer (A) requires **puniuntur** and (B) requires **punientur**. Answer (C) requires both an active verb and an object accusative. (See Chapter 28 for the jussive and Chapter 16 for the substantive.)

17. **(A)**

For several days correctly translates **complūrēs diēs**, an accusative extent of time. Answer (B) requires the ablative, (C) requires an accusative phrase with **abhinc**, and (D) requires the preposition **post**. (See Chapter 9 for extent of time with the accusative.)

18. **(B)**

Had been conquered translates the perfect passive infinitive **superātum esse** correctly after a main verb in the past tense ("past-past-*had*") in indirect statement. Answer (A) requires a main verb in the present tense; (C) requires the periphrastic form of the infinitive, **super-andum esse**; and (D) requires the present passive infinitive, **superārī**. (See Chapter 26 for infinitives and indirect statements.)

19. **(C)**

In Athens provides the proper meaning of the locative form **Athēnīs**, given the meaning of the main verb **occurrere**, *meet*, which eliminates (A) *from Athens*. Answer (B) *to Athens* requires **Athēnās,** and (D) requires *near Athens*, **prope Athēnās**. (See Chapter 10 for the locative case.)

20. **(B)**

In (B), *(happier) than dogs* correctly renders the ablative of comparison (**fēlīciōrēs**) **canibus**. Answer (A) *with dogs* requires **cum canibus**, (C) *by dogs* requires **ā canibus**, and (D) *as dogs* requires **canēs**. (See Chapter 10 for the ablative of comparison.)

21. **(A)**

This woman is the correct answer for the demonstrative pronoun **haec**, given a singular verb. **Haec** serves as the antecedent of the relative pronoun **quam**, which is the object of its verb **vidēs**. Answer (B) correctly translates **haec** as a neuter form, but the form is plural and requires a plural verb. Answer (C) *These women* is incorrect because it is also plural. Answer (D) *that thing* requires the neuter pronoun **illud** or **id.** (See Chapter 11 for demonstrative pronouns.)

22. **(C)**

Ōrātiōne habitā is an ablative absolute, which gives the translation *After the speech had been delivered* (i.e., the action is prior in time to that of the main verb.) Answers (A) and (B) do not translate actions that are prior in time to that of the main verb, and (D) *Having delivered the speech* incorrectly translates the perfect passive participle as active. Note the appearance of the supine **audītū**, after the Vergilian phrase **Mīrābile dictū!** This sentence also reflects language in Catullus's Poem 53. (See Chapter 24 for the ablative absolute.)

23. **(C)**

This sentence contains a fear clause with the subjunctive in second-ary sequence. Remember that in fear clauses, **nē** introduces a positive idea, and **ut** a negative one, therefore invalidating (A). Answers (B) and (D) incorrectly identify **frātrem suum**, respectively, as the subject of the subjunctive verb and of the indicative verb in the main clause. (See Chapter 30 for fear clauses.)

24. **(D)**

What kind of man Nero was correctly translates **quālis vir Nero esset**, which is an indirect question with the subjunctive verb in secondary se-quence. Answers (A) and (B) contain the wrong tenses, *is* and *had been*, and (C) mistranslates **quālis** as *who*. (See Chapter 31 for indirect questions.)

25. **(B)**

We must return home correctly renders the impersonal passive peri-phrastic construction **redeundum est**, which is accompanied by the da-tive of agent, **nōbīs**. Answer (A) mistranslates **redeundum est** as having a personal subject, (C) mistranslates the phrase as an active indicative verb, and (D) mistranslates it as a transitive verb requiring an object. (See Chapter 25 for the passive periphrastic.)

26. **(A)**

This sentence contains a past contrary to fact condition, with verbs in the secondary sequence. The sentence reads *If Caesar had not been killed, he would have been emperor*. This question unexpectedly requests the translation of the main or then-clause, rather than the subordinate or if-clause. Answer (B) requires the indicative **fuerat**; (C) requires that the contrary to fact condition be in present time (i.e., have a subjunctive verb in the imperfect tense); and (D) requires an active periphrastic with the subjunctive, **factūrus esset**, expressing future time. (See Chapter 29 for conditional sentences.)

PART D

27. **(A)**

The only pronoun that makes sense here is the reflexive form **sē**, giv-ing the meaning *The runaway knew that he (himself) had been spotted*. The ac-cusative case of the reflexive is required because the missing word serves as the subject of an indirect statement. The intensive pronoun **ipsum** also helps with this decision. The relative pronoun **quam**, the demonstrative **eam**, and the personal **nōs** do not make sense in this context. (See Chapter 15 for reflexives and Chapter 26 for indirect statements.)

28. **(B)**

Aeterna urbs is required to complete the meaning of *Rome is the eternal city*. **Aeterna urbs** serves as a predicate nominative in this sentence. Answer (A), the accusative **aeternam urbem**, is the most common error made with the predicate nominative, because the assumption is made that a direct object is needed; however, the verb **esse** and its forms cannot take a direct object. (See Chapter 6 for the predicate nominative.)

29. **(B)**

The sentence reads *The soldier wounded the enemy <u>with</u>* (i.e., *by means of*) *a sword*. This is an example of the ablative of means or instrument: **gladiō** is an object or implement used to carry out the action of the verb **vulnerāvit**. Always insert the English phrase *by means of* to ensure that the ablative without a preposition is indeed an ablative of means. (See Chapter 10 for the ablative of means.)

30. **(A)**

The appearance of the vocative form **discipulī** and the punctuation (comma and exclamation point) call for a verb in the imperative mood. Answer (C) is a present participle, and (D) is a present active infinitive, so both are incorrect. Because **discipulī** is plural, (B) **Tacē**, which is singular, is eliminated. (See Chapter 23 for the imperative.)

31. **(B)**

Hercules was a man <u>of great courage</u> requires either a genitive or ablative of description. The genitive does not appear as a choice (although **magnae fortitūdinī**, the dative, looks tempting!), so the ablative **magnā fortitūdine** is the correct answer. (See Chapters 7 and 10 for the genitive and ablative, respectively.)

32. **(C)**

Romulus knows that he (himself) (<u>has</u>) <u>killed</u> his brother. This sentence contains an indirect statement, which requires an infinitive, thereby eliminating (C) **necāvit** from consideration. Given that the subject of the infinitive is reflexive (**sē**), the passive infinitives **necārī** and **necātum esse** do not make sense. **Necāvisse**, the perfect active infinitive, is the only choice that fits the needs of both grammar and sense. (See Chapter 26 for indirect statements and Chapter 15 for reflexive pronouns.)

33. **(D)**
This sentence contains a subjunctive clause of result, **ut aqua (fieret) glaciēs**, which is triggered by **tam**. Answers (A) and (B) are not subjunctive (**fiēbat** is imperfect active indicative and **factus erat** pluperfect passive indicative), and (C) **fīat** is in the incorrect tense after the main verb **erat**. (See Chapter 30 for result clauses and Chapter 27 for sequence of tenses.)

PART E

34. **(B)**
The ablative of comparison, here **hāc**, may substitute for the **quam** comparison construction, here, **quam haec**. The sentence reads *That girl was much taller than this (one)*. Note the use of **multō (altior)**, an example of the ablative of degree of difference. (For the ablatives of comparison and degree of difference, see Chapter 10; for comparative constructions in general, see Chapters 16 and 17.)

35. **(C)**
Given the choices of answers, this question is asking you to substitute an indirect command with the verb **imperāre** for the infinitive phrase after **iūbet**. **Imperāre** takes the dative (**mīlitī**), and **iūbēre** takes the accusative (**mīlitem**) as an object. Answer (A) is incorrect because **imperāre** is not found with the infinitive. Answer (B) breaks the rule of sequence of tenses because it has a verb in the imperfect subjunctive (**invenīret**) following a main verb in the present tense (**imperat**). Answer (D) expresses the idea of necessity, which is not an alternative to the Latin underlined in the original sentence. (See Chapter 30 for indirect commands.)

36. **(D)**
This sentence expresses necessity through the use of **Necesse erat**. The sentence reads *It was necessary to do everything at the same time*. The only choices that fit this requirement are (B) and (D), the passive periphrastic. Because the main verb **erat** is in the imperfect tense, the past

tense is required in the periphrastic, hence **agenda erant**. (See Chapter 25 for the passive periphrastic.)

37. **(A)**

Hōc factō is an ablative absolute, for which various types of clauses may be substituted. Answers (B) and (C) are incorrect because they contain verbs in the imperfect tense, which expresses continuous action, whereas the action of the past participle **factō** in the ablative absolute expresses completed action. Answer (D) does not make sense in context, leaving **Cum hoc factum erat** (*When this had been done*) as the proper alternative to **Hōc factō**. (See Chapter 24 for the ablative absolute and Chapter 32 for **cum** clauses.)

38. **(C)**

Quī onera ferrent is an example of a relative clause of purpose. The antecedent of **quī** is **servōs**. The sentence reads *The master sent two slaves to carry the loads*. Answer (B) is a purpose clause, but has its verb in the incorrect tense (the main verb **mīsit** is in the past). The infinitive is not used to express purpose, eliminating (A), nor is the ablative absolute used in this way, eliminating (D). Answer (C) **ad onera ferenda**, a gerundive of purpose, is an appropriate substitute for the relative purpose clause. (See Chapter 31 for the relative purpose clause and Chapter 25 for the gerundive of purpose.)

PART F

Passage A

39. **(C)**

The adjective **proxima**, meaning *very close to*, requires the dative case, hence **marī**. The other answers require the prepositions **in** or **ad** to complete their meanings.

40. **(D)**

This sentence reads *At which place, there is glory and honor for the boys to be carried forth* (i.e., *to swim*) *very far out onto the deep*. The present passive infinitive **prōvehī** (see the word list for the passage) complements **est glōria et virtūs** as a subjective infinitive. Answer (B) translates an infinitive, but in the active voice. Answers (A) and (C), as an imperative and a finite verb, do not correctly translate **prōvehī.**

41. **(B)**

Answer (B) *those having swum* does not translate the present participle **natantēs** correctly. By the way, there is no perfect active participle of the verb **natāre.** The remaining three answers all translate **natantēs** as a substantive. (See Chapters 16 and 24 for substantives.)

42. **(C)**

Lines 2–3 read *That one is the winner, who not only has left behind the shore the farthest but also those swimming at the same time* (i.e., *with him*). Answers (A) and (B) are both grammatically correct, but they do not provide complete information. Answer (D) incorrectly translates **altissimē.**

43. **(A)**

Audentior cēterīs is an example of the ablative of comparison with a comparative adjective (here, modifying **puer quīdam**). Answer (A) gives the wrong translation of the comparative **audentior,** (B) translates **cēterīs** incorrectly, and (C) mistranslates the comparative as a superlative.

44. **(D)**

The sentence in lines 3–4 reads, *In this contest, a certain boy, more daring than the rest, went farther out.* Because the verb **tendēbat** is singular, (A), which has a plural subject, is eliminated. There is no information in the passage to warrant choosing (B) or (C).

45. **(B)**

A dolphin came to meet (him) is the correct translation of **Delphīnus occurrit.** The meaning of the word **delphīnus** may be derived from the title provided and from the context. The word *him* requires the assumption of the pronoun **eī,** in the dative case. The other answers incorrectly translate **delphīnus** as an object or give an inappropriate meaning of the verb **occurrit.**

46. **(C)**

The cited lines 4–5 are translated, *and now it* (i.e., *the dolphin*) *was going ahead of the boy, now following him, and now circling him.* . . . There is no information about the dolphin swimming *next to the boy,* as in (C). The infinitives here are examples of the historical infinitive, which may be translated using the imperfect tense of the indicative in narration (see the word list provided with the passage). **Delphīnus** serves as the subject of each infinitive. Note the anaphora, or repetition, of **nunc**.

47. **(B)**

The underlined Latin reads *at last (the dolphin) went under him, put him off, then went under him again.* . . . The idea is that the dolphin swam beneath the boy to lift him up, either in play or because the boy was exhausted from the swim. Answers (A) and (C) mistakenly assume that the boy is the subject (and is precipitating the action), and (D) gives a possible translation of the meanings of the verbs, with no regard to their grammatical forms.

48. **(A)**

The grammar and the logic of the situation require that the present participle **trepidantem**, *trembling (in fear)* modify **puerum** (line 5). Participles don't modify adverbs (**prīmum**), and it is unlikely that the sea (**altum**) would be trembling. Also, because **delphīnus** (line 4) is the subject of all of the verbs in these lines, it cannot serve as the object, as in (C).

49. **(C)**

Lines 6–7 read (*The dolphin*) *at first carried the trembling boy out into the sea, then turned toward shore and returned* [*him*] *to land and his comrades.*

Passage B

50. **(A)**

Vēnandī is a gerund in the genitive singular form and translates *of hunting*. The phrase **studio <u>venandī</u> fessus** translates (*the boy*), *weary (because of) his enthusiasm <u>of (for)</u> <u>hunting</u>* . . .

51. **(D)**

Speciēque locī fonteque motus translates as *Moved by the beauty of the place and the spring*. The word **speciēs** literally means physical appearance. The ablatives here are ablatives of cause or means. (See Chapter 10 for the ablative case.)

52. **(D)**

-**Que** . . . -**que** is the equivalent of **et** . . . **et**, *both* . . . *and*. It joins the phrase **speciē locī** to the word **fonte**. Answer (A) *either . . . or* requires **aut** . . . **aut** or **vel** . . . **vel**; (B) *whether . . . or* requires **utrum** . . . **an**; and

(C) *the one, the other* requires **alter . . . alter**. (See Chapter 35 for conjunctions and correlative phrases.)

53. **(A)**
    (**Puer**) . . . <u>vīsā</u> **correptus** <u>imāgine</u> translates as *The boy, seized <u>by the image that he had seen</u>* . . . The past participle **vīsā** modifies **imāgine**, which is an ablative of means rather than part of an ablative absolute. The participle is translated as a clause. (See Chapter 24.)

54. **(C)**
    The antecedent of the relative pronoun **quod** is **corpus**, which is neuter. This part of the line reads *he* (i.e., *the boy*) *thinks that* (*it*) *is a body* (i.e., *substantial, real*) *which is* (*in fact*) *a shadow.* The other nouns do not fit the necessary criteria of gender and case. (See Chapter 12 for the relative pronoun.)

55. **(B)**
    The correct answer to the previous question leads to the realization that what the boy sees in the pool he believes to be real. Lines 5–6 read *Captivated by the image that he had seen, he loved the image without a body* (i.e., *substance*) *and thought that what was a vision was actually a body* (i.e., *real*).

56. **(B)**
    The elision is found in line 6, **vultūque͜ immōtus**. (See Chapter 34.)

57. **(C)**
    Sibi is the dative form of the reflexive pronoun **sē**. The phrase reads *He* (*himself*) *is amazed at himself.* . . . (See Chapter 15 for the reflexive pronoun.)

58. **(C)**
    Vultū (**immōtus**) **eōdem** means (*transfixed*) *by the same face*, that is, the one Narcissus had seen in the pool, which was a reflection of his own.

59. **(A)**
    Ut here introduces a simile (*as* . . .), comparing Narcissus to a sculpture of white marble. The context should override your temptation to see **ut** as introducing a subjunctive clause, which is suggested by the other answers.

60. (D)
Narcissus stands frozen to the spot (**haeret**), as motionless as a statue.

Passage C

61. (B)
The past participle **servātā** modifies **patriā**. **In patriā** . . . **servātā** means literally (*in*) *the land* (*having been*) *often preserved by me*. (Note also that **Moriar** can also be translated as a form of the future tense, *I will die*, rather than *Let me die*.) Answers (A) and (C) exploit the typical confusion caused by the similarity of the verb **servō, servāre**, *save, preserve*, to **serviō, servīre**, *serve*. The translation in (D) ignores the preposition and so makes **mē** accusative instead of ablative.

62. (C)
Parātōs, an adjective deriving from a past participle, modifies **servōs** and completes the meaning of the infinitive **fuisse**, which must be translated *has been* given the present tense of the controlling verb, **constat**. Answer (A) *had been prepared* requires that the main verb be in the past tense; (B) *have prepared* requires **parāvisse**; and (D) requires a main verb in the past tense and the present passive infinitive, **parārī**. Look carefully at adjectives + **esse**, such as **laetus esse**, which could be mistakenly considered as forms of the perfect passive.

63. (A)
Ad dimīcandum is a gerund of purpose, which does not carry any of the meanings offered in choices (B), (C), or (D). This sentence (line 3) reads *It is well enough agreed that* (*Cicero's*) *slaves were prepared for* (*the purpose of*) *fighting*.

64. (A)
The clause **quod sors inīqua cōgeret** is a causal clause with the subjunctive, indicating that the reason given was Cicero's own (see Chapter 31). The clause reads *because an unjust fate required it*, that is, that his slaves put down the lectica and stand there patiently (**dēpōnī lectīcam et quiētōs patī**). Answers (B), (C), and (D) are logical but unsupported by the Latin.

65. **(C)**

The enclitic **-que** combines the two present participles **prōminentī** and **praebentī**. (See Chapter 34.) Answer (A) is a distractor because it may appear obvious that **-que** connects two words that are found next to one another, as in **lectīcā praebentīque**. This word position with **-que** occurs commonly; **praebentī** is in the dative case, whereas **lectīcā** is in the ablative. The words in (D) follow the **-que** and may be disregarded as an option.

66. **(B)**

The sentence in line 5 reads *With respect to him* (i.e., *While he was*) *sticking his neck out of the lectica and offering it without flinching, (Cicero's) head was cut off*. Given the meaning required by the correct translation, **cervīcem** must serve as the direct object of **praebentī**.

67. **(C)**

The relevant Latin in lines 5–6 reads *Nor was that enough <u>for the unfeeling cruelty</u> of the soldiers*. The words **stolidae** and **crūdēlitātī** suggest the tone.

68. **(C)**

The Latin in lines 5 and 6–7 informs us that Cicero's head (**caput praecīsum est**) and hands (**manūs quoque . . . praecīdērunt**) were both removed. There is no justification in the passage for the other answers.

69. **(D)**

Lines 6–7 read *They* (i.e., *the soldiers*) *cut off his hands, too, charging them <u>for having written something against Anthony</u>*. The present participle **exprobantēs** modifies **mīlitēs** (the understood subject of **praecīdērunt**) and introduces the indirect statement (**manūs**) **scrīpsisse**.

70. **(B)**

Dīmicandum is a gerund in a purpose construction, which makes it a noun, not a participle. It could be mistaken for a gerundive or future passive participle. Tricky! **Regressus** is the past participle of a deponent verb, and **prōminentī** and **exprobantēs** are present participles.

71. **(A)**

The final sentence in the passage reads *And so the head was brought back to Anthony and by his command was placed on the Rostra between (Cicero's) two hands*.

Translations of Passages

Passage A

There is in Africa a settlement very close to the sea. In this place there is glory and honor for boys to swim very far out into the deep: that one is the winner who not only has left the shore the farthest behind, but also his companion swimmers. In this contest, a certain boy, more daring than the rest, went rather far out. A dolphin came to meet him and now (swam) before the boy, now followed him and circled him, and finally went under him and then put him off, and did so again, and finally carried the trembling boy, first out into the sea, and then made for the shore and returned him to land and his comrades. (Pliny the Younger)

Passage B

Here the boy (Narcissus), weary because of his eagerness for hunting and because of the heat, lay down, entranced both by the beauty of the place and the pool, and while he desired to quench his thirst, another (type of) thirst arose, and as he drank, captivated by the image that he had seen (in the water), he loved the image without substance and thought that (that) which was a reflection had real substance. He wonders at himself, and, spellbound by the very same face (as his), remained (there) like a statue fashioned of Parian marble. (Ovid)

Passage C

Cicero, having gone back to his villa, said, "Let me die in the fatherland so often preserved by me!" It is well enough agreed that his slaves were ready to fight loyally and faithfully; (it is also agreed that) he himself ordered the lectica to be put down and for them to wait patiently, because an unjust fate required (it). While sticking his neck out of the lectica and offering it without flinching, (Cicero's) head was cut off. Nor was that enough for the unfeeling cruelty of the soldiers: his hands, too, they cut off, charging that they (the hands) had written something against Anthony. And so the head was brought back to Anthony and, by his order, was placed on the Rostra between (Cicero's) two hands. (Seneca the Elder)

SAT Latin Subject Test
Practice Test 1

ANSWER SHEETS

1. Ⓐ Ⓑ Ⓒ Ⓓ	25. Ⓐ Ⓑ Ⓒ Ⓓ	49. Ⓐ Ⓑ Ⓒ Ⓓ
2. Ⓐ Ⓑ Ⓒ Ⓓ	26. Ⓐ Ⓑ Ⓒ Ⓓ	50. Ⓐ Ⓑ Ⓒ Ⓓ
3. Ⓐ Ⓑ Ⓒ Ⓓ	27. Ⓐ Ⓑ Ⓒ Ⓓ	51. Ⓐ Ⓑ Ⓒ Ⓓ
4. Ⓐ Ⓑ Ⓒ Ⓓ	28. Ⓐ Ⓑ Ⓒ Ⓓ	52. Ⓐ Ⓑ Ⓒ Ⓓ
5. Ⓐ Ⓑ Ⓒ Ⓓ	29. Ⓐ Ⓑ Ⓒ Ⓓ	53. Ⓐ Ⓑ Ⓒ Ⓓ
6. Ⓐ Ⓑ Ⓒ Ⓓ	30. Ⓐ Ⓑ Ⓒ Ⓓ	54. Ⓐ Ⓑ Ⓒ Ⓓ
7. Ⓐ Ⓑ Ⓒ Ⓓ	31. Ⓐ Ⓑ Ⓒ Ⓓ	55. Ⓐ Ⓑ Ⓒ Ⓓ
8. Ⓐ Ⓑ Ⓒ Ⓓ	32. Ⓐ Ⓑ Ⓒ Ⓓ	56. Ⓐ Ⓑ Ⓒ Ⓓ
9. Ⓐ Ⓑ Ⓒ Ⓓ	33. Ⓐ Ⓑ Ⓒ Ⓓ	57. Ⓐ Ⓑ Ⓒ Ⓓ
10. Ⓐ Ⓑ Ⓒ Ⓓ	34. Ⓐ Ⓑ Ⓒ Ⓓ	58. Ⓐ Ⓑ Ⓒ Ⓓ
11. Ⓐ Ⓑ Ⓒ Ⓓ	35. Ⓐ Ⓑ Ⓒ Ⓓ	59. Ⓐ Ⓑ Ⓒ Ⓓ
12. Ⓐ Ⓑ Ⓒ Ⓓ	36. Ⓐ Ⓑ Ⓒ Ⓓ	60. Ⓐ Ⓑ Ⓒ Ⓓ
13. Ⓐ Ⓑ Ⓒ Ⓓ	37. Ⓐ Ⓑ Ⓒ Ⓓ	61. Ⓐ Ⓑ Ⓒ Ⓓ
14. Ⓐ Ⓑ Ⓒ Ⓓ	38. Ⓐ Ⓑ Ⓒ Ⓓ	62. Ⓐ Ⓑ Ⓒ Ⓓ
15. Ⓐ Ⓑ Ⓒ Ⓓ	39. Ⓐ Ⓑ Ⓒ Ⓓ	63. Ⓐ Ⓑ Ⓒ Ⓓ
16. Ⓐ Ⓑ Ⓒ Ⓓ	40. Ⓐ Ⓑ Ⓒ Ⓓ	64. Ⓐ Ⓑ Ⓒ Ⓓ
17. Ⓐ Ⓑ Ⓒ Ⓓ	41. Ⓐ Ⓑ Ⓒ Ⓓ	65. Ⓐ Ⓑ Ⓒ Ⓓ
18. Ⓐ Ⓑ Ⓒ Ⓓ	42. Ⓐ Ⓑ Ⓒ Ⓓ	66. Ⓐ Ⓑ Ⓒ Ⓓ
19. Ⓐ Ⓑ Ⓒ Ⓓ	43. Ⓐ Ⓑ Ⓒ Ⓓ	67. Ⓐ Ⓑ Ⓒ Ⓓ
20. Ⓐ Ⓑ Ⓒ Ⓓ	44. Ⓐ Ⓑ Ⓒ Ⓓ	68. Ⓐ Ⓑ Ⓒ Ⓓ
21. Ⓐ Ⓑ Ⓒ Ⓓ	45. Ⓐ Ⓑ Ⓒ Ⓓ	69. Ⓐ Ⓑ Ⓒ Ⓓ
22. Ⓐ Ⓑ Ⓒ Ⓓ	46. Ⓐ Ⓑ Ⓒ Ⓓ	70. Ⓐ Ⓑ Ⓒ Ⓓ
23. Ⓐ Ⓑ Ⓒ Ⓓ	47. Ⓐ Ⓑ Ⓒ Ⓓ	71. Ⓐ Ⓑ Ⓒ Ⓓ
24. Ⓐ Ⓑ Ⓒ Ⓓ	48. Ⓐ Ⓑ Ⓒ Ⓓ	

SAT Latin Subject Test
Practice Test 2

ANSWER SHEETS

1. Ⓐ Ⓑ Ⓒ Ⓓ
2. Ⓐ Ⓑ Ⓒ Ⓓ
3. Ⓐ Ⓑ Ⓒ Ⓓ
4. Ⓐ Ⓑ Ⓒ Ⓓ
5. Ⓐ Ⓑ Ⓒ Ⓓ
6. Ⓐ Ⓑ Ⓒ Ⓓ
7. Ⓐ Ⓑ Ⓒ Ⓓ
8. Ⓐ Ⓑ Ⓒ Ⓓ
9. Ⓐ Ⓑ Ⓒ Ⓓ
10. Ⓐ Ⓑ Ⓒ Ⓓ
11. Ⓐ Ⓑ Ⓒ Ⓓ
12. Ⓐ Ⓑ Ⓒ Ⓓ
13. Ⓐ Ⓑ Ⓒ Ⓓ
14. Ⓐ Ⓑ Ⓒ Ⓓ
15. Ⓐ Ⓑ Ⓒ Ⓓ
16. Ⓐ Ⓑ Ⓒ Ⓓ
17. Ⓐ Ⓑ Ⓒ Ⓓ
18. Ⓐ Ⓑ Ⓒ Ⓓ
19. Ⓐ Ⓑ Ⓒ Ⓓ
20. Ⓐ Ⓑ Ⓒ Ⓓ
21. Ⓐ Ⓑ Ⓒ Ⓓ
22. Ⓐ Ⓑ Ⓒ Ⓓ
23. Ⓐ Ⓑ Ⓒ Ⓓ
24. Ⓐ Ⓑ Ⓒ Ⓓ
25. Ⓐ Ⓑ Ⓒ Ⓓ
26. Ⓐ Ⓑ Ⓒ Ⓓ
27. Ⓐ Ⓑ Ⓒ Ⓓ
28. Ⓐ Ⓑ Ⓒ Ⓓ
29. Ⓐ Ⓑ Ⓒ Ⓓ
30. Ⓐ Ⓑ Ⓒ Ⓓ
31. Ⓐ Ⓑ Ⓒ Ⓓ
32. Ⓐ Ⓑ Ⓒ Ⓓ
33. Ⓐ Ⓑ Ⓒ Ⓓ
34. Ⓐ Ⓑ Ⓒ Ⓓ
35. Ⓐ Ⓑ Ⓒ Ⓓ
36. Ⓐ Ⓑ Ⓒ Ⓓ
37. Ⓐ Ⓑ Ⓒ Ⓓ
38. Ⓐ Ⓑ Ⓒ Ⓓ
39. Ⓐ Ⓑ Ⓒ Ⓓ
40. Ⓐ Ⓑ Ⓒ Ⓓ
41. Ⓐ Ⓑ Ⓒ Ⓓ
42. Ⓐ Ⓑ Ⓒ Ⓓ
43. Ⓐ Ⓑ Ⓒ Ⓓ
44. Ⓐ Ⓑ Ⓒ Ⓓ
45. Ⓐ Ⓑ Ⓒ Ⓓ
46. Ⓐ Ⓑ Ⓒ Ⓓ
47. Ⓐ Ⓑ Ⓒ Ⓓ
48. Ⓐ Ⓑ Ⓒ Ⓓ
49. Ⓐ Ⓑ Ⓒ Ⓓ
50. Ⓐ Ⓑ Ⓒ Ⓓ
51. Ⓐ Ⓑ Ⓒ Ⓓ
52. Ⓐ Ⓑ Ⓒ Ⓓ
53. Ⓐ Ⓑ Ⓒ Ⓓ
54. Ⓐ Ⓑ Ⓒ Ⓓ
55. Ⓐ Ⓑ Ⓒ Ⓓ
56. Ⓐ Ⓑ Ⓒ Ⓓ
57. Ⓐ Ⓑ Ⓒ Ⓓ
58. Ⓐ Ⓑ Ⓒ Ⓓ
59. Ⓐ Ⓑ Ⓒ Ⓓ
60. Ⓐ Ⓑ Ⓒ Ⓓ
61. Ⓐ Ⓑ Ⓒ Ⓓ
62. Ⓐ Ⓑ Ⓒ Ⓓ
63. Ⓐ Ⓑ Ⓒ Ⓓ
64. Ⓐ Ⓑ Ⓒ Ⓓ
65. Ⓐ Ⓑ Ⓒ Ⓓ
66. Ⓐ Ⓑ Ⓒ Ⓓ
67. Ⓐ Ⓑ Ⓒ Ⓓ
68. Ⓐ Ⓑ Ⓒ Ⓓ
69. Ⓐ Ⓑ Ⓒ Ⓓ
70. Ⓐ Ⓑ Ⓒ Ⓓ
71. Ⓐ Ⓑ Ⓒ Ⓓ

SAT Latin Score Conversion Table*

Raw Score	Scaled Score	Raw Score	Scaled Score	Raw Score	Scaled Score
71	800	39	600	7	410
70	800	38	590	6	410
69	800	37	580	5	400
68	800	36	580	4	400
67	800	35	570	3	390
66	800	34	560	2	390
65	800	33	550	1	380
64	800	32	550	0	380
63	790	31	540	-1	380
62	780	30	530	-2	370
61	770	29	530	-3	370
60	760	28	520	-4	360
59	750	27	520	-5	360
58	740	26	510	-6	350
57	740	25	500	-7	350
56	730	24	500	-8	340
55	720	23	490	-9	340
54	710	22	490	-10	330
53	710	21	480	-11	330
52	700	20	480	-12	320
51	690	19	470	-13	320
50	680	18	460	-14	310
49	670	17	460	-15	310
48	670	16	460	-16	300
47	660	15	450	-17	300
46	650	14	450	-18	300
45	640	13	440	-19	290
44	640	12	440	-20	290
43	630	11	430	-21	280
42	620	10	430	-22	270
41	610	9	420	-23	270
40	600	8	420		

*Scoring for REA's practice tests strongly approximates that for the actual test. Bear in mind, however, that scaled scores for different editions of the SAT Latin test are adjusted to take into account small shifts in content and in the overall performance of the test-taker population.

Index

O

P